Disability Politics in a Global Economy

Essays in Honour of Marta Russell

While the visibility of disability studies has increased in recent years, few have thoroughly examined the marginalization of people with disabilities through the lens of political economy. This was the great contribution of Marta Russell (1951–2013), an activist and prominent scholar in the United States and best known for her analyses of the issues faced by people with disabilities.

This book examines the legacy of Marta Russell, bringing together distinguished scholars and activists such as Anne Finger, Nirmala Erevelles and Mark Weber, to explicate current issues relevant to the empowerment of people with disabilities. Drawing from various fields including Law, Political Economy, Education and History, the book takes a truly interdisciplinary approach, offering a body of work that develops a dextrous understanding of the marginalization of people with disabilities.

The book will be of great use and interest to specialists and students in the fields of Political Economy, Law and Society, Labour Studies, Disability Studies, Women's Studies, and Political Science.

Ravi Malhotra is Associate Professor at the University of Ottawa, Faculty of Law, Common Law Section. He co-authored a piece with Marta Russell in the *Socialist Register* in 2001.

Marta Russell

Disability Politics in a Global Economy

Essays in Honour of Marta Russell

Edited by Ravi Malhotra

Routledge
Taylor & Francis Group
LONDON AND NEW YORK

First published 2017 by Routledge

2 Park Square, Milton Park, Abingdon, Oxfordshire OX14 4RN
711 Third Avenue, New York, NY 10017

Routledge is an imprint of the Taylor & Francis Group, an informa business

First issued in paperback 2018

British Library Cataloguing in Publication Data
A catalogue record for this book is available from the British Library

Library of Congress Cataloging in Publication Data
A catalog record for this book has been requested

ISBN: 978-1-138-88758-9 (hbk)
ISBN: 978-1-138-59094-6 (pbk)

Typeset in ITC Galliard by
Servis Filmsetting Ltd, Stockport, Cheshire

Contents

Foreword

Thoughts on responding to the left critique of disability rights law

Samuel R Bagenstos

The *Americans with Disabilities Act* is the crown jewel of the American disability rights movement. It is the product of decades of effort—in congressional back-rooms and hearing rooms, in policy seminars and on the streets—of committed activists with disabilities and their allies. And, as the UN Convention on the Rights of Persons with Disabilities exemplifies, it has served as a beacon of hope for disability rights activists around the world.

It's a cheeky move, then, for an American with a disability—one who calls herself a disability rights activist, no less—to criticize the ADA as fundamentally flawed. Yet that is precisely what Marta Russell did. In her extensive writings, Russell called the ADA a "free-market" civil rights law—one that not merely did not go far enough to address the problems of Americans with disabilities, but that actually entrenched the unequal status of members of that group.

Russell's critique of the ADA was sharp and bracing. It was and remains one that any disability rights activist—and, indeed, any advocate of civil rights law in the United States—must confront and take seriously. Russell's argument about the ADA, which might be extended to any American civil rights law, is that the operative force of antidiscrimination mandates creates equality only at the very tip of a social, economic, and political system that is rife with much deeper inequalities. But, she suggests, the *symbolic* force of antidiscrimination law lulls us into believing that we have solved our key problems of social justice. The ADA thus fails to address the fundamental problem of disability inequality at the same time as it relieves pressure to take steps that would address that problem.

This is not a mere heighten-the-contradictions argument—though there is a family resemblance. Russell was not arguing that the worse is the better. Rather, she was arguing that the ADA in the end did very little to advance its purported goals, and that such a small marginal benefit was not worth the cost in defusing mobilization for more effective action. Russell's argument operated in a long tradition of left-wing critiques of liberal reformism, but it had a particularly sharp edge because of Russell's own history of activism—and her own evident loss of faith in the civil rights strategy.

I do not agree with Russell's critique of the ADA. As a liberal (not left-wing) civil rights lawyer, I have spent a large chunk of my professional life enforcing, elaborating on, and studying the ADA. For two years, I supervised the enforcement of the statute at the United States Department of Justice. The ADA, and its civil rights approach, are my guiding light in addressing questions of disability inequality.

But 17 years after the publication of *Beyond Ramps: Disability at the End of the Social Contract*, it should be clear to all of us who consider ourselves disability rights advocates that Russell's critique contained much wisdom and prescience. The ADA's lack of success in the courts is well known. ADA employment cases have long been among the least successful classes of cases in the US federal courts. Although Congress amended the statute in 2008 to expand its definition of disability and reverse this trend, there is reason to believe that ADA employment plaintiffs continue to lose their cases at unusually high rates. And while plaintiffs have achieved notable successes under the titles of the ADA that deal with access to businesses and public services, many of the cases under those titles have resulted in defeats as well—and litigation against inaccessible businesses has provoked a major political backlash, even in California, the birthplace of the American disability rights movement.

Nor has the ADA eliminated the stigma attached to disability in the United States. When one considers the statements of leading politicians on the expansion of the Social Security disability rolls—statements that suggest that people with disabilities are using their conditions as an excuse for not working—the stigma seems as strong as ever. And, indeed, it may have gotten worse in some areas. As multiple-shooting incidents occur with sad and steady frequency, a common pattern of political response has emerged: liberals blame America's lack of restrictions on the purchase and possession of firearms, conservatives respond that the real problem is mental illness, and liberals allow that mental illness is a problem, too. The result is to increase stigma and fear of those with psychiatric disabilities.

Or, finally, consider the area of economic empowerment—a key focus of Marta Russell's own work. One of the principal aims of the ADA was to improve the pathetically low employment rates of Americans with disabilities. At the time President George HW Bush signed the statute into law, more than two-thirds of working-age adults with disabilities remained outside of the workforce. And that low employment rate actually *dropped* in the immediate aftermath of the ADA's adoption. Though the disability-employment picture improved some thereafter, people with disabilities experienced disproportionately large job losses during the Great Recession of 2007–2009. Today, employment rates for Americans with disabilities are roughly what they were when the ADA became law. If the ADA's goal was to achieve economic empowerment and independence for people with disabilities, the statute has failed.

These are facts with which all of us who support disability rights must contend—and they fit Marta Russell's critique of the ADA extremely well. Russell put her finger on a fundamental limitation of antidiscrimination laws: they take as a given the lion's share of the inequality and injustice that is baked into our political and economic system. An employment discrimination law can—if it's fully and effectively enforced—prevent an employer from refusing to hire a person with a disability whose conventional qualifications are better than those of her nondisabled competitors. But it doesn't address the situation where a person with a disability has conventional qualifications that are worse than those of her competitors. Because of extensive discrimination and the failure to take full account of the interests of people with disabilities, the latter situation is extremely likely to obtain.

Disability is a status that anybody can enter at any time, without warning. As a result, the experience of disability inequality is in some respects very different than the experience of inequality based on race or sex—statuses that generally accompany someone from childhood on. But regardless of when a person acquires a disability, that status is often accompanied by stigma, limitations, and discrimination that operate before she has a chance to apply for a job and that defy the antidiscrimination regime.

Consider a person who is born with a disability or acquires it in early childhood. Supports for medical needs and appropriate development are expensive, and in our system the government provides those supports to only a limited extent. A child growing up with a disability thus will often live in a family that experiences significant financial stress (a stress that is aggravated by higher rates of disability in poorer families)—and still is unlikely to get all of the services and supports necessary to promote full development of her talents and integration in the community. The family financial stress, and the lack of services and supports, will compound over the years to make her less likely to have the skills and experiences necessary to be the most qualified candidate when she applies for good jobs in adulthood.

Schooling creates an additional layer of inequality. Although the *Individuals with Disabilities Education Act* guarantees to every disabled child a free appropriate public education in the least restrictive environment, kids with disabilities are still too frequently shunted aside in separate, non-demanding classes that do not fully prepare them for life after leaving school. And repeated efforts—notably in the late, lamented No Child Left Behind law—to ensure that schools have high expectations for students with disabilities have provoked a viscerally intense and sustained reaction that betrays our society's continuing stigma and stereotypes about disability. Continually fighting through such stigma and stereotypes will necessarily make it harder to gain the same benefits from education as one's nondisabled peers. And, despite some recent improvements, the United States does a particularly poor job of facilitating the transition from school to work for young adults with disabilities.

Even for those who acquire disabilities later in life, our society imposes extremely significant barriers to work and economic empowerment that operate well before any employer has an opportunity to discriminate against a disabled applicant. One set of barriers involves transportation. The United States is a heavily car-dependent nation. Yet many people with physical disabilities, because of their disabilities, cannot drive cars. Many others lack the funds to own cars. Accessible public transit is therefore essential to ensure that Americans with disabilities can take advantage of job opportunities. But our metropolitan areas often have limited public transit, and far too little of that is accessible to those with disabilities. If you can't get to the workplace to apply for (and, eventually, perform) a job, an antidiscrimination law will not do much for you.

There is still a more pervasive barrier to employment for Americans with disabilities, one that Marta Russell herself often focused on—health insurance. In the United States, we have chosen to locate in the health care system many of the services and supports that are necessary for people with disabilities to experience integration and empowerment. To give Americans with disabilities the full opportunity to participate in the economic life of the nation, then, we must ensure that the health insurance system reimburses those key services and supports without imposing harmful limitations. Yet even after the important reforms of the *Affordable Care Act*, we still have a divided health insurance system. Working-age Americans typically get insurance through their workplace, and the ACA gives employers a substantial incentive to continue to provide that insurance. But employer-based health insurance often still fails to pay for key services on which people with a number of disabilities rely. To obtain those services, individuals with disabilities must default to the publicly-provided Medicare and (particularly) Medicaid programs, which contain substantial disincentives to working. Although the ACA has mitigated these problems, it has not resolved them.

Looking back, 25 years after the adoption of the ADA, it thus appears that Marta Russell's left critique has a lot to be said for it. The effects of the statute have been limited, in very much the ways she suggested they would be. And they have been limited precisely because the ADA merely layers an antidiscrimination rule on the surface of a system with deeply-entrenched systemic inequalities. If we don't challenge those inequalities, how can we ever hope to achieve the goal of full and equal citizenship for Americans with disabilities?

And yet. Despite the force of Russell's critique, and the undeniable disappointments, the last 25 years have seen substantial advances for Americans with disabilities. People with disabilities are visible members of the community to a far greater extent than they ever had before; disability equality has become a central commitment of public policy; and the result has been to expand disability policy beyond the antidiscrimination model of the ADA. Although No Child Left Behind provoked backlash, even the law replacing that statute retained a focus on ensuring that students with disabilities receive the same quality of education as their nondisabled peers. And notwithstanding its real limitations, the ACA contains a number of provisions that will mitigate the structural barriers to work for individuals with disabilities. These provisions include the statute's definition of "essential health benefits" and its expansion of the Medicaid program—which might prove to be the most important piece of policy promoting the integration and empowerment of people with disabilities ever. These (limited, incremental, but real) gains would not have been possible, I submit, without the change that the ADA made to American disability politics—moving from a model in which people with disabilities are passive recipients of charity and largesse to one in which people with disabilities are active citizens who claim entitlement to full participation in the life of the community.

Moreover, the ADA itself incorporates what might be understood as a radical expansion of the canonical model of antidiscrimination law. Unlike the laws prohibiting race and sex discrimination—which, within broad limits, take employers' definitions of job requirements as a given—the ADA effectively requires employers to justify those aspects of a given job that impose barriers to particular individuals with disabilities. An employer can no longer simply assert that answering the phones is an essential requirement for a secretary's job. Rather, a deaf applicant for that job can show that it would be possible to reallocate the phone-answering tasks to another employee, while reallocating other tasks (such as filing) to him. This is a major challenge to traditional managerial prerogatives and one that does not fit Russell's "free-market" epithet. And the ADA's challenge to the traditional property rights of business owners—which has made the physical accessibility of American civic and economic life the envy of disability rights activists around the world—marks a similar challenge to, rather than simple acceptance of, the market.

The ADA has also led to an expansion of the system of *public* supports for people with disabilities. The Supreme Court's 1999 decision in *Olmstead v LC* interpreted the statute's nondiscrimination requirement expansively to demand that states serve individuals with disabilities in the most integrated setting appropriate. Lower courts have read that decision to require states to fund adequate community-based services and supports for people with both physical and mental disabilities who might otherwise end up in institutions. Litigation under *Olmstead* has led states to significantly expand their community-based services systems, with tens of thousands of beneficiaries across the country.

Far from merely accepting the market as it is, the ADA represents a significant challenge to it. As the legitimacy of that challenge has been reinforced by bipartisan congressional action to expand the ADA in 2008, we have begun to see transgender individuals, pregnant individuals, and others invoke the statute's broad understanding of what antidiscrimination entails—whether by analogy or directly by claiming that transgender status, pregnancy, and so forth meet the law's criteria for disability. The ADA planted the seed for a move away from the conservative, "free-market" model of antidiscrimination law that Russell criticizes, and that seed has sprouted and begun to bear fruit.

But Russell was on to something incredibly important. The American disability rights movement has too often been in the thrall of language and argumentative frames that Russell would call "neoliberal." The movement has long focused on the achievement of what it has called "independence," and movement leaders have harshly criticized disability welfare programs in terms that resonate well with conservative critiques of the welfare state generally. In the campaign to enact the ADA particularly, the bill's supporters relied heavily on the claim that an antidiscrimination law would substitute for disability benefits programs and therefore save the taxpayers billions of dollars. This sort of rhetoric makes it difficult to secure support for interventions that require a substantial public investment—even if those interventions are necessary to ensure that people with disabilities can participate as full and equal members of our community. And to the extent that disability rights leaders authentically believe the anti-welfare arguments they are making—and they do—that understanding will necessarily limit the scope and prospects of success of the movement. It will also, as Russell emphasized, limit the disability rights movement's ability to create durable coalitions beyond disability lines. If universal health care, a universal basic income, and an extensive public commitment to housing and transportation are what is necessary to promote the equality and integration of people with disabilities—and Russell made a powerful case that they are—disability rights activists cannot readily achieve them through an individualistic *or* disability-specific argumentative frame.

Russell was right to see this problematic theme running through the campaign to enact the ADA, and she was right to call out its potential effects. But she was also right to understand that the disability rights movement, and the statute it parented, have been crucial in advancing the full and equal citizenship status of Americans with disabilities. She wanted the ambitions of the movement to extend beyond ramps, not for the movement to abjure ramps. The ADA has, as Russell predicted, proved a limited tool in achieving the goals of the disability rights movement. But it has changed our understanding of antidiscrimination laws, spurred expansions of public benefits programs, and provided a focal point for movements of individuals with disabilities around the world. It has also changed our politics. And savvy activists have come to realize that further advancements in disability equality depend on a commitment to public investment. Russell's critique offers a caution that all of us who care about equality and empowerment must continue to keep at the front of our minds.

This volume shows the influence and broad application of Russell's arguments, and I am proud to have this opportunity to contribute this foreword. The diverse contributions to this volume, by an equally diverse set of contributors, will no doubt spur interesting and important discussions in the years to come.

Preface

Ravi Malhotra

In late 2013, I was shocked to learn that disability rights advocate and scholar Marta Russell had died in California. Many years earlier, we had collaborated on a piece published in the journal *Socialist Register*. At the time, I was about to begin graduate work at Harvard Law School and begin a new chapter of my life. This piece, which we wrote early in my career despite the vast distances between us, has stuck with me for its emphasis on political economy and class. Too often, these themes have been marginalized in disability studies and Marta's work was pivotal in shaping my perspective. Early on, I decided I wanted to edit an anthology to honor Marta and received the enthusiastic support of the Russell family and from scholars in numerous disciplines including law, education, and English. The essays that appear in this volume all try to build on Russell's legacy in their respective fields. Two panels honoring Marta, which contained earlier versions of many of the contributions you will find within these pages were also held at the Society for Disability Studies' Annual Meeting in Atlanta in June, 2015 and the Canadian Law and Society Association Annual Meeting at the University of Ottawa, in Ottawa, Canada also in June, 2015.

A project like this inevitably takes on many debts. Katie Carpenter at Routledge has once again been endlessly supportive in providing timely editorial assistance. I cannot thank Steve Weiss (Marta's long-time partner and companion) and Georgia Scheele (daughter of Marta) enough for their tireless support of this initiative and their willingness to answer countless emails and phone calls. Professors Mark Weber and Anne Finger went out of their way to provide chapters well in advance to facilitate contract finalization. My former advisor at Harvard Law School, Professor Samuel R Bagenstos now of the University of Michigan, has been kind enough to write a foreword. Megan Rusciano and Lauren Lindsay provided valuable editing assistance. I also wish to thank the anonymous peer reviewers who gave of their time to review various chapters. Dean Nathalie Des Rosiers at the Faculty of Law, Common Law Section, University of Ottawa has been thoroughly supportive of this work and to social justice work in general. Finally, Christine Malone has been endlessly patient while I spent time revising this manuscript. I dedicate the volume to her.

A brief word on terminology. In order to emphasize disability pride, both disabled people and people with disabilities are used in the text as appropriate. This, I think, is in keeping with what Marta would have wanted.

Notes on contributors

Jihan Abbas, PhD sociology, has been involved in the disability movement for several years. Her research aims to build a more inclusive and equitable society and her interests include disability and the labor market, social policy, care, and exclusion.

Samuel R Bagenstos specializes in constitutional and civil rights litigation. From 2009–2011, he was a political appointee in the US Department of Justice, where he served as the Principal Deputy Assistant Attorney General for Civil Rights, the number-two official in the Civil Rights Division. His accomplishments included the promulgation of the 2010 Americans with Disabilities Act regulations—the first comprehensive update of those regulations since they were first promulgated in 1991—and the reinvigoration of the Civil Rights Division's enforcement of the Supreme Court's decision in *Olmstead v LC*, which guarantees people with disabilities the right to live and receive services in the most integrated setting appropriate. He led the negotiations of significant *Olmstead* settlements with the states of Delaware and Georgia, which guarantee appropriate, community-based services to thousands of people with disabilities. He also personally argued major cases in federal district courts and courts of appeals. He is Professor of Law at the University of Michigan Law School.

Liat Ben-Moshe is an Assistant Professor of Disability Studies at the University of Toledo. The co-editor of *Disability Incarcerated: Imprisonment and Disability in the United States and Canada* (Palgrave McMillan, 2014), she has written on such topics as deinstitutionalization and incarceration; the politics of abolition; disability; anti-capitalism and anarchism; queerness and disability; and inclusive pedagogy.

Michelle Bertrand holds her PhD in Social-Personality Psychology from Queen's University and is an Assistant Professor in the Criminal Justice Department at the University of Winnipeg. Her research and publishing interests are in the general area of Psychology and Law, with specific interests in the memory of eyewitnesses to crime, police eyewitness identification procedures, comprehensibility of Canadian judicial instructions, and conceptions of jury representativeness within the Canadian context.

David J Connor is a Professor and Chairperson of the Special Education Department, Hunter College, part of The City University of New York (CUNY). David is the author of several books: *Urban Narratives: Portraits-in-Progress—Life at the Intersections of Learning Disability, Race, and Social Class* (Peter Lang, 2008) and *Rethinking Disability: A Disability Studies Guide to Inclusive Practices,* co-authored with Jan Valle (McGraw-Hill, 2011). For more information, see: http://hunter-cuny.academia.edu/DavidJConnor.

April B Coughlin has worked as a high school teacher in New York City for six years and is currently pursuing a PhD in Inclusive Education at Syracuse University with a focus on disability, access and equality. April has been a paraplegic and wheeler for 28 years after a car accident at the age of six. She volunteers at rehabilitation centres speaking to newly spinal cord injured (SCI) individuals and provides support and guidance post-injury.

Nirmala Erevelles is Professor of Social and Cultural Studies in Education at the University of Alabama. Her teaching and research interests lie in the areas of disability studies; critical race theory, transnational feminism, sociology of education, and postcolonial studies. Specifically, her research focuses on the unruly, messy, unpredictable and taboo body—a habitual outcast in educational (and social) contexts. Erevelles has published articles in the *American Educational Research Journal*, the *Journal of Curriculum Studies*, *Disability & Society*, *Disability Studies Quarterly*, and the *Journal of Literary and Cultural Disability Studies*, among others. Her book, *Disability and Difference in Global Contexts: Towards a Transformative Body Politic* was published by Palgrave in November 2012.

Anne Finger is a writer of fiction and non-fiction. Her publications include the short story collection *Call Me Ahab* and the memoir *Elegy for a Disease: A Personal and Cultural History of Polio.* She lives in Oakland, California.

Richard Jochelson is an Associate Professor in the Department of Criminal Justice at the University of Winnipeg and holds his PhD in law from Osgoode Hall, York University. As of July 1 2016, he will be working at Robson Hall Law School at the University of Manitoba. He has published articles dealing with obscenity, indecency, judicial activism, police power, and disability in the criminal justice system. He is a member of the Bar of Manitoba and has co-authored three books—most recently, the *Disappearance of Criminal Law: Police Powers and the Supreme Court* (Fernwood, 2014).

Emily Perkins earned her PhD in English from the University of Alabama in 2012 where her dissertation, entitled *Re-figuring the Mestizo Body: Disability and Illness in Chicano Literature*, earned the University of Alabama's award for the most outstanding dissertation in the Arts and Sciences Division (2014). Perkins also writes creative nonfiction, much of which is based on her experiences with a high-level spinal cord injury, which she sustained from a life-altering car accident 20 years ago.

Zach Richter is a graduate student in UCSD's Communication Studies PhD Program. He is known for his continued work on queer and Marxian derivations of critical disability studies as well as his cutting-edge campaigns for communication accessibility in a variety of venues.

Matthew Smith is a graduate of the University of Ottawa Faculty of Law (2016). His research interests are in human rights, disability, labour and employment law. Matthew is currently articling with a civil litigation boutique in Ottawa.

Jean Stewart is the author of the acclaimed disability rights novel, *The Body's Memory* (St. Martin's Press) and has published stories, poems, and essays in *With Wings: An Anthology of Literature by and about Women with Disabilities* (Feminist Press), *Beyond Crisis: Confronting Health Care in the US* (Penguin), *Staring Back: The Disability Experience from the Inside Out* (Penguin), and *Voices from the Edge: Narratives about the Americans with Disabilities Act* (Oxford University Press), as well as in *Monthly Review* (with co-author Marta Russell) and other journals. Having engaged in disability rights activism in Cuba, India (where she co-organized a World Social Forum panel), Brazil, and Mexico, she is presently involved in a movement to stop a vast swath of California from being clear-cut and poisoned with pesticides.

Suzanne Stolz, EdD, serves at the University of San Diego as Academic Coordinator of the Online MEd and as faculty for the programme's Universal Design for Learning and Inclusive Education specialization. As a disabled woman, she has facilitated mentoring programmes for disabled young people and presented trainings for school districts on "What Graduates with IEPs Wish Their Educators Addressed".

Mark C Weber serves as Vincent de Paul Professor of Law at DePaul University in Chicago. He is the author of *Disability Harassment* (NYU Press), *Understanding Disability Law* (Lexis-Nexis), *Special Education Law Cases and Materials* (with Mawdsley and Redfield) (Lexis-Nexis), and *Special Education Law and Litigation Treatise* (LRP Publications); selected additional publications of his may be found at http://ssrn.com/author=83733.

Part I

Legal implications

1 The legal politics of Marta Russell: a Castoriadan reading

Ravi Malhotra

In this chapter, I explore the main intellectual ideas of the long neglected disability rights activist and scholar, Marta Russell (1951–2013), the subject of this anthology. I argue that Russell's identification of neo-liberal capitalism as the central problematic facing people with disabilities, exemplified in her landmark book, *Beyond Ramps: Disability at the End of the Social Contract*, is an original insight and major contribution to modern disability politics. By bringing the beginnings of a materialist analysis into the world of disability rights, Russell opened the door for the possibility of a fully-fledged counter-hegemonic theory of disablement that is so badly needed today. For too many legal scholars, amending the *Americans with Disabilities Act* (ADA) or transforming its case law is seen as the complete answer to the dilemmas faced by people with disabilities. For them, the social model, the idea that structural barriers are the main problem faced by disabled people today, is articulated exclusively through law. For many in American disability studies, an original interest in the symbolic interactionism of Erving Goffman (Shuttleworth and Meekosha, 2013: 351; Goffman, 1963) has degenerated into a focus primarily on culture and identity. Russell cogently argues in defense of a political economy approach. I suggest, however, that Russell's genuine insights can be fruitfully deepened by a critical engagement with the political thought of radical Greek-French philosopher, Cornelius Castoriadis. In Part I, I provide a short overview of Russell's life and introduce her to those new to her work. In Part II, I highlight the central ideas of her legacy, focusing particularly on the arguments contained in *Beyond Ramps.* In Part III, I provide a selective overview of some of the key ideas of Castoriadis. In Part IV, I argue that a Castoriadan reading of Russell's work provides the basis for a liberatory disability politics. Elsewhere, I have considered how other radical theorists, such as those associated with the Sojourner Truth Organization, might provide new insight into disability politics (Malhotra, 2014b) and others have examined the politics of disablement in the context of the autonomist Marxist tradition (Richter, this volume). However, in the interests of space, I confine myself here solely to Castoriadis. In Part V, I offer some potential law reforms that would undergird a Castoriadan reading of Russell's legacy. In Part VI, I provide an overview of the chapters that follow in this volume.

Part I: Marta Russell: a life of struggle and ideas

Marta Russell was born in 1951 near the town of Clarksdale, Mississippi in the Mississippi Delta (Clay, 2015). Disabled since birth and raised on a cotton farm, Russell was always integrated in regular classrooms despite the fact that she required leg braces and underwent periodic surgeries to attempt to improve her mobility. In an interview with noted disability advocate Laura Hershey, Russell comments on how she was given a tricycle to get between buses in an era when integration of students with physical disabilities was by no means the norm. Russell speculates that this may well have been in part because Mississippi was so poor that they did not have the institutional funding for a segregated school system for children born with disabilities (Hershey, 2000). As a child, Russell did not particularly self-identify as a disabled person. However, her impairments did preclude her participation in certain activities such as cheerleading, which all her friends did as children (Hershey, 2000). One might argue that, like many young girls with disabilities, her physical impairments freed her from certain ascribed gender roles that were dominant in the 1950s and 1960s to focus on more intellectual pursuits.

Russell had the good fortune to come of age at a time of enormous change in American society in general and in Mississippi in particular (Hamlin, 2012). The turbulent 1960s saw the destruction of the racist Jim Crow system that had dominated the South for nearly a century. The unpopular draft for the Vietnam War created massive unrest on college campuses throughout the United States. A participant in the emerging civil rights and anti-war movements, Russell grew up in a well-to-do family that included a Governor of Mississippi amongst her ancestors and attended the prestigious Lausanne boarding school for girls in Memphis, Tennessee during the late 1960s. Although Russell had physical impairments since birth, she had sufficient mobility in her youth to be included in this elite institution, notwithstanding the physically inaccessible environment that was common in private schools at the time (Clay, 2015). As a young woman, she was active as a volunteer for the American Civil Liberties Union (ACLU) in the enforcement of desegregation in Jackson, Mississippi and was friendly with activists who started an underground newspaper that drew the ire of the authorities (Hershey, 2000). In the early 1970s, she earned a bachelor's degree in visual arts from the Memphis College of Art (Malhotra, 2014a).

A major turning point in Russell's life came when she permanently moved to California in 1974 (Clay, 2015). In Los Angeles, she built a successful career as a photographer and graphic designer, and moved into the film industry, building her own company for title design and acting as a Supervisor for Disney's 1982 film *Tron*. During this busy time period, her daughter Georgia Scheele was born. Russell later created notable documentaries on visual effects and the disability community (Scheele, 2015). In the late 1980s, Russell gradually developed more mobility issues, necessitating the use of a wheelchair. Always the black sheep of the family and now divorced, she also found herself radicalized toward disability politics as her impairments made it increasingly difficult for her to work in the film industry, forcing her to eventually apply for Social Security Disability Insurance (SSDI) benefits (Weiss, 2015; Russell, 2005). From 1990 to 2005, Russell devoted her time to publishing both academic scholarship and activist articles about the socio-economic oppression of people with disabilities as neo-liberalism grew increasingly powerful after 1990. In 1994, she made the award winning video, "Disabled and the Cost of Saying I Do" on marriage disincentives for disabled people receiving social assistance (Russell, 1994a) that continue to plague American society more than 20 years later. She was also active in two organizations with occasionally conflicting belief systems. She played a role in the disability advocacy group, Not Dead Yet, which has been a stalwart voice in opposing physician assisted suicide because of concerns that vulnerable people with disabilities will be convinced to end their lives. They have been vocal in raising concerns about the activities of discredited physician Jack Kevorkian, among others (Russell, 1998: 29–30). She also served as a member of the Board of Directors of the Southern California chapter of the ACLU, an organization that has supported, *inter alia*, the right of individuals to end their own lives ("Marta Russell LinkedIn Profile"; "The Successes of the American Civil Liberties Union").

Russell also organized protests against telethons in Los Angeles that featured demeaning portrayals of people with disabilities. Many in the disability community have challenged the degrading way that telethons such as the Jerry Lewis Telethon have painted a picture of people with disabilities as helpless objects of pity (Shapiro, 1993; Longmore, 1997). She was also a participant in the activities of ADAPT, a militant direct action organization that in recent years has mobilized to demand appropriate funding to allow people with disabilities to live with appropriate attendant services in the community, rather than nursing homes (Hershey, 2000). Attendant services typically offer assistance with activities of daily living such as bathing, dressing, and toileting. I was privileged to co-author a piece with Marta on capitalism and disability that appeared in the journal, *Socialist Register* (Russell and Malhotra, 2001) and have the opportunity to present it at what was then known as the Socialist Studies Conference in 2002 in Manhattan on a panel that included noted public intellectual, Naomi Klein. Unfortunately, due to health issues, Russell ceased her writing career after 2005 until her untimely death in 2013. In all of her myriad political activities, Russell was one of a very small number of American disability rights advocates to focus again and again on disability discrimination through the lens of a political economy perspective. Where so many disability studies scholars have been distracted by issues of identity and culture, for Marta, class was central.

Part II: The disability politics of Marta Russell

Marta's political writings are extensive. They range in tone from scholarly to populist and activist. Unfortunately, they are scattered across a number of small circulation theoretical journals such as *Monthly Review* (Stewart and Russell, 2001; Russell, 2005), *Socialist Register* (Russell and Malhotra, 2001), and *Counterpunch*

(Russell, 2003) as well as magazines devoted to the disability community such as *The Disability Rag* (Russell, 1994b; Russell, 1994c). No central depository of her work exists as of this writing nor does there seem to be even a comprehensive listing of her publications. This poses serious challenges for researchers trying to study and appraise her work. For the purposes of this chapter, I will focus on her hard-hitting and pioneering if populist monograph, *Beyond Ramps: Disability at the End of the Social Contract*, published by Common Courage Press in 1998 (Russell, 1998). In primarily focusing on political economy and the role of people with disabilities in a free market economy, this text is emblematic of Russell's overall oeuvre.

In *Beyond Ramps*, Russell presciently anticipates the massive downsizing of the welfare state that has unfolded in the 15 years since its publication. In fact, one of her core messages is that people with disabilities essentially function as canaries in the coal mine. The marginalization that people with disabilities experience in (or more often outside) the labor market merely anticipates the dismal economic future of large sections of the working class if free market capitalism continues unchallenged. Sadly, with Donald Trump a serious Presidential candidate at this time of writing, anti-capitalist ideas remain almost as marginal today as they were in 1998. Divided into three parts, the book opens with an explanation of disability oppression and the use of the concept of normalcy to structure hierarchies predicated on ableism (Russell, 1998: Ch 1). Russell does this effectively through an exposition of the Nazi legacy of eugenics and its linkages to social Darwinism. She documents how eugenic ideas had influence in the United States as well (Russell, 1998: Ch 2). This leads to a discussion of the right to die movement and its ableist implications (Russell, 1998: Ch 3) and the Human Genome Project (Russell, 1998: Ch 4).

In the second part, Russell outlines the mechanics of poverty and how people with disabilities are marginalized in a system that is based first and foremost on profitability. She analyzes how the rise of the market required conformity to bodily standards to ensure efficient production in the factory system. This inevitably excluded disabled people who could not conform to those standards (Russell, 1998: Ch 5). Russell then details the hierarchies that are endemic to the social assistance system for people with disabilities in the United States. Not only are there a bewildering array of rules and regulations that can easily lead to a denial of benefits, there is a very clear class system that places injured veterans at the very top, disabled workers who are entitled to SSDI based on their past earnings and contributions in the middle, and those people with disabilities with no work history at the bottom who must survive on the most meagre social program known as Supplemental Security Income (SSI). The American social benefit system, which keeps disabled people with no work history in deep poverty, compares badly to the more generous welfare system on offer in Scandinavian countries such as Sweden. Russell also importantly draws attention to the layers of bureaucracy, including medical doctors, social workers and policy makers, which benefit through well-remunerated professional careers from the byzantine framework which people with disabilities must navigate daily (Russell, 1998: Ch 6).

She then devotes a chapter to the debilitating role that charity has played in the lives of disabled people. A particularly appropriate time for reflection as the Jerry Lewis Muscular Dystrophy Association Telethon, as of this writing, has finally come to a close, Russell documents how the Telethon portrayed disabled people as pitiful and helpless. At the same time, they maintained a vast bureaucracy staffed with many lavishly paid executives who were paid, in some cases, up to $300,000 a year in 1992, while spending relatively little on assistive devices that would benefit disabled patients. She also identifies the tax deductions associated with charitable giving, which benefit the wealthy (Russell, 1998: Ch 7).

Building on this theme of the commodification of disability, Russell turns her attention to the failings of the nursing home industry. She illustrates how the American nursing home industry generates huge profits from the institutionalization of people with disabilities who typically are not able to perform wage labor. At the same time, they are significant donors to politicians and have stymied the developments of more dignified (and ironically cheaper) alternatives, such as the development of personal attendant services that would enable people with disabilities to remain in their homes. She documents the tragic physical and emotional abuse that has been rampant in many institutions, often compromising the health of the residents, and the shocking number of citations that nursing homes have received for violating patients' rights (Russell, 1998: Ch 8). As she poignantly remarks, "[t]hose who have done time in nursing homes have exposed the rat-infested rooms, witnessed maggots crawling in open wounds, and counted the days inmates have lain neglected in feces" (Russell, 1998: 99). The deliberate choice of language referencing incarceration in penal institutions is unmistakable. As Russell notes, disability rights advocates have established organizations such as ADAPT which have used direct action tactics to confront nursing home operators and politicians about the abuses in the industry and the need for funded personal attendant services (Russell, 1998: 99).

In Chapter 9 of her book, Russell analyzes the deficiencies of the ADA, which she castigates as free market civil rights. She was among the first commentators to put forth the argument that many disability rights advocates were able to win essential Republican support for passage of the ADA by framing the issue as one of promoting independence, a key theme in American public discourse and historical imagination, and removing people from the welfare rolls. While legal scholars in more recent years have capably built on this theory to show how disability organizations embraced the welfare reform arguments (Bagenstos, 2003: 958–68), Russell was among the first to identify this clear libertarian discourse embedded in the philosophy of many disability advocacy organizations. A second problem is the fact that the onus lies on the disabled individual to file a complaint. Combined with woefully inadequate resources at the Equal Employment Opportunity Commission to process complaints, this leaves many disabled Americans without access to justice. Russell contrasts the legal status of African Americans and women, who are entitled to affirmative action, with disabled people who are excluded from such measures in the United States (Russell, 1998: Ch 9).

The third part of *Beyond Ramps* is devoted to a discussion of the ending of the social contract. By this, Russell means the Keynesian consensus at the end of the Second World War that offered full employment and prosperity for many Americans in exchange for cooperative labor relations. Of course, as is well-known, the American welfare state was never particularly generous in the first place. Unlike most Western countries, it never established a single payer health care system that provided universal health benefits to all. Russell makes the point that incrementalist change through civil rights cannot remedy the massive economic marginalization faced by people with disabilities. As many others have documented in many countries in the industrialized world (Supiot et al., 2001; Lobel, 2001; Fudge and Cossman, 2002), Russell also notes how full-time employees are expected to work longer hours while an army of contingent workers must get by on part-time employment with few benefits. American law also authorizes paying people with disabilities in some circumstances below the minimum wage and this has largely (and shamefully) not changed since Russell published her book (Russell, 1998: Ch 10). While I would argue some disabled professionals might benefit from the flexibility offered by the New Economy, Russell is accurate in suggesting this marks a massive decline in labor standards for the majority.

In Chapter 11, Russell is at her polemical best in outlining the efforts of both Congressional Republicans and Democrats alike to support cuts to the SSI program. These include initiatives by the Carter and Reagan administrations to arbitrarily dump large numbers of people from the disability benefits rolls. This took the form of Continuing Disability Reviews (CDRs) using independent physicians who did not necessarily understand the complexity of the patient's situation. This has to be understood in a context in which receiving entitlements in the first place is a harrowing process replete with significant delays. Again and again, Russell is crystal clear in marshalling the evidence that claims by Republicans of massive fraud in the SSI system are largely without merit. Instead, she insists that full employment for all must be the demand to counter neo-liberal trends that seek to exclude whole categories of people with disabilities from entitlements (Russell, 1998: Ch 11).

In Chapter 12, Russell begins another hard-hitting chapter by documenting the hostility of the late Mother Teresa toward wheelchair accessibility. Russell demonstrates how Mother Teresa did not support the installation of an elevator in a New York City homeless shelter because she regarded elevators as a luxury from a religious perspective. Yet, Russell shows how Mother Teresa ran a charitable business with tens of millions of dollars. She goes on to show how both Republicans and Democrats alike supported massive cuts during the 1990s to the Medicaid programs. Republicans have also enthusiastically supported devolution to the states, which endangers the notion of national standards of medical services for low income people with disabilities. Russell painstakingly documents the efforts of Republican governors in Michigan, New York, and Wisconsin to ruthlessly cut funding to the most vulnerable, in some cases in an effort to drive them out of the state altogether (Russell, 1998: Ch 12).

In Chapter 13, Russell shows how corporate donations have corrupted the democratic system in the United States. She connects this to the growing power of international institutions such as the World Trade Organization (WTO). At times, the analysis proffered by Russell can resemble a problematic return to nationalism. However, her overall critique by and large is accurate in showing the devastating impact that freer trade under NAFTA and other such agreements have had on employment. She legitimately identifies the corrupting role of money in the financial system (Russell, 1998: Ch 13). This leads in Chapter 14 to her proposals for social change entitled "Manifesto of an Uppity Crip." Russell advocates for democratic control of businesses; corporate accountability; campaign finance reform; increasing corporate taxes to 1950 levels; proportional representation (writing before the 2000 election crisis that saw the Supreme Court hand the outcome to George W Bush); greater participatory democracy; a shift away from growth to reflect green principles; citizen review of government agencies, which wield bureaucratic power; environmentally sustainable development; democratizing the corporate media; universal access of public and private spaces; single payer universal health care; redress of the enormous wealth gap in American society; fair corporate taxes without unreasonable loopholes; full employment funded through a tax on financial transactions; ecological assessment of new jobs; a living wage for all workers; ending penalties for people on disability benefits who wish to work; an expansion of personal assistance services; allowing people to work part time without penalty; increased government responsibility to promote equality; adequate funding for Social Security; quality education; quality child care services; clean air and water; effective occupational safety laws; preventing cuts to social programs to pay off deficits; and acting globally. This long list might be seen as a radical Keynesian program and I analyze it more closely later in the chapter. In her final short chapter, Russell advocates against a divisive identity politics and for a commitment to universalism. I now turn in Part III to explain the central ideas of the polymath Cornelius Castoriadis.

Part III: Into the labyrinth: the legacy of Cornelius Castoriadis

The political and philosophical legacy of Cornelius Castoriadis is both a contested one and not one that is easily summarized. In recent years, a large number of books and journal articles have appeared, devoted to debating the implications of his thought. What follows is inevitably selective and stylized. Born in Istanbul in 1922, still known as Constantinople at the time, his family moved to Athens, Greece when he was three months old (Dosse, 2014: 13). Castoriadis studied law, economics and philosophy at the University of Athens where he was a member of the Trotskyist movement. Faced with a dire threat to his personal security during the Greek Civil War by both the pro-capitalist and Stalinist forces that regarded Trotskyists as the enemy, he moved permanently to France in 1945 where he became an economist with the OECD (Dosse, 2014). Despite achieving a significant measure of professional success, he remained without French citizenship for many decades. He consequently used numerous pseudonyms in his radical political writing, including Paul Cardan and Pierre Chaulieu, which only complicates tracing the evolution of his thought. The first to translate Max Weber into the Greek language, he is perhaps best known for his 1975 magnum opus, *The Imaginary Institution of Society (IIS)*, which combines insights on transcending the Marxist tradition with his deepening interest in psychoanalysis. The power of imagination became a central theme in Castoriadis' thought (Adams, 2011: 226). He has also attracted a following for his earlier work in the 1950s and 1960s as a leading member and co-founder of the legendary anti-Stalinist radical group, Socialisme ou Barbarie, that is reputed to have influenced many activists who led the 1968 French General Strike (Adams, 2011: 226; Van Der Linden, 1997; Gabler, 2013). Yet, there is a connection between these two aspects of Castoriadis. It is no coincidence that one of the slogans of the 1968 General Strike was "power to the imagination" (Wolf, 2013: 186). Although the short-lived but highly creative Socialisme ou Barbarie group has only received modest attention among English language scholars (Hastings-King, 2014), it is fitting that the left-radical Syriza government that was recently elected to power in Greece has proposed putting Castoriadis on the 50 drachma note, in the event that Greece were to leave the European Monetary Union and adopt the drachma (Evans-Pritchard, 2015).

One of the central ideas in Castoriadis' thought is his commitment to struggle against bureaucracy in all its forms. Castoriadis believed that the "reason of rationalization obscured the function of the collective imagination" (Murphy, 2014: 141). For Castoriadis, the collective imagination was essential for the creative dynamism associated with capitalism. However, in modern bureaucratic societies, this creativity is deeply distorted by bureaucratic structures—whether of the free market variety of the West or the Stalinist bureaucracy of the East—whereby human beings become merely a means to the end of production. This is embodied in Castoriadis' famous quip, "Union of Soviet Socialist Republics, USSR: Four Letters, Four Lies" (Murphy, 2014: 148; Memos, 2014: 36). Castoriadis argues repeatedly for autonomy to combat the pernicious influence of bureaucracies. He contrasts the autonomous society with the vast majority of heteronomous societies in history. This can be seen in the day-to-day practices of the group, Socialisme ou Barbarie, which Castoriadis co-founded with Claude Lefort in 1949. Gabler notes how what she calls revolutionary work research was used to describe the possibilities and limitations of solidarity on the French shop floor such as the Renault factory at Billancourt. These were finely grained accounts of daily factory life. The writers were encouraged to both report and analyze their own experiences to break down any division between researcher and worker. Only they could understand and articulate their own experiences (Gabler, 2013: 159–61; Hastings-King, 2014).

Anticipating a generation of labor studies scholarship, the reports of Socialisme ou Barbarie activists such as Daniel Mothé and Philippe Guillaume indicate the extreme degree to which Fordist factory systems require the workers to follow orders obediently and learn as little as possible about the day-to-day operation of the factory. As Gabler remarks, "[t]he factory absorbs people arranging them in human poles of execution and management comparable to the tense relationship between anode and cathode" (Gabler, 2013: 163). Similar efforts to diagnose alienation and class exploitation in the United States were undertaken in the 1950s by the Johnson-Forest tendency led by the Trinidadian Marxist CLR. James and Raya Dunayevskaya, a former secretary of Leon Trotsky who immigrated to the United States from Russia as a young child (Glaberman, 1999; Hastings-King, 2014). Tellingly, the entire idea of initiative by workers was regarded by managers as a threat to the system (Gabler 2013: 165–66; Hastings-King 2014: Ch 6). There is therefore simultaneously the inclusion and exclusion of workers. They were disempowered because any acts of creativity were strictly regulated or prohibited. At the same time, their relatively secure financial status in the form of permanent employment at a well-remunerated rate gave them a stake in the system of wage labor. This contradiction was regarded by Castoriadis as the possible basis for building an autonomous alternative that put human needs first (Gabler, 2013: 171).

This perspective allowed Castoriadis to produce highly original insights that were largely ignored by the French and broader international left. By postulating worker control and self-management rather than state ownership as the key criterion for radical social transformation, the Socialisme ou Barbarie group were more or less unique on the international left in expressing solidarity with the outbreak of working-class resistance in the former East Germany in June, 1953, and in Poland and Hungary in 1956 (Hastings-King, 2014: 15). Castoriadis was unrelenting in pointing out the authoritarian features of life in Stalinist Russia and the malevolent role official Marxism played in dogmatically justifying this: the hidden patterns of worker resistance, the highly restrictive laws regulating production, and the use of violence and coercion to respond to threats from below. Despite the rhetoric of official Soviet Communism, sabotage, work slowdowns, and work stoppages were used by East German trade unionists to resist the restructuring of industry to accord to Soviet economic priorities (Hastings-King, 2014: 44, 82). Castoriadis was scathing in attacking scholars he perceived as apologists for the bureaucratic societies such as Althusser, seeing them as dangerously supporting authoritarian parties that claimed to possess the absolute truth while tyrannically trampling on the human rights of the citizens daily (Memos, 2012).

A second major aspect of Castoriadis' thought is his path-breaking focus on creativity and imagination. This requires the reader to appreciate Castoriadis' sometimes arcane terminology. Deeply influenced by Ancient Greek philosophers such as Aristotle as well as by the legacies of Maurice Merleau-Ponty and Martin Heidegger, Castoriadis argues that self-creation is the mode of being of the social-historical. In developing the concept of the social-historical, Castoriadis merges his notion of the social world with history (Adams, 2011). In the *IIS*, a work that reflects the evolution of his post-Marxist thought, Castoriadis defines the social-historical as "the anonymous collective whole, the impersonal-human element that fills every given social formation but which also engulfs it, setting each society in the midst of others, inscribing them all within a continuity in which those who are no longer, those who are elsewhere and even those yet to be born are in a certain sense present" (Castoriadis, 1987: 108).

Castoriadis later clarifies that his conception of self-creation or what he refers to as creation *ex nihilo* is not without constraints. Castoriadis acknowledges that there are biological and environmental constraints. Second, he notes that there are internal constraints on the psyche (Castoriadis, 1997a: 332–34). Reflecting Castoriadis' deep interest in psychoanalysis, he acknowledges that the psyche must be supplied with meaning through what he calls social imaginary significations. They are the answers to the big questions of society such as what do we desire and who are we (Castoriadis, 1997a: 334; Castoriadis, 1987: 146–47). In order to thrive, a society must first decide what is meaningful for the society (Klimis, 2013: 144). This emphasis reflects in part the phenomenological impetus of Castoriadis (Straume, 2013: 212–13). Third, there are historical constraints. The self-creation of society is shaped by the traditions and heritage of a given society, albeit in accordance with the social imaginary significations of the present (Castoriadis, 1997a: 334–35). Fourth, Castoriadis maintains that social imaginary significations have to be coherent within the context of socialized individuals. There may still be very real contradictions. He provides the example of a society where there may be construction of lavish pyramids as a tribute to deities while simultaneously peasants face starvation. Nevertheless, social imaginary significations have to be complete. By this, Castoriadis means that questions that undermine the social imaginary signification cannot be posed (Castoriadis, 1997a: 335–36). To provide an illustration, the idea that the market ought to be the central governing system for the allocation of wealth and power is frequently taken for granted by virtually all actors in the American political system.

In explicating his theory of social imaginary significations, Castoriadis distinguishes between two dimensions in which the institution of society unfolds. The first is the ensemblist-identitary dimension. This refers to how societal institutions act on the basis of set theory in mathematics. There are determined elements, classes, properties and relations. In contrast, there is the imaginary dimension. In the imaginary dimension, existence is signification, an ontological creation that may not be fully determined. Castoriadis refers to this as the creation of alterity, indicating that it is not reducible to its antecedents (Adams, 2008). The ensemblist-identitary and imaginary dimensions work together to create social imaginary significations. Building an autonomous society requires the creation of liberating social imaginary significations, which replace the hierarchical world that presently exists (Castoriadis, 2010: 52).

It also should be stressed that Castoriadis drew inspiration for many of his political ideas from the forms of direct democracy practiced in Ancient Greece. He was deeply immersed in studies of Ancient Greece in the 1980s and increasingly emphasized autocreation of the social-historical, in contrast to divine creation that has influenced theocracies (Adams, 2011: 28; Dosse, 2014: 285). This refers to the capacity of ordinary people to shape their destinies by reconstructing society for their own ends. For Castoriadis, it was critical to appreciate that the participatory democracy of Ancient Greece operated in a fundamentally different way than the representative democracies of the post-Enlightenment West, which he regarded as liberal oligarchies where generalized conformism prevailed (Klimis, 2013: 134). In modern liberal democracies, there is a sharp delimitation of the kinds of questions that may be typically posed because of institutions such as the market. Indeed, many questions that are absolutely vital to the flourishing of people with disabilities, such as the number of hours per week of attendant services a particular individual will be granted, are frequently seen as entirely apolitical decisions that must be resolved by deference to a particular bureaucratic authority. Yet, bureaucratic authorities in capitalist societies typically make these decisions by prioritizing a need to meet woefully inadequate budget targets, rather than promoting human needs. Radical democracy has been replaced with a much impoverished form of formal equality and deference to the outcomes of the market (Browne, 2014: 202–3).

Closely related to the development of a participatory democracy with a capacity for self-creating institutions is the emphasis that Castoriadis places on education and endless questioning by citizens. He regards education, using the Greek term *paideia*, as an essential prerequisite in order for individuals to develop the capacity to create and transform their society. In other words, they must be socialized to live in a world of autonomy where creativity, critical thinking skills and the transformation of their world are valued (Castoriadis, 1997b: 10). While this clearly leads to a paradox in that an autonomous society is required to adequately shape individuals to develop the capacities to create the autonomous society with a fulfilling education that allows creativity to flourish, Castoriadis relies on the fact that revolutionary transformations, such as the French Revolution, have previously shaken the core of existing societies to allow new social imaginary significations to take root (Straume, 2013: 212–25). The approach outlined by Castoriadis is in sharp contrast to the neo-liberal practices of recent years that have sought to make education more amenable to market forces. Indeed, Brant and Panjwani have effectively shown how neo-classical economics is the only economics taught to English high school students (Brant and Panjwani, 2015: 307).

I argue that the Castoriadan emphasis on creativity and imagination is precisely what is needed to reconstruct our economy from the ground up to fully include and empower disabled people. As Tormey expresses in his reading of Castoriadis, individuals have the capacity to recreate the world through a radical social imaginary that breaks free from the weight of an authoritarian past to embrace a future of liberation for all. Such a vision requires a transformation of the human psyche to transcend the alienation so endemic under capitalism (Tormey, 2014: 189). As scholars such as Sophie Klimis and the writing duo of Toula Nicolacopoulos and George Vassilacopoulos cogently maintain, reflective subjects are co-creators of their world in Castoriadis' vision. The key factor is imagination, which is the basis for both reflexivity and deliberate action (Klimis 2013: 142). Market capitalist institutions are thus capable of being replaced by radically democratic and innovative institutions (Nicolapoulos and Vassilacopoulos, 2014: 262). I now turn in Part IV to outline what a Castoriadan reading of disability politics might look like.

Part IV: A Castoriadan reading of disability politics

How might we envision a Castoriadan interpretation of Russell's work? How can we infuse a systemic challenge to ableism with the most valuable insights of Castoriadis? While I am certainly not the first to consider this question (Shuttleworth and Meekosha, 2013; Shuttleworth, 2014), the existing literature has largely tended to be framed in the context of analyzing very specific questions, such as the construction of disabled sexuality relating to the imaginary (Shuttleworth, 2014). Two governing principles that I think can be derived from Castoriadis' legacy are the importance of grassroots democracy and a willingness to use creativity and imagination to reshape institutions to serve human ends. In its emphasis on possible innovation in remodelling legal institutions, Castoriadis is similar to the work of noted legal scholar Roberto Unger, who has argued for a democratic experimentalism to allow policy reforms to reshape society in smaller or larger ways. Unger argues that institutional histories are contingent and that the market economy is a legally indeterminate form. Accordingly, radical reforms can imaginatively reshape how society functions if we take on the challenge of implementing innovative policies, be it tax reform or the promotion of equality (Unger, 1998: 23; Unger, 1996; Unger, 1987). A related theme is the need for an educated citizenry, which is capable of asking hard questions and pushing for democratic principles. In the context of disability rights and battling structural ableism, grassroots democracy would mean ensuring that services for disabled people are controlled by disabled people themselves. This is consonant with the well-known slogan in the disability rights movement, "Nothing About Us Without Us" (Charlton, 2000). Too often, bureaucratic structures delay the provision of assistive devices or attendant services, which a disabled person needs to flourish. In other cases, the service provided is inadequate or only available in a setting inappropriate to the person's needs: a nursing home. A Castoriadan reading melds with Russell's justifiably dire account of the state of disabled people in the United States to provide a genuine alternative.

In the world of Castoriadis, especially during his years as an activist in Socialisme ou Barbarie, there was a priority accorded to promoting workers' councils at the point of production in line with classical Marxist thinking about the fundamental role played by the proletariat in ushering in a revolution that would bring the new society (Hastings-King, 2014). In my reading of a Castoriadan program for the liberation of disabled people, workers' councils would remain important but would incorporate the task of evaluating the accessibility of each job and coming up with methods to make the job accessible. This approach relies on the expertise of the workers in the workplace who know the job best, rather than experts who too often, in the neo-liberal paradigm predominant throughout the West, may only recommend minimal alterations because of a concern about the impact on profitability. Councils must be adapted to ensure the development of accessibility outside the context of labor markets. This is particularly important because, as Russell reminds us, decades after the passage of the ADA, most disabled Americans remain outside the labor market (Russell, 1998). Services such as attendant services would be directed by councils of disabled people who have a direct stake in the quality of the care and are attuned to the potential for physical or emotional abuse. Advocating for accessibility in the community would no longer be handled in a piecemeal way, which requires a party to demonstrate that each request is reasonable and not undue hardship. Instead, accessibility councils would ensure that community services and amenities provided robust accessibility to wheelchair users and those with sensory impairments.

The overarching impetus of Castoriadis' intervention I think would be to ensure the democratic accountability of Russell's proposals. As I alluded to in Part II, her economic program is on the surface very radical. In many ways, she anticipated some 15 years ago social movements that have only recently garnered attention in the media and the popular imagination, including the living wage movement (Hewlett, 2005). She calls for a democratization of multiple spheres of life including the media, elections, corporate power as well as initiatives such as greening the economy. This is all tremendously valuable and a crucial step forward. I think, however, that the emphasis Castoriadis places on both democracy and imagination ensures that the proposals Russell makes are not simply reversed in the next election cycle. This has been a classic problem for reformist social democratic parties that face international pressure, as the left party Syriza in Greece is currently experiencing as it deals with repayment of the Greek debt (Kouvelakis, 2015). Castoriadis demands a deeper transformation in both society and the very individuals that make it up, ensuring that the change is long-term and that citizens have a real commitment to the program. By demanding more than just reformist Keynesianism, I think there is also a greater likelihood of long-term sustainability.

One important dimension that has to be addressed is the marginalization of workers who provide attendant services. In the United States and elsewhere, these workers are predominantly female, typically paid very low wages and have little job security. As a result, there is frequent turnover, which can be very disruptive in the life of a disabled person. It is not regarded as a valued career (Stacey, 2011). One way that could simultaneously empower both disabled people and attendants who work in this industry is to build structural institutions to reduce turnover. Instead of providing funding to community agencies or school boards to assist disabled people, the funding could be directly attached to the disabled person who would not have to constantly retrain new attendants nor argue with agencies about the merits of a particular attendant. The disabled person would be empowered to make the decisions about their care that affect their lives. This would provide greater stability for both the disabled person and job security for the service provider. A career ladder should retain more qualified individuals and ultimately offer greater wages and benefits for attendants (Malhotra and Rowe, 2014). This should result in greater dignity for both disabled users of attendant services and the women and men providing the service. Castoriadis' idea of a social imaginary signification is salient here. To truly embrace attendant services, one has to reimagine disabled people as autonomous and equal citizens who are capable of making their own choices. Current policy makers tend to see users of attendant services paternalistically and as incapable of knowing what is in their best interests (Krogh and Johnson, 2006). Yet, disability scholars have increasingly suggested that one ought to consider citizens to be interdependent. When one adopts such a lens, one sees the potential to build alliances between women with family responsibilities and people with disabilities who require personal assistance with activities of daily living (Watson et al., 2004: 340–41).

A second important point is how to build structured learning and education about ableism and disability discrimination into society. As I noted, Castoriadis stresses the importance of the educated citizen. To make real progress on the questions of inclusion for disabled people requires substantive education. Removing physical barriers will not result in genuine equality unless discriminatory attitudes about disabled people are rectified. Yet, the reality is many people have little knowledge of disability. Like gays and lesbians, disabled people are typically raised by parents who do not share their identity so there is not necessarily transmission within families about concepts such as disability rights, disability pride, and empowerment that are key to the flourishing of disabled people. Elsewhere, Morgan Rowe and I have suggested that the introduction of disability history into the school curriculum could be a valuable step in educating citizens about the importance of disability rights and disability equality (Malhotra and Rowe, 2014). If this were combined with a generally radical pedagogy that encouraged critical reasoning skills along the lines advocated by Castoriadis (Castoriadis, 1997b: 10), one could foresee school classrooms as laboratories where new forms of inclusion and empowerment for disabled people were discussed, debated, and proposed. These might include a much larger proportion of the population choosing to learn sign language or innovative approaches to modifying the latest technological developments to ensure that they are accessible to all disabled people (Roulstone, 1998). It might also entail lifelong education as a component of one's working life so that education no longer is this demarcated span of time at the end of adolescence. This would ensure that workers of all ages were exposed to ideas relating to ableism. However, I turn now to Part V to consider some law reform strategies that may bring a Castoriadan reading of Russell's political prescriptions into reality.

Part V: Some law reform strategies

Proposing law reform strategies that would remain true to the principles of Russell and Castoriadis is inevitably hazardous. It is difficult to capture the full range and complexity of their thought in the form of law reform proposals and there is a risk of oversimplification. Nevertheless, one valuable starting point may well be the work of American labor law scholar, Karl Klare. Klare has famously proposed redesigning the workplace through measures that enhance democracy in the workplace (Klare, 1988; Malhotra, 2015). He asserts, very much in the spirit of Russell and Castoriadis, that work should be "structured to provide opportunities for learning, self-discovery, growth and expression" (Klare, 1988: 8). He identifies three approaches: enhancing collective bargaining, democratizing the governance structure of firms, and democratizing labor markets among both unionized and non-unionized workers (Klare, 1988).

Enhancing collective bargaining is essential to revive unions, which are now in deep crisis. In both the United States and Canada, union density rates have declined, especially in the much beleaguered private sector (Galarneau and Sohn, 2013; Trottman, 2015). In order to strengthen the voice of workers, reversing this decline needs to become a leading priority for disability rights advocates. Strengthening unions will strengthen the capacity of workers to raise arguments about disability accommodations, even when a particular union has not had a history of championing disability rights. Empirical data from Canada using regression analysis has found that unionization is correlated with meeting accommodation needs (Shuey and Jovic, 2013: 190). Measures such as prohibiting replacement workers and granting better workplace access to union organizers would enhance collective bargaining, solidifying the position of unions which have largely been in retreat (Klare, 1988: 45–49). Granting better workplace access is particularly important in an Internet age in which unions may need to organize off-site workers who are not readily available or identifiable. Others have suggested that policy makers ought to consider minority unionism. Fairly common prior to the adoption of the *National Labor Relations Act* in the United States, often referred to as the Wagner model, minority unionism refers to the rights of union members who do not have majority support within a firm. In the United States, they may engage in protected concerted activity such as distributing union literature, retain the right to strike or picket and even bargain for their own members (Summers, 1990: 534–36). Given the significant barriers to winning certification elections, minority unionism has its attractions.

The second priority that Klare identifies is the need to democratize the governance structure of firms. Klare perceptively argues that workplaces require both participatory and adversarial institutional structures (Klare, 1988: 54). In so doing, he echoes the pioneering work of Castoriadis and his co-thinkers, such as Claude Lefort and, in the United States, CLR James, in identifying the deep alienation that factory workers experienced daily in the 1950s. A successful labor movement requires not simply negotiation of collective bargaining agreements but ensuring workers have a say in the governance of the firm in order to have a sense of dignity and confidence that their work is meaningful. This of course presupposes the inclusion of disabled workers in the firm in the first place. The precise mechanism might be membership on the firm's board of directors for union representatives or a direct ownership stake. Not only would this ensure that genuine inclusion of disabled people in the life of the firm is more likely to take place, it also makes it far more difficult for the owners to decide to relocate the plant (Klare, 1988: 53–55). It should be remembered that as Russell would remind us, disabled people face tremendous employment market barriers. Closure of a workplace has more negative effects on a disabled worker, who is less likely to be able to relocate than others.

Finally, Klare stresses the need to democratize markets. In his view, this entails raising wages and benefit demands and fighting against a segmented labor market to ensure labor market equality for women and racial minorities (Klare, 1988: 55–67). I agree but would argue that in the context of disability rights, it also means significant energies ought to be expended to ensure disabled people who want to work are provided with appropriate accommodations to enable them to work for the first time. Disabled people are structurally different from most minority groups in that the majority of disabled people across the Western industrialized world are not presently in the labor market. While the debates around commodification are complex (Taylor, 2004), I think it is reasonable to provide maximum support and technology for those who want to engage in the labor market, whether full-time or not, without stigmatizing those who choose to remain outside it. Ultimately, a society built on the principles articulated by Russell and Castoriadis would regard labor market entry as a personal inclination, rather than the stark moral, almost Calvinist, choice we are accustomed to viewing these issues today. One is reminded of Ursula Le Guin's iconic science fiction novel, *The Dispossessed*, which portrayed an anarchist planetoid, Annares, in which the word for work and play was identical (Le Guin, 1974). This unavoidably brief sketch will need to be supplemented by much greater scholarship on each aspect of market reconstruction. I conclude this introductory chapter with an overview of the contributions that follow in this volume.

Part VI: The chapters

The chapters that follow honor Russell's legacy in different ways and represent American and Canadian scholars from various disciplines such as law, sociology, education, and English. Both established academics and public intellectuals are featured. Part I of this book consists of legal contributions. In Chapter 2, Mark Weber provides an insightful account of legal issues relating to social insurance for workers with disabilities in the American context. Weber closely analyzes the SSDI program in the context of funding challenges and perceptions that the program is being abused. He provides a way to reconcile support for the SSDI program with the social model of disablement, which has stressed the empowerment and participation of people with disabilities in daily life. In Chapter 3, the writing duo Richard Jochelson and Michelle Bertrand discuss jury representativeness and people with disabilities. Writing in the Canadian context, Jochelson and Bertrand probe the issue of people with disabilities serving on juries and the implications that arise when people with disabilities are determiners of justice. In Chapter 4, which concludes this Part, Matthew Smith interrogates the use of zero tolerance policies in disciplining and discharging employees who face problems relating to drug and alcohol addiction.

Part II of this book addresses Russell's ideas within the realm of political economy. In Chapter 5, Liat Ben-Moshe and Jean Stewart explore issues faced by incarcerated disabled people and connect this back to Russell's ideas on political economy and the profound marginalization of disabled people under capitalism. In Chapter 6, Nirmala Erevelles' "The Political Economy of Disability at the Intersections of Difference" seeks to rescue the current impasse in disability studies by exploring how capitalism constitutes social difference within a number of historical contexts employing the ideology of disability imagined as "debilitating difference" to organize class divisions and preserve class antagonisms that benefit neo-liberal social arrangements in American society. She then explores transformative possibilities that a robust critique of capitalism from a materialist disability studies perspective can make possible. In Chapter 7, David J Connor and April B Coughlin's intervention, "Ramping it up: calling attention to dis/ability at the end of education's social contract" raises important issues about the American educational system and how it addresses disability accommodation and inclusion at a time of deep cutbacks. Connor addresses how he has used Russell's *Beyond Ramps* in courses in Disability Studies in Education, while Coughlin discusses her experiences as a teacher who uses a wheelchair and her research on students with mobility impairments.

In Chapter 8, Jihan Abbas analyzes issues relating to political economy and the social construction of intellectual disability. Building on and creatively extending Russell's framework, she argues that the social construction of intellectual disability may be traced to transformations in the economy. In Chapter 9, Zach Richter's contribution, "Autonomism and the disabled and able working classes: a class composition approach to histories of resistance and destructuration," argues that the opening of sanatoriums in 1885 represented a central shift in the move toward Fordist standardization through the establishment of sanity in the workforce. Richter sees this policy development as focused on maintaining ableness in the labor market, rather than primarily concerned with the health and welfare of the newly incarcerated. Finally, in Chapter 10, Suzanne Stolz concludes this Part with an intervention on the role of mentoring in facilitating empowerment, illuminating shared oppression and serving as a catalyst for change.

Part III, concerning Russell's relationship with the Humanities, begins with Emily Perkins' contribution on Benjamin Saenz's novel, *Carry Me Like Water.* In Chapter 11, Perkins explores narrative depictions of the deaf/mute/signing body in Saenz's novel to argue that the deaf/mute/signing body functions as a site of resistance to the oppression inherent in the capitalist economy's enforcement of oral language/English. It further argues that the deaf/mute/signing body can serve to foreground and disrupt class barriers. In Chapter 12, Anne Finger then presents a characteristic *tour de force* on eugenics in the Soviet Union, "The left hand of Stalin." Finger meticulously traces the shifts in eugenics policy in the early Soviet Union while Stalin was rapidly consolidating his power. As Finger demonstrates, eugenics was an idea that was supported by many, on both the left and the right. In the Appendix, I have chosen to reprint one of Marta's most insightful essays, "What disability civil rights cannot do" that was published in 2002 in the leading disability studies journal in the English language, *Disability & Society* (Russell, 2002). Here, we can read Marta in her own words as she outlines the limitations of a rights approach to alleviating systemic disability oppression in the labor market. Collectively, I hope that these contributions deepen the reader's understanding of disability studies and raise awareness of Marta Russell's continuing legacy.

Bibliography

Adams, S (2008) Towards a Post-Phenomenology of Life: Castoriadis' *Naturphilosophie. Cosmos and History: The Journal of Natural and Social Philosophy* 4: 1–2, available online at http://cosmosandhistory.org/index.php/journal/article/view/108/216# (last accessed August 5, 2015).

Adams, S (2011) *Castoriadis's Ontology: Being and Creation.* New York: Fordham University Press.

American Civil Liberties Union (no date) "The Successes of the American Civil Liberties Union," available online at www.aclu.org/successes-american-civil-liberties-union (last accessed July 27, 2015).

Bagenstos, S (2003) The Americans with Disabilities Act as Welfare Reform. *William and Mary Law Review* 44: 921–1028.

Brant, J and Panjwani, F (2015) School Economics and the Aims of Education: Critiques and Possibilities. *Journal of Critical Realism* 14(3): 306–24.

Browne, C (2014) Between Creative Democracy and Democratic Creativity. In Karalis, V (ed) *Cornelius Castoriadis and Radical Democracy.* Leiden, The Netherlands: Brill.

Castoriadis, C (1987) *The Imaginary Institution of Society*, trans by K Blamey. Cambridge: MIT Press.

Castoriadis, C (1997a) Radical Imagination and the Social Instituting Imaginary (1994). In Curtis, D (ed) *The Castoriadis Reader.* Malden, Massachusetts: Blackwell.

Castoriadis, C (1997b) Democracy as Procedure and Democracy as Regime. *Constellations* 4: 1–18.

Castoriadis, C (2010) Imaginary Significations. In Escobar, E, Gondicas, M, and Vernay, P (eds) *A Society Adrift: Interviews and Debates, 1974–1997*, trans by H Arnold. New York: Fordham University Press.

Charlton, JI (2000) *Nothing About Us Without Us: Disability Oppression and Empowerment.* Oakland: University of California Press.

Clay, M (2015) Interview, May 6.

Dosse, F (2014) *Castoriadis: Une Vie.* Paris: La Découverte.

Evans-Pritchard, A (2015) Humiliated Greece Eyes Byzantine Pivot as Crisis Deepens. *Telegraph*, February 28, available online at www.telegraph.co.uk/finance/economics/11441482/Humiliated-Greece-eyes-Byzantine-pivot-as-crisis-deepens.html (last accessed July 27, 2015).

Fudge, J and Cossman, B (2002) Introduction: Privatization, Law and the Challenge to Feminism. In Cossman, B and Fudge, J (eds) *Privatization, Law and the Challenge to Feminism.* Toronto: University of Toronto Press.

Gabler, A (2013) Artistic Critique? Socialisme ou Barbarie and Castoriadis's Concept of Revolutionary Work Research. In Straume, IS and Baruchello, G (eds) *Creation, Rationality and Autonomy: Essays on Cornelius Castoriadis.* Copenhagen: NSU Press.

Galarneau, D and Sohn, T (2013) Long-Term Trends in Unionization. *Insights on Canadian Society.* Ottawa: Statistics Canada, available online at www.statcan.gc.ca/pub/75-006-x/2013001/article/11878-eng.pdf (last accessed August 6, 2015).

Glaberman, M (1999) *Marxism For Our Times: C.L.R. James on Revolutionary Organization.* Jackson: University of Mississippi Press.

Goffman, E (1963) *Stigma: Notes on the Management of Spoiled Identity.* Englewood Cliffs, New Jersey: Prentice-Hall.

Hamlin, F (2012) *Crossroads at Clarksdale: The Black Freedom Struggle in the Mississippi Delta After World War II.* Chapel Hill: University of North Carolina Press.

Hastings-King, S (2014) *Looking for the Proletariat: Socialisme ou Barbarie and the Problem of Worker Writing*. Leiden, The Netherlands: Brill.

Hershey, L (2000) Is the ADA Enough? An Interview with Marta Russell. *Disability Life* July/August, available online at http://dljmlight.tripod.com/Text/Disability%20 Life%20Text/is_the_ada_enough__an_interview_with_marta_russell.htm (last accessed July 27, 2015).

Hewlett, D (2005) The Call for a Living Wage: Activists Fighting for Fair Wages Across the Country. *Canadian Dimension* May/June: 25–28.

Kouvelakis, S (2015) From the Absurd to the Tragic. *Jacobin*, July 10, available online at www.jacobinmag.com/2015/07/tsipras-syriza-greece-euro-debt/ (last accessed August 4, 2015).

Klare, KE (1988) Workplace Democracy and Market Reconstruction: An Agenda for Legal Reform. *Catholic University Law Review* 38: 1–68.

Klimis, S (2013) From Modernity to Neoliberalism: What Human Subject? In Straume, IS and Baruchello, G (eds) *Creation, Rationality and Autonomy: Essays on Cornelius Castoriadis*. Copenhagen: NSU Press.

Krogh, K and Johnson, J (2006) A Life without Living: Challenging Medical and Economic Reductionism in Home Support Policy for People with Disabilities. In Pothier, D and Devlin, R (eds) *Critical Disability Theory: Essays in Philosophy, Politics, Policy and Law*. Toronto: UBC Press.

Le Guin, U (1974) *The Dispossessed*. New York: Harper & Row.

Lobel, O (2001) Agency and Coercion in Labor and Employment Relations: Four Dimensions of Power in Shifting Patterns of Work. *University of Pennsylvania Journal of Labor and Employment Law* 4: 121–93.

Longmore, PK (1997) Conspicuous Contribution and American Cultural Dilemmas: Telethon Rituals of Cleansing and Renewal. In Mitchell, D and Snyder, S (eds) *The Body and Physical Difference: Discourses of Disability*. Ann Arbor: University of Michigan Press.

Malhotra, R (2014a) Honoring Marta Russell (1951–2013). *Against the Current*, available online at https://solidarity-us.org/site/node/4113 (last accessed July 27, 2015).

Malhotra, R (2014b) Beyond Wage Labor: The Politics of Disablement. *Tikkun* 29(4): 43–46.

Malhotra, R (2015) Karl Klare's Vision of Democratization in the Workplace and the Contradictory Evolution of Labour Law Jurisprudence in the Supreme Court of Canada. *Ottawa Law Review* 45(2): 303–41.

Malhotra R and Rowe, M (2014) *Exploring Disability Identity and Disability Rights Through Narratives: Finding a Voice of Their Own*. London: Routledge.

LinkedIn (no date) Marta Russell (profile), available online at www.linkedin.com/in/martarussell.

Memos, C (2012) Castoriadis on Althusser and the Crisis of Marxism. *Cosmos and History: The Journal of Natural and Social Philosophy* 8(2): 100–16.

Memos, C (2014) *Castoriadis and Critical Theory: Crisis, Critique and Radical Alternatives*. New York: Palgrave Macmillan.

Murphy, P (2014) Bureaucratic Capitalism and the Work of Cornelius Castoriadis. In Karalis, V (ed) *Cornelius Castoriadis and Radical Democracy*. Leiden, The Netherlands: Brill.

Nicolacopoulos, T and Vassilacopoulos, G (2014) Radical Democratic Subjectivity: Possibilities and Limits. In Karalis, V (ed) *Cornelius Castoriadis and Radical Democracy*. Leiden, The Netherlands: Brill.

Roulstone, A (1998) *Enabling Technology: Disabled People, Work and New Technology.* Buckingham, England: Open University Press.

Russell, M (1994a) *Disabled and the Cost of Saying I Do.* KCET Video.

Russell, M (1994b) The Back Door to Welfare 'Reform': Social Security has Found a Way to Make the ADA Pay. *The Disability Rag* (September–October): 29–31.

Russell, M (1994c) Wheeling through Mr. Bill's Neighborhood. *The Disability Rag* (November): 26–28.

Russell, M (1998) *Beyond Ramps: Disability at the End of the Social Contract.* Monroe, ME: Common Courage Press.

Russell, M (2002) What Disability Civil Rights Cannot Do: Employment and Political Economy. *Disability & Society* 17(2): 117–35.

Russell, M (2003) Extinguishing Frida Kahlo. *Counterpunch* (January 25–27), available online at www.counterpunch.org/2003/01/25/extinguishing-frida-kahlo/ (last accessed July 27, 2015).

Russell, M (2005) Targeting Disability. *Monthly Review* 56(11) (April), available online at http://monthlyreview.org/2005/04/01/targeting-disability/.

Russell, M and Malhotra, R (2001) Capitalism and Disability. In Panitch, L and Leys, C (eds) *Socialist Register 2002: A World of Contradictions.* New York: Merlin Press.

Scheele, J (2015) Email to Author, May 17.

Shapiro, J (1993) *No Pity: People with Disabilities Forging a New Civil Rights Movement.* New York: Times Books.

Shuey, KM and Jovic, E (2013) Disability Accommodation in Nonstandard and Precarious Employment Arrangement. *Work and Occupations* 40(2): 174–205.

Shuttleworth, R (2014) Conceptualising Disabled Sexual Subjectivity. In Pallotta-Chiarolli, M and Pease, B (eds) *The Politics of Recognition and Social Justice: Transforming Subjectivities and New Forms of Resistance.* New York: Routledge.

Shuttleworth, R and Meekosha, H (2013) The Sociological Imaginary and Disability Enquiry in Late Modernity. *Critical Sociology* 39(3): 349–67.

Stewart, J and Russell, M (2001) Disablement, Prison and Historical Segregation. *Monthly Review* 53(3) (July/August), available online at http://monthlyreview.org/2001/07/01/disablement-prison-and-historical segregation/ (last accessed July 27, 2015).

Stacey, CL (2011) *The Caring Self: The Work Experiences of Home Care Aides.* Ithaca: Cornell University Press.

Straume, IS (2013) Castoriadis, Education and Democracy. In Straume, IS and Baruchello, G (eds) *Creation, Rationality and Autonomy: Essays on Cornelius Castoriadis.* Copenhagen: NSU Press.

Summers, C (1990) Unions Without Majority—A Black Hole. *Chicago-Kent Law Review* 66: 531–48.

Supiot A, et al. (2001) *Beyond Employment: Changes in Work and the Future of Labour Law in Europe.* Oxford: Oxford University Press.

Taylor, S (2004) The Right Not to Work: Power and Disability. *Monthly Review* 55(10), available online at http://monthlyreview.org/2004/03/01/the-right-not-to-work-power-and-disability/ (last accessed August 8, 2015).

Tormey, S (2014) Between Modernism and Postmodernism: Castoriadis and the Politics of Heterodox Marxism. In Karalis, V (ed.) *Cornelius Castoriadis and Radical Democracy.* Leiden, The Netherlands: Brill.

Trottman, M (2015) Union Membership's Steady Decline. *The Wall Street Journal* (23 January), available online at www.wsj.com/articles/membership-rate-falls-for-u-s-unions-in-2014-1422028558 (last accessed August 6, 2015).

Unger, RB (1987) *False Necessity: Anti-Necessitarian Social Theory in the Service of Radical Democracy*. Cambridge: Cambridge University Press.

Unger, RB (1996) *What Should Legal Analysis Become?* London: Verso.

Unger, RB (1998) *Democracy Realized: The Progressive Alternative*. London: Verso.

Van Der Linden, M (1997) Socialisme ou Barbarie: A French Revolutionary Group (1949–65). *Left History* 5(1), available online at www.left-dis.nl/uk/lindsob.htm (last accessed July 27, 2015).

Watson, N, McKie, L, Hughes, B, Hopkins, D and Gregory, S (2004) (Inter)Dependence, Needs and Care: The Potential for Disability and Feminist Theorists to Develop an Emancipatory Model. *Sociology* 38: 331–50.

Wolf, H (2013) The Power of the Imaginary. In Straume, IS and Baruchello, G (eds) *Creation, Rationality and Autonomy: Essays on Cornelius Castoriadis*. Copenhagen: NSU Press.

Weiss, S (2015) Board and Political Action Committee President, Oregon State Council for Retired Citizens: Interview, May 5.

2 Social insurance for disability: contemporary challenges and insights from disability civil rights

Mark C Weber

A prominent part of Marta Russell's work was her opposition to efforts to scale back Social Security Disability Insurance benefits (Russell, 2005: 45). The threatened cutbacks were associated with George W Bush's drive to divert Social Security contributions into private accounts and diminish the already modest redistributive effects of the system. Ten years after that proposal's collapse in the face of widespread opposition, new challenges confront the United States system of social insurance for disability: fears that the disability trust fund will be unable to meet scheduled payouts at some point in the near future and allegations of abuse by people falsely claiming disability. Beyond those concerns is a lingering unease over whether a benefits system that depends on a medical definition of disability and appears to reward beneficiaries who separate themselves from the working economy is fully consistent with contemporary disability rights ideas. This chapter will provide background on the Social Security Disability Insurance (SSDI) program, discuss the challenges of the budget crunch and allegations of abuse, and explain why social insurance for disability is consistent with disability rights ideas. It will also suggest reforms to bring disability benefits more closely in line with disability rights insights.

Social insurance for disability

The basic idea behind social insurance is that workers contribute a share of their earnings to a central fund under government control, and this fund then provides support to the individuals when they lose their income because of old age, disability, unemployment, or other specified risks (DeWitt, 2010: 1). "Social insurance encompasses broad-based systems that help workers and their families pool risks to avoid loss of income due to retirement, death, disability, or unemployment, and to ensure access to health care" (National Academy of Social Insurance, 2015a). Fundamental principles of social insurance are: (1) entitlements are work-related in the sense of being based on work history or payment of specific taxes, and sometimes on recent paid employment; (2) means tests (income and assets maximums) are generally not imposed; (3) the program is fully or at least largely funded by the specific taxes collected from earnings; (4) participation is compulsory; (5) law defines benefit rights (Office of Research, Evaluation, and

Statistics, US Social Security Administration, 1997: 8–10). Prominent authorities outline the underlying philosophy:

> Social insurance rests on the widespread acceptance of the desirability of protecting workers and their families from dramatic losses of economic status brought on by a set of common risks to labor-market participation. Across virtually all advanced industrial societies, those risks are taken to include age (both youth and old age), illness, accident, and involuntary unemployment. Indeed, a strong historical case can be made that beginning with Otto von Bismarck's social insurance initiatives in the late nineteenth century, the social provision of income protection against these risks has been a fundamental precondition for the flourishing of industrial capitalism. Looked at historically, social insurance is a deeply conservative idea, the major viable alternative to state socialism.
>
> (Marmor and Mashaw, 2007: 126, footnote omitted)

As this description suggests, social insurance for disability is a conservative reform measure. Russell herself supported the American program and opposed cutbacks, but felt that the low level of benefits contributed to a "fear of destitution" that reinforced capitalists' control over workers: "Indeed SSDI is part solution and part problem for workers who can no longer work. American capitalism oppresses those who cannot work by shifting them onto a poverty-based social insurance program rather than allowing them a dignified stipend" (Russell, 2005: 50).

While protecting an earner against the risk of being unable to work enough to support oneself and one's family in the future, social insurance encourages working in the present, and it does so with a monetary incentive: within a range, the benefits depend on how much the beneficiary earns before disability, creating an incentive to work harder and earn more. At the same time, the program makes up for an imperfection in the market for insurance (Berkowitz, 1987: 52–53). Only those with the greatest risk of disability are likely to shop for insurance against it in the private marketplace, which makes for an unsustainable risk pool. In fact, when the United States' program began in the 1950s, private disability insurance was a rarity:

> During the Great Depression . . . [m]any companies stopped selling disability insurance, others failed financially, and the remainder made changes in their . . . practices to make themselves less vulnerable to loss. Sales of disability insurance began to increase after 1940, but the policies were very restrictive.
>
> (Kearney, 2006: 3)

Even now, disability insurance offered through employers or other nonpublic entities typically wraps around SSDI benefits, a practice that can cause problems if the insureds are required to apply for Social Security benefits for which they are not eligible (Walsh, 2008: B2).

SSDI is the principal American social insurance program protecting workers against disability-related loss of income (Silverstein, 2000: 1700–04). Employees and employers contribute payroll taxes to the Social Security Disability Trust Fund (USC 26: § 3111(a)). If a person works a sufficient number of calendar quarters to become insured (based on earnings per year rather than actual quarters of work) during his or her lifetime and up to shortly before the onset of disability (USC 42: § 414), the person receives monthly payments from the fund in rough proportion to past taxed earnings (USC 42: § 423(d)(4)(A)). Limited benefits are also available to spouses and children (Social Security Administration, 2015a). About three-quarters of the working-age population has "insured" status (Rupp et al., 2008: 9). There is a slight redistribution effect in which persons who are at the lower end of the earnings spectrum obtain more compared to their contributions than those at the higher end, and maximum and minimum monthly payment limits, but those characteristics of the program are consistent with conventional principles of social insurance. As with old-age benefits, payouts need not be strictly proportional to pay-ins as long as some essential connection exists between benefits and work-related tax contributions (Berkowitz and McQuaid, 1988: 135–36). For purposes of the program, disability is inability to "engage in any substantial gainful activity by reason of any medically determinable physical or mental impairment which can be expected . . . to last for a continuous period" of a year or result in death (USC 42: § 423(d)(1)(A)). Generally speaking, substantial gainful activity means earning more than an average of $1,070 per month after impairment-related work expenses (Social Security Administration, 2015b), but there are various special rules and exceptions (CFR 20: § 404.1574). In February 2015, the number of disabled workers receiving SSDI was 8,941,000, with an average monthly amount of $1,165.11, exclusive of spousal and child benefits (Social Security Administration, 2015c).

Most SSDI beneficiaries need their payments to survive. The monthly benefit amount constitutes between 75 and 100 percent of income for more than half of all beneficiaries (Bailey and Hemmeter, 2014: 3). Most SSDI beneficiaries subsist on less than $20,000 per year total income. Nearly 32 percent of beneficiaries are on the Supplemental Nutrition Assistance Program (the successor to the food stamp program); nearly 20 percent of beneficiaries are in poverty even with receipt of SSDI, and half of all beneficiaries would be in poverty without the benefits (Bailey and Hemmeter, 2014: 3).

The SSDI program has a storied past. As early as the 1930s, President Franklin Roosevelt's Committee on Economic Security proposed a social insurance program for temporary disability and called for study of a program for permanent disability (Witte, 1963: 208). The proposals were deferred, but the Roosevelt and Truman administrations continued to advocate for them (Kearney, 2006: 5). In the early 1950s, Congress approved a "Disability Freeze," by which workers who became disabled after working enough to earn old-age Social Security benefits at age 65 received protection from loss of their old-age benefits as a result of low or no earnings in the years between the onset of disability and when they reached retirement age (Berkowitz, 1987: 71–72). Implementation of the freeze showed that a program entailing individual determinations of disability was workable, as did the success of other civilian disability-related programs, such as one for civil-defense workers (Kearney, 2006: 6, 9–10). Disability insurance for work-related accidents came about much earlier. "Historically, workers' compensation has been the first social insurance program adopted in developed countries. In the US most states adopted workers' compensation laws in a relatively short period between 1910 and 1920" (National Academy of Social Insurance, 2015b).

In 1956, Congress established the SSDI program and gave it the basic form that it has today (Pub L No 84–880). The Eisenhower Administration opposed it, but with some ambivalence (Corning, 1966: 28), and eventually supported the elimination of the minimum age requirement (age 50) that was a feature of the original program (Berkowitz, 1987: 109–10). Under welfare reform legislation adopted in the 1970s, persons who do not meet the SSDI earnings requirements before becoming disabled, but who meet the SSDI disability standard and are impoverished, may qualify for Supplemental Security Income (SSI) (USC 42: §§ 423(d)(1)(A), 1382); Berkowitz and McQuaid, 1988: 207), as may those who are poor and disabled whose SSDI amount is lower than the SSI amount plus a $20 income disregard (Social Security Administration, 2015d).

Recent challenges for Disability Insurance

The Social Security Administration pays out benefits from trust funds that combine revenue from workers' payroll taxes with interest on government bonds in which the funds are invested (Social Security Administration, 2015e: 10), though the economic stimulus program in effect during 2011–12 entailed a temporary reduction in payroll taxes, during which general revenues were substituted for the lost payroll taxes to make up the difference (Board of Trustees, 2013: 2). The most recent problem with this method of funding is that the benefits being paid out have been growing faster than the revenue in the disability insurance fund, with the result that the reserves were expected to be depleted in 2016 and full payouts could not be maintained unless changes were made. The 2013 Report of the Board of Trustees states:

> The Trustees project that the asset reserves of the OASI [Old-Age and Survivors Insurance] Trust Fund and of the combined OASI and DI Trust Funds will be adequate over the next 10 years under the intermediate assumptions. However, the projected reserves of the DI Trust Fund decline steadily from 85 percent of annual cost at the beginning of 2013 until the trust fund reserves are depleted in 2016. At the time reserves are depleted, continuing income to the DI Trust Fund would be sufficient to pay 80 percent of scheduled DI benefits. The DI Trust Fund does not satisfy the short-range test of financial adequacy.
>
> (Board of Trustees, 2013: 2)

A study of enrollment trends over nearly 40 years before the latest recession found that three causes—population growth, the increased proportion of women covered by SSDI, and the gradual movement of the large baby boom birth cohort into the ages when people are most likely to become disabled—explain 90 percent of the program's growth from 1972 to 2008 (Pattison and Waldron, 2013: 25). These demographic factors accounted for even more of the growth (94 percent) from 1990 to 2008 (Pattison and Waldron, 2013: 25).

Knowledgeable observers pointed out these facts years ago:

> [T]he [Social Security] trustees estimated in 1995 that the number of people receiving disabled worker benefits would nearly double between 1995 and 2010 – from 4.2 million to 7.9 million. This predicted increase was based largely on known demographic trends, including: a growing labor force . . . [t]he aging of the baby boomers . . . [and] the increase in Social Security's full retirement age from 65 to 66. . . . In 2010 the actual number of disabled worker beneficiaries – 8.2 million – was slightly higher than the 1995 projection of 7.9 million. This difference was due in large part to two economic recessions after 2000.
>
> (Reno et al., 2013: 3, footnotes and italics omitted)

The increase in the retirement age necessarily affects disability payouts:

> When DI beneficiaries reach the full retirement age, they shift from disability to retirement benefits. The increase in the retirement age from 65 to 66 has delayed that shift. In December 2012, 455,700 disabled workers aged 65 and 66—more than 5% of all disabled worker beneficiaries—received disability benefits, whereas under the rules of 10 years ago they would have received retirement benefits instead.
>
> (Reno et al., 2013: 3)

Thus, the shortfall is due not to any newfound generosity of those making disability determinations nor to a sudden rise in benefit levels. It is simple demographics, compounded by recent economic crises. Though the test for disability may seem objective, in fact eligibility depends heavily on economic conditions, for the availability of work in significant numbers in the national economy will expand or contract with the business cycle, technological change, and other circumstances affecting the availability of jobs. The proponents of the SSDI program realized this fact from the beginning (Berkowitz, 1987: 43–49), and events confirmed it: "Disability claims have risen during every economic recession since the late 1960s—with the one exception of the early 1980s, when unprecedented retrenchment policies offset those effects" (Disability Policy Panel, 1994: 58). Even the latest recession was hardly an unpredictable shock to the system. At the height of President Bush's drive to privatize Social Security, which made much of a prediction that the fund would run out in 2052, the Center for Economic Policy Research put out a report listing events that would occur before the fund ran dry.

Among the predictions was that the housing bubble would burst, destroying $5.2 trillion in wealth and causing a serious recession (Baker, 2005: 6).

A permanent solution to the anticipated shortfall in the SSDI fund would be to raise the worker's and employer's payroll tax rate by 0.2 percentage points each, thus increasing the contribution from 0.9 percent to 1.1 percent of the worker's income subject to Social Security tax (Reno et al., 2013: 5). The total percentage of covered income paid by the worker in Social Security taxes is currently 6.2 percent, so his or her contribution would go up to 6.4 percent. This step would make SSDI solvent for at least the next 75 years (Manchester, 2013: 7). Another means to increase revenue would be to raise the portion of income subject to the Social Security payroll tax; the earnings of workers at the higher end of the income range have risen so much faster than that of others that the share of all earnings covered by the tax slipped from 90 percent in 1983 to 83 percent in 2011 (Manchester, 2013: 7).

An alternative, a more temporary fix would be to keep the Disability Insurance tax rate as it is but reallocate money from the Old-Age fund. Because the Old-Age fund is so much larger, there would be little impact on the sustainability of Social Security as a whole: "Reallocating part of Social Security's tax rate to the DI trust fund to equalize the two funds would not affect the long-term financing of the combined Social Security . . . system. The two funds are usually discussed together, and the combined funds' reserve depletion date would remain 2033," after which ongoing tax income would cover 77 percent of the combined programs' costs into the future indefinitely (Reno et al., 2013: 6). Reallocation worked before. One researcher comments:

> In 1994, the Congress acted to reallocate a portion of the combined OASDI payroll tax rate from the OASI program to the DI program, in order to avert near-term trust fund exhaustion for the DI program. Then, as now, the OASI program had more favorable actuarial status. Given the possibility that comprehensive reform for the OASDI program might not be completed by 2020, a small reallocation of 0.1 percent to 0.2 percent of the existing 12.4 percent tax rate [combining employee and employer contributions] to the DI fund would again be possible to more nearly equalize the financial status of the OASI and DI Trust Funds. It is for this reason, and because of the simplicity of considering the OASDI program on a unified basis, that most analysis of the actuarial status of the Social Security program is done on a theoretical basis where the two trust funds are considered on a combined basis.
>
> (Goss, 2010: 116)

Whether it would work in 2015 was in serious doubt, however, for the House of Representatives majority came out strongly against a transfer (Hall, 2015):

> With a little-noticed proposal, Republicans took aim at Social Security on the very first day of the 114th Congress. . . . The largely overlooked change

> puts a new restriction on the routine transfer of tax revenues between the traditional Social Security retirement trust fund and the Social Security disability program. The transfers, known as reallocation, had historically been routine.
>
> (Scott, 2015)

It is thus remarkable that in the Bipartisan Budget Act of 2015, signed into law on November 2, 2015, a majority of the House and the Senate agreed to reallocate Old-Age fund and Disability fund revenues so as to preserve the existing disability benefits payment schedule until 2022 (Pub L No 114–74: § 833; Pear, 2015). Ultimately, there may need to be an adjustment to tax rates or benefit rates for both the Old-Age and Disability programs, but Congress apparently recognized that there was no reason to cut benefits now, in the face of a slow economic recovery generating too few employment opportunities for everyone, including those with disabilities. The worst that could happen would be a benefits cutback years later. One economist-opinion writer commented:

> [Some] insist that we must move right now to reduce scheduled benefits. But I've never understood the logic of this demand. The risk is that we might, at some point in the future, have to cut benefits; to avoid this risk of future benefit cuts, we are supposed to act pre-emptively by . . . cutting future benefits. What problem, exactly, are we solving here?
>
> (Krugman, 2013: A21)

A second challenge to SSDI is that inevitably, there are some who abuse the program by falsely claiming disability, and various cases of fraud have recently generated headlines. Not all reports concern SSDI. The Social Security Administration's program has a much better record on fraud and abuse than other, less professionally run disability determination operations (Neas, 2014; Bagdanich, 2014). Nevertheless, reports of fraud in one disability program have a way of spilling over to damage the reputations of other programs, regardless of the actual facts about those programs. The best available evidence is that the level of fraud in SSDI is less than 1 percent (Colvin, 2014: 1).

Is there a solution to the problem? Perhaps there is an irony in the fact, but fraud may well decline over time due to the gradual disappearance of personal privacy in an increasingly cyber-scrutinized American society. Tellingly, a prominent recent investigation for Social Security Disability fraud relied in part on information taken from recipients' Facebook pages (Rashbaum and McKinley, 2014: A1). One Social Security Administrative Law Judge has proposed that Facebook and other social media be investigated routinely during the initial eligibility determination process, a step that has not yet been taken (Frye, 2014: A17). Other, quite limited steps might diminish whatever abuse currently exists. Disability determinations are typically outsourced to state disability determination services, but only about half of the states make use of a Cooperative Disability Investigation Unit (CDIU), which has greater investigative capacity than individual disability examiners have, and which can make appropriate referrals to the Office of Inspector General for a full inquiry. Enlarging the presence of CDIUs should decrease incidence of fraudulent and other improper receipt of benefits (Nottingham, 2014). The Bipartisan Budget Act provides for expansion of CDIUs and imposes stringent new penalties on persons who engage in conspiracy to commit Social Security fraud (Pub L No 114–74: §§ 811, 813; Pear, 2015). In addition, an increase in SSDI applications has coincided with retirements and hiring freezes for disability examiners, with the result that there are fewer people at every step of the process that is used to determine whether benefits should be paid. A recent increase in the number of personnel authorized to be hired should help alleviate improper payment of benefits due to inadequate attention to the merits of claims (Nottingham, 2014). Continued funding of these positions should pay for itself in more accurate eligibility determinations.

Disability benefits and disability rights: a paradox?

Thus SSDI can easily be preserved. Should it be?

Among the most important of the social movements emerging in the late twentieth century was the concerted drive for disability rights. The militant disability rights movement might be said to begin in the late 1960s with Ed Roberts and other students with physical impairments—many of them polio survivors—who roomed in the University of California-Berkeley hospital, which was the only residence on campus that could accommodate them (Shapiro, 1994: 41–53). Even earlier than that, the League of the Physically Handicapped demonstrated against the disqualification of workers with disabilities from jobs programs implemented by the New Deal (Longmore, 2003: 68–85). In the 1970s, activists occupied the office of the Health, Education, and Welfare Secretary and demonstrated all over the country to force the administration to adopt final regulations to implement Section 504 of the *Rehabilitation Act* of 1973, which forbids disability discrimination in federally funded programs and activities (Cook, 1991: 394; Malhotra, 2001). During the Reagan era, demonstrators challenged proposed changes that would have weakened federal disability discrimination regulations and the refusal to appoint a deaf president for Gallaudet University; some disability militants chained their wheelchairs to public transit facilities; others undertook a litigation campaign over accessibility (Burgdorf, 2008: 294–95; Fleisher and Zames, 2001: 57–70; Sacks, 1989: 125–59).

The social movement transformed the law both nationally and internationally: first the *Americans with Disabilities Act* of 1990 (ADA) (Pub L No 101–336), and more recently, the *ADA Amendments Act* of 2008 (Pub L No 110–325), and the *United Nations Convention on the Rights of Persons with Disabilities* (United Nations, 2007). As might be suspected from the account of early disability rights activism, federal laws against disability discrimination go back even earlier and supply the background against which the ADA was adopted (Weicker, 1991: 387–90). A 1948 statute forbade employment discrimination based on physical disability in the Civil Service (Pub L No 617: Ch 434). The *Architectural*

Barriers Act, which requires accessibility for federal public spaces, was enacted in 1968 (42 USC: §§ 4151–57). A watershed was the passage of the disability discrimination provisions of the *Rehabilitation Act* in 1973 (Pub L No 93–112).

A fundamental insight behind the disability rights movement is that physical and mental conditions do not necessarily disable: disability instead arises from the relationship between those conditions and physical and attitudinal barriers that exist in the human environment (Hensel, 2005: 150). Thus, a person who uses a wheelchair is not disabled but for stairs, curbs, and attitudes that keep the individual from full participation in society. This social approach to disability contrasts with a medical approach, which emphasizes the impairment and identifies it, rather than society's response, as the critical marker of disability (Crossley, 1999: 649–53). "While it acknowledges the existence of biologically based differences, the social-political model locates the meaning of these differences—and the individual's experience of them as burdensome—in society's stigmatizing attitudes and biased structures rather than in the individual" (Berg, 1999: 9). A medical model directs attention to fixing bodily or mental conditions. The social model focuses instead on the social and environmental barriers, and directs attention to changing them. This social model of disability points towards a civil rights approach to disability law reform, in which political action and social regulation are used to alter physical and attitudinal barriers that discriminate against people with disabilities (O'Brien, 2001: 207–21; Weber, 2011: 2490–91).

SSDI depends heavily on the medical approach. The qualifying standards for disability are framed in medical terms, complete with listings of medical conditions, even specification of medical tests and outcomes (Stone, 1984: 90–117; Bloch, 2007: 225). Even the functional disability tests, which apply if a claimant does not meet the medical listings, are medically based: "While functionalism folded into disability certification some consideration of social context and individual disadvantage, it was essentially an adaptation of the medical perspective" (Erkulwater, 2006: 227). SSDI originated long before the social model achieved influence. As one scholar states, "[S]ocial welfare programs were premised on the assumption that a disabled person was helpless, and the state offered support out of a sense of charity or pity" (Erkulwater, 2006: 61). The paradox of social insurance for disability is that it reinforces the impression that disability is a medical condition, a life hazard anyone would avoid, or if the person is not able to do that, insure against.

> There is . . . an enormous tension between the major disability benefits programs—which excuse people with disabilities from the obligation to work and pay them a steady cash benefit simply because they have a disability—and the notion that individuals with disabilities should test their skills in the world and experience the "dignity of risk."
>
> (Bagenstos, 2003: 997–98)

The reality is of course that social insurance protects against the loss of income caused by the medically determined defect in the person with the disability, even though the social model insists that what matters is the impairment in relation to social attitudes and conditions. If disability is not necessarily a hazard, and does not have to cause separation from the work force, except for the pervasive failure of employers to adapt their workplaces and attitudes, the insurance would seem unnecessary. Does it make sense to insure against the negative attitudes of employers?

The answer, perhaps paradoxically, is yes. Social insurance keeps workers who become disabled from suffering the worst effects of the failure to provide accommodations by potential employers (Weber, 2009: 595–96). Even traditional government programs of old-age pensions and welfare for impoverished families are to a significant degree addressed to discrimination (Weber, 2009: 590–92). Adequate remunerative work was near impossible to find for single mothers in the era when Aid to Families with Dependent Children came into being, and hard to find for elderly workers in the period when the Social Security Old-Age program was adopted (Douglas, 1939: 5–6). Social insurance for workers with disabilities—a class of individuals who experience overwhelming levels of discrimination in employment—insures against the social condition of discrimination as much as it insures against anything else. Professor Jacobus tenBroek, a pioneer of disability civil rights, discussed public support as a form of compensation for disability discrimination:

> [C]ertainly special weight must be given to the circumstances of those who are kept out of the labor market so largely by social arrangements and public attitudes. This is the case of many of the disabled. Do not they have a right which derives from the social barriers which prevent their engaging in productive labor? . . . [I]s it not a reciprocal duty on the part of organized society to keep the path to the labor market free of socially created road blocks? If society fails to discharge this duty and men are thereby prevented from engaging in productive work, should not society compensate for its remissness and nonperformance by according a right of equal status to those who have thereby been denied access to the main social and economic channels of the community?
>
> (tenBroek and Wilson, 1954: 248–49)

A further aspect of social conditions is that political consensus so far has permitted legislation only for "reasonable" accommodations, and even that duty has been unduly narrowly read by many courts (Porter, 2014: 73–78; Bagenstos, 2004: 35). A weakness of relying on a reasonable accommodation model is that it uses the non-disabled as the norm, requiring only limited departures from existing practices. The social model is by no means limited to reasonable accommodations, but the law is, and that greatly restricts the work opportunities for people with disabilities. Even the fact that the economic system under which most of the world operates requires people to sell their labor in order to live might be characterized as an aspect of the environment that disadvantages (to put it mildly) those whose physical or mental conditions make them unable to find a buyer for their services under current levels of accommodation. Physical incapacities or limits on stamina diminish what persons with disabilities may have to sell in the labor market (Wendell, 1997: 271). Highly mechanized economies where the fastest growing sectors deal in information may provide openings to those with physical impairments, but offer few opportunities to those with severe cognitive impairments (Disability Policy Panel, 1994: 61). SSDI compensates for the whole range of labor market-related barriers.

SSDI also protects against risks other than those related to the ability to find a job. Living with a disability typically entails higher medical and related costs: "The disabled make nearly three times as many physician visits a year and purchase more than four times as many prescriptions as individuals with no activity limitations" (Oi, 1991: 37). Time that might be devoted to paid work is lost while the medical expense is incurred (Oi, 1991: 40). The social model would deem these risks a form of discrimination as well. In a society built on social justice principles, the extraordinary costs of survival would not be placed on a disadvantaged class of individuals when the very cost contributes to their disadvantage (Weber, 2000: 920). The expenses of adapting to structures of society created without people with disabilities in mind would decrease if a society committed to anti-subordination replaced those structures with better ones (Colker, 2007: 1447). For the moment, however, what exists is social insurance against those costs. The government disability insurance system relies on medical categories and determinations, but the problems it addresses are social ones.

Improving social insurance for disability

The absence of any contradiction between disability rights and disability benefits is not the end of the story. Disability rights ideas suggest possible improvements in the American system of social insurance for disability. These reforms would include closer attention to stigma's role in rendering individuals unable to work in the present labor market, consideration of partial and temporary disability benefits, and greater incentives for beneficiaries to undertake work they might be able to do under current levels of accommodation.

1. Eligibility standards adjustments

The social model suggests that the standard for SSDI should account for the stigma that keeps people who might otherwise be able to work from being offered jobs. The attitudes that disable should affect the coverage of disability benefits laws. People with mental disabilities—both intellectual disability and mental illness—face attitudes that present strong barriers to employment: "People suffering from mental conditions are typically 30–50% less likely to be employed than those with other health problems or disability" (OECD, 2009: 10). People with some other conditions, mostly congenital ones, are also likely to encounter stigma and discrimination, limiting opportunities (Baldwin and Johnson, 1998: 46–47, 56). Thus, standards for disability benefits for people with those conditions ought to be made easier to meet. Disability standards for those conditions might be raised for impairments that do not confer stigma and for which accommodations are more readily supplied.

Moreover, in general the SSDI eligibility standard is unduly severe, and does not adequately consider the difficulty of obtaining the adaptations people need if they are to work. Many cases uphold denials of benefits to individuals with severely debilitating impairments (e.g., *Tommasetti v Astrue*; *Eichstadt v Astrue*; *Bradley v Astrue*). Of all the individuals placed on the SSDI rolls in any given year, one out of eight dies within two years (Oi, 1996: 113). The proportion of individuals who die during their first six months on SSDI is 14 times that of elderly individuals during their first six months on the Social Security Old-Age program (Ycas, 1996: 171). SSDI's disability standard is more extreme than those of disability insurance programs in other countries (Erkulwater, 2006: 237). A lower disability threshold would not undermine the incentives to work that currently exist in the national economy.

2. Temporary and partial disability insurance

Temporary and partial disability benefits were part of the early American social insurance agenda (President's Message, 1948: 2490–91), and are widely found in the advanced world (Erkulwater, 2006: 237). Partial and temporary disability benefits are also the rule in the United States with regard to impairments related to specific causes, as with service-connected benefits for veterans, injuries and diseases at work covered by workers' compensation, and tortious injuries. Benefits of this type have the advantage of not discouraging work, and in fact make employment dramatically easier for those who have limits on stamina or conditions that are episodic or progressive. To that extent, they fit well with the social model, because they operate to strengthen integration of people with disabilities into the working economy on a plane of equality with others. Experts, even those critical of partial disability benefits, identify inducing people to delay leaving the work force as the most effective way to reduce SSDI expenditures (Mashaw and Reno, 1998: 254–55).

3. Work incentive enhancements

Much has been written in recent years about work incentives in disability benefits programs, but one reform that holds promise and is closely tied to social insurance principles is the Disabled Workers Tax Credit (DWTC). Like the Earned Income Tax Credit (EITC), which provides low-income workers a credit against taxes, and typically gives a cash award in the form of a tax refund for a low-wage worker (USC 26: § 32; Lipman, 2003: 443), the DWTC would furnish a tax credit for people with sufficiently severe disabilities who work and earn income. It would enhance the financial reward for their efforts and make up for some of the discrimination and lack of accommodation that currently diminishes their earnings (Lipman, 2003: 447–51; Mashaw and Reno, 1998: 254–55). In addition or alternatively, the EITC could be enhanced to provide special benefits on the basis of disability (Fremstad, 2009: 16).

If it survives the ministrations of Congress and the Supreme Court, the *Patient Protection and Affordable Care Act* will be a major improvement in the array of work incentives for people with disabilities, and one consistent with social insurance principles (Pub L No 111–48; Graetz and Mashaw, 2013: 356–59). Present and potential SSDI enrollees will be able to obtain (or retain) eligibility for Medicaid in participating states even if they substitute a modest earned income from employment for the SSDI benefits. Moreover, if they earn too much and lose Medicaid eligibility, they will be able to obtain private insurance without preexisting conditions exclusions and with community rating rather than with the exclusions and at higher rates.

Congress recently enacted the *Achieving a Better Life Experience (ABLE) Act*, a law that allows people with disabilities to retain up to $100,000 of savings and keep eligibility for Medicaid and related benefits, as well as be free from having to pay federal tax on interest on the funds (Pub L 113–295). This measure will be highly useful for individuals who are contemplating starting businesses, or making other plans that require accumulating capital in order to enter or re-enter a working economy in which many employers continue to resist providing accommodations (Diament, 2014).

Conclusion

Social insurance for disability protects people against the loss of income that occurs when they can no longer do their jobs or other remunerative work, but it also protects against the harms of discrimination caused by the social barriers that keep persons who have disabilities from participating in the workplace on a plane equal to that of others. Though it depends on medical categories and concepts, it is consistent with disability rights thinking, which recognizes the role that environmental and attitudinal obstacles play in making physical and mental differences disabling.

Problems of financial shortfalls and occasional abuse are real, but hardly insurmountable. They should not divert attention from the need for the SSDI program and the social good that could be achieved if modest improvements were made.

Bibliography

Bagdanich, W (2014) Flaws Persist in L.I.R.R.'s Disability Claims, a Report Finds. *New York Times*, February 21, available online at www.nytimes.com/2014/02/22/nyregion/flaws-persist-in-lirrs-disability-claims-a-report-finds.html?src=recg (last accessed April 30, 2015).

Bagenstos, SR (2003) The Americans with Disabilities Act as Welfare Reform. *William and Mary Law Review* 44: 921–1028.

Bagenstos, SR (2004) The Future of Disability Law. *Yale Law Journal* 114: 1–84.

Bailey, MS and Hemmeter, J (2014) Characteristics of Non-institutionalized DI and SSI Program Participants. *Office of Retirement and Disability Policy Research Note*

(February), available online at www.ssa.gov/policy/docs/rsnotes/rsn2014-02.pdf (last accessed April 30, 2015).

Baker, D (2005) Things That Will Happen Before Social Security Faces a Shortfall. *Center for Economic and Policy Research*, June, available online at http://research.policyarchive.org/20738.pdf (last accessed May 1, 2015).

Baldwin, ML and Johnson, WG (1998) Dispelling the Myths about Work Disability. In Thomason, T (ed) *New Approaches to Disability in the Workplace*. Madison, WI: Industrial Relations Research Association.

Berg, PE (1999) Ill/legal: Interrogating the Meaning and Function of the Category of Disability in Antidiscrimination Law. *Yale Law and Policy Review* 18: 1–52.

Berkowitz, E (1987) *Disabled Policy*. Cambridge: Cambridge University Press.

Berkowitz, E and McQuaid, K (1988) *Creating the Welfare State: The Political Economy of Twentieth-Century Reform*. 2nd edition, New York: Praeger.

Bloch, FS (2007) Medical Proof, Social Policy, and Social Security's Medically Centered Definition of Disability. *Cornell Law Review* 92: 189–234.

Board of Trustees of the Federal Old-Age and Survivors Insurance and Federal Disability Insurance Trust Funds (2013). *Annual Report*. Washington, DC: Government Printing Office, available online at www.ssa.gov/oact/tr/2013/tr2013.pdf (last accessed April 30, 2015).

Bradley v Astrue, 528 F.3d 1113 (8th Cir. 2008).

Burgdorf, RL Jr (2008) Restoring the ADA and Beyond: Disability in the 21st Century. *Texas Journal on Civil Liberties and Civil Rights* 13: 241–365.

Code of Federal Regulations ("CFR") (2015) Washington, DC: Government Printing Office.

Colker, R (2007) Anti-Subordination Above All: A Disability Perspective. *Notre Dame Law Review* 82: 1415–84.

Colvin, CW (2014) Follow-up Report on Anti-Fraud Efforts Requested at the January 16, 2014 Hearing on Disability Fraud, February 14, available online at www.ssa.gov/legislation/SSA_Report_to_Chairman_Johnson_2_14_2014.pdf (last accessed April 29, 2015).

Cook, TM (1991) The Americans with Disabilities Act: The Move to Integration. *Temple Law Review* 64: 393–469.

Corning, PA (1966) Interview with Roswell Perkins. *Social Security Administration Project*, Part IV, No 160 (2 April), Oral History Research Office: Columbia University.

Crossley, M (1999) The Disability Kaleidoscope. *Notre Dame Law Review* 74: 621–716.

DeWitt, L (2010) The Development of Social Security in America. *Social Security Bulletin* 70(3): 1–26, available online at www.socialsecurity.gov/policy/docs/ssb/v70n3/v70n3p1.pdf (last accessed April 29, 2015).

Diament, M (2014) Congress Eyeing Tax-Free Disability Savings Accounts. *Disability Scoop*, February 22, available online at www.disabilityscoop.com/2014/02/21/congress-eyeing-savings/19134/ (last accessed May 1, 2015).

Disability Policy Panel, National Academy of Social Insurance (1994) Rethinking Disability Policy: The Role of Health Care, Rehabilitation, and Related Services in Fostering Independence. *Social Security Bulletin* 57(2): 56–62, available online at www.socialsecurity.gov/policy/docs/ssb/v57n2/v57n2p56.pdf (last accessed April 30, 2015).

Douglas, PH (1939) *Social Security in the United States*. 2nd edition, New York: Whittlesey House.

Eichstadt v Astrue, 534 F.3d 663 (7th Cir. 2008).

Erkulwater, JL (2006) *Disability Rights and the American Social Safety Net*. Ithaca: Cornell University Press.

Fleisher, DZ and Zames, F (2001) *The Disability Rights Movement*. Philadelphia: Temple University Press.

Fremstad, S (2009) Half in Ten: Why Taking Disability into Account is Essential to Reducing Income Poverty and Expanding Economic Inclusion. *Center for Economic and Policy Research*, September, available online at www.cepr.net/documents/publications/poverty-disability-2009-09.pdf (last accessed May 1, 2015).

Frye, DR (2014) Fixing Disability Courts. *New York Times*, 20 January, available online at www.nytimes.com/2014/01/20/opinion/fixing-disability-courts.html?ref=socialsecurityus (last accessed April 30, 2015).

Goss, SC (2010) The Future Financial Status of the Social Security Program. *Social Security Bulletin* 70(3): 111–25, available online at www.ssa.gov/policy/docs/ssb/v70n3/v70n3p111.pdf (last accessed April 30, 2015).

Graetz, MJ and Mashaw, JL (2013) Constitutional Uncertainty and the Design of Social Insurance: Reflections on the Obamacare Case. *Harvard Law and Policy Review* 7: 343–66.

Hall, CT (2015) Good Planning, GOP. *Social Security News*, 14 April, available online at http://socsecnews.blogspot.com/search?updated-max=2015-04-24T06:00:00-04:00/ (last accessed April 30, 2015).

Hensel, WF (2005) The Disabling Impact of Wrongful Birth and Wrongful Life Actions. *Harvard Civil Rights-Civil Liberties Law Review* 40: 141–96.

Kearney, J (2006) Social Security and the "D" in OASDI: The History of a Federal Program Insuring Earners Against Disability. *Social Security Bulletin* 66(3): 1–26, available online at www.ssa.gov/policy/docs/ssb/v66n3/v66n3p1.pdf (last accessed April 29, 2015).

Krugman, P (2013) The Geezers Are All Right. *New York Times*, June 3, available online at www.nytimes.com/2013/06/03/opinion/krugman-the-geezers-are-all-right.html (last accessed April 30, 2015).

Lipman, FL (2003) Enabling Work for People with Disabilities: A Post-Integrationist Revision of Underutilized Tax Incentives. *American University Law Review* 53: 393–458.

Longmore, PK (2003) The League of the Physically Handicapped and the Great Depression. In Longmore, PK (ed) *Why I Burned My Book and Other Essays on Disability*. Philadelphia: Temple University Press.

Malhotra, R (2001) *The Politics of the Disability Rights Movements*. Available online at https://zcomm.org/znetarticle/the-politics-of-the-disability-rights-movement-by-ravi-malhotra/ (last accessed May 1, 2015).

Manchester, J (2013) The Social Security Disability Insurance Program. *Testimony before the Subcommittee on Social Security, House Committee on Ways and Means* (14 March), available online at http://waysandmeans.house.gov/uploadedfiles/manchester_testimony.pdf (last accessed April 30, 2015).

Marmor, TR and Mashaw, J (2007) Understanding Social Insurance: Fairness, Affordability, and the "Modernization" of Social Security and Medicare. *Elder Law Journal* 15: 123–52.

Mashaw, JL and Reno, V (1998) Social Security Disability Insurance: A Policy Review. In Thomason, T (ed) *New Approaches to Disability in the Workplace*. Madison, WI: Industrial Relations Research Association.

National Academy of Social Insurance (2015a) *Mission*. Available online at www.nasi.org/about/mission (last accessed April 16, 2015).

National Academy of Social Insurance (2015b) *An Overview*. Available online at www.nasi.org/learn/workerscomp/overview (last accessed April 16, 2015).

Neas, K (2014) Social Security Disability Fraud Is Rare, *Congress Blog*, *The Hill*, January 16, available online at http://thehill.com/blogs/congress-blog/economy-budget/195559-social-secuity-disability-fraud-is-rare (last accessed April 30, 2015).

Nottingham, J (2014) *Statement of the President, National Association of Disability Examiners, to the House Committee on Oversight and Government Reform, Subcommittee on Energy Policy, Health Care & Entitlements*, April 9, available online at www.nade.org/NADEadvocateTESTIMONY.htm (last accessed April 30, 2015).

O'Brien, R (2001) *Crippled Justice: The History of Modern Disability Policy in the Workplace*. Chicago: University of Chicago Press.

Office of Research, Evaluation and Statistics, US Social Security Administration (1997) *Social Security Programs in the United States*. Washington, DC: Government Printing Office.

Organization for Economic Cooperation & Development ("OECD") (2009) *Sickness, Disability and Work: Keeping on Track in the Economic Downturn*. Available online at www.oecd.org/dataoecd/42/15/42699911.pdf (last accessed May 1, 2015).

Oi, WY (1991) Disability and a Workfare-Welfare Dilemma. In Weaver, CL (ed) *Disability and Work: Incentives, Rights, and Opportunities*. Lanham, MD: AEI Press.

Oi, WY (1996) Employment and Benefits for People with Diverse Disabilities. In Mashaw, JL (ed) *Disability, Work and Cash Benefits*. Kalamazoo, MI: WE Upjohn Institute for Employment Research.

Pattison, D and Waldron, H (2013) Growth in New Disabled-Worker Entitlements, 1970–2008. *Social Security Bulletin* 73(4): 25–48, available online at www.ssa.gov/policy/docs/ssb/v73n4/v73n4p25.pdf (last accessed April 30, 2015).

Pear, R (2015) Agreement Is Seen as Short-Term Relief for Medicare and Social Security *New York Times*, October 27, available online at www.nytimes.com/2015/10/28/us/agreement-is-seen-as-short-term-relief-for-medicare-and-social-security.html?_r=0 (last accessed November 12, 2015).

Porter, NB (2014) The New ADA Backlash. *Tennessee Law Review* 82: 1–82.

President's Message to Congress on Social Security Expansion ("President's Message") (1948). *United States Code Congressional Service*. St Paul, MN: West.

Public Law ("Pub L") No 617, Ch 434 (1948), 62 Stat 351, Washington, DC: Government Printing Office.

Public Law ("Pub L") No 84–880 (1956), 70 Stat 815, Washington, DC: Government Printing Office.

Public Law ("Pub L") No 93–112 (1973), 87 Stat 394, Washington, DC: Government Printing Office.

Public Law ("Pub L") No 101–336 (1990), 104 Stat 327, Washington, DC: Government Printing Office.

Public Law ("Pub L") No. 110–325 (2008), 122 Stat. 3553, Washington, DC: Government Printing Office.

Public Law ("Pub L") No 111–148 (2010), 124 Stat 119, Washington, DC: Government Printing Office.

Public Law ("Pub L") No 113–295 (2014), 128 Stat 4056, Washington, DC: Government Printing Office.

Public Law ("Pub L") No 114–74 (2015), 129 Stat 584, Washington, DC: Government Printing Office.

Rashbaum, WK and McKinley, JC Jr (2014) Charges for 106 in Huge Fraud Over Disability. *New York Times*, January 7, available online at www.nytimes.com/2014/01/08/nyregion/retired-new-york-officers-and-firefighters-charged-in-social-security-scheme.html (last accessed April 30, 2015).

Reno, VP, Walker EA, and Bethell, TN (2013) Social Security Disability Insurance: Action Needed to Address Finances. *National Academy of Social Insurance* (June), available online at www.nasi.org/sites/default/files/research/SS_Brief_041.pdf (last accessed April 30, 2015).

Rupp, K, Davies, PS, and Strand, A (2008) Disability Benefit Coverage and Program Interactions in the Working-Age Population. *Social Security Bulletin* 68(1): 1–30, available online at www.socialsecurity.gov/policy/docs/ssb/v68n1/68n1p1.pdf (last accessed April 29, 2015).

Russell, M (2005) Targeting Disability. *Monthly Review* 56(11) (April), available online at http://monthlyreview.org/2005/04/01/targeting-disability/.

Sacks, O (1989) *Seeing Voices: A Journey Into the World of the Deaf*. New York: Vintage.

Scott, D (2015) New GOP Congress Fires Shot at Social Security on Day One. *Talking Points Memo*, January 6, available online at http://talkingpointsmemo.com/dc/social-security-di-house-rules-change (last accessed April 30, 2015).

Shapiro, J (1994) *No Pity: People with Disabilities Forging a New Civil Rights Movement*. New York, NY: Three Rivers Press.

Silverstein, R (2000) Emerging Disability Policy Framework: A Guidepost for Analyzing Public Policy. *Iowa Law Review* 85: 1691–806.

Social Security Administration (2015a) *Disability Benefits*. Available online at www.ssa.gov/pubs/EN-05-10029.pdf (last accessed April 16, 2015).

Social Security Administration (2015b) *Disability Planner: How We Decide If You Are Disabled*. Available online at www.ssa.gov/dibplan/dqualify5.htm#a0=0> (last accessed April 16, 2015).

Social Security Administration (2015c) *Monthly Statistical Snapshot*. Available online at www.ssa.gov/policy/docs/quickfacts/stat_snapshot/index.html?qs#table2 (last accessed April 16, 2015).

Social Security Administration (2015d) *Supplemental Security Income (SSI)*. Available online at www.ssa.gov/pubs/EN-05-11000.pdf (last accessed April 16, 2015).

Social Security Administration (2015e) *What You Need To Know When You Get Social Security Disability Benefits*. Available online at www.ssa.gov/pubs/EN-05-10153.pdf#page=3 (last accessed April 16, 2015).

Stone, DA (1984) *The Disabled State*. Philadelphia, PA: Temple University Press.

tenBroek, J and Wilson, RP (1954) Public Assistance and Social Insurance—A Normative Evaluation. *UCLA Law Review* 1: 237–302.

Tommasetti v Astrue, 533 F.3d 1035 (9th Cir. 2008).

United Nations (2007) General Assembly Resolution 611, UN GAOR, 61st Sess, Supp No 49, UN Doc A/RES/61/106 (January 24), available online at www.un.org/disabilities/documents/convention/convoptprot-e.pdf (last accessed May 1, 2015).

United States Code ("USC") (2012) Washington, DC: Government Printing Office, available online at http://uscode.house.gov/.

Walsh, MW (2008) Disability Insurer Found Guilty of Social Security Fraud. *New York Times*, October 23, available online at www.nytimes.com/2008/10/24/business/24disability.html?_r=0 (last accessed April 29, 2015).

Weber, MC (2000) Disability and the Law of Welfare. *University of Illinois Law Review* 2000: 889–956.

Weber, MC (2009) Disability Rights, Disability Discrimination, and Social Insurance. *Georgia State Law Review* 25: 575–605.

Weber, MC (2011) Disability Rights, Welfare Law. *Cardozo Law Review* 32: 2483–532.

Weicker, LP Jr (1991) Historical Background of the Americans with Disabilities Act. *Temple Law Review* 64: 387–92.

Wendell, S (1997) Toward a Feminist Theory of Disability. In Davis, LJ (ed) *The Disability Studies Reader*. New York, NY: Routledge.

Witte, E (1963) *The Development of the Social Security Act*. Madison, WI: University of Wisconsin Press.

Ycas, MA (1996) Patterns of Return to Work in a Cohort of Disabled-Worker Beneficiaries. In Mashaw, JL (ed) *Disability, Work and Cash Benefits*. Kalamazoo, MI: WE Upjohn Institute for Employment Research.

3 Justice making: scrutinizing Canada's jury representativeness guarantees while ameliorating Stewart and Russell's conceptions of "social wreckage" for Canadians with disabilities

Richard Jochelson and Michelle Bertrand

Introduction

Amongst Marta Russell's many contributions to disability advocacy was her indictment of the criminal justice complex in America, and its criminalization, in particular, of people with mental illnesses. Her work has been instrumental in demonstrating the ways in which the criminal justice system manufactures disability through deprivation, which leads to "acute or chronic physical and psychological disabilities" (Stewart and Russell, 2001; see also Liat Ben-Moshe and Jean Stewart, this volume.). Broader issues of incarceration, trial and charging rates have occupied the policy landscape of criminal justice studies. Few studies have focused on disabled persons as determiners of justice. The Canadian jury selection process aims to select a representative jury—a jury that corresponds to a cross-section of society. The carceral punitivity of the criminal justice system towards persons with disabilities and its production of disability remain tragically unresolved. Perhaps some disruption is possible through valuing justice making by disabled persons.

Jury research is an under-studied area within the Canadian context. This absence may largely be due to the fact that the study of ex-jurors is essentially prohibited by the *Criminal Code of Canada*. Section 649 states that jurors are prohibited from disclosing the content of their deliberations except for examining the workings of a jury. While the prohibition seems to allow some study of jury work, the work has been undertaken in a very general manner and has been largely ignored by academics. This is because the studies have been limited to general questions since any study of deliberation itself has been prohibited—the realm of deliberation is sacrosanct. The Supreme Court of Canada has itself spoken of this chilling of jury research in Canada:

> More comprehensive and scientific assessment of this and other aspects of the criminal law and criminal process would be welcome. Should Parliament reconsider this prohibition, it may be that more helpful research into the Canadian experience would emerge. But for now, social science evidence

> appears to cast little light on the extent of any 'generic prejudice' relating to charges . . . [and the relationship of charges] . . . to jury verdict.
> (*R v Find* 2001: para. 87; see also *R v Williams* 1998 and *R v Spence* 2005: para. 55)

Within this tightly constrained legal culture perhaps the only way to gain insight into juror understanding of legal concepts is through the development of experimental and survey-based trials on the basis of limited questions. In addition to the interrogation of a juror's assessment of reasonableness, empirical studies may allow us to question the rationality and tolerance of juror decision-making.

In this chapter we delve into the work of Marta Russell and her collaboration with Jean Stewart as a source of inspiration for the study of disability as a central concern in the response of criminal justice institutions. Stewart and Russell provided a powerful political economic critique of corrections in the United States and squarely addressed issues of disability within the prison. This same focus on disability would surely illuminate other critical interrogations of criminal justice responses to criminality at both formative and carceral phases. Under-studied in the Canadian context is the role of disability in the justice-making process—in the work of judges and juries. In this chapter, we seek to take Stewart and Russell's focus and use it in the study of jury formation. Jury work is contested terrain for people with disability. The barriers to service include issues of physical accessibility. However, socio-legal barriers exist as well. A review of leading cases suggests that the Canadian legal terrain remains one that doctrinally works against participation of persons with disabilities in the justice-making process. Second, a study of almost two hundred participants also demonstrates that social conceptions of participation in justice making also contribute to barriers for persons with disabilities in the context of jury service. Ultimately, Stewart and Russell provide a framework for thinking about the production of disability and the reification of partial citizenship for persons with disabilities who wish to partake in the justice-making process.

We organize this chapter into four parts. First, we review Stewart and Russell's important work on imprisonment and disability. Second, we explore the notions of jury representativeness in Canada and then review salient elements of the recent case law. Third, we share the results of a survey study in which we attempted to delineate the degree of participation our sampled population would accept in jury work in respect of persons with disabilities. We end the chapter with a discussion of our findings and the ways in which Stewart and Russell's work can continue to inform the study of the justice system.

Background and influence

In 2001, Jean Stewart and Marta Russell wrote *Disablement, Prison, and Historical Segregation*. The article was prescient and anticipated a tremendous amount of critical criminological scholarship. The piece, published in the independent socialist magazine *Monthly Review*, was not cited vociferously in the extant academic literature; indeed, currently, it is only cited 34 times on Google Scholar. It has, however, influenced the work of new notable scholars like sociologist Liat Ben-Moshe (Ben-Moshe et al., 2014; Ben-Moshe, 2013). It has also had an impact on various studies in public health journals (Ghai, 2009; Eliason et al., 2004). In the Canadian critical criminological literature we see echoes of the work in later scholarship about imprisonment, and criminalization of women (see Comack and Balfour, 2004; Hannah-Moffatt and Shaw, 2000). Certainly, in the Canadian literature the intersection of criminalization and disability is now relatively well-mined. In addition to academic explications, notable reports have been produced by advocacy associations like the John Howard Society indicating the challenges facing inmates with disabilities (see John Howard Society of Alberta, 2002; Boland et al., 1998; Canadian Human Rights Commission, 2003).

Stewart and Russell's article contains lasting observations and critiques that should inform all critical criminologists in their work. Stewart and Russell note that alarmingly high rates of physical illness, disability, cognitive disabilities, and mental illness occur in the prison population and they also note the intersection of these disabilities with poverty (Stewart and Russell, 2001). The authors write of the brutal socio-economic dimensions of incarceration in America: In order to manage and contain its surplus populations and poorest classes, American capitalism has developed paramilitary forms of segregation, containment, and repression (Stewart and Russell, 2001; Parenti, 1999).

Stewart and Russell also write of the ways in which the social world is generative of disability noting that thinking of disability as socially contested and manufactured corrects the myth that we should "blame a disabled person's inability to participate fully in the economic life of our society on their physiological, anatomical, or mental limitations rather than on economic or social forces" (Stewart and Russell, 2001).

They also describe the move towards institutionalization of disabled persons as a progression that has been galvanized by changes in industrialization and in the movement towards capitalism. They write that:

> While one cannot claim that working-age disabled persons in pre-capitalist societies had achieved full integration and economic well-being, many occupied a niche in small workshops and family-based production, where they could contribute according to their ability. . . . Disabled workers were increasingly excluded from paid employment on the grounds that they were unable to keep pace with the new, mechanized, factory-based production system.
>
> (Stewart and Russell, 2001 (citing Finkelstein, 1980); Oliver, 1990; Russell, 1998; Ryan and Thomas, 1980)

The result of industrialization and the expansion of capitalism served to create "a class of proletarians and a class of 'disabled' whose bodies did not conform to the standard worker physique and whose labor-power was effectively ignored"

(Stewart and Russell, 2001). At the same time industrialization further manufactured disability by increasing the risk of work related accidents (Stewart and Russell, 2001).

The authors also noted that the "medical industry pathologized traits such as blindness, deafness, and physical and mental impairments that have naturally appeared in the human race throughout history" and thus medicalization and institutionalization relegated "disabled persons to isolation and exclusion from society" (Stewart and Russell, 2001). The resultant impact has been institutional and carceral and reveals itself in educational, employment and earnings outcomes, all of which are poorer for persons with disability (Stewart and Russell, 2001).

Noting that in many jurisdictions, "jails have become the primary 'treatment' provider for poor people with mental illnesses" Stewart and Russell explicate the acuteness of the "criminalization of mental illness" (Stewart and Russell, 2001). They note that persons with mental illnesses occupy a disproportionate share of the homeless population (Stewart and Russell, 2001). The authors argue that as the welfare state was slowly being dismantled the "mental institution [wa]s being replaced with yet another institution, the prison"; incarcerated persons with mental illnesses were mere "social wreckage" that contributed to the Gross Domestic Product of America "by supporting thousands of persons associated with expanding and maintaining the prison industry" (Stewart and Russell, 2001).

Stewart and Russell claimed that once incarcerated, persons with disabilities faced unique problems within the prison system. People with disabilities often face accessibility barriers in prison, confront oppression and abuse by the prison system and its workers, and routinely are not accommodated in order to meet basic needs (Stewart and Russell, 2001). The authors argue that these failures are made all the more troubled by problems of "overcrowding" and the rapidly expanding "prison industrial complex" (Stewart and Russell, 2001).

The intersection of criminalization and disability is now well-worn and explored in the Canadian and US literature. It has ironically spurred a new line of rehabilitative initiatives, often under the rubric of therapeutic jurisprudence. For example, calls to bring mental health courts to more segments of the criminalized population, including Indigenous offenders, under the auspices that courts together with social services practitioners can therapeutically administer services to accused persons in exchange for guilty pleas (Ferrazzi et al., 2013).

Stewart and Russell, then, manage to explain the ways that criminalization and disability intersect in the carceral environment. Indeed, many studies of intersectional oppressions and criminalization seem to occur at the site of incarceration or policing (see Comack, 2000; Balfour and Comack, 2014). Some studies focus on these intersections in the context of alternative courts, such as drug courts in Canada (Moore, 2007). Indeed, broader issues of incarceration, trial, and charging rates have occupied the policy landscape of criminal justice studies and have been highlighted by scholars. Hosts of cultural, social and economic issues are at play prior to the criminal legal process.

In Canada, the procedural aspects of legal process remain understudied in the context of persons with disabilities. Part of the criminalization process includes decisions of fact—the deliberations of judges and juries. Few studies have focused on persons with disability as determiners of justice, or the impacts of their roles in Canadian juries. The Canadian jury selection process aims to select a representative jury. The vast majority of the literature on jury work in Canada and the USA tends to focus on race and ethnicity. Below, we review some of these interrogations of jury work and race because this is the main body of literature that has developed in respect of notions of representativeness. We then explore recent cases on representativeness in order to understand the legal duties of the state in achieving a representative jury.

Representativeness studies in North America and case law—from race to disability

Certainly in the United States, studies of juries and their representativeness are well-worn, an observation which reflects the frequency of jury trials in America. Studies on the representativeness of jury rolls can be found in major jurisdictions (Kairys et al., 1977). The Canadian context is less prolific in the area of jury representation. The Manitoba (Aboriginal Justice Inquiry) and Ontario (The Iacobucci Report) reports are regrettably amongst the only sources regarding issues of representation (Aboriginal Justice Inquiry, 2001; The Iacobucci Report, 2013). Other major Canadian studies have not attempted to investigate the Canadian populace's views on representation, a matter all the more important given that the courts seem to want representativeness to align with how the reasonable Canadian would react to the administration of justice in a given case.

Within the last 25 years there have been academic calls for jury reform, usually in the context of race-based discussions. Petersen asserted that white jurors are more likely to be influenced by racial stereotypes and contended that juror challenges that removed prospective jurors from the jury exacerbated the bias and representative issues of a given jury (Petersen, 1993). Petersen contended that Canada should revisit its laws on peremptory challenges and the author was prescient in her advocacy for suggesting that questions for racist and prejudicial attitudes should be permitted (see *R v Williams*; *R v Parks*; *R v Gayle*).

Roach studied the cases of *R v Parks* and *R v Williams*, and outlined legal tools that could be used to prevent the risk that jury deliberations would be sullied by racial prejudice and stereotypes (Roach, 1995). Roach argued that the decisions should make clear that racial prejudices may apply to accuseds and complainants and calls for closer interrogation of whether the law should scrutinize for bias in the context of age- or gender-based distinctions (Roach, 1995: 426). Roach argues that Canada should strive to avoid the American model of jury vetting in which defence and prosecution struggle to obtain a favorable jury to ensure easy wins (Roach, 1995: 426). Nonetheless, Roach noted that understanding of personal and institutional racism were critical investigations for future legal cases, though Roach remained wary of the claim that singular questions could cleanse a jury of bias (Roach, 1995: 426).

Israel (2003) examined the specific issues of Indigenous underrepresentation in the jury panel and described the roots of the issue through historic discrimination (Israel, 2003). Israel explored the problems that exacerbate the representation issues including the use and administration of non-representative lists, the broad Sheriff discretion in finding eligible members for a jury, the problems of using mail, issues related to qualification (including criminal records), and the rolling nature of jury service (which favours non-Indigenous response) (Israel, 2003). Israel notes that Ontario and Manitoba studies such as the Manitoba Aboriginal Justice Inquiry, Law Reform Commission of Saskatchewan, Donald Marshall Jr Inquiry, and Commission on Systemic Racism in the Ontario Criminal Justice System irrefutably establish underrepresentation as a problem and that legal reform was a necessity (Israel, 2003: 43).

Morton (2003) studied the *R v Gayle* decision and noted that while the Court paid lip service to the notion of representativeness, it provided a formalistic legal decision that created a very high burden on an accused to demonstrate that the jury was either biased or unrepresentative (Morton, 2003). The process of assembling the list of potential jurors (i.e. the array of names) and its randomness together with the lack of misconduct on the part of the Sheriff seemed to satisfy formalistic interpretations that a jury was representative (Morton, 2003). Morton asserted that the Canadian courts have generally ascribed to conceptions of formal, not substantive, equality in ensuring jury representativeness and lack of bias.

Psychological studies have considered the race and decision-making of juries, albeit in the United States context (Sommers, 2007; Hastie, et al., 1983). Sommers notes that most studies focus on the race of the accused, rather than the jury. In general, jury studies have found that juries which are authoritarian hand out harsher punishments (McGowen and King, 1982), that jurors who can be evaluated as highly ethnocentric are more likely to judge people who are of different race more harshly (Kemmelmeir, 2005), and that white jurors are more likely to convict dark-skinned than light-skinned accused persons (Foley and Bjamblin, 1982). In cases with ambiguous evidence, jurors of both races were harsher towards other-race defendants, showing a strong "in-group, out-group" effect (Ugwuegbu, 1979). Other studies have found that race works in complex ways, but that different contexts will produce a race-based effect in mock trial scenarios (Sommers and Ellsworth, 2000; Mazella and Feingold, 1994). Race-based effects have been found in a number of other studies, as well (Bowers et al., 2001; Bernard, 1979; Hans and Vidmar, 1982; Jones and Kaplan, 2001; Marder, 2002; Mitchell et al., 2005; and Perez et al., 1993). In short, the litany of American psychological studies shows that race does, across a variety of contexts, influence juror decision-making.

The Canadian literature on juries is somewhat scant in terms of empirical studies, but, as we have discussed above, major jurisdictions are reporting representation and jury bias issues. For example, the two most recent major reports establish as social fact that jury representation is a major obstacle facing Indigenous accused persons in Canada.

Iacobucci notes that the jury is a fact finder that protects against oppressive laws and that it acts as an "educator" because it helps to legitimize the criminal justice system by acting as the conscience of the community in criminal proceedings (The Iacobucci Report, 2013: 20). These functions were adopted by the Supreme Court of Canada in *R v Sherratt* (1991). The importance of representativeness in Canada was constitutionalized in 1982 but seemed to be apprised of the values of "fairness" and "random selection" (The Iacobucci Report, 2013: 30). *R v Sherratt* served to link the *Charter* right to be tried by a jury under s. 11(f) and the presumption of innocence under a fair and public hearing in s. 11(d) to the principles of representativeness (*Charter*, 1982). Iacobucci contends that the *Sherratt* decision serves notice that the jury's role is essentially one that mirrors the community's commitment to justice, including its conceptions of representation (The Iacobucci Report, 2013: 31).

It is surprising—given the public reports, the Supreme Court's findings in *Sherratt*, and the psychological literature on race, representativeness, and bias—that there are no Canadian studies analyzing the opinions of Canadians regarding juror representation. If a jury stands as a proxy for the Canadian conscience, surely the content of that conscience, in respect of issues of representation, must be examined. Given this context we developed a questionnaire in order to gather information on Canadian conceptions of representativeness.

It has been well-established in the Canadian jurisprudence that the jury is to act as something of a moral arbiter in criminal cases, one that balances the administration of justice including the needs of an accused for due process and the state's interest in maintaining a secure society. It is worth noting that the conception of representativeness is derived from the *Charter* as opposed to explicitly within its enumerated terms. No Canadian study has attempted to understand if the conception of representativeness is a value that prospective jurors hold. Our literature search did not uncover any instance in which a Canadian sample was canvassed regarding attitudes and relative value of the conception of representativeness. Given the dearth of research on the topic, our survey provides some content and context to the relative importance that representativeness has to populations. It is notable that while courts have been reluctant to give too much weight to the representativeness claims of accused persons, the two major public inquiries find major deficiencies in the implementation of representation rights. If the public perception were that representativeness was an acceptable value, the case for law reform would be strengthened considerably.

The idea of representativeness is a troubled one. The Canadian jury selection process strives for a representative jury—one that corresponds to a cross-section of society and the large or wider community (*R v Kokopenace*, 2013). Claims by accused that they did not receive a fair trial due to representativeness issues have in the main resulted in failure. A recent study demonstrated that virtually all claims by accused that a jury was not representative have met with failure in

Canadian adjudication (Jochelson et al., 2014). Factors which result in a less than representative jury include difficulty in finding lists that reflect a proportional share of the vulnerable population, inability, unwillingness or slower speed of action by the vulnerable population in responding to requests for jury pool data, delayed reimbursement for travel costs, discretionary state processes that eliminate members of the pool due to a determination that a juror may lack comprehension abilities, and deliberate or negligent composition of jury lists by state officials creating the jury pool (AJI, 2001; The Iacobucci Report, 2013). In the case of Indigenous persons, the AJI made sweeping recommendations to rectify problems of representation:

> [W]hen a Sheriff exempts an Indigenous person from service they should be replaced by a member from the same community; stand aside and peremptory challenges should be eliminated; rulings for challenges for cause should be made by the presiding judge; jurors in rural communities should be drawn from within 40 km of the trial location where practicable or from locations that are more functionally representative; and that translation services be provided for prospective jurors who speak only Indigenous languages and that the provincial legislation be amended to allow service of these individuals.
>
> (AJI, 1991; Jochelson et al., 2014: 7)

The AJI and the Iacobucci Report did not seem to influence the behaviors of high courts in assessing the issue of representativeness in general. No reports have been conducted examining representativeness issues of the disability community in Canada. This is not to suggest that accommodations are not afforded to prospective jurors with disabilities in Canada.

Boyle writes of the some of the positive changes that Canada has made in accommodating disability in the juror context and notes that Canada expressly allows persons who are deaf or blind to serve on the jury (Boyle, 2011). In addition, Boyle notes that the *Criminal Code of Canada*, the *Canadian Evidence Act* and the *Canadian Human Rights Act*, amongst others, provide an architecture of support for equality rights, support the removal of discriminatory barriers and encourage participation (Boyle, 2011). For example the *Criminal Code of Canada* in s 627 provides that "The judge may permit a juror with a physical disability who is otherwise qualified to serve as a juror to have technical, personal, interpretative or other support services" (*Criminal Code of Canada*, 1985: s 627). However, it must be stated that this architecture of support though, does little to ensure representativeness of the jury itself.

Two Maritime cases are emblematic of the possible ways a Court can trouble representativeness in Canada in the context of disability. These cases are exceptional, and their persuasiveness is in significant question in light of the Supreme Court of Canada's decision in *R v Kokopenace* (*R v Kokopenace*, 2015). *R v Francis*, 2007 was a Nova Scotia case involving a request for a change of venue in order to accommodate persons with disabilities who would not have been able to serve on a jury if the original trial location had been maintained for reasons of inaccessibility (*R v Francis*, 2007). While the accused was not disabled, he argued that the location of the trial, due to its inaccessibility, meant that the jury could not be representative because it would exclude disabled persons. The accused was relying on the conception of representativeness under the *Canadian Charter of Rights and Freedoms* as well as the provincial jury legislation. Justice Warner noted that, "the accused is denied a statutory right to a jury panel randomly selected from the entire adult population of the jury district if the jury panel does not include persons with physical disabilities" (*R v Francis*, 2007: paras 28–30) Justice Warner noted that:

> the jury must not exclude a spectrum of society, if possible, without that exclusion being based upon a reason logically connected with, and justifiable under, the criminal trial process. . . . Exclusion of a group, which has been randomly selected to the jury list or the jury panel . . . whether excluded by intent or by effect, and where accommodation is possible without undue hardship, negates randomness, breaches the statutory right of the accused, and infringe [sic] on trial fairness.
>
> (*R v Francis*, 2007: para 29)

Similarly, in *Buckingham v The Queen* 2007 the use of motor vehicle registries for a juror pool was found by the Newfoundland court to violate representativeness rights because the lists systematically excluded persons with disabilities (*Buckingham v The Queen*, 2007). The Court relied on the Supreme Court case of *R v Sherratt* 1991 in articulating its vision of representativeness, citing Justice L'Heureux-Dubé:

> The jury, through its collective decision making, is an excellent fact finder; due to its representative character, it acts as the conscience of the community; the jury can act as the final bulwark against oppressive laws or their enforcement; it provides a means whereby the public increases its knowledge of the criminal justice system and it increases, through the involvement of the public societal trust in the system as a whole. . . . The modern jury was not meant to be a tool in the hands of either the Crown or the accused and indoctrinated as such through the challenge procedure, but rather was envisioned as a representative cross-section of society, honestly and fairly chosen.
>
> (*Buckingham v The Queen*, 2007: para 9)

The Court in *Buckingham* found that using motor vehicle registries to form jury lists was too exclusive of a variety of populations, including "persons of disability who do not have a driver's licence or own a motor vehicle" (*Buckingham v The Queen*, 2007: para 16). These exclusions violated the guarantee of representatives found in s 11 of the *Canadian Charter of Rights and Freedoms*.

These decisions and their influence on troubling conceptions of representativeness in the context of disability have been effectively overruled by the recent

Supreme Court of Canada case of *R v Kokopenace* (*R v Kokopenace*, 2015). While this case does not expressly deal with issues of disability, it does demonstrate the links that the right of representativeness has to the *Charter*, and the difficulties of challenging this right in the context of challenges to process on the basis of exclusion of disability as a value inherent to representativeness.

Kokopenace was a case that involved the conviction for manslaughter of an Indigenous man from a reserve community. The accused's counsel learned of potential problems of including on-reserve Indigenous persons in the district where the trial was held (Kenora). On appeal, the majority of the Ontario Court of Appeal found that the accused's ss 11(d) and 11(f) rights of the *Charter* had been violated and ordered a new trial. The majority of the Supreme Court of Canada did not find a representativeness violation under the *Charter* and explicated the criteria for showing a *Charter* violation in future cases.

The majority of the Supreme Court of Canada makes clear that the *Charter* right to jury representativeness stems from "the s. 11 (*d*) right to a fair trial by an impartial tribunal and the s. 11 (*f*) right to a trial by jury" (*R v Kokopenace*, 2015: para 1). The different rights correspond to different aspects of the guarantee. Section 11(d) raises issues of independence and impartiality of the jury, and representativeness's relationship to these values. (*R v Kokopenace*, 2015: para 48). The test for representativeness under this branch of the right is "whether a tribunal is impartial, the question is whether a reasonable person, fully informed of the circumstances, would have a reasonable apprehension of bias" at the institutional and individual levels (*R v Kokopenace*, 2015: para. 49). Citing *R v Lippé*, 1991, the majority notes that the representativeness guarantee under "s. 11(*d*) will be violated if the process used to compile the jury roll raises an appearance of bias at the systemic level" (*R v Kokopenace*, 2015: para 49). However, the majority is careful to note that:

> The narrow way in which representativeness is defined in Canadian jurisprudence means that impartiality is guaranteed through the process used to compile the jury roll, not through the ultimate composition of the jury roll or petit jury itself. A jury roll containing few individuals of the accused's race or religion is not in itself indicative of bias.
>
> (*R v Kokopenace*, 2015: para 51)

The majority also noted that representativeness could be troubled under a second branch using s 11(f) of the *Charter* which relates to "the jury's role as the 'conscience of the community' and promotes public trust in the criminal justice system" (*R v Kokopenace*, 2015: para 55; *Sherratt*, 1991: 523–25). For the majority, the conscience of the community requirement mandates representativeness through an "adequate jury selection process" (*R v Kokopenace*, 2015: para 56). The absence of representativeness will undermine the right to a trial by a jury under s 11(f) of the *Charter*. On some occasions when that representativeness issue also affects impartiality, s 11(d) will also be violated (*R v Kokopenace*, 2015: para 58).

The majority then used its analysis to rearticulate a legal test for jury representativeness. The test is highly contextual and will differ from situation to situation. The majority explains the legal test as follows:

> To determine if the state has met its representativeness obligation, the question is whether the state provided a fair opportunity for a broad cross-section of society to participate in the jury process. A fair opportunity will have been provided when the state makes reasonable efforts to: (1) compile the jury roll using random selection from lists that draw from a broad cross-section of society, and (2) deliver jury notices to those who have been randomly selected. In other words, it is the act of casting a wide net that ensures representativeness. Representativeness is not about targeting particular groups for inclusion on the jury roll.
>
> (*R v Kokopenace*, 2015: para 61)

The majority notes that it is "the quality of the state's efforts that will determine if the process is adequate" as opposed to a standard of objective adequacy (*R v Kokopenace*, 2015: para 63). Where a population does not cooperate with the state to create appropriate juror lists, the representativeness guarantee is not triggered (*R v Kokopenace*, 2015: para 63). The majority also rejected that through the representativeness guarantee "the state is obliged to address the distressing history of estrangement and discrimination" (*R v Kokopenace*, 2015: para 64). The majority notes that the state need only provide "a fair opportunity for participation" (*R v Kokopenace*, 2015: para 64). Indeed, the majority wrote that using representativeness to address historic wrongs was inappropriate. Such goals while "socially laudable,"

> are by definition an attempt to target a particular group for inclusion on the jury roll. Requiring the state to target a particular group for inclusion would be a radical departure from the way the Canadian jury selection process has always been understood.
>
> (*R v Kokopenace*, 2015: para 64)

Since the right of representativeness is held by an individual and not a social group, "the state's constitutional obligation is satisfied by providing a fair opportunity to participate—even if part of the population declines to do so" (*R v Kokopenace*, 2015: para 65). However, while deliberate state exclusion of a subset of society would violate representativeness, unintentional exclusion requires a determination of whether the state made "reasonable efforts" (*R v Kokopenace*, 2015: para 66). If a state has made reasonable efforts but a particular population declines to cooperate, the State will have respected the *Charter* (*R v Kokopenace*, 2015: para 66). If the State failed to make reasonable efforts the size of the excluded population will be relevant—if the excluded population is small in size this will not violate the representativeness guarantee (*R v Kokopenace*, 2015: para 66).

The majority found that the efforts of Ontario to establish a representative juror list were adequate in light of the reserve communities' failure to participate in aiding with the formation of the list. The majority found that Ontario committed itself to improving the representation of Indigenous people on juries:

> the province did not simply throw up its hands upon learning of the problems with delivery. Rather, it took an aggressive approach. After consulting . . . it increased the number of notices sent to on-reserve residents by nearly 50 percent.
>
> (*R v Kokopenace*, 2015: para 121)

The majority noted that, "the state's constitutional obligation stops when it has provided a fair opportunity for a broad cross-section of society to participate in the jury process. It has done so" (*R v Kokopenace*, 2015: para 126).

Members of disability communities may face similar barriers to participating in jury work that would preclude an accused from arguing issues of representativeness. In *Kokopenace*, the majority was troubled that the reserve communities were not cooperating in formulating prospective juror lists with the province's requests. This lack of compliance was fatal to the claims of representativeness flaws because in this context the province was seen to be making reasonable efforts. The Iacobucci report suggests that the failures of reserve communities to respond relate to suspicions of the state's motives, and a sense that the criminal justice apparatus is fundamentally foreign to Indigenous cultural heritage (The Iacobucci Report, 2013; Jochelson et al., 2014). Disability communities may similarly face barriers in responding to state requests for names. Disability communities are likely less organized than on-reserve communities, and just as suspicious of the state's requests to form lists of names from their population. Disability communities may also face structural barriers to agreeing to a jury process and err on the side of non-cooperation in list formation. Without knowing that travel would be accommodated, made accessible, and that the process throughout would be accommodating, systemic barriers to participation would obviously inure. The representativeness guarantee as it is currently articulated may be of little assistance to participation in justice making by persons with disabilities.

Yet, the link between s 11(f) of the *Charter* and the need for the jury to act as the "conscience of the community" suggest that conceptions of representation are important in articulations of Canadian justice. The wider community should be represented on the jury by an appropriate cross-section of society. Challenging this notion legally may, after *Kokopenace*, prove to be difficult. Nonetheless, the problem of jury participation issues raises interesting questions about public perceptions of representativeness. In the context of disabilities, do public perceptions align with ideals of representativeness?

Inspired by Stewart and Russell's work in outlining the barriers that incarcerated persons with disabilities face in corrections institutions, we undertook a study to understand how public perception is articulated in relation to the participation of different marginalized groups in justice making and court room participation. One area of marginalization we explored was the perception of participants in respect of persons with disabilities and the nature of participation as justice makers that the participants thought appropriate in the Canadian justice context.

We understood the issue of the jury acting as the conscience of the community to be a pivotal concept to which Canadians would relate. Further, the legal phrase that a jury ought to be the conscience of the community raises the specter of the importance of Canadian opinion of the matter of representativeness and disability.

The study's demographics

In our study we sampled 188 participants in a student sample pool. The pool began with 211 participants, but as only 188 identified as Canadian citizens, and were therefore eligible for jury duty, we limited our analysis to Canadian citizens. The average age of the participants was 20.89 years, and the age range of participants was between 18 and 54 years of age. The participants identified as 61.7 percent female, 37.8 percent male and 0.5 percent of unspecified gender. Participants were provided with other options for gender, but with the exception of one unspecified, all identified as either male or female. The study spanned a wide ethnic ancestry range with self-identification of ethnicity as follows: Aboriginal: 5.3 percent; African: 2.7 percent; East Asian: 1.6 percent; South Asian: 4.8 percent; Southeast Asian: 4.3 percent; European: 67.6 percent; Hispanic: 2.1 percent; Middle Eastern: 3.2 percent; Pacific Islander: 2.1 percent; and mixed ancestry: 6.4 percent. The approximate household income of participants also varied quite markedly. The participants described their household income as follows: 35.1 percent earned $0–25,000; 15.7 percent earned $25–50,000; 15.1 percent earned $50–75,000; 11.9 percent earned $75–100,000; 5.9 percent earned $100–125,000; 2.7 percent earned $125–150,000; 3.8 percent earned $150–175,000; 2.2 percent earned $175–200,000 and 7.6 percent earned above $200,000.

Information provided to participants

Some very basic information was provided to all the participants. All participants were told that according to Canadian case law, "a representative jury is one that corresponds to a cross-section of the larger community as far as is possible and appropriate in the circumstances."

The participants were also provided with the following classifications of mental disability in an attempt to avoid clinical understandings of mental disorders. The categories were designed so that mild mental disorder would be understood to be persons who were roughly as capable as the average juror in undertaking jury work. The definitions we provided are as follows:

Mild mental disability in this case includes having some difficulty reading or understanding very complex material on one's own, but generally being able to understand what the average person could understand.

Moderate mental disability in this case includes greater difficulties reading or understanding very complex material on one's own, including some material that the average person could understand.

Severe mental disability in this case includes having substantial difficulty reading and understanding material on one's own, including most material that the average person could understand.

Questions

We asked a number of questions about jury work that are beyond the scope of this chapter. However we asked questions pertaining to disability and jury work and courtroom access that potentially illuminate some public perceptions on the issue.

In terms of jury work, we asked participants to state their level of agreement, with 0 being complete disagreement and 100 being complete agreement, in respect of the following statements:

1 The "larger community" should include, at least in part, proportionate jury membership of people with physical disabilities;
2 The "larger community" should include, at least in part, proportionate jury membership of people with mild mental disability;
3 The "larger community" should include, at least in part, proportionate jury membership of people with moderate mental disability;
4 The "larger community" should include, at least in part, proportionate jury membership of people with severe mental disability.

In terms of courtroom work and attendance, using the same method, we asked for level of agreement with the following statements:

1 The courthouse should be accessible to all people with physical disabilities;
2 The courthouse should be accessible to all people with mental disability;
3 The courthouse should be accessible to all people with mild mental disability;
4 The courthouse should be accessible to all people with moderate mental disability;
5 The courthouse should be accessible to all people with severe mental disability.

Results

Jury work

Table 3.1 Effects of disability on participants' definition of "larger community" for the purposes of jury membership

Statement regarding inclusion on jury	*Mean agreement level*	*Minimum level of agreement*	*Maximum level of agreement*	*Standard deviation*
Inclusion of physical disabilities	64.51	0	100	26.18
Inclusion of mild mental disabilities	51.19	0	100	25.98
Inclusion of moderate mental disabilities	43.96	0	100	26.49
Inclusion of severe mental disabilities	34.97	0	100	27.42

In our assessment of jury representativeness, we found statistically significant differences in the responses (P<0.001). The participants' support was clearly distinguished between whether the identified disability was physical (64.51) or mental (51.19, 43.96 and 34.97 for mild, moderate and severe mental disability respectively). Participants viewed participation on the jury for a person with a physical disability with, on average, moderate support. The participants very weakly supported people with mild mental disability (51.19) despite that the definition made clear that this category could complete mental tasks that the average juror could undertake. As the mental disorder was described progressively more seriously, participants began to disagree with including mental disability as a category that should inform the notions of larger community.

Accessibility

Table 3.2 Effects of disability on participants' agreement with courtroom accessibility

Statement regarding access to the courtroom	*Mean agreement level*	*Minimum level of agreement*	*Maximum level of agreement*	*Standard deviation*
All physical disabilities	80.63	0	100	23.7
All mental disabilities	61.31	0	100	28.2
Mild mental disabilities	66.86	0	100	27.57
Moderate mental disabilities	60.95	0	100	29.34
Severe mental disabilities	49.08	0	100	32.87

In our assessment of court work and courtroom accessibility, we also found significant statistical differences (P<0.001). Participants agreed (80.63) that the court should be accessible to people with physical disabilities (though as noted before they agreed less that people with physical disabilities should serve on a jury). When considering all mental disabilities they weakly agreed (61.31) that this category should have courtroom accessibility. When the mental disorder was described as mild, the level of agreement of accessibility rose slightly (66.86). When we asked about moderate and weak mental disability we found some modest support for moderate mental disorder accessibility (60.95) and weak lack of support for severe mental disorder accessibility (49.08).

For both our jury and accessibility questions, participants used the entire range of agreement levels with some recording 0 and others recording 100 on each question. The standard deviations reflect this wide variability in response range.

Understanding these results

Our results do not show a tremendous amount of enthusiasm by participants for inclusion of persons with disability into the work of jurors. Even persons described with no cognitive deficits, described as physically disabled, evoked only mild support for jury work (65.51). Our participants were more willing to let people with physical disabilities have access to the courtroom (80.63). When it came to mild mental disability, which we described as roughly comparable to the cognitive abilities of the average juror, we were surprised that our participants evoked bare support for jury work (51.19) and even weak to moderate support for access to the courtroom (66.86). These revelations make the disagreement with participation for jury work and courtroom access for the categories of moderate and severe disability less surprising.

Several other observations are warranted in light of the results. Simply using the word disability seems to result in a discriminatory effect for juror participation and access for people with disabilities for our participant pool. The qualifier of the word "mental" before disability seems to further prejudice agreement for jury work and access by our participants, regardless of whether we described that mental disorder as somewhat benign in respect of ability to perform juror functions. Mental disorders evoked weak support for jury work, and surprisingly weak responses to access to the courtroom for those individuals. This is somewhat shocking, given that courthouses are generally considered to be amongst the most open and public places in Canada.

While it would be difficult to extrapolate our findings with this participant pool to the Canadian population at large, the results are suggestive of a lingering discrimination against persons with disabilities in jury work and court-room access. These sentiments align with the recent Supreme Court of Canada's decision in *Kokopenace* as a difficult environment in which to hope for a representative jury replete with participation with members from disabled communities. The Supreme Court does not seem to want to hold the state to high standards of seeking out representativeness in the jury pool, preferring to limit them to a "reasonable efforts" standard. Our participant pool suggests that the public sentiments are not strong on the issue of disability representation on the jury, or even in seeking courtroom access.

Unlike Indigenous representation on the jury, there have been no public reports in Canada investigating the problems with disability representation on the Canadian jury. The nature of the problem has never been explored in any meaningful sense. Most of the discussion has been limited to studies of accommodation for disabled persons who manage to serve on a jury. There are good empirical reasons to scrutinize the issue of representation on the jury for persons with disabilities. In 2012, Statistics Canada undertook a study of disability in Canada entitled *Canadians in Context: People with Disabilities* (Statistics Canada, 2013). According to the report, 3.8 million Canadians reported having a disability in 2012; this corresponds to 13.7 percent of Canadians (Statistics Canada, 2013). If one compares this to Statistics Canada data in 2011, the only ethnic groups, which rank higher in terms of percentages in Canada than persons with disabilities, are those who identify as Canadian (32.16 percent), English (19.81 percent), French (15.42 percent), Scottish (14.35 percent), and Irish (13.83 percent) (Statistics Canada, 2011). Indigenous identification including First Nations, Metis, and Inuit amounted to 4.3 percent according to 2011 Census data (Statisics Canada NHS, 2011). The percentage of persons with disabilities in Canada who are of age to participate in justice making is high—for example 16.1 percent of people aged between 45 and 64 reported being persons with disabilities. For Canadians over 75, disability rates climb to 42.5 percent, indicating that almost half of Canadians will be persons with disabilities in their lifetimes (Statistics Canada, 2013). These are staggeringly high numbers of people to not study definitively in terms of intersections with the justice system and its apparatuses, including jury work. Furthermore, these numbers potentially translate to extremely low proportions of representation on the Canadian jury. Populations of people with disabilities are far less likely to participate in state activities unless they are assured of accessibility. Indeed, many persons with disability are likely to request exemption from jury service for reasons relating to accessibility, and often, tremendous efforts are required to participate. This phenomenon, while not studied in Canada, is well established in the US literature. In certain states, prospective jurors with disabilities may choose not to serve. Elderly Americans have access to these exemptions in 21 states, and people with mental or physical disabilities can do so in at least Georgia, Tennessee, and Texas (Bleyer et al., 1995). In addition, 32 states include juror excuse legislation for undue hardship or extreme inconvenience, and 17 allow physical or mental infirmity to excuse service (Bleyer et al., 1995).

In Canada, similar disqualifying options also inure (undue hardship, etc). A prosecutor or an accused is entitled to challenge service on the ground that a juror, even with the aid of accessibility services provided to the juror under s 627 of the *Criminal Code of Canada*, is physically unable to perform properly the duties of a juror (Boyle, 2011). In addition, persons with disability find additional risks in using accessibility support persons. If any support service worker of a juror with a physical disability discloses information of the trial, the support worker may be found guilty of a summary conviction offence (Boyle, 2011). The legislative and social conditions are therefore in place to systematically exclude or dissuade disabled persons from juror service.

Yet, the philosophy behind jury representativeness strives to maintain a cross-section of society represented in the jury. As the majority of the Supreme Court in *Kokopenace* has determined that lack of cooperation in serving from a particular pool of jurors would obviate the State's requirement to make reasonable efforts to lead to a representative juror pool, it is likely that solutions which seek to place more persons with disabilities in a position to be determiners of justice (i.e. on the jury) are destined to face significantly formidable legal and social opposition.

These observations lead us back to the opening salvo of this paper, that the work of Stewart and Russell needs to be injected into more investigations of the criminal justice system. In our study, we see that public perceptions of persons with disability are generally not enthusiastic about their jury service or even courthouse accommodation. We also see a general lack of interest in our participant pool about proportional representation on the Canadian jury for persons of disability, a matter further evidenced by the scarcity of serious academic treatment in the Canadian literature. We see a legislative and legal scheme that is largely willing to accommodate disability to an extent but which at the same time provides a number of opportunities for dismissal that allow persons with disabilities to excuse themselves from jury service. What is lacking in the administration of jury work in Canada is a positive commitment to forming a representative jury, since typically all that is required of the State is reasonable efforts, no deliberate exclusion of targeted populations, and the inability to claim lack of representation when a community does not cooperate in the formation of jury lists. Persons with disabilities are likely to be impacted under each of these prongs in ways which would result in chronic underrepresentation on the jury, and in ways that other populations are not so challenged.

The message that this socio-legal policy regime sends is that persons with disabilities are, indeed, social wreckage whose participation on the jury is open for those only with the will, the resources, the intellect, and the drive to advocate for the accessibility they need in order to participate in the justice-making process. Participation in jury work is already difficult for many persons with disabilities, but the structural and legal barriers are in place to further disincentivize persons with disabilities from engaging in participation. The lack of proactive socio-legal encouragement to participate, supports the view that persons with disabilities are less able to be fully-formed citizens capable of weighing in on pivotal questions of liberty in the criminal trial in particular. Thus, the socio-legal context further constructs persons with disabilities as less well-formed citizens, whose reluctance to participate is evidence of their inability to perform basic civic functions, and which also serves to justify the State's claim that it has met its representativeness burdens. In short, the current environment does little but "blame a disabled person's inability to participate fully in the economic life of our society on their physiological, anatomical, or mental limitations rather than on economic or social forces" (Stewart and Russell, 2001).

Bleyer et al. make a number of cogent recommendations for enabling access for jurors with disabilities. The list provided is extensive and includes: the availability of court materials in alternate formats at all stages of the proceedings; advanced courthouse orientation services in order to facilitate accommodation;

the recording and captioning of all proceedings informing the panel; requiring questions that seek to determine ability to comprehend rather than focusing on particulars of disabilities; the use of private sidebars to get into more detailed questions about juror understanding; jury box physical and cognitive accessibility protocols; the arrangement of interpreters for people with sight, hearing and cognitive impairments; the use of hearing systems in the infrastructure of the court house; real-time computer assisted transcriptions; the ability to stand, move, or wheel as necessary during the proceedings; and the use of simple language in the courtroom (Bleyer et al., 1995).

For those who have spent time attending a Canadian jury trial, it is obvious that few of these accommodations are in place and that the accommodations that are present are not well publicized. These represent, then, further structural and mental barriers to juror representation. The availability of this suite of services may be cost-prohibitive to the State and this tension is then supportive of not extending representativeness-based interests deep into the pool of prospective jurors with disability. Concomitantly, these factors discourage participation from recalcitrant jurors with disabilities whose unwillingness to serve further reifies the reasonableness of the state's representativeness duties. In short, the economic, legal and social terrains all conspire to exclude justice making by persons with disabilities through juror work.

Concluding thoughts

Stewart and Russell's salvo on imprisonment in 2001 was a stinging rebuke of the prison industrial complex and how politics, class, and economics co-agitate to marginalize incarcerated persons in a manner that was constructive of disability. Stewart and Russell succeeded in explaining how the socio-political landscape forms and creates disability in the prison, and how further marginalized the inmate with disabilities becomes in the carceral environment. These probing observations lead scholars of criminal justice to consider other ways in which the persons with disabilities are further removed from participation in the justice-making process. There has been a plethora of work in this regard in respect of race and ethnicity, but representation on the criminal jury for persons with disability has been understudied, particularly in the Canadian context.

Obviously accessibility issues which stand in the way of service on a jury for persons with disabilities continue to be a significant challenge. That jury representativeness now appears to be an impossible site of legal challenge provides further barriers for participation in jury work for Canadians with disabilities. Our study indicates that these barriers are acceptable for our participant pool. Given the legal architecture and the results of our study, one can see how the service of persons with disabilities on juries continues to be undervalued. Further, the barriers to participation for persons with disabilities would be overwhelming for those with few resources. The lack of participation suggests less currency in the "conscience of the community" and supports conceptions of members of the community with disabilities possessing less agency, and as having less citizenship than other Canadians. Even in justice-making exercises, persons with disabilities become part of the constellation of social wreckage, a notion that Stewart and Russell admonish in their 2001 salvo on imprisonment. Further, this constellation seems to extend from the social realities of Canadians with disabilities to within the justice system, whether these persons face criminal accusation or are discouraged from participating in Canadian justice making.

Bibliography

Balfour, G and Comack, E (eds) (2014) *Criminalizing Women: Gender and (In)justice in Neo-liberal Times* (2nd edition). Halifax: Fernwood Publishing.

Ben-Moshe, L (2013) Disabling Incarceration: Connecting Disability to Divergent Confinements in the USA. *Critical Sociology* 37(7): 385–403.

Ben-Moshe, L and Meiners, E (2014) Beyond Prisons, Mental Health Clinics: When Austerity Opens Cages, Where Do the Services Go? *Public Eye*, available online at www.politicalresearch.org/2014/10/09/beyond-prisons-mental-health-clinics-when-austerity-opens-cages-where-do-the-services-go/# (last accessed June 24, 2015).

Ben-Moshe, L, Chapman, C and Carey, A (eds) (2014) *Disability Incarcerated: Imprisonment and Disability in the US and Canada.* London: Palgrave McMillan Press.

Bernard, JL (1979) Interaction Between the Race of the Defendant and that of Jurors in Determining Verdicts. *Law and Psychology Review* 5: 103–11.

Bleyer, K, McCarty, KS, and Wood, E (1995) Jury Service for People with Disabilities. *Judicature* 78(6): 273–75.

Boland, FJ, Burrill, R, Duwyn, M, and Karp, J (1998) Fetal Alcohol Syndrome: Implications for Correctional Service. *Correctional Service of Canada*, available online at www.faslink.com/FASImplicationsforCSC.htm (last accessed June 15, 2015).

Bowers, WJ, Steiner, BD, and Sandys, M (2001) Death Sentencing in Black and White: An Empirical Analysis of Jurors' Race and Jury Racial Composition. *University of Pennsylvania Journal of Constitutional Law* 3: 171–275.

Boyle, C (2011) A Consideration of the Eligibility of Blind or Deaf People for Jury Service in Ireland. *Hibernian Law Journal* 1: 10–81.

Buckingham v The Queen, 2007 NLTD 107.

Canadian Human Rights Commission (2003) *Protecting Their Rights: A Systemic Review of Human Rights in Correctional Services for Federally Sentenced Women*, available online at www.caefs.ca/wp-content/uploads/2013/05/fswen.pdf (last accessed June 15, 2015).

Canadian Charter of Rights and Freedoms, Part I of the Constitution Act, 1982, being Schedule B to the Canada Act 1982 (UK), 1982, c 1.

Comack E (2000) The Prisoning of Women: Meeting Women's Needs? In Hannah-Moffat, K and Shaw M (eds) *An Ideal Prison? Critical Essays on Women's Imprisonment in Canada*. Halifax: Fernwood Publishing, 117–27.

Comack E (2003) *Racialized Policing: Aboriginal People's Encounters with the Police.* Halifax: Fernwood Publishing.

Comack, E and Balfour, G (2004) *The Power to Criminalize: Violence, Inequality, and the Law*. Halifax: Fernwood Publishing.

Criminal Code of Canada, RSC 1985, c C-46 s 745.

Eliason, MJ, Taylor, JY, and Williams, R (2004) Physical Health of Women in Prison: Relationship to Oppression. *Journal of Correctional Health Care* 10(2): 175–203.

Ferrazzi, P, Krupa, T, and Lysaght, R (2013) Mental Health Courts, Court Diversion, and Canada's Obligations under the United Nations Convention on the Rights of Persons with Disabilities. *Canadian Journal of Community Mental Health* 32(4): 43–57.

Finkelstein, V (1980) *Attitudes and Disabled People: Issues for Discussion*. New York, NY: World Rehabilitation Fund.

Final Report of the Aboriginal Justice Implementation Commission "Aboriginal Justice Inquiry" (2001) *Aboriginal Justice Implementation Committee*, available online at www.ajic.mb.ca/reports/final_toc.html (last accessed June 23, 2015).

First Nations Representation on Ontario Juries, Report of the Independent Review Conducted by the Honourable Frank Iacobucci "The Iacobucci Report" (2013), available online at www.attorneygeneral.jus.gov.on.ca/english/about/pubs/iacobucci/pdf/First_Nations_Representation_Ontario_Juries.pdf (last accessed June 23, 2015).

Foley, LA and Chamblin, MH (1982) The Effect of Race and Personality on Mock Jurors Decisions. *Journal of Psychology* 112: 47–51.

Ghai, A (2009) Disability and the Millennium Development Goals: A Missing Link. *Journal of Health Management* 11(2): 279–95.

Hannah Moffat, K and Shaw, M (2000) Gender, Diversity and Risk Assessment in Canadian Corrections. *Probation Journal* 47(3): 163–72.

Hans, VP and Vidmar, N (1982) Jury selection. In Kerr, NL and Bray, RM (eds), *The Psychology of the Courtroom*. New York, NY: Academic Press, 39–82.

Hastie, R, Penrod, S and Pennington, N (1983) *Inside the Jury*. Cambridge, MA: Harvard University Press.

Israel, M (2000) Juries, Race and the Construction of Community. In Goldsmith, Andrew, and Israel (eds), *Criminal Justice in Diverse Communities. Law in Context Special Issue* 17(1): 96–112.

Israel, M (2003) The Underrepresentation of Indigenous Peoples on Canadian Jury Panels. *Law & Policy* 25(1): 37–62.

Jochelson, R et al., Revisiting Representativeness in the Manitoban Criminal Jury. *Underneath the Golden Boy* 37(2): 365–98.

John Howard Society of Alberta (2002) *Inmate Education* 1–4, available online at www.johnhoward.ab.ca/pub/respaper/educa02.pdf (last accessed June 15, 2015).

Jones, CF and Kaplan, MF (2001) The Effects of Racially Stereotypical Crimes on Juror Decision-making and Information-Processing Strategies. *Basic and Applied Social Psychology* 25: 1–13.

Kairys, D, Kadane, JB and Lehoczky, JP (1977) Jury Representativeness: A Mandate for Multiple Source Lists. *California Law Review* 65(4): 776–827.

Kemmelmeier, M (2005) The Effects of Race and Social Dominance Orientation in Simulated Juror Decision Making. *Journal of Applied Social Psychology* 35: 1030–45.

Marder, NS (2002) Juries, Justice & Multiculturalism. *University of Southern California Law Review* 75: 659–726.

Mazzella, R and Feingold, A (1994) The Effects of Physical Attractiveness, Race, Socioeconomic Status, and Gender of Defendants and Victims on Judgments of Mock Jurors: A Meta-Analysis. *Journal of Applied Social Psychology* 24: 1315–44.

McGowen, R and King, GD (1982) Effects of Authoritarian, Anti-authoritarian, and Egalitarian Legal Attitudes on Mock Juror and Jury Decisions. *Psychological Reports* 51: 1067–74.

Moore, D (2007) Translating Justice and Therapy: The Drug Treatment Court Networks (January). *The British Journal of Criminology* 47(1): 42–60.

Morton, E (2003) Two Conceptions of Representativeness in the Canadian Jury Selection

Process: A Case Comment on R. *v Gayle*. *University of Toronto Faculty of Law* 61(1): 105–31.

Mitchell, TL, Haw, RM, Pfeifer, JE, and Meissner, CA (2005) Racial Bias in Mock Juror Decision-making: A Meta-analytic Review of Defendant Treatment. *Law and Human Behavior* 29: 621–37.

Oliver, M (1990) *The Politics of Disablement*. New York, NY: St. Martin's Press.

Parenti, C (1999) *Lockdown America*. London: Verso.

Perez, DA, Hosch, HM, Ponder, B, and Trejo, GC (1993) Ethnicity of Defendants and Jurors as Influences on Jury Decisions. *Journal of Applied Social Psychology* 23: 1249–62.

Petersen, C (1993) Institutionalized Racism: The Need for Reform of the Criminal Jury Selection Process. *McGill Law Journal* 38: 147–79.

R v Find, 2001 SCC 32, [2001] 1 SCR 863.

R v Francis, 2007 NSSC 108.

R v Gayle, 2001 CanLII 4447 (ON CA).

R v Kokopenace, 2013 ONCA 389.

R v Kokopenance, 2015 SCC 28.

R v Lippé, [1991] 2 SCR 114.

R v Parks (1993), 84 CCC (3d) 353.

R v Sherratt, 1991 CanLII 86 (SCC), [1991] 1 SCR 509.

R v Spence, [2005] 3 SCR 458, 2005 SCC 71.

R v Williams, [1998] 1 SCR 1128.

Report of the Aboriginal Justice Inquiry of Manitoba (1991). *Aboriginal Justice Implementation Commission*, available online at www.ajic.mb.ca/volume.html (last accessed June 23, 2015).

Roach, K (1995) Challenges for Cause and Racial Discrimination. *Criminal Law Quarterly* 37: 410–27.

Russell, M (1998) *Beyond Ramps: Disability at the End of the Social Contract*. Monroe, ME: Common Courage Press.

Ryan, J and Thomas, F (1980) *The Politics of Mental Handicap*. New York, NY: Penguin.

Sommers, SR and Ellsworth, PC (2000) Race in the Courtroom: Perceptions of Guilt and Dispositional Attributions. *Personality and Social Psychology Bulletin* 26: 1367–79.

Sommers, SR (2007) Race and The Decision Making of Juries. *Legal & Criminal Psychology* 12(2): 171–87.

Statistics Canada (2011) *National Household Survey (NHS) Profile*. Canada, available online at www12.statcan.gc.ca/nhs-enm/2011/dp-pd/prof/index.cfm?Lang=E (last accessed October 30, 2015).

Statistics Canada (2013) *Disability in Canada: Initial Findings From the Canadian Survey on Disability*. www.statcan.gc.ca/pub/89-654-x/89-654-x2013002-eng.pdf (last accessed June 23, 2015).

Stewart, J and Russell, M (2001) Disablement, Prison and Historical Segregation. *Monthly Review* 53(3) (July/August), available online at http://monthlyreview.org/2001/07/01/disablement-prison-and-historical segregation/ (last accessed July 27, 2015).

Ugwuegbu, DCE (1979) Racial and Evidential Factors in Juror Attribution of Legal Responsibility. *Journal of Experimental Social Psychology* 15: 133–46.

4 The duty to accommodate drug and alcohol addiction in the workplace

Matthew Smith

This chapter will focus on the dismissal of drug- and alcohol-addicted employees. Canadian and American courts have recognized that addiction is a disability for the purposes of human rights legislation. Although this is not an exercise in comparative law, this chapter recognizes that the duty to accommodate is a legal principle common to both countries. This chapter will first provide an overview of Canadian arbitral jurisprudence and how Canadian arbitrators have interpreted the duty to accommodate addiction. Second, this chapter will explain why zero-tolerance policies are discriminatory. The foundational principles of the duty to accommodate are frustrated when drug- and alcohol-addicted employees face automatic termination for violating workplace policies. Third, this chapter will argue that violations of last chance agreements should not warrant the automatic dismissal of drug- and alcohol-addicted employees. Even where employers make accommodation efforts, these efforts are not always serious or conscientious. In many cases, collective bargaining values have been given preference over human rights values. Nowhere is this more readily apparent than in the imposition of last chance agreements. In conclusion, this chapter will advocate for a novel approach to invalidating inflexible and discriminatory last chance agreements.

Introduction

Disabled persons are among the most marginalized identity groups in North America. They face significant structural and attitudinal barriers to health care, housing, transportation, education, and employment. More than 2.3 million working-age Canadians (roughly 10.1 percent of the Canadian population) self-identified as disabled in 2012 (Statistics Canada, 2013: 4). Yet, despite representing a considerable segment of the population, disabled persons are extremely underrepresented in formal employment (Wilton, 2006: 129). Since the 2008 recession, the employment rate of disabled persons has dropped dramatically in Canada (House of Commons Standing Committee on Human Resources, 2013). A confluence of factors is to blame for the undervaluing of disabled persons in the workplace. Shifts in production, the restructuring of traditional forms of employment, and the desire of employers to cut down on labor costs, has resulted in disabled persons working less and making less than non-disabled persons (Wilton, 2006: 130).

Unfortunately, micro-economic discrimination (Russell and Malhotra, 2002: 214) and concern for the bottom line has resulted in long-term unemployment for disabled persons. Disabled persons who cannot be accommodated are tasked with re-entering a hostile and market-driven workforce, in which they are statistically less employable than non-disabled persons. Prospective employers inevitably rely on "labor market signals, such as prior employment history or employment references" (Verkerke, 2003: 921) when hiring. Discharge may "signal to prospective employers that a particular employee is unproductive" (Verkerke, 2003: 921) even if he or she could be profitably employed in the future. Incomplete information about an individual's disability can further stigmatize, and discriminate against, a disabled person.

Regrettably, labor market status is one of the most fundamental and defining characteristics of personhood. Having and maintaining a job is arguably the surest path towards social inclusion and economic security (Malhotra, 2006: 71). Discriminatory labor practices that threaten the job security of disabled persons should be challenged, then, on the basis that they further marginalize an already disadvantaged group in society.

The legislation

The Canadian human rights system is a complex web of human rights commissions, tribunals, and public agencies that are tasked with enforcing human rights legislation in the provinces and territories. Human rights legislation applies to the interactions of individuals in relation to things like employment, goods and services and accommodation. Between roughly one-third and one-half of all human rights complaints in Canada involve disability (Eliadis, 2014: 113). Further, most of the human rights complaints citing disability as a ground for discrimination are filed as a result of discrimination experienced in the workplace. There are pressing reasons for combating disability discrimination, particularly when it results in a disabled person losing his or her job.

Addiction as a disability

Canadian human rights tribunals and arbitrators have been willing to afford fairly broad and inclusive interpretations of human rights legislation. Adjudicators have recognized that disabled persons are a diverse identity group, and this has opened the door for less-recognizable disabilities. Only recently have Canadian courts, tribunals, and arbitrators begun to identify mental health, chronic pain, obesity, and drug and alcohol addiction as disabilities (Lynk, 2002: 72).

Addiction has often been disputed as a ground for disability. Innumerable commentators have maintained that addiction is not a disability. They argue that addiction is mutable. They argue that addiction, unlike other disabilities, can be *overcome*. Alcoholism and drug addiction are likely discredited as disabilities because they are so often moralized and derogated (Room, 2005: 146). In a WHO study conducted in 2002, for example, 11 out of 14 countries ranked being a drug addict as "more disapproved or stigmatized than having a criminal record for burglary" (Room, 2005: 147). Mainstream conceptions tend to reduce addiction to vice or moral weakness (Room, 2005: 146) and, in doing so, ascribe some level of agency to addicts.

Contrarians are apt to discount the complexities of addiction and ignore the lived experiences of disabled persons. These narrow conceptions of disability are largely responsible for the discrimination experienced by drug- and alcohol-addicted employees. An essentialist conception of addiction has the effect of reducing addicts to a limited number of personal characteristics that make them less deserving than other disabled persons. This distinction was not lost on Marta Russell, who admonished the disability community for dismissing the issues of addiction as not related to disability. In her seminal text *Beyond Ramps: Disability at the End of the Social Contract*, Russell was critical of ADAPT (American Disabled for Attendant Programs Today) co-founder and national organizer, Michael Auberger (Russell, 1998: 124). In a 1994 *Newsweek* article titled "Who are the disabled?", Auberger noted that he "would like to see recovering alcoholics, drug abusers and some people with back pain excluded from the ranks of the disabled" (Kaufman-Rosen, 1994: 80). He expressed concerns that businesses would retaliate and hurt the people the law was supposedly intended to help (Kaufman-Rosen, 1994: 80). Rightfully so, Russell criticized Auberger:

> The people you want to eliminate from the ranks of the disabled are not taking jobs away from you; corporate America is doing that. Perhaps people with 'traditional' disabilities aren't successfully using the law yet because it doesn't work for them.
>
> (Russell, 1998: 124)

Implicit in Auberger's criticism of the ADA is the belief that recovering alcoholics and addicts are less deserving of protection. From Auberger's comments it would appear that there is something morally reprehensible about an addict claiming protection and being treated the same as someone with a traditional disability. The only discernible differences between a traditional disability and an addiction are the perceived failings of the addict and the presumed impermanence of the impairment.

Particularly disconcerting is that moral judgments and punitive sanctions have found expression in anti-discrimination legislation. The *Americans with Disabilities Act* (ADA) is the civil rights legislation in the United States prohibiting discrimination against, and ensuring equal opportunities for, disabled persons in employment. Despite the ADA's stated goal of protecting disabled persons, the legislation makes a legal distinction between those entitled to, and those disqualified from, accommodation and social assistance. For example, employees with addictions are only protected under the ADA once they have stopped using illegal drugs. Active users of illegal drugs are not protected by the Act. These laws discriminate not only between drug addicts and alcoholics, but between those addicted to legal drugs and those addicted to illegal drugs. By definition, addiction involves the uncontrollable use of legal or illegal substances or both (Le Fauve, 2011: 1462). By excluding active users of illegal substances, the Legislature is sending a punitive message to those breaking criminal laws (Le Fauve, 2011: 1462). The social prejudice experienced by disabled persons takes on an extra-criminal dimension under the ADA, lending further credibility to the contention that addiction may be more stigmatized than criminal behavior. This attitude towards criminality has no place in legislation intended to address discrimination.

Under the ADA, addicts must also "meet the same standards other employees are held to, even if their unsatisfactory behavior is attributable to their use of substances" (Le Fauve, 2011: 1463). The American approach, in many respects, runs contrary to the entire purpose of anti-discrimination legislation in Canada, which is to achieve substantive equality amongst all Canadians. The very notion of treating all alike, "including those with demonstrable social advantage" (Riddle and Rioux, 2011: 44), does not achieve the objective of substantive equality. Disabled persons should not bear the entire burden of ensuring that their fundamental human rights are upheld. The formal equality approach of treating likes alike is an inherently flawed conception of equality.

Legislators and some disability advocates like Auberger have failed to appreciate the diversity of disability. Not all disabled persons are the same, just as not all addicts are the same. The prevailing opinion on addiction as a disability amongst Canadian human rights lawyers and disability rights advocates is one based on logic. An individual who has received medical treatment for an addiction does not automatically transcend his or her disability. The overwhelming evidence of post-rehabilitation relapse logically infers that addiction may, and often does, persist well beyond treatment. Disabilities have varying degrees of mutability, with impairment being temporary, long-term or permanent (Lynk, 1999: 185). It would also be inaccurate to reduce addiction to entirely neurobiological factors or genetic predisposition—those aspects of a person's health that might be treated by medicine. Rather, there has been a strong push from legal practitioners and those in the disability rights community to recognize addiction as the "interaction between environmental context and neurobiological and genetic factors" (Le Fauve, 2011: 1459). Addiction as a category of disability is largely indeterminate because of the multiplicity of inherent and extrinsic factors that can contribute to one's addiction.

Social and scientific evidence concerning the validity of addiction as a disability—however interesting a topic of scholarship—is not the subject matter of this chapter. This chapter proceeds from the legal presumption that drug and alcohol addiction are valid disabilities.

The duty to accommodate

The duty to accommodate has found expression in both American and Canadian legislation. The ADA, as previously noted, prohibits employers from discriminating against disabled persons. The United States has its own evolving body of case law that might properly be the subject of its own chapter. Although the American jurisprudence serves as a valuable comparator, the primary focus of the remainder of this chapter is on the interpretation of anti-discrimination legislation in Canada.

The duty to accommodate has evolved from the passage and amendment of Canadian human rights legislation and a developing body of jurisprudence. This legal duty, as Michael Lynk explains, is straightforward to state: "employers and unions in Canada are required to make every reasonable effort, short of undue hardship, to accommodate an employee who comes under a protected ground of discrimination within human rights legislation" (Lynk, 2002: 58). The duty to accommodate has shifted the burden that might previously have been placed upon the employee and has instead placed that burden on the employer. An employee is no longer required to match the demands of the workplace; rather, once an employee establishes a *prima facie* disability requiring accommodation, the onus is placed on the employer to "determine whether existing positions can be adjusted, adapted or modified for the employee, or whether there are other positions in the workplace that might be appropriate" (Lynk, 2002: 58). An employer is only relieved of its duty if it can establish that accommodation would result in undue hardship.

The Supreme Court of Canada clarified the duty to accommodate and the extent to which an undue hardship defence could be merited in the case of *British Columbia v BCGSEU*, which is commonly referred to as *Meiorin* (*British Columbia v BCGSEU (Meiorin)*, 1999). The principles from this case have since been imported into labor arbitration decisions. In *Meiorin*, a female firefighter—despite being able to adequately perform the duties of her job—was dismissed after failing an aerobic test. The Court found that the testing was based on standards set for male firefighters. The Court determined that, in cases in which a complainant could establish that a workplace rule or policy was discriminatory, the onus would be placed upon the employer to justify the rule or policy as a *bona fide* occupational requirement ("BFOR") (*Meiorin*, 1999: para 54). An employer is required to show that accommodation would be impossible without causing undue hardship.

The Supreme Court of Canada has recognized that a comprehensive definition of undue hardship is unnecessary, and has instead created a non-exhaustive list of factors relevant to an appraisal of undue hardship (*Central Alberta Dairy Pool v Alberta (Human Rights Commission)*, 1990). These factors include—but are not limited to—financial cost, disruption of a collective agreement, problems of morale of other employees, interchangeability of workforce and facilities, and the health and safety of the workplace (*Central Alberta Dairy Pool*, 1990: 521).

The task of interpreting the duty to accommodate in labor disputes falls primarily to labor arbitrators. It is important at this juncture to note that labor arbitrators adjudicate the majority of Canadian labor disputes. Those unfamiliar with Canadian labor relations might be surprised by the voluminous body of labor arbitration case law, which can be explained in part by union density rates. Thirty percent of all Canadian workers are covered by collective agreements (Statistics Canada, 2014). These statistics are significantly higher than in the United States and other Commonwealth nations. Social science evidence has drawn a negative correlation between union density and inequality. Countries with higher union density rates generally have more centralized collective bargaining and more closely mirror international labor norms (International Labour Organization, 2008: 86). Greater accessibility to grievance arbitration and other dispute resolution mechanisms is generally thought to provide increased protection against exploitation and unfair labor practices (Statistics Canada, 2003: 31–7). Increased union density might help to explain why labor disputes are so often arbitrated in Canada.

It is also important to understand where arbitrators find their authority to rule on matters relating to the duty to accommodate. Labor arbitrators have concurrent jurisdiction, which means they have the authority to rule on disputes arising out of the interpretation and administration of collective agreements, as well as the authority to interpret and apply human rights and other employment-related statutes (see *Weber v Ontario Hydro*, 1995; *Parry Sound (District) Social Services Administration Board v OPSEU, Local 324*, 2003). The human rights principles established in cases like *Meiorin* have consequently been imported into labor arbitration decisions.

Arbitrators on drug and alcohol addiction

Arbitrators, for the most part, have treated addiction as they would any other disability protected by human rights legislation. Arbitrators have fairly consistently ruled that an employer only has the right to dismiss an employee with an addiction if it can prove the following: the employee's condition adversely affects their work, the employee has not responded to efforts to accommodate and the employee is not, in the foreseeable future, likely to improve. The standard for employers is relatively high. However, there are a number of disconcerting examples of arbitrators adhering to a just cause standard when reviewing the discipline and dismissal of drug- and alcohol-addicted employees. Under the just cause standard, it is arguably legally permissible for an employer to ignore the causal connection between the employee's misconduct and his or her disability.

Just cause standard

The case most often cited in support of the just cause standard is commonly *BC (Public Service Agency) v BCGSEU* (*Gooding*, 2008). In this case, an alcoholic employee (Gooding) was caught stealing liquor from his workplace. Gooding was subsequently terminated and filed a grievance. The arbitrator, at first instance, upheld the termination. On appeal to the British Columbia Labour Relations Board, the arbitrator was ordered to reconsider his initial decision. On a second hearing, the arbitrator found that the employee's termination was *prima facie* discriminatory. He determined that Gooding's alcoholism was a contributing factor in the theft. Gooding was reinstated and ordered back pay.

The arbitrator's decision was subsequently appealed to the BC Court of Appeal. The Court of Appeal reversed the arbitrator's final decision and overturned Gooding's reinstatement. In delivering her judgment, Justice Huddart stated the following:

> I can find no suggestion in the evidence that Mr. Gooding's termination was arbitrary and based on preconceived ideas concerning his alcohol dependency. It was based on misconduct that rose to the level of crime. That his conduct may have been influenced by his alcohol dependency is irrelevant if that admitted dependency played no part in the employer's decision to terminate his employment and he suffered no impact for his misconduct greater than that another employee would have suffered for the same misconduct.
>
> (*Gooding*, 2008: para 15)

The Court of Appeal's decision in *Gooding* has since been followed by a number of arbitrators in other provinces. In *Toronto Transit Commission v CUPE, Local 2* a grievor was similarly terminated for a number of thefts in the workplace (*Toronto Transit Commission*, 2011). The employee in this case had a drug and alcohol addiction, but the employer maintained that the employee's misconduct was not the result of his addiction. The arbitrator, applying the same reasoning in the *Gooding* Court of Appeal decision, determined that the employer had just cause to dismiss the employee. The employee was terminated like any other employee would have been on the same facts.

Legal scholars and disability rights advocates have taken the *Gooding* decision to task. Brian Etherington, for example, has been extremely critical of the BC Court of Appeal's decision, stating that the decision is "inconsistent with the purpose underlying [adverse effects discrimination]—to eliminate facially neutral rules or practices that constitute barriers to equality in employment" (Etherington, 2013: 403). Etherington goes on to note that, if the reasoning of the majority in *Gooding* is followed, "employers will no longer have to justify the implementation and enforcement of zero-tolerance policies against persons with disabilities as a BFOR under the principle accepted in *Meiorin*" (Etherington, 2013: 410). *Gooding* and *Toronto Transit Commission* have significantly undermined the effects-based approach to discrimination. These cases have lent credibility to the primacy of workplace policies over human rights laws in labor arbitration cases. The employers in both cases were not required to provide accommodation or some other form of non-disciplinary action.

The *Gooding* decision also reinforced a number of stereotypes—primarily the stereotype that addicts have complete control over, and should bear full responsibility for, their actions. The Court of Appeal prevented Gooding from defending his actions in any meaningful way by denying the role played by his addiction. It was illogical for the Court of Appeal to suggest that an alcohol-dependent employee's theft of alcohol was in no way related to his alcohol dependency.

There is no indication from the facts of this case that Gooding stole anything other than alcohol. In fact, his misconduct coincided with an increased consumption of and dependency upon alcohol, which lends credibility to the connection between the misconduct and his addiction. The employer was able to avoid the normal accommodation measures made for disabled persons by refusing to recognize a causal connection between Gooding's addiction and the theft. The duty to accommodate should persist, despite employers' zero-tolerance policies.

The grievors in *Gooding* and *Toronto Transit Commission* were also unnecessarily tasked with proving that zero-tolerance policies were informed by stereotypes about addiction. A *prima facie* case of discrimination should be made where a person with a disability is adversely affected by a policy, regardless of whether that policy is informed by stereotypical or prejudicial thinking. It is of little consequence whether a policy is facially neutral or intentionally discriminatory. The essence of adverse-effects discrimination is to say that no distinction should be made between the two when providing accommodation.

Gooding and *Toronto Transit Commission* abide by the same principles upon which Title VII of the US Civil Rights Act is founded. Substantive equality is a Canadian innovation that Title VII does not recognize to the same degree. Substantive equality recognizes that policies and practices meant to treat similarly situated persons the same may result in indirect and systemic discrimination. Title VII, however, is founded on principles of formal equality. Under the Title VII regime, employers must treat all races and both sexes equally (Weber, 2007: 31). As Marta Russell once remarked, formal equality is very much an appeal to the myth of rugged individualism. Formal equality equates individual failings to personal shortcomings (Russell, 2002: 122), rather than structures that are built to reflect and accommodate privileged norms (Riddle and Rioux, 2011: 44). The Court in *Gooding* remarked that the employer had treated the offending employee the same as they would any other employee for the same misconduct. Although equality may mean identical treatment in the United States, Canadian courts are guided by the principles of substantive equality.

The American judiciary has limited the potential for accommodation by maintaining the like-treatment model of equality. American judges have viewed requests for accommodation as "*special* benefits and treatment instead of equal rights" (Russell, 2002: 119). Accommodation in the Canadian legal context should not be confused with formal equality. Accommodation is an individualized process that requires employers to treat certain employees differently in order to achieve equality in the workplace.

The hybrid approach

In spite of the decisions in *Gooding* and *Toronto Transit Commission*, many labor arbitrators have applied a so-called hybrid approach to assessing discipline and termination. Arbitrators applying the hybrid approach attempt to separate the culpable and non-culpable parts of an employee's misconduct. Most notably, in *Rio Tinto*, a BC arbitrator found that an employee's marijuana addiction played a role in his breach of a zero-tolerance workplace policy (*Rio Tinto*, 2008). The arbitrator applied the hybrid approach pre-dating the Court of Appeal decision in *Gooding*, and found that the employee's disability was causally connected to his violation of a zero-tolerance workplace policy.

The arbitrator's decision to reinstate the employee in *Rio Tinto* recognizes the concurrent jurisdiction of arbitrators to import human rights law principles into their analyses (Etherington, 2009: 287). In accordance with a just cause approach, it might be appropriate to dismiss an employee for having violated a zero-tolerance policy. Under the hybrid approach, due consideration must be given to the causal connection between the employee's disability and his or her misconduct. The hybrid approach does not completely deny the role of agency; however, it allows for the possibility that some workplace misconduct is the result of an overwhelming dependency upon drugs and alcohol. By framing an analysis in this manner, arbitrators can compel employers to craft non-disciplinary remedies that accommodate employees' disabilities.

Last chance agreements

A last chance agreement is one non-disciplinary tool available to employers to accommodate employees with disabilities. Arbitrators have made last chance agreements conditions of their orders for reinstatement, and have consistently upheld their use by employers as a form of accommodation (see *Stelco Inc v UWSA*, 2000; *UFCW, Local 832 v Maple Leaf Meats*, 2000). When an employee has displayed problematic behavior in the workplace, unions, employees, and employers can sign a last chance agreement (Lynk, 1999: 214). Last chance agreements take many different forms, "but they usually state that if there is any repetition of the problematic behavior, the employee is automatically dismissed and there is no right to grieve or arbitrate the firing" (Lynk, 1999: 214). Last chance agreements vary depending on the circumstances of an employee's misconduct, but many contain similar provisions. Some last chance agreements address initial treatment and after-care, testing, the timing of return to work and abstinence from mood altering substances (Charlton, 1994: 448). Last chance agreements are ultimately consistent with the principles of progressive discipline. They provide drug- and alcohol-addicted employees with another opportunity to rehabilitate and become productive members in the workplace.

Often, last chance agreements set standards for job performance based on a single workplace standard. Unfortunately, ableist notions of satisfactory job performance can inform these standards. A single approach to setting workplace standards in last chance agreements is unsatisfactory given the complicated nature of disabilities. Future attendance requirements in last chance agreements, for example, are extremely controversial. In cases of innocent absenteeism, it is common practice for employers to reinstate employees "on terms and conditions related to future attendance at work" (Pothier, 2010: 28). Future attendance standards are often determined by reference to average attendance records of an employee's coworkers. Disabled persons may be adversely affected by measurements based on the average attendance records of predominately non-disabled employees. By creating boilerplate language in last chance agreements, an employer may dismiss an employee for an infraction only tangentially related to the employee's initial problematic behavior. Attendance management programs and strict adherence to other job performance standards likely fail to provide appropriate accommodation for disabled persons.

Relapse

The preceding reflection on attendance standards illustrates the inflexibility of last chance agreements. One standard for attendance is discriminatory and based on presumptions about ability. Similarly, last chance agreements that do not provide for the possibility of slip or relapse ignore the complexity and indeterminacy of drug and alcohol addiction. In *Health Employers' Assn of British Columbia* (*Health Employers' Assn of British Columbia on Behalf of Castlegar & District Hospital v BCNU (Bergen Grievance),* 2000), a drug-addicted nurse was terminated for violating the terms of a last chance agreement. The nurse relapsed one year after signing a last chance agreement, which led him to steal drugs from the hospital and submit false urine samples. The arbitrator in this case accepted the testimony of an expert called by the union. The expert stated that "relapse . . . was a powerful negative reinforcement, making it less likely that it will happen again" (*Health Employers' Assn*, 2000: para 63). The arbitrator determined that the last chance agreement was not binding. It was necessary for the arbitrator to consider "all of the circumstances . . . to see whether the employer would incur undue hardship if required to give the employee another chance" (Adell, 2000: 217). *Health Employers' Assn* suggests that a finding of undue hardship may not be met where rehabilitation is likely. In *Health Employers' Assn*, the nurse could have been given duties that did not involve distributing drugs to patients. Similarly, he could have been moved to a part of the hospital where he did not have access to drugs or was under the supervision of management.

Merrick v IPSCO Saskatchewan—a Saskatchewan Human Rights Tribunal case—relied on the same analysis and expert testimony from *Health Employers Assn* (*Merrick v IPSCO Saskatchewan*, 2008). Merrick (the employee) signed a last chance agreement, which required him to take steps to rehabilitate a drug addiction. Soon after signing the agreement, Merrick relapsed. He was dismissed for violating the conditions of the agreement. When his union refused to take his grievance to arbitration, Merrick complained that the respondent company and union violated Saskatchewan's human rights legislation. The Tribunal ultimately found that enforcing a last chance agreement was discriminatory in light of Merrick's drug dependency. Accordingly, the Tribunal ordered Merrick's reinstatement and awarded him damages. The Tribunal stated that, "slip/relapse is an integral part of the disease of addiction . . . [and] there is a duty to accommodate a slip/release to the point of undue hardship" (*Merrick*, 2008: para 331). The Tribunal cited *Health Employers' Assn* as an authority on the duty to accommodate relapse, acknowledging that, "[s]everal relapses is the rule rather than the exception" (*Merrick*, 2008: para 330).

Health Employers' Assn and *Merrick* point out the inadequacies of last chance agreements to accommodate relapse. Both cases show that even after an addiction is treated and an employee is rehabilitated, the addiction persists. By failing to accommodate relapse—an integral part of the disability—employers unfairly discriminate against their employees. Many last chance agreements should not be enforced given the prevalence of post-rehabilitation relapse. It would be naive for employers to ignore the pervasiveness of drug and alcohol addiction, and more particularly the prevalence of addiction relapse.

Many Canadian employers already provide Employee Assistance Programs (EAPs), which are meant to deal with a wide range of personal issues affecting performance in the workplace. In the private sector, EAPs are often contracted for through a business' insurance company. Employment Assistance Services (EAS), operating under Health Canada, similarly provides organizational health and employee wellness programs for government employees. Employers are well aware of the mental health and addiction issues affecting employees. They should not, then, be able to eschew the normal accommodation process by failing to allow for contingencies. In recent years, unions have argued that relapse is almost inevitable, and that "something like a 'subject to relapses' exception" (Adell, 2000: 216) should be read into last chance agreements. Last chance agreements that do not provide for contingencies are unconscionable. Progressive discipline programs that allow for the eventuality of a relapse and the ultimate dismissal of a drug- or alcohol-addicted employee can hardly be said to constitute accommodation.

There are many misconceptions about the effectiveness of rehabilitation programs and addiction in general. In *Health Employers' Assn*, for example, the employer did not provide for any contingencies in its last chance agreement. The last chance agreement was the final accommodation in the eyes of the employer. The successful completion of a rehabilitation program was sufficient evidence for the employer that the employee had overcome his addiction. Any subsequent relapse, then, would be the employee's responsibility and the result of his own failings. The employer in that case relied on the stereotype that addiction is overcome once the employee has completed a rehabilitation program. Employers' assumptions about the long-term success of rehabilitation programs inevitably dictate the form and extent of accommodation given to an employee upon his or her return to the workplace. These assumptions can unfairly prejudice employees who are often held to unrealistic standards.

Repeated attempts are often required to stop addictive behavior. Addiction persists long after consumption. Zero-tolerance policies and last chance agreements that fail to accommodate relapse are discriminatory, as they punish addicts for behavior that is uncontrollable. These policies also punish addicts for a future outcome that is, in most cases, certain. Multiple "attempts to change and multiple treatment events are the norm rather than the exception in recovery from addiction" (DiClemente et al., 2011: 765). In any cohort of individuals seeking treatment for substance abuse, "the majority, between 60 and 80 percent, return to the problematic behavior after some period of success" (DiClemente et al., 2011: 765). The process of cycling through stages of change may actually be a negative reinforcement for addicts, as was stated in *Merrick*.

The rhetoric used by the employer in *Health Employers' Assn* is the same rhetoric that has plagued obesity discrimination cases in Canada. In *Vogue Shoes*, a sales clerk filed a complaint with the Ontario Human Rights Commission, which claimed that she had been discriminated against based on her weight. She left her employment after being told she must lose 35 pounds within six weeks (*Ontario (Human Rights Commission) v Vogue Shoes*, 1991). The Board of Inquiry "attempted to draw a distinction between uncontrollable medical conditions and controllable behaviour" (Nowell-Smith and O'Reilly, 2003: 684). Unfortunately, the Board "presumed that obesity must be caused either by a medical condition over which a person has no control or by behaviour, which a person can control" (Nowell-Smith and O'Reilly, 2003: 684). In light of increased social and scientific evidence on obesity, "it no longer makes sense to say obesity is controllable" (Nowell-Smith and O'Reilly, 2003: 685). Like drug and alcohol addiction, there is a confluence of factors that contribute to someone's weight. Just as many people can temporarily lose weight but ultimately struggle to do so long-term, addicts struggle with abstinence.

It is unfair to say that addiction is controllable. There are countless reasons why an employee might relapse that are largely out of his or her control (Standing Committee on Social Affairs, 2006). Many of these reasons can be found in the workplace itself, which is often the site of consumption, distribution, and temptation for vulnerable and recovering addicts (Shain, 1994: 292). Last chance agreements that do not account for contingencies, such as relapse, cannot in all circumstances be said to accommodate to the point of undue hardship. The predominant view amongst the social and scientific communities is that substance abuse is the result of potentially innumerable personal and neurobiological characteristics, as well as an individual's environment (Frone, 2013: 55). Judges and arbitrators require a greater appreciation for the social and environmental causes of workplace addiction.

Cross-role and within-role stressors are significant contributing causes of addiction in the workplace. The "notion that exposure to work stressors promotes employee substance use (i.e., one type of behavioral strain) is widely accepted and has been explored in many studies" (Frone, 2013: 75). As Michael Frone notes, a review of literature relating to health care professionals concluded that "increased access to drugs at work was an important risk factor for illicit drug use" (Frone, 2013: 72). Decisions such as *Gooding* are extremely troubling given the relationship between "physical availability of substances at work and employee substance abuse" (Frone, 2013: 71).

The majority of cases cited in this chapter have considered the employee–employer relationship in institutional and industrialized workplaces. However, most—if not all—of the case law previously cited has failed to consider how rigid and out-dated work environments affect substance abuse. Work demands and the organization of work often interfere with social and familial responsibilities. Missing important family events because of an inflexible or indeterminate work schedule may cause considerable cross-role stress, which is a known and precipitating cause of addiction (Frone, 2013: 76). Similarly, the nature of one's job, including "aversive work conditions, such as a high level of work demands, repetitive work, exposure to noxious physical work environments, and overly simple or complex work" (Frone, 2013: 76) can induce stress-related substance abuse. Continued exposure to work stress "leads to more frequent experience of negative emotions and other forms of tension, which then causes more frequent and heavier [substance abuse]" (Frone, 2013: 76). Employers should be prevented from punishing substance abusers if work demands and the structuring of the work environment are significant contributing causes of substance abuse.

The dilemma for arbitrators

Arbitrators often face difficult decisions when ruling on the enforceability of last chance agreements. Last chance agreements "represent one of the most frequent areas of conflict between collective bargaining values and human rights values, and also provide one of the clearest examples of the importance of individualization" (Adell, 2000: 215). Arbitrators have been reluctant to overturn decisions made by employers based on the terms of settlement agreements, especially when employees, unions, and employers have voluntarily entered into those agreements. In *Port Coquitlam (City) and CUPE, Local 498*, an arbitration board noted that the "industrial relations value" of last chance agreements "would be severely impaired were employers' decisions routinely set aside by arbitrators" (*Port Coquitlam*, 1998: para 99). The fear amongst arbitrators is that employers will lose the incentive to settle disciplinary disputes through last chance agreements. The policy concern expressed by arbitrators is, perhaps, best articulated in *Kimberly-Clark Forest Products*. Arbitrator Levinson noted the following policy reasons for enforcing last chance agreements:

> [t]he importance of the parties being able to rely on the terms of the last chance agreements they negotiate, the fostering and promoting of confidence in the parties' ability to resolve their disputes and to fashion their own solutions instead of having a third party impose one.
>
> (*Kimberly-Clark Forest Products v Paper, Allied Industrial Chemical and Energy Works International Union*, 2003: para 17)

Arbitrators have consistently upheld last chance agreements on one or more of these policy concerns.

Despite the policy concerns cited in *Kimberly-Clark*, the Supreme Court of Canada has unequivocally ruled that last chance agreements cannot oust human rights legislation (see *Weber v Ontario Hydro*, 1995; *Parry Sound*, 2003). When there is a fundamental human rights issue relating to a disability, arbitrators must factor into their analyses the duty to accommodate. Arbitrators must determine on the facts of each case whether the employer's duty to accommodate and the employee's duty to facilitate accommodation (*Central Okanagan School District No 23 v Renaud*, 1992: para 20) have been met. As the arbitrator in *Re Labatt Breweries* stated, "[w]hat amounts to undue hardship is a question of fact in every case" (*Re Labatt Breweries*, 2002: para 141).

The question, then, is why employers have so aggressively resisted reinstating employees in cases where providing accommodation is neither prohibitively expensive nor does it pose an overarching health and safety concern. With considerable regularity, drug- and alcohol-addicted employees' requests for reinstatement have been denied, even when those employees have successfully completed rehabilitation programs. In 1995, the Supreme Court of Canada dealt with the scope of arbitrators' authority to substitute lesser penalties in cases where dismissed employees submitted post-discharge evidence of rehabilitation and good conduct (*Cie minière Québec Cartier v Quebec*, 1995). Unfortunately, *Quebec Cartier* "has not provided the certainty that parties to a collective bargaining relationship were hoping for" (Devine et al., 2000: 161). In the majority decision, Justice L'Heureux-Dubé stated the following:

> An arbitrator can rely on [post-discharge evidence], but only where it is relevant to the issue before him. In other words, such evidence will only be admissible if it helps to shed light on the reasonableness and appropriateness of the dismissal under review at the time that it was implemented.
>
> (*Cie minière Québec Cartier*, 1995: para 13)

These remarks would suggest that post-discharge evidence of rehabilitation is inadmissible, as employers would not have been apprised of such evidence at the time of dismissal.

The majority of arbitral decisions respecting post-discharge evidence have applied Justice L'Heureux-Dubé's reasoning. This reflection on the admissibility of post-discharge evidence demonstrates the obstinate and uncooperative attitudes of employers—and some arbitrators—towards human rights legislation and human rights values. Arbitrators often ignore post-discharge evidence of good behavior, even though an employer's accommodations might fall below the threshold for undue hardship.

The preceding cases also reflect the adversarial process of grievance arbitration, as noted by Joan McEwen:

> All too often, the employer's focus appears to be aimed, not at helping the employee deal with his or her illness, but at gathering facts which it can marshal against the employee so that it can succeed at the arbitration hearing.
>
> (McEwen, 1994: 422)

There are a number of reasons an employer might be hesitant to reinstate an employee in light of post-discharge evidence. Less persuasive arguments suggest that reinstating problematic employees will lower morale and reduce productivity.

Employers often resist reinstatement because of its precedential value, and not because the employee will pose an undue hardship on their business. These conscious decisions made by employers are discriminatory and unfairly prejudice employees with disabilities. Unless an employer can show that accommodation reaches the point of undue hardship, they should not be able to rely on such defences.

Fashioning a potential remedy for dismissed employees

If employers and arbitrators attach such significance to collective bargaining rights and the freedom of parties to voluntarily reach agreements, then the law of contractual defects should be available to aggrieved employees. Arbitrators have consistently shown deference to last chance agreements. They have reasoned that failing to enforce such agreements will result in fewer employers offering them at all. Unfortunately, respect for the principles of contract law has demonstrated a "systematic tendency to marginalize the interests of workers" (Malhotra, 2009: 15). There are significant power imbalances and inequalities between employers and employees, despite the presence of unions. The doctrines of duress and unconscionability have developed as defences to suits in contract in an attempt to balance inequalities of bargaining power between parties. In non-unionized workplaces, courts have been willing to render agreements between employers and employees voidable based on these doctrines. Claims of duress and unconscionability have the potential to render last chance agreements voidable.

Duress

Duress, in its simplest form, is coercion of will which vitiates consent. The doctrine provides the basis for repudiating consent previously given in an agreement. As a general principle, contract law will not hold weaker parties to every single bargain they make. Duress was previously limited to a number of narrow circumstances, whereby a contract could only be set aside if it was agreed upon as a result of actual or threatened force. The doctrine has since expanded to include economic duress. In the employment law context, employees have been afforded some protection against economic duress. In the case of *Puiia v Occupational Training Centre*, an employee was faced with the choice of signing an agreement, which derogated his rights to notice, or having his employment terminated (*Puiia v Occupational Training Centre*, 1983). The PEI Court of Appeal ruled that the termination was unenforceable, as the economic pressure applied by the employer meant that the employee had not given true consent.

The doctrine of duress is relevant to a discussion of last chance agreements, as many drug- and alcohol-addicted employees feel compelled to sign them. Ravi Malhotra explains the predicament faced by employees in such circumstances:

> [M]ost individuals in a modern capitalist economy must seek employment in order to earn the wages necessary to purchase the goods necessary for survival. To the extent that workers with disabilities typically have even fewer options to change careers . . . they are even more likely to be able to demonstrate duress.
>
> (Malhotra, 2009: 16)

Employees have no realistic alternatives. They must choose between signing a last chance agreement and maintaining their employment, or not signing and being terminated for having failed to facilitate accommodation. Union jobs are highly desirable and difficult to come by. It can hardly be said that there is a choice at all for employees. Failing to sign a last chance agreement will result in the termination of employment. With that comes economic uncertainty should the dismissed employee choose to admit herself into a rehabilitation facility. By signing a last chance agreement, the employee can say with certainty that a job will be waiting for her when she returns. Should an employee choose not to sign a last chance agreement and ultimately face dismissal, the offending incident may stigmatize the employee and follow him or her to any new workplace. Employees often choose the lesser of two evils—a program that is often intrusive and provides little in the way of actual accommodation.

Regrettably, trial judges have set a fairly high standard for establishing economic duress. In many cases, the standard would be too high for any employee trying to claim the defence of economic duress. For example, it is uncertain how protest from the affected party might play out, particularly if the employer considers protestation to violate the terms and conditions of a last chance agreement. Also, there are very few instances in which a last chance agreement has been signed without the advice of an employee's union. Even if an employee's union is present, there is nothing to say that a third-party's presence will absolve unions and employers of liability for discriminatory conditions in last chance agreements (*Ryan v St. John's City*, 2007). This area of labor arbitration is largely uncertain; however, grievors are not precluded from raising the defence of economic duress.

Unconscionability

The standard for meeting the test for unconscionability, much like duress, is relatively high. Early on, the Canadian courts adopted a narrow approach to unconscionability, whereby two elements must be present: (1) an improvident bargain and (2) an inequality between the parties (Ben-Ishai and Percy, 2009: 697). The traditional doctrine of unconscionability stands for the presumption that "no person should be allowed to take advantage of the severe physical or situational disadvantage of another" (Ben-Ishai and Percy, 2009: 704). There are significant physical and psychological dimensions to drug and alcohol addiction. Drug and alcohol dependencies can impair an individual's capacity for reasoned judgment and decision-making. Such impairment has the potential to severely disadvantage parties to last chance agreements.

Last chance agreements are often entered into soon after an offending incident or upon admission into a rehabilitation program. There are serious questions about the capacity of addicts to consent to last chance agreements that are offered soon after offending incidents. An employee might still be reeling from the workplace incident resulting in his or her dismissal. The employee might have been conditionally reinstated, but has yet to rehabilitate his or her addiction. The employee is arguably in his or her most vulnerable state at this point. Bait and switch tactics that encourage addicts to agree to terms they ultimately cannot live up to should be condemned. Last chance agreements that recognize the likelihood of slip or relapse but fail to accommodate that eventuality are unconscionable, as they reflect the need of the weaker party to agree to terms and conditions that are substantially unfair.

The common law has developed to recognize that contracts can be rescinded where a contracting party is incapacitated and lacks the requisite amount of consent needed to reach *consensus ad idem*. The standard, again, is relatively high. The affected party must have been intoxicated to the point that they could not appreciate what they were doing or agreeing to, and the other party must have been aware of that fact. An employer's position of power may be used to take advantage of an employee's impaired capacity for reasoned judgment and decision-making. The success of this defense is largely determinative of the evidence presented by experts. It might be difficult to show that the affected party was sufficiently intoxicated at the time he or she signed a last chance agreement. Greater social and scientific evidence relating to the residual effects of alcohol and drugs might be marshalled to show that drug- and alcohol-addicted employees lack the capacity to reach fair agreements with their employers.

Conclusion

In this chapter, I suggested that a more nuanced approach to evaluating the duty to accommodate might result in fewer drug- and alcohol-addicted employees being dismissed from the workplace. I noted that zero-tolerance policies are discriminatory and fail to provide adequate accommodation for drug- and alcohol-addicted employees. Last chance agreements, then, have served as a tool for what is referred to as progressive discipline. Arbitrators have fairly consistently found that last chance agreements are accommodative. However, arbitrators have also paid lip service to the industrial relations value of upholding such agreements. I reviewed a number of Canadian labor arbitration cases in which last chance agreements were found to be an appropriate form of accommodation. I argued, though, that the conditions of last chance agreements are often disingenuous. Many last chance agreements impose conditions that an employee with an addiction is unlikely to satisfy. By failing to account for relapse, employers are essentially contracting for the eventuality that an employee will relapse and ultimately be dismissed from the workplace. This is hardly accommodative. I suggested that slip and relapse are significant aspects of an addiction and should also be accommodated. Finally, I noted that the circumstances under which employees sign last chance agreements create significant inequalities and power imbalances. Although the standards for establishing duress and unconscionability are fairly high, arbitrators should factor into their analyses the disproportionate levels of bargaining power between employers and employees. Arbitrators should question both the seriousness and conscientiousness of accommodations made by employers, as well as the capacity of employees to consent to the conditions imposed by last chance agreements.

Bibliography

Adell, B (2000) Jurisdictional Overlap Between Arbitration and Other Forums: An Update. *Canadian Labour & Employment Law Journal* 6: 179–230.

Ben-Ishai, S and Percy, D (2009) *Contracts: Cases and Commentaries.* Toronto, ON: Carswell.

British Columbia (Public Service Employee Relations Commission) v BCGSEU, [1999] 3 SCR 3, 176 DLR (4th) 1 [*Meiorin*].

British Columbia (Public Service Agency) v BCGSEU, 2008 BCCA 357, 298 DLR (4th) 624 [*Gooding*].

Central Alberta Dairy Pool v Alberta (Human Rights Commission), [1990] 2 SCR 489, 72 DLR (4th) 417.

Central Okanagan School District No 23 v Renaud, [1992] 2 SCR 970, 95 DLR (4th) 577 [*Renaud*].

Charlton, S (1994) 'Trade Union Concerns About Substance Abuse in the Workplace', *Canadian Labour & Employment Law Journal*, 2: 439–50.

Cie minière Québec Cartier v Quebec (Grievances arbitrator), [1995] 2 SCR 1095, 125 DLR (4th) 577.

Devine, H, MacPherson, R, and Palayew, D (2000) The Use of Medical Evidence at Arbitration: A Management Perspective. *Labour Arbitration Yearbook* 151–73.

DiClemente, C, Holmgren, M, and Rounsaville, D (2011) Relapse Prevention and Recycling in Addiction. In Jonhson, B (ed) *Addiction Medicine*, New York, NY: Springer.

Eliadis P (2014) *Speaking Out on Human Rights: Debating Canada's Human Rights System.* Montreal: McGill-Queens University Press.

Etherington, B (2009) The Accommodation of Disability that is a Contributing Cause in the Commission of Disciplinary Misconduct in Canadian Arbitration Law. *NAARB Arbitration* 279–90.

Etherington, B (2013) Recent Developments in the Duty to Accommodate Disabilities. *Labour Arbitration Yearbook.* Toronto: Lancaster House, 403–31.

Frone, MR (2013) *Alcohol and Illicit Drug Use in the Workforce and Workplace.* Washington, DC: American Psychological Association.

Health Employers' Association of British Columbia on Behalf of Castlegar & District Hospital v BCNU (Bergen Grievance) (2000), 86 LAC (4th) 81, [2000] BCAAA No. 9 [QL] (Arbitrator: Larson).

House of Commons Standing Committee on Human Resources, Social Development and the Status of Persons with Disabilities (2013) *Exploring Employment Opportunities for Persons with Disabilities.* Ottawa: Standing Committee on Human Resources, Social Development and the Status of Persons with Disabilities.

International Labour Organization (2008) Income Inequalities in the Age of Financial Globalization. In Hofman Öjermark, M (ed) *World of Work.* Geneva: ILO.

Kaufman-Rosen, L (1994) Who are the disabled? *Newsweek*, November 7: 80.
Kimberly-Clark Forest Products v Paper, Allied Industrial Chemical and Energy Works International Union, Local 7-0665 (2003), 115 LAC (4th) 344 (Arbitrator: Randy Levinson).
Le Fauve, C (2011) Disability and Addiction. In Johnson, B (ed) *Addiction Medicine*, New York, NY: Springer.
Lynk, M (1999) Accommodating Disabilities in the Canadian Workplace. *Canadian Labour & Employment Law Journal* 7: 183–247.
Lynk, M (2002) Disability and the Duty to Accommodate: An Arbitrator's Perspective. *Labour Arbitration Yearbook.* Toronto: Lancaster House, 51–122.
Malhotra, R (2006) Justice as Fairness in Accommodating Workers with Disabilities and Critical Theory: The Limitations of a Rawlsian Framework for Empowering People with Disabilities in Canada. In, Pothier, D and Devlin, R (eds), *Critical Disability Theory: Essays in Philosophy, Politics, Policy, and Law.* Toronto, ON: UBC Press.
Malhotra, R (2009) The Implications of the Social Model of Disablement for the Legal Regulation of the Modern Workplace in Canada and the United States. *Manitoba Law Journal* 33(1): 1–40.
McEwen, J (1994) Addressing Chemical Dependency-Related Issues in the Workplace: A Proposed Model for Workplace Health and Productivity. *Canadian Labour & Employment Law Journal*, 2: 421–38.
Merrick v IPSCO Saskatchewan Inc (2008), 65 CHRRD/220.
Nowell-Smith, H and O'Reilly, H (2003) A Triumph of Substance Over Form in How Discrimination Law Treats Obesity. *Canadian Bar Review* 82(3): 681–710.
Ontario (Human Rights Commission) v Vogue Shoes (1991), 14 C.H.R .R . D/425 (Ont. Bd. Of Inquiry) [*Vogue Shoes*].
Parry Sound (District) Social Services Administration Board v OPSEU, Local 324, 2003, SCC 42, 2 SCR 157.
Port Coquitlam (City) and CUPE, Local 498 (Re) (1998), 54 CLAS 134 (Arbitrator: Robert Diebolt).
Pothier, D (2010) Tackling Disability Discrimination at Work: Toward a Systemic Approach. *McGill Journal of Law and Health* 4(1): 17–37.
Puiia v Occupational Training Centre (1983), 43 Nfld & PEIR 283, 127 APR 283.
Re Labatt Breweries Ontario and Brewery, General and Professional Workers' Union, Local 304 (2002), 107 LAC (4th) 126 (Arbitrator: Barrett).
Riddle, C and Rioux, M (2011) Values in Disability Policy and Law: Equality. In Rioux, M, Basser, L and Jones, M (eds) *Critical Perspectives on Human Rights and Disability Law*, Boston, MA: Martinus Nijhoff Publishers.
Rio Tinto Alcan Primary Metal (2008), 180 LAC (4th) 1, 96 CLAS 133 (Arbitrator: Steves).
Room, R (2005) Stigma, social inequality and alcohol and drug use. *Drug and Alcohol Review* 24: 143–55.
Russell, M (1998) *Beyond Ramps: Disability at the End of the Social Contract*, Monroe, ME: Common Courage Press.
Russell, M (2002) What Disability Civil Rights Cannot Do: Employment and Political Economy. *Disability & Society* 17(2): 117–35.
Russell, M and Malhotra, R (2002) Capitalism and Disability. In Panitch, L and Leys, C (eds) *Socialist Register 2002: A World of Contradictions.* New York: Merlin Press.
Ryan v St John's City (2007), 60 CHRR D/134 (QL).

Senate, Standing Committee on Social Affairs, Science and Technology (2006) *Out of the Shadows at Last: Transforming Mental Health, Mental Illness and Addiction Services in Canada.*

Shain, M (1994) The Extent and Nature of Drug-Related Problems in the Canadian Workplace. *Canadian Labour & Employment Law Journal* 2: 291–309.

Statistics Canada (2003) Unionization and the grievance system. In Akyeampong, E (ed) *Perspectives on Labour and Income.*

Statistics Canada (2013) *Disability in Canada: Initial Findings.*

Statistics Canada (2014) *Union Coverage in Canada, 2013.*

Stelco Inc v UWSA, Local 1005 (Re) (2000), 61 CLAS 111 (Arbitrator: Maureen K Saltman).

Toronto Transit Commission and CUPE, Local 2 (2011), 210 LAC (4th) 268 (Aribtrator: John Stout).

UFCW, Local 832 v Maple Leaf Meats (2000), 95 ACWS (3d) 496, 145 Man R (2d) 114, Ont CA.

Verkerke, JH (2003) Is the ADA Efficient? *UCLA Law Review*, 50: 903–58.

Weber v Ontario Hydro, [1995] 2 SCR 929, 125 DLR (4th) 583.

Wilton, R (2006) Working at the Margins: Disabled People and the Growth of Precarious Employment. In Pothier, D and Devlin, R (eds) *Critical Disability Theory: Essays in Philosophy, Politics, Policy, and Law*, Toronto: UBC Press.

Part II

Marta Russell and political economy

5 Disablement, prison and historical segregation: 15 years later

Liat Ben-Moshe and Jean Stewart

Going back to the origin

Liat: In 2001, Marta Russell and Jean Stewart co-wrote what would become a foundational text on disability, political economy, and imprisonment, titled *Disablement, Prison and Historical Segregation.* It had a profound impact on a variety of audiences, from academics to activists who viewed it as a means of understanding, and charting a path out of, the political/economic segregation and oppression of people with disabilities (and disabled prisoners). I will first review the key tenets of the original piece and discuss its importance, and then Jean and I will examine what developments over the past 15 years have significantly impacted the forces of "disablement, prison and historical segregation."

We begin with three important definitions. The *materialist* view of history, at the core of the original article, posits that a society's mode of production (its means of producing the physical necessities of life) fundamentally determines its organization and development. *Disablement,* as used by Stewart and Russell, refers to the exclusion of disabled persons from full participation in society by means of segregation, containment, and repression. *Surplus population* refers to those who, within a capitalist system, are deemed unproductive, including the unemployed and underemployed.

As its title suggests, the original article focused on the triad of disablement, imprisonment (people with disabilities in the prison system), and the segregation of disabled people in a variety of facilities, such as nursing homes. The piece powerfully impacted me and many others because it was the first scholarly account (in a popular venue) to connect these three components, arguing that they are interlocking and inseparable.

As Stewart and Russell painstakingly explore, prisoners exhibit a startlingly high prevalence of disability, not only because people entering prison already have high rates of disability but because the prison/jail environment is itself disabling. The authors point to political economy as the root cause of disability. In the US, socioeconomic class and race are interconnected and are linked with higher rates of imprisonment; and disability is linked with class/poverty. Therefore, it should not surprise us that so many people who end up in jails and prisons have disabilities. In addition, prison functions to support the accumulation of capital and the social control of surplus populations, within which disabled people and people of color figure prominently. Thus, Stewart and Russell contributed to the burgeoning field of prison-industrial-complex scholarship/activism, a critical analysis of disability as a socioeconomic construct, rather than a medical diagnosis or deficit.

The article links disablement, as a materialist process, with other forms of segregation and incarceration, especially for profit. It argues that the process by which people with disabilities are forged into a surplus population is not merely a by-product of the capitalist system but one of the foundations on which capitalism rests. Stewart and Russell show the ways in which institutionalization not only segregates people with disabilities but creates a variety of industries which profit from this segregation. I call this the ***institutional-industrial complex*** (Ben-Moshe, 2013), or *Dis. Inc.,* blending "disability incarcerated" and "Disability Incorporated". "Dis Inc" simultaneously captures the corporatization of disability for profit by carceral institutions (e.g. nursing homes and prisons) and the incorporation of disability into the mainstream by assimilation. This analysis demands a scrutiny of the carceral state within which disabled people live their lives, and a rethinking of solutions from a materialist/disability justice perspective. It suggests that legislative, judicial, or policy changes, or changes in the built environment, will not maintain people with disabilities in their homes or communities even if supports are provided, as long as the capitalist system remains intact (Russell, 1998).

Stewart and Russell link disability to a materialist analysis of imprisonment, and imprisonment to other forms of segregation or incarceration. Incarceration and segregation thus become a continuum (from school to work/sex/recreation to the nursing home/prison/institution) in the lives of disabled people, rather than an exception that can be remediated on a case-by-case basis. Failure to acknowledge this historical reality of continuous segregation of disabled persons dooms us to an insufficient and inaccurate understanding of the lived experience of people with disabilities.

Disablement, imprisonment, and resistance: 2001–2015

Jean and Liat: In the 15 years since publication of the original piece, many changes have occurred in the legislative, economic, activist, and scholarly arenas. We will review some of these developments and the ways in which they have impacted the lives of disabled people who have been, are presently, or perhaps will be incarcerated; we'll also look at ways to resist such forms of incarceration. In short, we will view the original article through the lens of the present, posing the question: how might the article be different if it were written not in 2001 but today?

The original article discussed the following themes: historical segregation and social control; capitalist accumulation and unemployment; prison labor; commodification through institutionalization; deinstitutionalization and neoliberalism; oppression of disabled prisoners; and finally, ways to resist capitalist segregation. We loosely follow these themes to expose shifts that have occurred over the last 15 years and offer a new, revised analysis of the current state of incarceration, segregation and disablement.

> **Jean:** Because of space constraints, Marta and I were unable to include in our original article the personal, lived realities and hardships of the prisoners with whom I worked and for whom I advocated, as founder of the Disabled Prisoners' Justice Fund. In belated rectification of this gap, I have interspersed in this chapter two thumbnail prisoner sketches, at junctures where they seem to illuminate relevant points.* In doing so, I hope to give voice to a group not often heard in public discourse: our incarcerated disabled comrades.
>
> * Since I'm no longer in touch with these individuals and thus cannot get permission to tell their stories, I've changed their names.

Disability and oppression behind bars: then and now

One reality remained constant from 2000 to 2015: the incarceration rate in the US has continued its overall ascent. According to the US Bureau of Justice Statistics (BJS), 2,266,800 adults were incarcerated in US federal and state prisons, juvenile facilities, and county jails at year-end 2011—almost 1 percent of US adults. Additionally, 4,814,200 adults were on probation or on parole (BJS, 2013). By comparison, in 2000, when the original article was written, the United States incarcerated 2,071,686 persons (BJS, 2001).

Unfortunately, reliable data on the ratio of those incarcerated who are disabled remains elusive. Some states have begun to mandate the collection of such statistics, mostly as an outcome of class action lawsuits relating to negligent health care or mental health care in prisons. As more class actions are successfully litigated, perhaps a national picture of the disabled inmate population will emerge. Meanwhile, nonprofit advocacy organizations have begun to collect data on specific disabled populations in prison. For example, HEARD (Helping Educate to Advance the Rights of the Deaf), which advocates for the rights of deaf/Deaf[1] individuals caught up in the criminal justice system, tries to collect data on deaf/Deaf inmates.

Several recent news items dramatically update Russell and Stewart's argument regarding the disabling nature of prison. Rakia (2015) reported the following story:

> In 2000, the Pennsylvania government broke ground on a new maximum-security men's prison on 237 acres of land in La Belle that it received from Matt Canestrale Contracting, Inc. The plot of land where the new prison would be was shared with MCC's main business, a coal-refuse site with a coal-ash dump and two coal-slurry ponds that served a nearby mine.
>
> (Rakia, 2015)

1 When capitalized, Deaf refers to those who embrace the culture of the Deaf community, the keystone of which is American Sign Language. Small letter deaf simply refers to those with hearing/auditory impairment.

In 2014, a report titled "No Escape" outlined the health issues people were experiencing in the Fayette prison that was built in the town of La Belle, including skin conditions, throat and respiratory illnesses, thyroid issues, and tumors (McDaniel et al., 2014). According to the report, 11 of the 17 prisoners who died at Fayette between 2010 and 2013 passed away from cancer. Spurred by the economic downturn and the decline of the coal industry, capitalists have found a profitable use for these toxic sites by building prisons atop them, with inevitably disabling results.

Additionally, over the past 15 years, epidemics have become both more frequent and more virulent within carceral settings. Valley Fever, for example, has swept through prisons in central California, leaving profound damage in its wake. This highly contagious soil-borne fungus, known to affect over 150,000 people annually, is potentially deadly; for some reason, Black, Latino, and Filipino inmates are especially susceptible. Of inmates in California, 8.6 percent have contracted the disease, for which there is at this point neither cure nor vaccine (Take Two, 2015). Because of the high number of infected inmates and former inmates, and because of the high cost of treatment, the epidemic has the potential to radically transform the economy of the Central Valley. According to a recent television documentary, a one-month supply of fungicide medication costs $3,500–$4,000, a cost which must be borne for the rest of one's life ("Deadly Dust," 2015). Thus generations of released prisoners who have contracted Valley Fever return to their communities dependent on a medication which few if any of them can afford. One could hardly ask for a clearer (and crueler) example of the interlocking of multinational pharmaceutical corporations, disablement, and the prison industrial complex.

One former inmate who contracted Valley Fever recently filed suit against the state *under a hate crimes law* (the *Bane Act*). Claims brought under the *Bane Act* can be tried in state court, and "qualified immunity" does not apply. This is precedent-setting; until now, prison officials have had the protection of "qualified immunity" in many other lawsuits. The lawsuit charges that by placing this inmate, who is African American, in that particular prison—where Valley Fever was known to be rampant, and black and Hispanic inmates were known to be especially susceptible—prison officials willfully and knowingly exposed him to an epidemic they could have prevented, thus endangering his life.

Jean: As an example of the disabling potential of prison, one prisoner with whom I visited and for whom I advocated, Charlene, had MS. While in prison she was treated to unimaginable abuse by contemptuous officials who were convinced she was faking. On the advice of the prison doctor, who believed he could "flush her out of her act" by denying her services, correctional officers refused to bring meals to her bedside, refused to help her with toileting, denied her basic hygiene supplies like sanitary napkins (thus leaving her lying in a pool of blood when she was menstruating), etc. The prison doctor denied her a specific medication recommended by her personal doctor, on the grounds that it was too expensive. The withholding of this medication caused her to lose her sight and the use of her legs; when I visited her, she was legally blind and paraplegic. Once she was released from prison and began to take the medication, her vision returned and she was able to walk with the help of crutches.

Prisons cause not only bodily harm but long-term psychiatric damage. The high rate of suicide within American prisons and jails has unfortunately held steady since 2001. Suicide remains the leading cause of jail inmate deaths; the picture is not much different in state prisons. According to BJS (2012), between 2001 and 2010, suicide was among the five leading causes of death in prison in all but two years (BJS, 2012).[2] Why is the suicide rate so high in carceral spaces? Perhaps the case of Howard Andrews, a California prisoner who requested physician-assisted suicide, might shed light. Andrews requested PAS not because he found life as a quadriplegic unbearable, but because he found life as a quad *in prison* unbearable. Rather than address the issues of abusive treatment and deplorable conditions raised by his case, the judges—citing American foundational texts (John Stuart Mill) extolling the nobility of independence—granted him permission to end his life. Interestingly, by the time of their decision, Andrews had apparently changed his mind and opted for life, but in an ironic, bitter twist of fate, he died anyway, unintentionally, due to prison conditions (a botched catheterization) (Stewart, 1998). Thus, disablement (as opposed to *disability*) and imprisonment converged and intertwined.

Recent research and legislation in the area of sexual assault further illustrate the ways in which disablement functions as a core characteristic of the prison system. The 2003 *Prison Rape Elimination Act* (PREA) discusses the high incidence of rape and sexual assault in prison. The act mentions the overrepresentation of people with disabilities, especially psychiatric disabilities, in the prison system and their vulnerability to sexual abuse. In addition to disabled individuals, LGBTQ and gender-variant people are highly susceptible to sexual assault while incarcerated, especially in men's facilities. But as Beth Ribet points out, prison sexual assault is disabling and has long-term impact on those who experience it. In Ribet's words: "The relationship between disability and prison rape actually entails a tri-part dynamic, as it may be first a precursor to incarceration, then a basis for the sexual assault, and then again the additional or compounded consequence of experiencing rape" (Ribet, 2010: 295). Whether or not correctional institutions, advocacy groups or the judicial system view sexual assault survivors as disabled, and thus entitled to the protections of disability law, is a different matter.

Recently the carceral state reinvented itself with a new form of segregation and containment: the immigration detention center. Fed by a burgeoning tide of

2 When considering inmate suicide statistics, one should bear in mind a tendency on the part of some prison officials to attribute many prisoner deaths to "suicide" which, upon investigation by outside sources, are discovered to be the result of police/correctional officer brutality. The July 2015 suspicious death of Sandra Bland, while still unresolved at the time of writing, raises this question.

xenophobia, these centers are now springing up throughout the nation. Among the detainees held captive in these facilities are thousands of immigrants with mental health differences who, until a federal court ruling in 2013, were expected to represent themselves in immigration proceedings, which they were unable to do (Preston, 2013). Segregated away from family and community supports, held in frequently abusive conditions for sometimes years on end, detainees' mental stability inevitably worsens. Their disabilities range from trauma (as a result of persecution or war in their home countries) to severe depression brought on by the conditions and length of their detention, and from cognitive deficits to mental health challenges.

Jean: Antwan, a black paraplegic Jamaican, was the first prisoner on whose behalf I advocated. I corresponded with him for several years and visited him many times at various upstate New York facilities. He was serving 25 to life, but midway through his sentence, a wave of anti-immigrant hostility began to sweep the country. Politicians decided that non-citizens who have been convicted of a crime should be the first to go, and Antwan was deported to back to his homeland. Ironically, since this was his only way out of prison, he welcomed it; once he arrived in Jamaica, he became a free man.

Unemployment, segregation and legislative/judicial developments

2015 marks the 25th anniversary of the *Americans with Disabilities Act*, a law which was touted as "the civil rights bill for disabled people." But as disability legal scholar Arlene Kanter (2015) suggests: "the ADA's limited success in achieving equality for people with disabilities is likely due to the fact that it was never intended to achieve equality; rather, it sought (only) to move people from reliance on government benefits to employment by prohibiting discrimination" (Kanter, 2015: 819). Alas, even this modest proposal has not been achieved, as unemployment figures suggest.

"Ten years after passage of the Americans with Disabilities Act," Stewart and Russell wrote in 2001, "the unemployment rate of disabled people has barely budged from its chronic 65–71 percent" (Stewart and Russell, 2001: 65). In 2014, according to the US Bureau of Labor Statistics, 17.1 percent of persons with disabilities were employed, compared with 64.6 percent of nondisabled persons (Bureau of Labor Statistics, 2014). If we compare with rates from 1990, the year the ADA was enacted, the picture is even gloomier. In 2013 only 14 percent of working-age Americans with a work-limiting disability were employed, compared with 29 percent in 1990 (Thomson-DeVeaux, 2015).

Given the recent recession and rise in unemployment nationwide, we should perhaps not be surprised by these figures, as marginalized populations are always harder hit by economic downturns. Stewart and Russell explain the ADA's failings by reminding us that unemployment, underemployment and the forging of disability into a defining characteristic of a surplus population (along with race, gender/sexuality, and nationality/citizenship) are necessary for the maintenance of capitalism. Under the capitalist mode of production, disability becomes a social class, an administrative category, an abject population, and a commodity for a whole category of professionals.

Why have laws failed to move people with disabilities into employment? Because that is not their function. Litigation and rights discourse appeals to the state to remedy social ills of its own creation. Dean Spade addresses this conundrum: "Various social movements have had to contend with why legal change in the form of rights has not brought the deep transformation they were seeking, why disparities in life chances have increased during a period when we have seen the elimination of formal segregation and the advent of policies prohibiting discrimination on the basis of sex, race and disability" (Spade, 2011: 20). Appealing to the law for protection presupposes that the State is a level playing field from which the upright citizen can seek redress. But Spade reminds us: "since US law has been structured from its inception to create a racialized-gendered distribution of life chances that perpetuates violence, genocide, land theft, and exploitation, we will not resolve those issues solely by appealing to the law" (Spade, 2011: 27). This dismal conclusion is equally true in the arena of institutionalization and incarceration.

As of 2015, people with disabilities are *still* fighting for passage of legislation which would eliminate institutional bias by guaranteeing people with disabilities the necessary supports to live independent, integrated lives in the community. (The Community Integration Act is the current iteration of this struggle.) Thus, the Supreme Court's *Olmstead* decision—which held that unjustified segregation of persons with disabilities constitutes discrimination, in violation of the ADA—is ignored hundreds of times every day, in every state of the union.

Neoliberal shift, deinstitutionalization, and incarceration

In their original article, Russell and Stewart closely examined the high prevalence of individuals with mental disabilities in prisons and jails, a phenomenon which many activists, scholars and journalists attribute to deinstitutionalization. Such proponents argue that when psychiatric hospitals and institutions for people with intellectual disabilities closed, many former residents landed on the streets and, ultimately, in jails and prisons, often for minor offenses. Thus went the formula: A led to B, B led to C, therefore A caused C. But if we examine closely *why B followed A*, i.e., what economic and sociopolitical factors prevailed from the mid-1950s (when mental institutions began to close) to the 1970s (closure of institutions for people with intellectual disabilities), we discover the fallacy in this syllogism.

What caused people who had formerly resided in institutions to become homeless when those facilities shut down? Stewart and Russell (2001: 69) parse this meticulously: a change in economic policies shrank the US social safety net, leaving no funds for community mental health, affordable housing, food assistance etc. Thus neoliberalism (and its predecessors) gave rise to poverty and homelessness by failing to offer any socioeconomic supports. This does not mean that deinstitutionalization was a bad idea. Recent calls for a "return to the asylum" (to quote the title of a widely-circulated editorial by Sisti et al. in the 2015 Journal of the American Medical Association), or the reopening of psychiatric facilities to deal with the large number of prisoners with mental disabilities, cannot be justified fiscally, politically, medically, or ethically.

But let's look at the second half of the syllogism, "B→C." Why do so many homeless people end up in jail/prison? Are they simply more prone to crime? Well, yes, if by "crime" one refers to eating, sleeping, sitting, seeking employment, and other life-sustaining activities which have been criminalized by specific social policies. Law enforcement carries out sweeps in urban areas where homeless people live, confiscating personal property, including tents, bedding, clothing, and medications. Panhandling is declared illegal, as is the sharing of food with homeless persons in public spaces. Politicians, heavily influenced by chambers of commerce and business associations, enact "quality of life" ordinances relating to hygiene and public activity—such as sitting or lying on sidewalks.

While it's true that disabled street "beggars" have been criminalized in the US as far back as the mid-nineteenth century (Schweik, 2009), over the years since the publication of "Disablement, Prison, and Historical Segregation," such policies have spread throughout the US, becoming broader in scope and more lethal in severity, even fanning the flames of anti-immigrant sentiment by declaring it illegal for day laborers to seek work from passing motorists. If virtually every life-sustaining activity of a homeless person is outlawed, and neoliberals have shredded social supports, it's not hard to understand why so many homeless individuals land in jail.

How does this relate to disability? The fact is, homelessness disables. The streets, like prisons, are disabling, psychologically as well as physically. The constant noise, diesel fumes, cold/heat, lack of privacy, the anxiety of not knowing where the next meal will come from, fear of attack, fear of being routed or arrested by police—all this combines to destabilize even the strongest of psyches. And the psyches of deinstitutionalized individuals have already been destabilized by the disabling environment of institutions. Life on the streets only exacerbates whatever downward spiral has already been set in motion. Furthermore, due to practices like mandatory minimum sentencing and solitary confinement, even those who did not enter prison with a psychiatric disability will very likely experience one during incarceration (see Ben-Moshe, 2013).

Political economy and disablement: disability and incarceration for profit

To reiterate a central thesis of Stewart's and Russell's original article, disabled bodies/minds are worth more to the Gross Domestic Product in an institutional bed than in their own beds (Stewart and Russell, 2001: 68). This reality has unfortunately not changed since 2001, though the institutional population continues to decline, especially in large state residential facilities. If we specifically look at residential facilities for people with intellectual and developmental disabilities (I/DD), we see that life in an institution carries a heavy price not only in terms of the rights and freedoms of those incarcerated, but in monetary terms as well. In 2013, the (national) average annual amount paid (by state or federal funds) for institutional care was $255,692 per person; for care in a group home of six people or less, the average was $130,685. By contrast, the average annual cost (in 2013) of living at home with the help of paid caregivers was $26,708 (Braddock et al., 2015). Thus disability continues to generate high profits for the nursing home industry, whether in group "homes" or larger residential settings.

One might reasonably assume that caring for institutionalized people with I/DD would cost more because they have more complex needs; however, if we examine institutional closures, we find that this assumption falls apart. By 2013, 14 states had closed all their large (over 16 people) state institutions for people labeled I/DD (Braddock et al., 2015). The residents of those facilities (including those with very complex needs) were not exiled to another state; on the contrary, officials in those states learned how to assist and support disabled people without reliance on large institutional settings. Some of these closures came about as a result of ideological opposition to the segregation of people with disabilities, and some resulted from pressure to reduce spending (see Ben-Moshe and Meiners, 2014).

To the credit of so many who fought for deinstitutionalization, most people with I/DD no longer reside in institutions. As of 2013, 71 percent resided with a family member. But in terms of political economy, the policy and financial picture has not changed much from the heyday of institutionalization. Since little profit can be generated by investing in homecare performed by a family member, it should not surprise us that less than 0.5 percent of families who support a loved one with an I/DD label actually get paid for their labors (Braddock et al., 2015). The likelihood of strong financial support for family caregivers recedes further when one considers the gendered dynamics of caregiving and the ways in which women's work in the private sphere remains devalued.

Unfortunately, disabled employers of homecare workers have occasionally found themselves pitted against the organized force of their homecare workers' unions around issues of institutionalization. Marta Russell recounts one such faceoff (Russell, 2000), describing SEIU's (Service Employees International Union) strong support for San Francisco's nearly $300 million rebuilding of Laguna Honda, the world's largest nursing home (Russell, 2000). Russell compared the wages paid by Laguna Honda workers at the time (reportedly $14–15 per hour, with full benefits) with the wages earned by In-Home Supportive Services workers ($5.75 minimum wage at that time, with no benefits). Despite massive protests, a lawsuit filed by Laguna Honda residents, and the intervention of numerous disability rights organizations, the new 1,200 bed facility was built.

A more recent situation in which disabled employers of homecare workers have found themselves pitted against homecare workers' unions has been the struggle over the so-called "companionship exemption," a provision in the *Fair Labor Standards Act* (FLSA) which exempts homecare workers from overtime and minimum wage requirements. In 2013 the US Department of Labor, backed by the Obama administration, extended minimum wage and overtime protections to the nation's homecare workers, a move for which homecare worker unions had fought long and hard. But disability rights organizations pointed out that disabled and elderly individuals who require homecare—a statistically extremely low-income group—would be unable to afford the enormous increase in wages; that such a change would reduce the pool of available attendants, would force people with disabilities to cut the hours of longtime attendants, and would ultimately drive disabled people into institutions. People with disabilities (they argued) are, as a group, as economically and socially marginalized as domestic workers, equally at risk of exploitation and abuse, but with the added unique threat of medically unnecessary institutionalization and segregation. As of this writing, the matter is in the courts and is unresolved.

Prison profiteering: prison labor and private prisons

Since publication of Russell's and Stewart's article, activists and scholars have devoted considerable focus to the issue of profiteering private prisons and prison labor. But private prisons house only a small fraction of the prison population (see Gilmore, 2015). By 2010, 8 percent of all prisoners were held in private facilities, and in federal prisons, the figure was 16 percent (Gottschalk, 2015). Although prison privatization is a small minority in federal and state prisons, that is not the case for all carceral spaces. Immigration detention centers provide a huge windfall profit for the corporations that run them, e.g. GEO, which has a longstanding contract with Immigration and Customs Enforcement (ICE). By 2011, nearly half of all immigration detention facilities were private, up from 10 percent the previous decade (Gottschalk, 2015).

In updating Stewart's and Russell's exploration of the disabling nature of prison labor, one might start with the 4,000 California inmates who, as of this writing, are being used to fight the state's unprecedented, climate-change-exacerbated wildfires, at a pay rate of $1 an hour (Geiling, 2015). "This might be beyond slavery, whatever this is," one firefighting inmate told a BuzzFeed reporter, comparing the foremen to overseers. "They don't have a whip. That's the difference," he said (Lewis, 2014). In addition to the obvious threat posed by fire and chainsaws, this dangerous job involves breathing hazardous particulate matter, which permanently damages the lungs. It is unclear who will pay these inmates' ongoing medical bills after the fires have subsided. In the short run, the state is saving, according to one estimate (Lewis, 2014), one billion dollars a year (regular civilian firefighters make $9 per hour minimum wage). However, down the road, these inmates' medical costs will be borne by the state.

Prison labor has also been used to clear-cut forests and apply herbicide to the stumps of trees—again, dangerous work involving chainsaws, falling trees, and exposure to pesticides (Day, 1996). One final example of the capitalist state's deployment of prison labor played out in 2010, when BP used prisoners to clean up the Gulf Coast oil spill. A reporter working for *The Nation Magazine* offered the following account:

> Prisons and parish jails provide free daily labor to the state and private companies like BP. . . . Work release inmates are required to work for up to 12 hours a day, 6 days a week, sometimes averaging 72 hours per week . . .

> performing what may arguably be the most toxic job in America. Although the dangers of mixed oil and dispersant exposure are largely unknown, the chemicals in crude oil can damage every system in the body, as well as cell structures and DNA.
>
> (Young, 2010)

The political economy of decarceration

As we have shown, incarceration of people with disabilities is profitable. But apparently, so is decarceration. One area that has grown significantly in the past 15 years is the expanding market for so-called alternatives to incarceration. If capitalism found a clever way to profit from disabled people by placing them in institutional beds (Stewart and Russell, 2001), in 2015 it has also found a way of turning a profit by releasing disabled people from said beds.

Deinstitutionalization created a need, and later a market, for the placement of disabled people in settings outside the walls of institutions and hospitals. But while activists advocate for supported living at home, considerable money is now spent on placing disabled people in smaller "community" settings. What constitutes "community living" is a highly contested arena (Ben-Moshe, 2011); people with disabilities define the term expansively, to include full participation in all areas of life, including recreation and sexuality. Unfortunately, the so-called "community" housing arrangements that many disabled persons find themselves in are simply smaller versions of the old institutions (such as nursing homes), or they continue the logic of the institution in an ostensibly non-institutional setting (e.g., living with family while being denied basic rights and freedoms).

What has shifted, in the years since Russell and Stewart published the original article, is this: it's no longer enough to focus on the ways in which the private sector sustains institutionalization and incarceration of disabled folks; we must now apply the same critical lens to deinstitutionalization and decarceration. Rehabilitation programs, day habitation, treatment facilities, and supervised residential settings are all promoted as alternatives to incarceration and institutionalization, though in fact they often represent a back-door expansion of incarceration for profit.

Private corrections companies now diversify their portfolios by expanding into probation, parole, re-entry, and other so-called "community" areas. A report titled "Treatment Industrial Complex" (Isaacs, 2014) details the incarceration industry's shift into areas such as forensic mental hospitals, halfway homes, house arrest and civil commitment. Civil commitment is a legal process whereby a person designated as mentally ill is court-ordered into treatment in a psychiatric hospital or in the community. Certain criminal offenders can be civilly committed to a secure facility indefinitely, after serving out their full prison sentences. In addition, because of lawsuits alleging negligent health care, correction departments and states have begun contracting out medical care delivery to private companies, thus creating a new commodity for profit: the bodies of sick and disabled prisoners (which, as we have seen, comprise a large segment of the incarcerated population).

As one example, the above-mentioned report cites the GEO group, the second largest private prison company in the US, as a trendsetter in terms of this pivot toward the marketing of so-called alternatives to incarceration. In 2012, GEO created a subsidiary euphemistically called "GEO Care," which provides mental health services in prison, in addition to operating state psychiatric hospitals with forensic units. The irony of a for-profit company providing mental health services to counter the disabling effects of its own prisons should not be lost here. The report also cites a private company in Connecticut which contracted, in 2013, to create a nursing home specifically for aging and disabled state prisoners. The authors refer to this as "cradle to grave" control services (Isaacs, 2014: 10). GEO calls it "the correctional lifecycle," including addiction and mental health treatment and electronic monitoring (Gottschalk, 2015). In 2010, GEO acquired Behavioral Interventions Inc, maker of ankle bracelets. Of course, electronic monitoring, house arrest or forced psychotropic drugs comprise alternatives to *prison* without providing a meaningful alternative to *incarceration*.

Beyond the profit-making problematic of what Marta Russell called Handicapitalism, there is also an ideological problem at the heart of these so-called alternatives to incarceration, in that what is touted as treatment and medical help is often no less coercive than other forms of incarceration. What does "treatment" mean in neoliberal times? For instance, the psychiatric survivor movement fiercely challenges and resists the widespread use of psychopharmaceuticals as a "treatment alternative" to incarceration (see Fabris, 2011). Similarly, placing people in psychiatric wards as a "treatment alternative" is equally questionable.

Stopping the capitalist juggernaut/resisting incarceration

Concomitant with the expansion of both incarceration/institutionalization and their "alternatives", resistance to such expansion has also grown. In particular, prison abolition has gained prominence, calling not only for criminal justice overhaul, but for the eradication of a fundamentally racist and profiteering carceral system. An analysis of the prison industrial complex as an extension of slavery and of the convict lease system (see Lichtenstein, 1996; Davis, 2000) has gained widespread credibility in recent years, due to the popularization of critiques of incarceration which incorporate a racial framework, such as Michelle Alexander's *The New Jim Crow*. Alexander delineates a social construction of criminality by which men of color are turned into criminals through federal policies (e.g., the war on drugs), although they sell no more drugs and exhibit no more criminal tendencies than other groups. She also discusses the ways in which individuals exiting prisons are accorded second-class status for the rest of their lives, thus becoming an undercaste (Alexander, 2010). The US has enacted Jim Crow, she argues, while maintaining the myth of a colorblind society.

Unfortunately, such powerful and compelling critiques often lack intersectional analysis, ignoring the relationship of ability, gender/sexuality and other factors to the carceral state. Excellent recent works, too numerous to cite here, have showcased the importance of bringing a robust analysis of gender expression to the incarceration arena.[3] The recent widely-publicized case of Chelsea Manning highlights connections between gender, the medical industrial complex, the politics of disablement, and incarceration. Manning, a US army soldier, was convicted in July 2013 of *Espionage Act* violations for sending military documents (classified and unclassified), particularly about the US military involvement in Iraq and Afghanistan, to WikiLeaks, an open-source website publishing intelligence information from anonymous sources. Manning was sentenced to 35 years for revealing so-called sensitive military information. Like many other transgender individuals, Chelsea was forced to accept a diagnosis of "gender dysphoria," listed in the *Diagnostic and Statistical Manual of Mental Disorders* (DSM) as a "psychiatric disorder", in order to have her sex reassignment surgery and hormones—now categorized as hormone "therapy"—paid for by the army. Without a designation of "therapy" or "disorder," transgendered people are unable to access surgeries or treatments that are gender-affirming.

Resistance to the capitalist juggernaut has also focused in recent years on police killings of people of color, including transgendered women of color. The years since the 2013 acquittal of George Zimmerman in the shooting death of African-American teen Trayvon Martin have seen the rise of *Black Lives Matter*, a powerful social movement which has sparked activism across the country, profoundly impacting public discourse around issues of incarceration, police militarization, and racism in general. While "Disablement, Prison, and Historical Segregation" unfortunately failed to address racism as a major component of incarceration or disablement, many victims of police violence are disabled, including many people of color. Often the police have been summoned by family members seeking help for their disabled loved one. While public outcry is mounting against the systemic racism that underlies police violence against people of color, less well known is the litany of names of disabled people of color killed or injured by police.[4]

The case of Teresa Sheehan had particular significance in light of its potential to impact certain protections of the Americans with Disabilities Act. Sheehan is a woman in her mid-fifties with a history of psychiatric disability. In 2008, in the midst of a psychotic episode, she brandished a knife and barricaded herself inside her room in the San Francisco group home where she lived. Her caseworker called the police and requested help in dealing with the situation. The city police department maintained a team of officers trained in proven de-escalation techniques designed to assist people in psychiatric crisis. Unfortunately, instead of waiting for back-up from properly trained officers, two police entered Ms. Sheehan's room with guns drawn and proceeded to shoot her five times.

3 These include writings by Angela Davis (*Are Prisons Obsolete?*) and Beth Richie (*Arrested Justice: Black Women, Violence, and America's Prison Nation*), as well as the collections *Global Lockdown: Race, Gender, and the Prison-Industrial Complex*; and *Captive Genders: Trans Embodiment and the Prison Industrial Complex; and Queer (In)Justice: The Criminalization of LGBT People in the United States.*

4 Leroy Moore of *Krip Hop Nation* has been documenting recent cases of police brutality against disabled people of color in an effort to create more intersectional accountability and analysis around these issues.

Amazingly, despite being shot in the face, she survived. Eventually she sued San Francisco for violating her ADA rights; the city appealed to the US Supreme Court. In agreeing to hear the case, the High Court addressed the question of whether the ADA applies to encounters with police, thus setting the stage for a possible derailment of crucial ADA protections. Civil rights and disability rights organizations from around the country weighed in, asking the city to withdraw its appeal. Despite widespread public outcry, the case went forward; to the relief of the disability community, the Court left the ADA's protections intact.

While the ADA comes under sharp criticism by Russell and Stewart (in the original article) for its failure to adequately address economic discrimination, a dismantling of the ADA's protections in criminal justice situations would undoubtedly have led to a far greater rate of incarceration, particularly for people with psychiatric disabilities (Emslie and Bale, 2014).

The fact that the ADA failed to protect Teresa Sheehan reinforces our argument regarding the inability of a litigation/rights approach to bring about deeply transformative justice, while underscoring the urgent need for intersectionality between the disability rights movement and the campaign to end police brutality. It also reinscribes our concerns regarding the carceral dimension of group homes. In a facility specifically intended to house people with mental disabilities, psychiatric crisis is surely commonplace. Why, then, was Sheehan's caseworker so ill-equipped to deal with a psychiatric emergency that he felt it appropriate to call the police and risk escalating the situation?

An analysis of incarceration which takes into account race, gender, ability and class informs recent work on what has come to be known as "the School to Prison Pipeline." Across the US, the last decade has seen an explosion in organizing and scholarship surrounding this troubling trend. Disturbingly, the funneling of vulnerable youth toward incarceration starts very early; the practices of "special education" all too frequently ensure carceral futures for youth. Often labeled as emotionally disturbed or intellectually disabled, African-American and Latino males in particular are overrepresented in special education. They are also frequently stigmatized and isolated from the rest of the population in self-contained classes which embrace a behavioral curriculum that reinforces racialized and gendered constructions of compliance and conformity. Our present public education system denies these youth the education they need in order to receive high school diplomas, thus limiting their opportunities upon leaving school. Students with disabilities, as well as those from working class or poor families, immigrants, racial or ethnic minorities, and LGBT students may find it difficult to conform or meet the expectations of a system that devalues them as individuals. Special education thus forges marginal youth into "surplus populations" destined for carceral sites (Adams and Meiners, 2014).

According to the US Department of Education Office for Civil Rights (2014), Students with disabilities (served by IDEA, the Individuals with Disabilities Education Act) are more than twice as likely to receive an out-of-school suspension (13 percent) as nondisabled students (6 percent). In addition, they represent a quarter of students arrested and referred to law enforcement, though they comprise only 12 percent of the overall student population.

The capitalist juggernaut has been particularly industrious in its approach to the education of Deaf youth. In a burst of neoliberal zeal, state governments across the country have been closing, or attempting to close, Deaf schools, claiming that they're not cost-effective. The state marketed its strategy by singing the praises of "integration," as if placement of a single Deaf child in an all-hearing classroom were somehow the moral equivalent of desegregation in the South.

Resisting such closures has become a rallying cry for the Deaf community, which views these schools as the repositories and transmitters of Deaf language and culture, buttressing Deaf children against the isolation they experience within the larger hearing society and energizing their sense of Deaf pride. The community regards the (hearing) State's closure of Deaf schools in favor of "mainstreaming" as cultural imperialism, whereby a people's language and culture are expunged. They argue that when a Deaf child is forced to sit in a class with a roomful of hearing kids and a hearing teacher, that child is cut off, *segregated* from the world that gives her life meaning (sign language interpreter notwithstanding). One cannot help but think of administrative segregation, as prison officials euphemistically refer to solitary confinement. Adopting similar reasoning, Deaf prisoners have fought for the right to be housed in the same cell-block, instead of being scattered throughout the general population. Thus we circle back to Russell's and Stewart's foundational thesis: segregation = disablement = imprisonment.

We want to emphasize that the point is not, "the Deaf community supports segregation." Our point is that the Deaf community assigns a different meaning to the word. As scholars/activists, we must avoid a one-size-fits-all approach when considering the definition of segregation, always bearing in mind that language and meaning derive from sometimes bitterly painful cultural experience. If we approach disability as an analytic, a way to view the world, we need to rethink what disability, segregation or incarceration mean.

Conclusion

We have attempted herein to update and reactivate the still-timely arguments contained in "Disablement, Prison, and Historical Segregation." The original article argued that segregation in a variety of institutions has been the forced historical reality for disabled persons, and that these institutional settings, taken together, constitute a carceral state. In thus segregating people with disabilities, capitalism enacts *disablement* upon their bodies and minds, transforming them into a profit-generating commodity, an administrative category, and a surplus population, to be exploited and discarded. Prison—in all its iterations, including prison labor—is disabling, and disablement is a core characteristic of the prison system. Without an understanding of the forces of disablement—including nursing homes/group homes and other segregated settings—we cannot analyze and resist systems of incarceration.

In updating the original article, we have shown that over the intervening 15 years since its publication, attempts to improve the lives of disabled persons have had limited success because of their reliance on a legislative/judicial approach which leaves the root cause of the problem—capitalism and its varied impacts relative to race/gender/sexuality/ability—intact. Meanwhile the carceral state has expanded to include not only immigration detention centers but a variety of decarceral settings and initiatives.

In closing, we want to point out that while popular media continue to frame disability as a form of incarceration in itself ("trapped in her body," etc), in fact the disability community has evolved a thriving culture of resistance, countering not only negative media stereotypes but also incarceration itself, in all its iterations. While we hope that over time, it will expand to take on capitalism itself and adopt an intersectional approach that incorporates ability, race, class, and gender analyses, we admire and embrace this spirited resistance as it presents itself in 2015.

Bibliography

Adams, D and Meiners, E (2014) Who Wants to be Special? Pathologization and the Preparation of Bodies for Prison. In Nocella II, A, Parmar, P, and Stovall, D (eds) *Critical Urban Education: Dismantling the School to Prison Pipeline*. New York: Peter Lang.

Alexander, M (2010) *The New Jim Crow: Mass Incarceration in the Age of Colorblindness.* New York, NY: The New Press.

Ben-Moshe, L (2011) The Contested Meaning of "Community" Discourses of Deinstitutionalization and Community Living in the Field of Developmental Disability. *Research in Social Science and Disability* 6 (Special issue on Disability and Community): 241–64.

Ben-Moshe, L (2013) Disabling Incarceration: Connecting Disability to Divergent Confinements in the USA. *Critical Sociology* 39(3): 385–403.

Ben-Moshe, L and Meiners, E (2014) Beyond Prisons, Mental Health Clinics: When Austerity Opens Cages, Where Do the Services Go? *Public Eye*, available online at www.politicalresearch.org/2014/10/09/beyond-prisons-mental-health-clinics-when-austerity-opens-cages-where-do-the-services-go/# (last accessed June 25, 2015).

Braddock, D, Hemp, R, Rizzolo, MC, Tanis, ES, and Haffer, L (2015) *The State of the States in Developmental Disabilities 2015.* Boulder: Department of Psychiatry and Coleman Institute, University of Colorado and Department of Disability, and Human Development, University of Illinois at Chicago.

Bureau of Justice Statistics (2001) *Prisoners in 2000.* Washington, DC: Bureau of Justice Statistics.

Bureau of Justice Statistics (2012) *US, Mortality in Local Jails and State Prisons, 2000–2010—Statistical Tables.* Washington, DC: Bureau of Justice Statistics.

Bureau of Justice Statistics (2013) *Prisoners in 2012: Trends in Admissions and Releases, 1991–2012.* Washington, DC: Bureau of Justice Statistics.

Bureau of Justice Statistics (2014) *Prisoners in 2013.* Washington, DC: Bureau of Justice Statistics.

Bureau of Labor Statistics (2014) *Persons with a Disability: Labor Force Characteristics Summary*, available online at www.bls.gov/news.release/disabl.nr0.htm (last accessed August 1, 2015).

Davis, AY (2000) From the Convict Lease System to the Super-max Prison. In James, J (ed) *States of Confinement: Policing, Detention, and Prisons.* New York, NY: St. Martin's Press.

Davis, AY (2011) *Are Prisons Obsolete?* New York, NY: Seven Stories Press.

Day, B (1996) *Cut-Stump Treatment of Saltcedar (Tamarix Spp) Using Alternative Labor Sources: Successful Venture?* National Invasive Species Information Center. Portland, OR: US Fish and Wildlife Service, available online at www.invasivespeciesinfo.gov/docs/news/workshopSep96/index.html (last accessed September 1 2015).

Emslie, A and Bale, R (2014) More Than Half of Those Killed by San Francisco Police Are Mentally Ill. *KQED News*, 30 September, available online at ww2.kqed.org/news/2014/09/30/half-of-those-killed-by-san-francisco-police-are-mentally-ill (last accessed September 5, 2015).

Fabris, E (2011) *Tranquil Prisons: Chemical Incarceration under Community Treatment Orders.* Toronto: University of Toronto Press.

Geiling, N (2015) Thousands Of Firefighters in California Are Inmates, Being Paid $1 An Hour On The Line. *Thinking Progress*, August 13, available online at http://thinkprogress.org/climate/2015/08/13/3691283/inmates-are-fighting-californias-wildfires/ (last accessed September 1 2015).

Gilmore, RW (2015) The Worrying State of the Anti-Prison Movement. *Social Justice: A Journal of Crime, Conflict & World Order*, February 23, available online at www.socialjusticejournal.org/the-worrying-state-of-the-anti-prison-movement/ (last accessed March 17, 2016).

Gottschalk, M (2015) *Caught: The Prison State and the Lockdown of American Politics.* Princeton: Princeton University Press.

Isaacs, C (2014) *The Treatment Industrial Complex: How For-Profit Prison Corporations are Undermining Efforts to Treat and Rehabilitate Prisoners for Corporate Gain.* American Friends Service Committee, Grassroots Leadership and the Southern Center for Human Rights, available online at https://afsc.org/sites/afsc.civicactions.net/files/documents/TIC_report_online.pdf (last accessed October 30, 2015).

Kanter, AS (2015) Americans with Disabilities Act at 25 Years: Lessons to Learn from the Convention on the Rights of People with Disabilities. *The Drake Law Review* 63: 819–83.

Lewis, AC (2014) The Prisoners Fighting California's Wildfires. *BuzzFeed News.* October 30, 2014, available online at www.buzzfeed.com/amandachicagolewis/the-prisoners-fighting-californias-wildfires#.nxPL7V6Rq (last accessed July 2, 2015).

Lichtenstein, A (1996) *Twice the Work of Free Labor: The Political Economy of Convict Labor in the New South.* London: Verso.

McDaniel, DS, Grote, B, Fiorillo, B, Cohen, D and Cozzens, Q (2014) *No Escape: Exposure to Toxic Coal Waste at State Correctional Institution Fayette.* Abolitionist Law Center & Human Rights Coalition, available online at https://abolitionistlawcenter.files.wordpress.com/2014/09/no-escape-bw-1-4mb.pdf (last accessed August 1, 2015).

Mogul, JL, Ritchie, AJ, and Whitlock, K (eds) (2011) *Queer (in) justice: The Criminalization of LGBT People in the United States.* Boston, MA: Beacon Press.

Preston, J (2013) In a First, Judge Orders Legal Aid for Mentally Disabled Immigrants Facing Deportation *New York Times*, April 23.

Rakia, R (2015) Coal Ash May Be Making Pennsylvania Inmates Sick, and Now They're Fighting to Shut Their Prison Down. *Vice Magazine*, 18 May, available online at www.vice.com/read/ashes-to-ashes-0000651-v22n5 (last accessed August 20, 2015).

Ribet, B (2010) Naming Prison Rape as Disablement: A Critical Analysis of the Prison

Litigation Reform Act, the Americans with Disabilities Act, and the Imperatives of Survivor-Oriented Advocacy. *Virginia Journal of Social Policy & the Law*, 17: 281–317.

Richie, BE (2012) *Arrested Justice: Black women, Violence, and America's Prison Nation*. New York, NY: NYU Press.

Russell, M (1998) *Beyond Ramps: Disability at the End of the Social Contract*. Monroe, ME: Common Courage Press.

Russell, M (2000) Stuck at the Nursing Home Door: Organized Labor Can't Seem to Get Beyond the Institutional Model. *Ragged Edge Online*, Jan/Feb 2000, available online at www.raggededgemagazine.com/0100/a0100ft1.htm (last accessed May 15, 2014).

Schweik, SM (2009) *The Ugly Laws: Disability in Public*. New York, NY: NYU Press.

Sisti, DA, Segal, AG, and Emanuel, EJ (2015) Improving Long-term Psychiatric Care: Bring Back the Asylum. *JAMA 313*(3): 243–44.

Spade, D (2011) Normal life: Administrative violence, Critical Trans Politics, and the Limits of Law. Brooklyn, NY: South End Press.

Stanley, EA and Smith, N (eds) (2011). *Captive Genders: Trans Embodiment and the Prison Industrial Complex*. Oakland, CA: AK Press.

Stewart, J (1998) Life, Death and Disability Behind Bars. *New Mobility*, 9 (June).

Stewart, J and Russell, M (2001). Disablement, Prison, and Historical Segregation. *Monthly Review* 53(3): 61–75.

Sudbury, J (ed) (2005) *Global Lockdown: Race, Gender, and the Prison-industrial Complex*. New York, NY: Routledge

Take Two (2015) *8.6 percent of California Inmates Test Positive for Valley Fever*. Southern California Public Radio, February 2, available online at www.scpr.org/programs/take-two/2015/02/02/41370/8-6-percent-of-ca-inmate-test-positive-for-valley/ (last accessed August 5, 2015).

Thomson-DeVeaux, A (2015) Has The ADA Broken Its Economic Promises To People With Disabilities? Employment and Wage Gaps Persist 25 years Later. *FiveThirtyEight Blog*, available online at http://fivethirtyeight.com/features/has-the-ada-broken-its-economic-promises-to-people-with-disabilities/ (last accessed August 28, 2015).

Young, AL (2010) BP Hires Prison Labor to Clean Up Spill While Coastal Residents Struggle. *The Nation*, July 21, available online at www.thenation.com/article/bp-hires-prison-labor-clean-spill-while-coastal-residents-struggle/ (last accessed September 1, 2015).

ViewFinder (2015) *Deadly Dust: Valley Fever in the West* (DVD). KVIE PBS.

US Department of Education Office for Civil Rights (2014). *Data Snapshot: School Discipline*, available online at http://ocrdata.ed.gov/Downloads/CRDC-School-Discipline-Snapshot.pdf (last accessed October 30, 2015).

6 Beyond Ramps/against work: Marta Russell's legacy and politics of intersectionality

Nirmala Erevelles

It is a cliché to begin this chapter bemoaning the fact that we are living in murderous times. In the USA, state violence against black and brown citizens, several of them disabled, has become a daily occurrence. No sooner than the cries of protest against this violence have softened to a silent roar than our attention swerves towards the heartbreak of more black and brown bodies—this time refugees—fleeing from political and economic violence, struggling to cross borders of nation-states that then decide who deserves recognition of their humanity as global citizens. Costly wars waged overseas producing even more death, destruction, and disability are continued again at home extending beyond the horror of police turning their guns against the unarmed to also target its poor and disabled citizens through cutbacks in the meager economic safety net as health care costs rise, wages fall, and the struggle for bare subsistence takes its toll on the physical and mental health of these citizens. If Marta Russell were alive today, her writing would have confronted this terrible cliché with a passionate and political response that would have refused to read these murderous circumstances as inevitable fact. Rejecting naturalizing discourses that mourn the inevitability of this rather dismal future, while at the same time refusing to restrict her analysis to the descriptive, Russell would have offered up a materialist explanation that would have foregrounded the historical social relations and economic conditions that have produced death and disability on such a massive scale. But Russell would not have stopped there. Recognizing that social class also implicates race, gender, and disability, Russell's writing can be extended beyond merely acknowledging intersectional difference. Rather, her work has the potential to explain how identity gets constituted at the intersections of difference and the terrible implications transnational capitalism has for bodies located at those violent and exploitative intersections. And it is in the pursuit of what such explanations would look like, that I write this chapter for the book that commemorates Marta Russell's work.

Marta Russell's analysis of political economy and disability has explained how the antagonisms of social class have impacted disabled people in US society. Her work spanning the prison industrial complex and the medical industrial complex and her critique of the liberal failures rooted in the American with Disabilities Act (ADA) have powerful implications not just for disabled people but also for the working class living at the volatile intersections of race, class, gender, and sexual identity. In this chapter, I engage Marta Russell's published work to foreground the politics of intersectional difference in contemporary social theory. Discussions of difference in contemporary social theory have devolved into a conflicting web of identity politics where social difference has been constituted solely in cultural and discursive terms. Disability studies has also fallen prey to this problematic phenomenon in social theory. I will argue in this chapter that Marta Russell's deployment of the political economy of disability offers a way out of this problematic. Drawing on the different venues where Marta Russell situated her work, I will explore how capitalism constitutes social difference within diverse historical contexts using the ideology of disability imagined as "debilitating difference" to organize class divisions and maintain class antagonisms that benefit neoliberal social arrangements in US society. I will conclude the chapter by exploring transformative possibilities that a robust critique of capitalism from a materialist disability studies perspective can make possible.

Against work: historical materialist analyses of disability

In *Beyond Ramps: Disability at the End of the Social Contract*, Marta Russell (1998) has argued convincingly that just like the canary in the coal mine, disability and disability policy become the barometers for "progress" or its lack thereof in US society. Central to Russell's argument is the examination of how economic policies underlie social oppression and, in doing so, Russell has questioned the political wisdom of using labor (work) as the central measure of human worth in capitalist economies. While a historical materialist critique of capitalism offers an explanation as to how alienation through labor and the appropriation of labor power have organized hierarchical oppressive social relations (class), this critique has very rarely explored the implications for labor (work) continuing to be crucial to defining citizen subjects located within the exploitative class relations of capitalism. Russell is not alone in deploying a historical materialist analysis in disability studies. In fact, there are a few others (Oliver, 1990; Charlton, 2000; Erevelles, 2011; Malhotra, 2014) who have also sought to redefine disability as constituted within the social relations of production and consumption within capitalism rather than as a medical condition or a socio-cultural identity. But I argue that Russell has made the most extended argument that has sought to re-examine the centrality of work in anti-capitalist critiques from the critical standpoint of a historical materialist disability studies.

Russell's historical materialist analysis of disability located within antagonistic class relations in capitalism is also clearly an intersectional analysis, even though it has not been identified as such. Rejecting a liberal politics of inclusion that leaves unquestioned the social relations that support oppressive hierarchies, Russell's critique of disability oppression begins with a discussion of how mainstream adherences to normative ideologies and ways of being are painfully oppressive to disabled people who are perceived as less than human. These ideologies have made it easy to justify inhumane policies that construct disabled people as disposable. One of these troubling ideologies is the overvaluation of work in capitalist society. Within capitalism, Russell (1998) pointed out, the working class is expected to work for another's profit. Discussing the historical shift from feudalism to capitalism, Russell argued that capitalism's focus on efficient accumulation required a workforce with particular bodily specifications (what she termed "physicalism" and in disability studies is more broadly constituted by ableism) to meet its productive requirements—normative specifications that excluded disabled bodies from productive/paid labor. Thus, refusing the mainstream insistence that work be the defining quality of disabled people's lives, Russell wrote:

> Employability and aptitude for earning money are not the measure of what it means to live, to be part of the human race. The goal of social justice is to ensure the dignity of each and every person. To buy into capitalist propaganda that work is god, that people are laborers first and human beings second, serves to oppress us all.
>
> (Russell, 1998: 83)

This critique is especially relevant for the US based Disability Rights Movement (DRM) in light of its celebration of the 25th anniversary of the *American with Disabilities Act* (ADA) on July 26 2015. Almost 10 years earlier Russell presciently questioned whether the ADA could really pave the way for social and economic parity for disabled people with its overwhelming focus on access and inclusion into mainstream society—what she termed "free-market civil rights" (Russell, 1998: 114). The ADA's central focus, as Russell pointed out, has been the granting of civil rights to disabled people if and only if it costs little to nothing to the institutions/businesses that recognize/enable these rights. Thus, according to Russell, the ADA's insistence on inclusive gestures, like, for example, building more ramps if and only if they are cost-effective does nothing to challenge the "physicalism" (and ableism) that is inherent in the imperative that work be central to disability emancipation. Moreover, the ADA only requires that disabled people have an equal opportunity to be included in employment in the economic market place with little or no funding to ensure that this indeed takes place. As a result, the ADA, while still a legislative necessity, is nevertheless invested in free market ideologies that Russell argued has continued to constitute the disability community as a "fettered people" in capitalist economies.

When cost-effective economic inclusion is not possible (notwithstanding the ADA), disabled people have had little choice but to become recipients of social welfare. And with the growth of the welfare state, disability once again is defined in relation to capitalist labor. As a result, social welfare policy continues to fetishize a "physicalism" (and ableism) built to serve the market economy instead of members of society. Russell (1998) explains this further:

> Laissez-faire sociologists and anthropologists used biological determinism to argue against implementing reforms that would better the living conditions of the poor, claiming that biology conferred a non-correctable individual

> condition, that could not be solved by social reform. By erecting these "logical" barriers against humane social policy, Social Darwinists could make the case for a bare-bones government, and use futility as a reason to curtail the role of government in society, to oppose socialized medicine, and to make public expenditures unpopular.
>
> (Russell, 1998: 64)

Such Darwinist perspectives on disability as intransigent biology supported eugenic policies that sought to restrict, control, dehumanize, and destroy disabled lives. A more "humane" version of Social Darwinism manifested itself in the conceptualization of the welfare state. But here too, the conceptualization of disability as failed biology continued to persist. Echoing Deborah Stone's (1984) argument in *The Disabled State*, Russell wrote that through social welfare programs, disability now conceptualized as the inability to engage in substantial work activity became the primary criteria to distinguish the deserving from the non-deserving poor. Thus, in order to ensure that social welfare could never be an attractive and easy alternative to work, social welfare policies were instituted such that disability-related claims were not easily attainable. In fact Russell observed that in the early days when social security was established, private insurance companies as well as Chambers of Commerce believed that "[i]f workers were provided with a federal social safety net that adequately protected them through unemployment, sickness, impairment, and old age, then business would have less control over the work force because labor would gain a stronger position from which to negotiate their conditions of employment, such as fair wages, reasonable accommodations, and flexible work hours" (Russell, 1998: 72). As a result, Russell (1998) argued that the over-valuing of work and the celebration of this particular US-styled work ethic became a mode of social control such that capitalists could continue to control labor even within the context of social welfare.

With disability being central to the workings of the welfare state, Russell (2005) decried the welfare state's propensity to continue to locate disability in a "moral economy" (Russell, 2005: 50)—a location that does not guarantee a decent standard of living for disabled people. Updating Russell's figures from a decade earlier, the monthly stipend that Supplemental Security Income (SSI) provides disabled people (18–64 years) is $559.19 and for those who are over 65 years, this stipend is $433.19 (Social Security, July 2015). In light of these sobering statistics, it seems imperative that disabled people's struggle for recognition as bona fide citizens needs to extend beyond ramps (physical access) to dismantle ableist social ideologies and economic structures that constitute them as non-productive citizens (a terminology very akin to the depiction of disabled people in Nazi Germany as "useless eaters").

Russell's critique of the centrality of work in emancipatory discourses on disability is also echoed by disability activist, artist, and scholar Sunaura Taylor (2004) who has also critiqued ableist ideologies that construe disabled workers as "inefficient workers . . . [such that] inefficient is the antithesis of what a good worker should be." Taylor writes:

> Western culture has a very limited idea of what being useful to society is. People can be useful in ways other than monetarily. The individuals who I marched with may not have paying jobs, but they spend hours each day organizing protests and freeing people from lives in institutions. Isn't this a valuable way to spend one's time? Disabled people have to find meaning in other aspects of their lives and this meaning is threatening to our culture's value system. Though education, legislation, and technological developments may work to level the employment field for some impaired individuals, we should keep some fundamental insights from Marxist economic theory in mind, particularly the theory of surplus value, which dictates that higher profits result from the ability to pay less for labor power than the value imparted by the worker. The same rule that often excludes the impaired from the traditional workplace also exploits the able-bodied who have no other choice but to participate. The right not to work is an ideal worthy of the impaired and able-bodied alike.
>
> (Taylor, 2004: 44)

I quoted Taylor at length to demonstrate how Russell's argument against work, nearly a decade earlier, still has resonance today, especially in light of the austerity measures that have had devastating effects on disabled people, especially in Europe (Crow, 2012; Runswick-Cole and Goodley, 2015; Beatty and Fothergill, 2015). These austerity measures have sought to cull disabled people from welfare rolls on the assumption that many of them are either "fraudsters" or "scroungers" (Crow, 2012). Here, refusing the imperative to work within the exploitative regimes of capitalism or being unable to meet its profit-directed demands for efficiency has inspired these pejorative designations. Crow describes these two designations as follows:

> [Fraudster] . . . is a portrayal of working age non-disabled people charged with defrauding the state through benefits secured for non-existent impairment. Family snapshots and grainy surveillance video show claimants 'caught' taking pleasure in leisure activities most likely precluded by their alleged impairment: playing golf, digging gardens, on a rollercoaster.
>
> Scrounger reporting, in contrast, focuses on 'work shy' disabled people 'languishing' on benefits in preference to work, in a shift of gaze from non-disabled fraudster to disabled parasite.
>
> (Crow, 2012: 170)

What becomes apparent in Crow's definitions is how the inclusion of disabled people in a profit-oriented work-based economy demonstrates once again the astuteness in Russell's critique of work. In the next section I will explore the relevance of Russell's argument in the intersectional context where race, class, and disability intersect.

Working Jim Crow: disability at the intersections

Russell and Taylor's argument about the right "not to work" has implications for people living at the complex intersections of race, class, and disability. Historically, discussions of intersectionality have explored how the boundaries of identity are not discrete, but instead overlap, producing more nuanced and complex subject positions (Collins, 2000; Crenshaw, 2000). While these arguments have focused mostly on the sociological trinity of race, class, and gender, some disability scholars have explored what happens to theories of intersectionality when disability is added to this conglomeration of social identities (Erevelles, 2011; Annamma, et al., 2013). In this section, however, instead of identity as the fulcrum about which discussions on intersectionality turn, I substitute the construct of work (labor) for identity. In other words, I will argue in this section, that Marta Russell's analysis of work using historical materialism opens up a conceptual space to critically engage identity at the intersections of race, class, and disability.

In her book, *The New Jim Crow*, Michelle Alexander (2010) has argued that racial caste in the US that was upheld by Jim Crow laws continues today with the criminal justice system disproportionately imprisoning communities of color. Because of their criminal history, when released, the legal discrimination against these former prisoners continues in the context of employment, housing, education, and public benefits, as well as in the denial of the right to vote and serve on juries, upholding what Alexander calls the "New Jim Crow." Alexander argues that this new racial under-caste has "functioned relatively automatically, and the prevailing system of racial meanings, identities, and ideologies [are naturalized and] . . . explained in race neutral terms" (Alexander, 2010: 56–57). While Alexander claims that this group is defined largely by race, I have argued that this group is defined at the crucial intersection of race, class, and disability (Erevelles, 2014) and echoes in many ways ideologies of physicalism (Russell, 1998) used to exclude disabled people from the work force. Interestingly, Alexander almost intuitively gestures towards a similar analysis when she writes that, "the degraded status of Africans was justified on the grounds that Negroes, like the Indians, were an uncivilized lesser race, perhaps even more lacking in intelligence and laudable human qualities than the red-skinned natives" (Alexander, 2010: 25). Here, Alexander seems unaware that disability as deviant pathology (physicalism/ableism), was utilized to simultaneously assign African slaves a degraded self-worth and yet at the same time justifying their value as slave labor. This unawareness results in Alexander's non-recognition of the constitutive relationship of race and disability where racialized bodies become disabled and disabled bodies become racialized within the specific historical conditions of a burgeoning capitalism (Erevelles, 2011).

In my book, *Disability and Difference in Global Context* (Erevelles, 2011), I have argued that the locus of this constitutive relationship between race and disability is the context of labor (work) and, in particular, slave labor. To make this argument, I have used literary theorist Hortense Spillers's (1987) essay, "Mama's Baby, Papa's Maybe: Notes on an American Grammar" where she locates the "origins" of African-American subjectivity in the (trans)Atlantic slave trade which started with the unimaginable violence during the Middle Passage, continued through the dehumanization of slavery, and finally concluded by exposing dominant conceptualizations of the contemporary "Black Family" as a tangle of pathology. Spillers describes scenes of both the procurement and then the exploitation of slave labor as "scene[s] of *actual* mutilation, dismemberment, and exile" (Spillers, 1987: 67) that I have argued produce disabled bodies—black disabled bodies without gender, without genitalia, without subjectivity—who are transformed into commodities that are exchanged in the market for profit. Here, *black* and *disabled* are not just linguistic tropes used to delineate difference, but are, instead, materialist constructs used to justify slave labor that produced unimaginable profits for the proto-capitalists—the slave masters.

It is important to also recognize that the actual participation in slave labor produced disability when slaves were subjected to the most brutal violation of the flesh with "eyes beaten out, arms, backs, skulls branded, a left jaw, a right ankle, punctured; teeth missing, as the calculated work of iron, whips, chains, knives, the canine patrol, the bullet" (Spillers, 1987: 67). Here, impairment that the slaves acquired was not just biological/natural; it was also produced in a historical, social, and economic context that constructed the enslaved body as a dehumanized commodity. Thus, rather than posing a simple causal effect (namely that slavery produces disability), I have argued that centering labor (work) in an intersectional analysis treats social identities like disability and race as neither biological nor discursive, but rather as materialist categories constituted by the exploitative conditions of labor in transnational capitalism.

Thus, even though it has been customary to perceive segregationist Jim Crow laws as emerging from racist ideologies, I argue instead, that these ideologies emerge from the economic context where intersecting categories of race, class, and disability revolve around the exploitative fulcrum of labor/work. Alexander herself, implicitly gestures towards a similar analysis when she argues that the origins of Jim Crow arose from attempts to control free black workers as a backlash against the gains earned by the former slaves during the Reconstruction Period enacted by the southern elite plantation class. Following the civil war, the dearth of social laws and customs to maintain white social and economic control gave rise to white elite fears of a possible insurrection by former slaves. Here, vagrancy laws, as well as laws accusing African-Americans of "mischief" and "insulting gestures" (physicalism/ableism) were utilized to incarcerate large numbers of African-American men who then became part of the convict labor force and who thus re-entered into yet another system of extreme repression and control. Here once again, labor becomes the linchpin around which racialized social hierarchies were preserved at the same time that the labor power of former slaves continued to be appropriated for free (convict labor) or for minimal wages (exploited labor). As a result, by the turn of the century, every state in the South supported Jim Crow laws that sanctioned racial ostracism in virtually every aspect of social life that extended to schools, churches, hospitals, prisons, cemeteries, and asylums that enabled even lower class whites to maintain some sort of superiority (ableism) over African-Americans.

Different historical conditions produce different material outcomes for the working and non-working poor. While before Reconstruction, the forced inclusion of black bodies within the material context of labor produced the mutually constitutive constructs of race and disability, in the contemporary historical context, racialized bodies perceived as disabled because of an ascribed deviant pathology continue to be excluded from participation in the mainstream economy, and are therefore forced to make a living in an alternative underground (and illegal) economy in the urban ghetto. The sociologist Loic Wacquant (2009) has likened the ghetto to an "ethnoracial prison" and the prison to a "judicial ghetto" (Wacquant, 2009: 205), both of them being "socio-spatial device[s] that enable a dominant status group . . . to simultaneously ostracize and exploit a subordinate group endowed with negative symbolic capital" (Wacquant, 2009: 204). Here, the concurrent loss of jobs in the inner city, and the gradual retrenchment of social welfare in response to the neoliberal policies of less government intervention and their corresponding association with social stigma, has created "a redundant population of younger black men (and women) . . . in a self-fulfilling cycle of social and legal marginality" (Wacquant, 2009: 207) and therefore functions "as an ancillary institution for caste preservation and labor control" (Wacquant, 2009: 207). Here, Wacquant's analysis once again echoes Russell's argument that labor (work) is the fulcrum around which the exclusion of bodies located at the intersections of race, class, and disability revolves.

Economic segregation and incarceration at the intersections

To demonstrate how labor (work) or the lack thereof is central in critical discussions of intersectionality, I turn to the violent oppression experienced by residents in the urban ghettos as an example. On April 19 2015, Freddie Gray, a 25 year old African-American male, was severely injured when police arrested him and transported him to the jail in Baltimore, Maryland, where he died a week later, in hospital, as the result of a broken neck. Following the news of Grey's death, protests broke out in Baltimore that mirrored the protests in Ferguson, Missouri that had occurred nearly nine months earlier in reaction to the killing by police of another unarmed African-American teenager, Michael Brown, which gave birth to the social movement *Black Lives Matter*. After the Baltimore protests, when the tear gas cleared and the community sought a brief reprieve, the public for a moment focused on the conditions that created the seemingly insurmountable impasse between the State and its minority residents living in the urban ghettos in US cities like Baltimore. And what was once again brought to the fore was the economic and social segregation on account of exclusionary policies in the context of labor, education, and housing, and the impact of this exclusion on the social identities of the residents of these urban ghettos.

For example, an editorial in the *New York Times* (NYT Editorial Board, May 9, 2015) attributed the poverty and isolation to decades of housing segregation and economic exploitation experienced by its African-American residents. Young residents growing up in urban ghettoes in Baltimore earned 28 percent less than 26 year olds in other parts of the country. Here, housing segregation was maintained via Jim Crow-like policies practiced in the rural south. For example, in 1910, to prevent a black Yale educated lawyer from moving to the white neighborhood, Mount Royale, an ordinance was passed where "no black person could occupy a home on a block where more than half the people were white; no white person could move into a block where more than half the residents were black" producing what was "the most pronounced 'Jim Crow' measure in record" (NYT Editorial Board, May 9, 2015). African-American residents who were part of the working poor were unable to get reasonable loans to buy homes and were forced to turn to loan sharks. Many of them, as a result, were unable to maintain their properties and often lost their homes. Additionally, during the housing boom from 1930–1950, they were unable to acquire home equity, experiencing what was tantamount to financial apartheid.

Clearly, discrimination on the basis of employment and housing produced the extreme marginalization of residents in these urban ghettoes. However, rather than focusing on the material conditions that produced this marginalization, many of these analyses located the causes of this marginalization in biology (physicalism/ableism). Thus, for example, Orlando Patterson (2015), a Harvard University sociologist, locates the real problem in "the vicious tangle of concentrated poverty, disconnected youth and a culture of violence among a small but destructive minority in the inner cities; and, on the other hand, of out-of-control law-enforcement practices abetted by a police culture that prioritizes racial profiling and violent constraint" (Patterson, 2015: 6). Here, Patterson slips into the lazy analysis of a culture of poverty that naturalizes the conditions within which young African-American inner-city youth live.

Ironically, Patterson inadvertently gestures to a materialist analysis located at the intersection of race, class, and disability when he mentions "contemporary conditions like poverty, racial discrimination, chronic unemployment, single parenting and a chemically toxic, neurologically injurious environment, like the lead paint that poisoned Freddie Gray" (Patterson, 2015: 6). But no sooner does he highlight these material realities than he quickly turns to medical/pathological interventions such as moralistic exhortations as well as rehabilitative interventions that are behavioral and punitive. Thus, rather than keeping the focus on the destructive context of labor and its role in the creation of the inner city, Patterson's version of social transformation uses the most pernicious ideologies at the intersection of racism and ableism when he describes black survival as dependent on the "reduction in the number of kids born to single, usually poor, women," increasing what he argues is "the greatly increased risk of prolonged poverty, child abuse, educational failure and youth delinquency and violence, especially among boys, whose main reason for joining gangs is to find a family and male role models" (Patterson, 2015: 6).

Echoing Russell's critique of physicalism/ableism, I argue here that similar pathological discourses of disability are used to justify the oppressive binary cultural constructions of normal/pathological, autonomous/dependent, competent citizen/ward of the state, and the social divisions of labor (Erevelles, 2011). Moreover, just like disability, these pathologies are so intimately embedded in black bodies that it is difficult to disentangle the intersectional strands of race, class, and disability. Here again, Alexander (2010) inadvertently refers to this phenomenon when she writes:

> [W]hat it means to be a criminal in our collective consciousness has become conflated with what it means to be black. . . . For black youth, the experience of being "made black" often begins with the first police stop, interrogation, search, or arrest. The experience carries social meaning – *this is what it means to be black*. . . . For the [racial caste] system to succeed . . . black people must be labeled criminals before they are formally subject to control. . . . Thus black youth must be made – labeled – criminals. This process of being made a criminal is, to a large extent, the process of "becoming" black.
>
> (Alexander, 2010: 195)

I have argued elsewhere (Erevelles, 2014) that when Alexander describes "becoming" black in the above quote, she is referring to a "body-based disqualification" (Snyder and Mitchell, 2006: 400) that presumes an in-built inferiority/deviance which being biologically encoded would therefore be almost impossible to transcend. Here, disability serving as the "master trope of human disqualification" (Mitchell and Snyder, 2003: 3) is deployed to give oppressive credence to this flawed equation: criminal = black youth. Here, remapping the historical continuities with earlier times, the simultaneous process of "becoming black" AND "becoming disabled" described uncritically as "natural" deviance, foregrounds a complex intersectional politics of race, class, and disability that is used to justify first the exclusion from the workforce and the incarceration of "outlaw" bodies that eventually become profitable commodities in the neoliberal prison-industrial-complex of late capitalism (Erevelles, 2014).

Further, the historical continuities between Jim Crow and the contemporary context of mass incarceration mirror in many ways eugenic ideologies that imagined a "uniquely modern utopian fantasy of a future world uncontaminated by defective bodies—either disabled, racialised, and/or both at the same time" (Mitchell and Snyder, 2003: 861). It is these eugenic ideologies that are now used to consign entire communities of color to what La Paperson (2010) has theorized as the "post-colonial ghetto." Because of its feared pathology, there is also always the move to destroy the ghetto, to always shift its inhabitants someplace else—such that it becomes a space that is always open for continuous dispersal; of going "nowhere for good" (Paperson, 2010: 21). Thus, the "ghetto" is not just a space but "a portable status that can be cast onto bodies—some are temporarily and selectively branded, others inescapably so" (Paperson, 2010: 19), "[such that if mapped] . . . it would be a palimpsest, a map of absences—of what used to be there—or perhaps a map of the condemned" (Paperson, 2010: 21).

The dis-locating procedure of the ghetto is echoed in Russell and Stewart's

(2001) thought-provoking essay, "Disablement, Prison and Historical Segregation." Citing Christian Parenti who pointed out that capitalism is both threatened as well as dependent on poor people, Russell and Stewart, like Patterson, also foreground the toxic physical, economic, and social conditions that create disability in the first place among poor people, and then sentence them to lifetimes of incarceration. Russell and Stewart argue that institutional life, whether in prisons, nursing homes, hostels, mental institutions, or segregated schools always limit the lives of inmates held against their will in these spaces (Stewart and Russell, 2001: 63). In fact, each of these segregated spaces produce institutions that warehouse those bodies that are both necessary for and yet threatening to capitalist appropriation. Russell and Stewart expose the limits of Patterson's argument when they describe how capitalism on the one hand produces disability via industrialization (labor) as a result of impairments caused through black lung disease, industrial accidents, and repetitive action injuries while, at the same time, relocates these now disabled workers as part of the industrial reserve army and creates them as redundant to the economy.

Russell and Stewart (2001) are quick to point out that prison labor as well as labor in sheltered workshops becomes another form by which capitalism generates profits off the labor of those already victimized by the system. Being an inmate in an institution also contributes to capitalist appropriations. Nursing homes become spaces where disabled people as "valued commodities" are "worth more to the Gross National Product when occupying institutional 'beds' rather than in their own homes" (Stewart and Russell, 2001: 68). When incarcerated in these spaces, the access needs of disabled prisoners in terms of physical assistance, assistive technologies, and necessary medical treatments such as counseling and help with substance abuse, are denied. The psychological and medical abuse experienced in prison further exacerbates impairments or even serves as an onset for them—such that disability becomes a "by-product" of the prison industrial complex. Here, once again, it is possible to see how labor (work) becomes the fulcrum around which social identities are constituted at the intersection of race, class, and disability.

Conclusion

Russell's (1998) historical materialist critique that decentralizes work in the quest for social transformation pushes the emancipatory envelope, not just for disability liberation but also for other liberation movements as well. Her argument reminds us that "social power relations control the nature of work" (Russell, 1998: 66) with its focus on efficiency and profit rather than principles of cooperation and equality. As a result, disabled people become "social casualties of the system" (Russell, 1998: 68). Quoting the economist Karl Polyani, Russell argued that "[i]nstead of the economy being embedded in social relations, social relations are embedded in the economic system" (Russell, 1998: 68) and, as a result, human beings are subject to economic tyranny. Russell's argument, however, is not deterministic but rather pushes us to radically re-imagine social change because "we are not at the mercy of some 'natural law' but are part of a social order which is by no means fixed, but needs democratizing to offer a counterforce to the dominant market 'society'" (Russell, 1998: 68). Following Russell's urge for us to re-think the centrality of work in the context of our collective emancipation offers us an opportunity to also radically rethink how we understand intersectionality.

Bibliography

Alexander, M (2010) *The New Jim Crow: Mass Incarceration in the Age of Colorblindness.* New York, NY: The New Press.

Annamma, S, Connor, D, and Ferri, B (2013) Dis/ability Critical Race Studies (DisCrit): Theorizing at the Intersections of Race and Dis/ability. *Race Ethnicity and Education* 16(1): 1–31.

Beatty, C and Fothergill, S (2015) Disability Benefits in an Age of Austerity. *Social Policy & Administration* 49(29): 161–81.

Charlton, J (2000) *Nothing About Us Without Us: Disability Oppression and Empowerment.* Berkeley, CA: University of California Press.

Collins, P (2000) *Black Feminist Thought: Knowledge, Consciousness, and the Politics of Empowerment,* (2nd edition). New York, NY: Routledge.

Crenshaw, K (2000) Demarginalizing the Intersection of Race and Sex: A Black Feminist Critique of Antidiscrimination Doctrine, Feminist Theory and Antiracist Politics. In James, J and Sharpley-Whiting (eds) *The Black Feminist Reader,* Malden, MA: Blackwell Publishers, 208–38.

Crow, L (2012) Scroungers and Superhumans: Images of Disability from the Summer of 2012. *Journal of Visual Culture* 13(2): 168–81.

Erevelles, N (2011) *Disability and Difference in Global Contexts: Towards a Transformative Body Politic.* New York, NY: Palgrave Macmillan.

Erevelles, N (2014) Crippin Jim Crow: Disability and the School to Prison Pipeline. In Ben-Moshe, L, Chapman, C, and Carey, A (eds) *Disability Incarcerated Imprisonment and Disability in the United States and Canada.* Basingstoke, UK: Palgrave Macmillan, 81–99.

Malhotra, R (2014) Beyond Wage Labor: The Politics of Disablement. *Tikkun,* 29(4): 43–6.

Mitchell, D and Snyder, S (2003) The Eugenic Atlantic: Race, Disability, and the Making of an International Eugenic Science, 1800–1945. *Disability & Society* 8(7): 843–64.

NYT Editorial Board (2015) How Racism Doomed Baltimore. *The New York Times,* May 9, available online at www.nytimes.com/2015/05/10/opinion/sunday/how-racism-doomed-baltimore.html?_r= (last accessed September 20, 2015).

Oliver, M (1990) *The Politics of Disablement: A Sociological Approach.* New York, NY: Palgrave MacMillan.

Paperson, L (2010) The Postcolonial Ghetto: Seeing Her Shape and His Hand. *Berkeley Review of Education* 1(1): 5–34.

Patterson, O (2015) The Real Problem with America's Inner Cities. *The New York Times Sunday Review,* (May 9): 6.

Runswick-Cole, K and Goodley, D (2015) Disability, Austerity and Cruel Optimism in Big Society: Resistance and "The Disability Commons". *Canadian Journal of Disability Studies* 4(2): 162–86.

Russell, M (1998) *Beyond Ramps: Disability at the End of the Social Contract*. Monroe, ME: Common Courage Press.

Russell, M (2005) Targeting Disability. *Monthly Review* 56(11): 45–53.

Snyder, S and Mitchell, D (2006) Eugenics and the Racial Genome: Politics at the Molecular Level. *Patterns of Prejudice* 40(4/5): 399–412.

Social Security (July 2015) *Research, Statistics and Policy Analysis*, available online at www.ssa.gov/policy/docs/quickfacts/stat_snapshot (last accessed September 20, 2015).

Spillers, H (1987) Mama's Baby, Papa's Maybe: An American Grammar Book. *Diacritics: A Review of Contemporary Criticism* 17(2): 65–81.

Stewart, J and Russell, M (2001) Disablement, Prison, and Historical Segregation. *Monthly Review*, 53(3): 61–75.

Stone, D (1984) *The Disabled State*. Philadelphia, PA: Temple University.

Taylor, S (2004) The Right Not to Work: Power and Disability. *Monthly Review* 55(10): 30–44.

Wacquant, L (2009) *Punishing the Poor: The Neoliberal Government of Social Insecurity*. Durham, NC: Duke University Press.

7 Ramping it up: calling attention to dis/ability at the end of education's social contract

David J Connor and April B Coughlin

Introduction

This chapter focuses upon ways in which Marta Russell's ideas expressed in the iconic text *Beyond Ramps: Disability at the End of the Social Contract* (1998) have influenced our thinking and work within the field of Disability Studies in Education (DSE). In brief, we use the analytical tools that Marta provided us to critically engage with the field of education. We begin by elaborating how her central message to challenge existing social structures is more pertinent than ever in confronting the limitations placed upon children, youth, and adults with disabilities within education systems. Next, we share our own personal insights about the following areas: (1) David's use of Marta's book in teaching courses on inclusive education; (2) his use of Marta's ideas in helping develop key ideas within DSE; (3) April's experiences as a wheelchair-using teacher in public school; and (4) her research on students who use wheelchairs, walkers, and other mobility devices in public schools. Subsequently, we discuss ways in which Marta's ideas that helped originally ground us, continue to influence our ongoing work in DSE as it relates to theory, research, practice, and policy. We conclude by recognizing Marta as a major influence who contributed to paving the way for DSE to challenge the deficit-based master narrative of special education and disability in schools by questioning restrictive notions of normalcy while advocating for accessible structures and systems in the name of social equality.

Outrage at structural inequalities

The first thing we noticed about *Beyond Ramps: Disability at the End of the Social Contract* was its subtitle, *A Warning from an Uppity Crip*. This "in your face" statement serves as a harbinger of Marta's style: unfiltered, unrestrained, provocative. She made no pretense of genteel manners because it would not serve her purpose, as Marta was outraged at the inequalities within American society—specifically in relation to its disabled citizens. This book was her opportunity to describe the world in the way she saw it—filled with glaring discrepancies in how people are (mis)perceived, (mis)understood, and (de)valued—clearly illustrate such discrepancies and the material consequences of them; and suggest ways in which to create a more socially just society.

One of the features that distinguished Marta's work was her critical engagement with issues of social class, an area that is under-addressed in a country that often conflates socialism with communism. To question unfettered capitalism in the USA—and the subsequent effects it has on the entire population—can be seen as irrelevant at best and traitorous at worst. Marta renders capitalist economics, what most people believe to be "the natural order of things," instead as a phenomenon that prizes productivity over humanity, a system that by its very nature is founded on competition, not community, and therefore creates a world of winners and losers. She notes, "[t]o philosopher Descartes, the body was a machine; to the industrialist striving for more profits, people's bodies were valued for their ability to function like machines. The capitalists used labor to generate larger output to accumulate more wealth" (Russell, 1998: 60). A "byproduct" of such a system will always be a sub-population of people who are not needed and/or are unable to execute specific tasks required of a worker, raising the question: what does society do with its "surplus" population?

This question lies at the heart of Marta's analysis of society. It allows her to foreground Social Darwinism, predicated upon Charles Darwin's theory of life, namely "the survival of the fittest" as the natural order of things. Although the concept was developed to describe the animal kingdom, it has also been applied to human society. In sum, those that "make it" do so because of a combination of superior genes, intelligence, and the ability to adapt to function within an environment. Conversely, the rationale for those who do not "make it" can be attributed to inferior genes, poor intelligence, and the inability to adapt and function within an environment. For Marta, this way of thinking justified inhumanity by promoting selfishness and neglect. She writes, "[s]ocial Darwinism provided the business class who controlled the means of production with the justification to leave the surplus population in poverty to die, rather than design an economic system that would accommodate all of society" (Russell, 1998: 65). In contrast, Marta claimed the value of being a humanist. She explained:

> in the humanist view, work is not the defining quality of our worth. Employability and aptitude for earning money are not the measure of what it means to live, to be part of the human race. The goal of social justice is to ensure the dignity of each and every person. To buy into the capitalist propaganda that work is god, that people are laborers first and human beings second, serves only to oppress us all.
>
> (Russell, 1998: 83)

As a disabled person and an advocate of disabled rights, Marta critiqued the notion of "employability" as a primary goal to prove one's value. Additionally, disabled citizens face the contradiction of being denied access to resources and opportunities that lead to employment provided to non-disabled people. The disabled population is automatically viewed as an inevitable part of the "surplus" population, not quite fully human, unable to participate in society, at best a burden and at worst a drain. Thus—despite well-intended laws to protect civil rights—disabled citizens are summarily discounted in terms of employment, social services, transportation, leisure, and so on. Marta notes, "We have only to look at social democracies like Sweden to see how punitive our system is and how badly America fails to meet the basic needs of [all] its citizens" (Russell, 1998: 83).

It is this challenge to existing social structures that incited our interest in Marta's work, and her desire to look both *within* American society and *outside* of it in order to reimagine possibilities for change. Throughout her text, as Marta systematically took on philosophical, historical, scientific, cultural, and legal aspects of disability, we could not help but relate these ideas to our primary field of interest—education. As career-long educators we experience first-hand the structures and systems that limit children, youth, and adults with disabilities. In the following sections, we narrate the ways in which our personal connections to Marta's work have helped us develop as teachers and academic activists.

Using *Beyond Ramps* in teacher education

As a former New York City high school teacher, I (David) worked in the Department of Special Education. I had never experienced "a call" to teach, but rather fell into it by chance—as many people do. However, after a tough first year in which I was told by a student, "Take your flat white ass back to where it belongs," I managed to persevere and grew to enjoy teaching very much. At the same time, I quickly came to realize that I worked in a deeply flawed system. What do I mean by this? For example, I could not understand why: students identified as disabled had to be in separate classes on a separate floor; labels such as Learning Disabled or Emotionally Disturbed were vague and unhelpful; students were not informed of what their label meant; faculty and staff underestimated the stigma associated with "special," a euphemism for "not normal"; a staggering number of professionals "served" a small number of students, many of whom had poor attendance or dropped out; all students in my classes were African-American or Latino; individualized instruction was expected, but rarely delivered; a bifurcated system reified an "us" and "them" mentality between special and general education that influenced both teacher and student identities.

It did not take long to realize that *I* was stigmatized too. There were comments about special educators not being *real* teachers. Teachers in special education openly joked when they made a mistake, "I'm special ed., after all." Some students that were friendly in class would walk by me on the street, fearing identification with a special education teacher. Other students would place their desks against the wall, outside the view of passers by who peered through the classroom door. When I spoke to students, the majority of them wanted to be in mainstream classes with their friends that travelled from the same neighborhoods. All of these things impacted how I came to view the system in which I worked. One of the most interesting developments, however, was the beginning of inclusive classes in which two teachers—a general and a special educator—were paired to collaborate in teaching a class comprised of non-disabled and disabled students. To cut a long story short, I had a positive experience in such classes—and so did students. This fact confirmed my thinking that the vast special education system in which I worked was not justifiable in so many ways. Teaching a diverse body of students could be improved when two teachers worked closely together, committed to problem solving with a view to providing support needed by all students.

Fast-forward several years. I began teaching graduate level teacher education courses in inclusive education. By then I realized that the institution of special education had a monopoly on thinking about the paired concepts of disability *and* education. The foundation of special education was then, as it is now, predicated upon scientific, medical, and psychological knowledge. However, I had grown aware of how these fields always posited human differences as abnormalities, flaws, or deficits that had to be fixed, remediated, or cured. The problem with such a view of disability was that I could not think this way about all of the people I had ever taught and known who had a disability. They were complete individuals as they were. As Simi Linton, another vociferous disability self-advocate wrote, "special education is not a solution to the 'problem' of disability, it is the problem" (Linton, 2006: 161).

I came to recognize that, as well-intended as special education purported to be, it was actually responsible for creating and reifying differences among humans that separated them into two types—the "regular" and the disabled. This binary was also synonymous with normal/abnormal, desirable/undesirable, and unproblematic/problematic. As a gay man, I have always questioned the concepts of normal and abnormal, as the latter had been used to justify positioning gay people as unnatural and inferior in comparison to their heterosexual counterparts. Similarly, I could see how notions of abnormality that were inscribed upon people identified as disabled were equally oppressive, with the potential to create significant psychological damage. Marta's book was one of the first that I read in which the author asked, "Why be normal?" (Russell, 1998: 13).

In her typical style, Marta points out how "'Normalcy' [is used] as a mechanism for social control" (Russell, 1998: 13) and dismisses the status of 'normal' as not only being "overrated" (Russell, 1998: 16) but complicit in the oppression of others. She notes that:

> The danger of the 'normal' construct is that it serves to make disabled people seem *less than human*. When disabled people are not seen as fully human, it is easy to justify continuing inhumane policy towards us, to cut us out of the social contract, even to eliminate us at political will. We become too easily disposable.
>
> (Russell, 1998: 17)

By calling attention to how the idea of what is "normal" becomes ingrained into laws, policies, and institutions, Marta illustrates ways in which these systems operate to deny full humanity to those identified as disabled. Like Simi Linton's classic text *Claiming Disability* (1998), Marta makes a case for "non-normals" to recognize and embrace their affinity, unifying to redress the inaccuracies perpetrated about them and injustices perpetrated against them. As Marta asserts, "[b]eing disabled/impaired is not a negative, not something to be ashamed of, rather it is a shared identity amongst those who have the common experience of being disabled in a world dominated by nondisabled people" (Russell, 1998: 14).

The narrative above is a roundabout way of sharing why, for many years, I used Marta's book as a required text in the graduate class on *Methods to Support Students with Disabilities in Inclusive Classrooms.* Although *Beyond Ramps* does not address education *per se*, Marta's basic philosophical grounding and critical stance of existing societal structures, practices, and beliefs allowed me to use her text as a tool to stimulate discussions around the who, why, when, what, where, and how of educating not just potential teachers, but rather *all* the population about disability. I was able to utilize a pivotal quotation she includes by Thomas Kuhn that reads, "To try to change the outward attitudes and behaviors does very little good in the long run if we fail to examine the basic paradigms from which those attitudes and behaviors flow" (Russell, 1998: 69). These words resonated with me as they reinforced Marta's thrust to deconstruct the seemingly stable base on which current knowledge about disabled people and their "position" in society rested.

Likewise, in education, a number of critical special educators began to embrace the writings of activists and/or scholars in the interdisciplinary fields of disability studies who advocated for different understandings of disability. Using Marta's book in classes of 25 teachers provided great leverage to address the often-contentious issues around inclusive education. Although I am recalling from over a decade ago, I do remember many students being shocked at learning the often-untaught histories of the Eugenics movement. In addition, I also recall their outrage that Marta denounced cultural icons such as Jerry Lewis and Mother Theresa for benefitting from charities that perpetrated stereotypes of the disabled. Above all, I remember when students experienced small—but crucially important—epiphanies when they understood that their *disposition* toward human differences, more than any other factor, influenced the success of all students in their classes. As Marta succinctly stated, "The issue is not what causes disability but the reaction to it" (Russell, 1998: 16).

Developing disability studies in education

Although the interdisciplinary field of Disability Studies had taken root in the 1970s, and flourished in subsequent decades, its intersection with *education* did not formally emerge until the beginning of the millennium (Danforth and Gabel, 2006). It can be argued that Disability Studies was wary of education, given that special education continues to define disability as a deficit, disorder, or dysfunction. That said, critical special educators had been arguing for alternative understandings of human differences in which the label of disability was seen as *created* by beliefs, systems, and structures rather than being something *innate* to be identified and labeled (see Brantlinger, 1997; Danforth and Rhodes, 1997; Gallagher, 1998; Heshusius, 1984; Skrtic, 1995; Tomlinson, 1982; Ware, 2001).

Marta's claim that disability is a social construct was radical for the time, and appealed to critical special educators. In *Beyond Ramps*, she was able to convey the historical and social location of disability—claiming it as a phenomenon that occurs within the dynamics of a cultural context. Marta illustrates how malleable disability can be when she critiques governmental categories that reveal the politics of defining it. She wrote, "[o]ne day you are disabled, the law changes, and the next day you aren't. How can that be? Historically, the definition of 'disability' has been kept flexible precisely so that government could restrict or expand the program in response to economic or political directives" (Russell, 1998: 158). As has been noted before, the fluidity of what constitutes disability becomes apparent when definitions change, such as when the label of "Mental Retardation" was shifted from being an intelligent quotient (IQ) of one standard deviation below the Bell Curve norm (85 IQ cut off), to two deviations (70 IQ cut off), revealing the arbitrary nature of societal decisions (Gallagher, Connor, and Ferri, 2014).

Marta's critiques of society ensured that *Beyond Ramps* was part of a constellation of works (see also Garland-Thomson, 1996; Linton, 1998; Oliver, 1990; Longmore and Umansky, 2001; Barnes, Mercer, and Shakespeare, 1999) that encouraged dissatisfied special educators working within educational systems to establish and develop the growing field of Disability Studies in Education. In portraying disability as a social construct, Marta drew together a body of knowledge that revealed the unarticulated history of people with disabilities, the economic impact of being disabled, and the inadequate response of society-at-large toward disabled people, their rights, and needs.

As part of a group of scholars who strove to articulate the tenets of Disability Studies in Education, influenced by a constellation of DS works, I recall Marta's writing coming to mind as DSE scholars hosted a year-long discussion online to make sure we did the best we could to capture our collective thinking. In reviewing the tenets of DSE, I am unsurprised at how compatible they are with Marta's disposition and politics conveyed within *Beyond Ramps*:

> The tenets of DSE center on engagement in research, policy, and action that:
>
> - contextualize disability within political and social spheres;
> - privilege the interests, agendas, and voices of people labeled with a disability/disabled people;
> - promote social justice, equitable and inclusive educational opportunities, and full and meaningful access to all aspects of society for people labeled with disability/disabled people; and
> - assume competence and reject deficit models of disability
>
> (Connor et al., 2008: 447–48)

Here, there is clear evidence of an alignment of thinking designed to help educators reframe what disability is, and the importance of how they respond to it. Similarly, Connor et al. (2008) articulated examples of approaches to theory, research, and practice in DSE that are compatible with core values expressed within *Beyond Ramps*. A sample of these approaches is shared below.

> Examples of approaches to theory in DSE include:
>
> - Contrasts medical, scientific, psychological understandings with social and experiential understandings of disability.
> - Engages work that discerns the oppressive nature of essentialized/categorical/medicalized naming of disability in schools, policy, institutions, and the law while simultaneously recognizing political power that may be found in collective and individual activism and pride through group-specific claims to disabled identities and positions.
> - Recognizes the embodied/aesthetic experiences of people whose lives/selves are made meaningful as disabled, as well as troubles the school and societal discourses that position such experiences as 'othered' to an assumed normate.
>
> (Connor et al., 2008:,448)

> Examples of approaches to research in DSE include:
>
> - Recognizes and privileges the knowledge derived from the lived experience of people with disabilities.
> - Challenges research methodology that objectifies, marginalizes, and oppresses people with disabilities.
>
> (Connor et al., 2008: 448–49).

> Examples of approaches to practice in DSE include:
>
> - Disability is primarily recognized and valued as a natural part of human diversity.
> - The Disability Rights Movement is studied as part of the civil rights movement.
>
> (Connor et al., 2008: 449)

All of these and other examples convey the sentiment of Marta, as we attempted to "play forward" many of her ideas. At the same time, while it was gratifying to help articulate these tenets to further an academic agenda, we remained acutely aware of the material realities of people with disabilities in society. Such realities are illustrated within the following section in which April shares elements of her own story.

A wheelchair-using teacher in public school

From the age of six, I knew I (April) would become a teacher. I learned early on that when you have a visible, physical disability, you are constantly placed in a position of having to educate and prove to others what you *can* do. This is because of the way society constructs disability as being "less than" or "not normal" (Russell, 1998: 15). Growing up as a paraplegic and "wheeler," I quickly learned that I would have to fight for my rights if I wanted to get anywhere in life. As a high school senior, I had to attend Village Hall meetings as part of the requirement for my Participation in Government class.

When I arrived at the first meeting, I found that the Village Hall and Courthouse were not wheelchair accessible. Naturally, my senior project turned into a letter writing campaign to the mayor requesting that both public spaces be made accessible. Within a year, an elevator was installed and wheelers could finally have their place at the local political table and their day in court. I grew up in a supportive environment where I was instilled with the belief that having a disability meant not only that I *belonged* and was *valued* in society, but also that I could make a difference from a stature of three feet and nine inches, with a titanium frame and four wheels. When I became a teacher in New York City, while attempting to hold the attention of 35 seventh-graders during my first week, I noticed some commotion going on outside of my classroom door between a parent and a teacher. I learned afterwards that the parent had looked into my classroom and said, *"I don't want someone in a wheelchair teaching my child."* A few weeks later, in an effort to try and figure out why my students seemed to be listening to and respectful of their *other* teachers, but not *me*, I approached the topic with my class. One student responded, *"We don't have to show you respect like other teachers because you're in a wheelchair."* Well, there certainly is something refreshingly unique about the blatant honesty of a seventh grader. However, it is important to note that the student and parent in these separate events were *not* related. At the time, I had no idea about the field of Disability Studies, nor had I ever heard of Marta Russell or the concept of ableism. I just knew that I had my work cut out for me, and that work reached *far* beyond teaching English Language Arts.

In my second year of teaching, I encountered a whole new set of barriers. This time they were more physical than attitudinal. I was hired at a high school in New York City that was housed on the third floor of the building. The *good* news—there were two elevators. The *bad* news—one elevator was broken nearly half the time. On a few occasions, *both* elevators were broken and I resorted to teaching my class in the cafeteria, out on the baseball field, or in the auditorium with an inaccessible stage. None of these environments were very conducive to teaching English, especially with all of my supplies still up in my classroom on the third floor.

My school was, however, given a site accessibility status of *functionally accessible* by the New York City Department of Education, which is defined as thus:

> Functionally accessible schools are schools in which an individual with a disability may enter and access all relevant programs and spaces in the building, including science laboratories, library, cafeteria, auditorium, and the gymnasium. In some cases school classes or activities may be relocated to accommodate access. At least one restroom is accessible.
>
> (2014–2015 Directory of NYC Public High Schools: 13)

Interestingly, schools given the site accessibility status of "*not accessible* cannot provide access to all relevant programs and spaces within a building" (2014–2015 Directory of NYC Public High Schools: 13). However, according to the NYC Department of Education:

> Some schools are located in *partially accessible buildings* that do not provide access to all relevant spaces and services in a school. For example, these schools may be in partially accessible buildings and may or may not have an elevator [or] ramp, but may be able to meet limited mobility needs.
>
> (2014–2015 Directory of NYC Public High Schools: 13)

It is important to note here that of the 435 public high schools in New York City, 30 percent of them are assigned the status of *not accessible*. While 70 percent of schools are labeled *functionally accessible*, 87 percent of those schools are housed in *partially accessible* buildings (NYC DOE Accessibility Building Designation, September 2014) and only 13 percent are in *fully accessible* buildings (NYC DOE Accessibility Building Designation, September 2014).

The most problematic finding among these statistics is that for the 2014–2015 school year, six "new" public high schools opened in New York City that are *not accessible*. In addition, from the 2013–2014 to 2014–2015 school year, six high schools went from a rating of *functionally* accessible to *not accessible*. Although New York City does have many schools housed in older buildings that could take years to make fully accessible, creating "new" schools that are inaccessible in 2014 does not seem like the right direction we should be moving in as a society. In sum, in terms of accessibility, in many ways it appears as if time has stood still.

In light of this disappointing finding, allow me to move back to my story to share some things that *can* be achieved. Although I taught English, I suppose I always had a secret disability agenda tucked into nearly every lesson plan. Whether it was starting my classes out with a quick anecdote about a daily disability access issue I encountered, bringing in guest speakers with disabilities, or supplying books to my students that included characters with disabilities, I made sure to constantly infuse disability as diversity and social justice into my lessons. Sometimes this was unintentional, like when we took field trips. In New York City, most schools use the subway for student transport. For my classes it was no different. My students would begin the trip by opening a subway map to plan out our route. Despite the fact that there was a subway stop two blocks from our school, my classes would have to walk four avenues and eighteen streets (about one and three-quarter miles) to get to a wheelchair accessible subway entrance. Rain, wind, snow, or heat, it didn't matter, my students learned first-hand about the limited number of accessible subway stops that the Metropolitan Transit Authority had to offer. Several times, we arrived at our stop and the elevator was "out of service." There was no time to call for the police who would then call the fire department (which is the protocol in New York City) to lift me up the stairs and out of the station. We had a destination to get to! Without hesitation, my students lifted me and my chair up the stairs.

While they could see that our society was in many ways not built with disabled people in mind, they also were not going to let that prevent their teacher from fully participating in every part of it.

My students learned about the need for equality and social justice movements and even took it upon themselves to start their own. When they got tired of having English class in other locations due to a broken elevator, they started a petition to fix the elevator and obtained 300 signatures in one day. As a teacher with a disability, I was in the unique position of being able to educate and empower my students to go out and make a difference and get others to join in their efforts. Instead of a broken elevator being *their [the disabled's]* problem, while everyone else went about their lives and used the stairs, it quickly became *our [both disabled and non-disabled]* problem that needed to be solved so that everyone could get up to the third floor with dignity and be fully included. Marta Russell refers to this concept as "social solidarity" (Russell, 1998: 233), explaining it as, "build[ing] upon mutual respect and support without dismissing or diluting difference. For instance, to move beyond ramps, we must first agree that ramps are indisputably necessary. That would be making a common political 'home,' blending difference into commonality" (Russell, 1998: 233).

After six years of teaching in New York City, I decided to return to graduate school for a degree in Disability Studies. Marta Russell's *Beyond Ramps: Disability at the End of the Social Contract* was one of the first books I picked up. I just had to hear what another "uppity crip" had to say. As I read through, I began to re-examine my own journey with disability and many of the experiences of my "wheeler" friends. I learned the basics such as the attitudes that I encountered in my first year of teaching were evidence of "ableism" and "physicalism" (Russell, 1998: 15), and that the original American with Disabilities Act had been compromised, watered-down and weakened with loopholes to get it passed into law. One area that really resonated with me was when Russell wrote, "disabled people are witnessing a race to the bottom in after-injury care" (Russell, 1998: 179). She stated this in 1998 and when I read it nearly 13 years later, I thought about all of the newly spinal cord injured individuals I meet each year, whose post-injury rehabilitation is cut drastically short and are sent home before learning the basics of self-care or wheelchair mobility. I was reminded of all the young men and women today with spinal cord and traumatic brain injuries who are still being transferred to and "warehoused" in nursing homes for years on end without receiving crucial physical or occupational therapy services. As Russell states, "disabled people are 'worth' more to the GDP [Gross Domestic Product] as a slot in a nursing home bringing in $50,000 a year than we are living in our own homes. The horrible end result is a society that reduces personhood to a commodity, diminishing human dignity and eroding the human substance of the culture" (Russell, 1998: 213).

Marta's book caused me to reflect on the ever-present struggle that continues for equal access to public buildings like the iconic James A Farley federal post office in Manhattan. As of today, the separate "Mobility Impaired Access" (as the sign reads on the door) entrance is only open until 5pm each day and 4pm on Sundays. However, the main *inaccessible entrance* is open until 10pm Monday through Friday, 9pm on Saturdays and 7pm on Sundays. When wheelchair users protested this inequality they were told by the post office, "You'll just have to mail your package by 5pm or find someone to bring the package up the steps for you." This is just one of many tangible examples that support Marta's assertion that "disabled people have not been brought fully into the human race" (Russell, 1998: 229). Above all, the field of Disability Studies and Russell's *Beyond Ramps* provided me with the language and framework to think critically about and describe the inequalities that my disabled comrades and I still experience everyday. They also influenced how I originally conceived of, and shaped, my research.

Researching students who use wheelchairs (and walkers/other mobility devices) in public schools

Much like Marta did, I have years of personal experience with disability as well as the social capital to ensure that my voice is heard when it comes to issues of access and equality. As a teacher, whether it was the need for an accessible classroom, bathroom, parking space, or entrance, I could assert my rights or rally my students to effect change. What led me to my current research and ultimately to pursue a PhD was a moment that occurred day after day. I arrived at work one morning and was greeted with an "out of service" sign on both elevators. As I devised my plan to once again conduct my English class on the baseball field, I saw a group of *students* who used wheelchairs and walkers being ushered into a small, separate room down the hall, in the basement. This not only caught my attention, but disturbed me to my deepest disability-advocate-core. I observed these students being brought to this separate room day after day until eventually the elevator was fixed *weeks* later. No one ever asked why these students were being segregated. No one seemed to be bothered by or care about the fact that these students were separated from their non-disabled peers and forced to miss their regular classes for weeks at a time, simply because of a broken elevator. I began to think about all of the other students with physical disabilities that are put in situations like this across the city at *"functionally accessible"* schools and wondered where *their* voices were in all of this exclusion and segregation. I knew my experiences of disability (in)access from my own *teacher* perspective, but I needed to find out what it was like from the *students'* point of view, particularly from those who use wheelchairs or walkers to move around on a daily basis.

From the interviews conducted, I have gained valuable insight into these students' lived experiences. They have shared stories of two-hour commutes, both to and from school on the "special bus" despite living in the same borough as their school. Many students have expressed not being able to participate in after-school activities because, "[t]he school bus will only come at 3pm and if I stay for an activity I won't have a ride home."

Students have shared descriptions of their daily entrance to the school building, and having to enter through the *separate accessible backdoor*, wheeling over old milk cartons and between garbage dumpsters. They have drawn diagrams of the *separate accessible tables* in the lunchroom where they sit with "the other students that are like me," meaning that they too have physical disabilities. Despite many schools' efforts towards inclusion, these students' first-hand accounts demonstrate that there is still a very present underlying culture of segregation and exclusion when it comes to students with disabilities.

Many students have expressed resistance at being labeled "disabled" or "special ed." and wonder, "Why do we need to have these labels in the first place?" When asked about paraprofessionals, every student has been assigned one, whether they want it or not. When asked what specific things the paraprofessional does to help them, some have responded, "She helps me get my bag off of my chair and get my notebook out." When asked if the paraprofessional does anything else, they responded, "She walks with me to my classes and she gets my lunch on the lunch line." Some students reported trying to "get rid" of their paraprofessional, but are pressured into keeping them, and/or made to feel guilty when told by administration, "Well, if you don't have the para, she'll be out of a job." Students have shared stories of trying to converse with peers in class "like a normal teenager" while their paraprofessional reprimands them publicly for not being on task. All students reported having to rely on their paraprofessional or school staff to use the elevator, which requires key access.

Every student reported having to take "adaptive physical education," which is a separate gym class for students with disabilities. While most describe it as a "favorite part of the day because I feel equal to my other [disabled] classmates" some say that "[t]here's not really much I can do in the class because there's no adaptive equipment."

Hearing these stories, I reflect back on my own experiences as a wheelchair-using teenager in school. I recall being fully included in general education gym class with all of my non-disabled peers and never having a paraprofessional required to shadow me. I recall utilizing my *peers* for assistance in getting my bag off of my chair, moving classroom furniture so I could participate in group work or helping to push me up a steep ramp. I remember having my own key to the elevator in school and being trusted that I could ride it alone. Most of all, I recall the friendships I made participating in afterschool activities, gaining self-advocacy skills to assert my needs, and the administration and teachers ensuring that I had the opportunity to be fully included in everything.

In my research to date, there seems to be little evidence of opportunity for self-advocacy building offered to these students and instead, much dependence being instilled in them by the school system. I cannot help but question what will happen when these students leave high school unprepared to advocate for their rights and face challenges such as obtaining accommodations in college, finding affordable accessible housing, accessing necessary healthcare, experiencing disability discrimination when applying for a job, or having the post office tell them, "[s]orry, the *accessible* entrance is closed, come back tomorrow during business hours."

Marta's legacy: playing it forward

In *Beyond Ramps* Marta articulated what disability-related topics should be part of everyone's curriculum. In terms of history, for example, she informed a new audience about the development and growth of American eugenics that led to Nazi Germany's systematic euthanasia of what was officially described as "useless eaters" (Proctor, 1995). Such dehumanization was not even recognized by legal institutions, as Marta shares a Post-World War II response:

> The Nuremberg court did not view disabled people as equal citizens against whom it would be illegal to commit a crime. The treatment of disabled people by the court was discriminatory; no reparations were ever made to the families of those killed, no one was punished for their murders.
>
> (Russell, 1998: 28)

Generally speaking, her writing calls attention to the *worth* of all lives. She questions the medical establishment's desire to eradicate children with disabilities through the aggressive use of amniocentesis, asking, "What kind of society makes parents believe that having a child with a disability is not an option for them? What kind of culture views disability as a burden placed on society, stigmatizing children who happen to have one?" (Russell, 1998: 50). Marta also rallies against "The Right to Die Movement," because—instead of benevolence—she sees society as, "willing to step in and help a disabled person die rather than provide the means to live" (Russell, 1998: 32). In brief, she brings into focus ways in which society mobilizes to prevent disabled children entering into the world and expedites disabled people's exit. In doing so, Marta questions society's values through its attitudes toward disability, writing, "With neo-Nazism on the rise and with scientists capable of manipulating genes, the primacy of IQ, the production of the perfect baby, and the quest for physical perfection need to be scrutinized" (Russell, 1998: 47). In sum, Marta makes a compelling case for including disability history throughout the curriculum. Failure to do so signals being complicit in continuing to sweep under the carpet what is, in essence, a fascinating, integral strand of our collective history (Baynton, 2001; Kudlick, 2003; Longmore and Umansky, 2001; Stiker, 1999).

In addition to her foregrounding of disability history that should be part of K-12 and college level curriculum, Marta's work continues to influence our way of thinking as we work in the field of education. For example, Marta's demythologizing of what is considered normal, by whom, and for what purpose has led us to unpack the myth of the normal child promulgated throughout educational discourses (Baglieri et al., 2011) and advocate for ways to increase and support classrooms that are accessible to all students (Valle et al., 2011). Although length restrictions prohibit a detailed discussion, we will touch upon ways in which elements within Marta's work continue to offer an important critique of educational theory, research, practice, and policy that impacts all citizens.

In terms of theory, for example, the field of special education continues to be entrenched in deficit-based understandings of human differences that primarily conceives of disability through a medicalized lens of deficit, disorder, or dysfunction that needs perpetual remediation, curing, or fixing (Danforth and Gabel, 2006). Stalwarts of the field are vociferous in their denunciation of alternative conceptualizations of disability to the point of being aggressive and relentless, as well as disingenuous (Anastasiow and Kauffman, 2011, 2012, 2013). However, through the work of Marta and others like her, we have the tools for "talking back" to attempts of institutional silencing by deconstructing the questionable knowledge base on which special education is founded and justified (Gallagher et al., 2014). As Simi Linton has stated in the documentary *Invitation to Dance*:

> If I hear the term 'people with special needs' one more time I want to punch somebody. His needs are not special. His needs for rights for education for living in the community . . . he ain't special. The more they say *that* phrase, the more it seems that the burden is on us to keep up. We must constantly monitor the language that we use and that we use about us.
>
> (Von Tippleskirch and Linton, 2014)

Like Marta, Simi questions the fundamental premise of a "special" or "exceptional" child—and instead views everyone as citizens with needs and rights.

In terms of research, for example, the journals within the field of education are divided into general and special categories, reifying the concept of someone with a disability as a separate type of person. Key special education journals have repeatedly declined to publish works by scholars in DSE who view disability primarily as a social construction located within historical, cultural, and social contexts. Because of the special education field's unwillingness to examine the ideologies of what constitutes "special" (Brantlinger, 1997), a noticeable lack of pluralism in what is recognized as research (Connor et al., 2011), and a sense of maintaining separation and insularity at all cost (Anastasiou and Kauffman, 2011), many critical scholars working within it transitioned into DSE in the hope of changing how disability is conceptualized and taught within education (Baglieri and Shapiro, 2012; Connor, 2014; Ware, 2004).

In terms of practice, for example, gains have been made over the past few decades in regard to making more schools and classrooms accessible for all students (Salend, 2010). However, we note that while concepts such as the principles of Universal Design for Learning and the practice of differentiated instruction are widely known, these are not sufficiently implemented within all classrooms. Recent changes in national and state policy such as the Common Core Standards, Response to Intervention, and mandated Regents Diploma tracks have served to place a strain on the inclusive schools movement because children and youth are penalized if they do not achieve certain academic standards at specified grade levels, therefore not fitting the desired standardized "norm" expected of all children. Marta potently questioned such pulls and pressures, challenging us with a question as pertinent now as it was then, "[w]ill we submit to the insurance company profiteers, the genetic capitalists, and sub-human corporate-driven social policy, or will we create and insist on social policy which is people-centric and assures all, disabled and temporarily-abled alike, the resources to live to our potential?" (Russell, 1998: 55).

In regard to educational policy, this is arguably where changes need to occur in order to ***articulate what should be***—in terms of moving in a direction toward people with disabilities having greater access to all aspects of society. As an advocate of promoting the general welfare, Marta asked: "What if the US practiced an equality of results where every poor person in this rich country—white, red, yellow, black, and disabled—was guaranteed a livable annual income in addition to civil rights?" (Russell, 1998: 142). Using Marta's premise of social concern, we are compelled to ask: what if the US practiced equality in the provision of a quality education to all of its citizens? Furthermore, what if it also ensured all citizens having access to jobs that allowed them to earn a reasonable wage? Issues of social class (Tomlinson, 2013) and race (Ladson-Billings, 2006) are central to these questions, and combined with disability issues, point toward the need for an intersectional approach in understanding the complex lives of all citizens, and the universal right to be included in education as part of all aspects of society.

Some concluding thoughts

Undoubtedly, Marta's work has had a significant impact upon scholars within the field of DSE. She has been a major influence upon both of us and many other educators who continue to challenge the deficit-based master narrative of special education and disability in schools by questioning restrictive notions of normalcy while advocating for accessible structures, systems, and practices in the name of social equality.

Marta's cautionary, caustic words remind us to slice through a contemporary world of individuals seemingly multi-tasking in perpetuity, filling time with vapid amusements and ironically isolating themselves via "social media," lest we lose sight of mobilizing for long overdue changes. She notes that:

> the information society has produced another phenomenon—overload—where the truth is obscured by so much information, disinformation, and holes in our information that it is difficult to make sense of it all, so many just tune out. That effectively thwarts meaningful political action
>
> (Russell, 1998: 234).

Cautioning further, Marta writes, "in addition, we are precariously positioned in a 'society' of consumers, lulled by their products and technology into the drug of entertainment, where meaningful public discourse is not even a topic of interest" (Russell, 1998: 234).

Such powerful comments by Marta haunt us. Why? As teacher educators, we hear our graduate students recognize the undeniable inequities in school policies and practices. However, many also articulate that they can do very little about such things if they want to be successfully evaluated, gain tenure, and manage the myriad of other issues and responsibilities within each day of the job. Still, we take hope in the graduate students we know who realize that they *must* negotiate schools as they are currently configured, are invested in moving toward a more socially just system, and being part of that movement. As Marta has asked, "The essential question is, do we want public relations civil rights or civil rights that deliver?" (Russell, 1998: 123). We argue for the latter, as we continue to advocate for real change within education—and the world at large.

Bibliography

Anastasiou, D and Kauffman, JK (2011) A Social Constructionist Approach to Disability: Implications for Special Education. *Exceptional Children* 77(3): 367–84.

Anastasiou, D and Kauffman, JK (2012) Disability as Cultural Difference: Implications for Special Education. *Remedial and Special Education* 33(3): 139–49.

Anastasiou, D and Kauffman, JK (2013) The Social Model of Disability: Dichotomy Between Impairment and Disability. *Journal of Medicine and Philosophy* 38(4): 441–59.

Baglieri, S and Shapiro, A (2012). *Disability Studies and the Inclusive Classroom.* New York, NY: Routledge.

Baglieri, S, Bejoian, L, Broderick, A, Connor, DJ and Valle, J (2011) [Re]claiming "Inclusive Education" Toward Cohesion in Educational Reform: Disability Studies Unravels the Myth of the Typical Child. *Teachers College Record* 113(10): 2122–54.

Barnes, C, Mercer, G and Shakespeare, T (1999) *Exploring Disability: A Sociological Introduction.* Cambridge, UK: Polity Press.

Baynton, D (2001) Disability and the Justification of Inequality in American History. In Longmore, LK and Umansky, L (eds) *The New Disability History: American Perspectives.* New York, NY: New York University, 33–57.

Brantlinger, EA (1997) Using Ideology: Cases of Non-recognition of the Politics of Research and Practice in Special Education. *Review of Educational Research* 67(4): 425–59.

Connor, DJ (2014) The Disability Studies in Education Annual Conference: Explorations of Working Within, and Against, Special Education. *Disability Studies Quarterly* 34(2).

Connor, DJ, Gallagher, D and Ferri, B (2011) Broadening our Horizons: Toward a Plurality of Methodologies in Learning Disability Research. *Learning Disability Quarterly* 32(2): 107–21.

Connor, DJ, Gabel, SL, Gallagher, D and Morton, M (2008) Disability Studies and Inclusive Education—Implication for Theory, Research, and Practice: Guest Editor's Introduction. *International Journal of Inclusive Education* 12(5-6), 441–57.

Danforth, S and Gabel, S (eds) (2006) *Vital Questions Facing Disability Studies in Education.* New York, NY: Peter Lang.

Danforth, S and Rhodes, WC (1997). Deconstructing Disability: A Philosophy for Inclusion. *Remedial and Special Education,* 18(6): 357–66.

Directory of NYC Public High Schools (2015) 2014–2015 Directory. Available online at: http://schools.nyc.gov/NR/rdonlyres/6EBFAB79-2001-48FA-8680-E494DF2CE20C/0/20142015HSD_FullDirectory.pdf

Gallagher, DJ (1998) The Scientific Knowledge Base of Special Education: Do We Know What We Think We Know? *Exceptional Children* 64(4): 493–502.

Gallagher, DJ, Connor, D, and Ferri, BA (2014) Beyond the Far Too Incessant Schism: Special Education and the Social Model of Disability. *International Journal of Inclusive Education* 18(11): 1120–42.

Garland-Thomson, R (1996) *Extraordinary Bodies: Figuring Physical Disability in American Culture and Literature*. New York, NY: Columbia University Press.

Heshusius, L (1984) Why Would They and I Want To Do It? A Phenomenological Theoretical View of Special Education. *Learning Disabilities Quarterly* 7: 363–7.

Kudlick, CJ (2003) Disability History: Why We Need Another "other." Available online at www.historycoop.org/journals/ahr/108.3/kudlick.html (last accessed October 30, 2015).

Ladson-Billings, G (2006) From the Achievement Gap to the Education Debt: Understanding Achievement in US Schools. *Educational Researcher* 35(7): 3–12.

Linton, S (1998) *Claiming Disability*. New York, NY: New York University Press.

Linton, S (2006) *My Body Politic: A Memoir*. Ann Arbor, MI: University of Michigan Press.

Longmore, PK and Umansky, L (eds) (2001) *The New Disability History: American Perspectives*. New York, NY: New York University Press.

Oliver, M (1990) *The Politics of Disablement*. Basingstoke, UK: Palgrave Macmillan.

Proctor, RN (1995). The Destruction of "lives not worth living." In Terry, J and Urla, J (eds) *Deviant Bodies*. Bloomington, IN: Indiana University Press, 170–96.

Russell, M (1998) *Beyond Ramps: Disability at the End of the Social Contract*. Monroe, ME: Common Courage Press.

Salend, S (2010) *Creating Inclusive Classrooms: Effective and Reflective Practices* (7th edition). Upper Saddle River, NJ: Pearson.

Skrtic, TM (1995) The Special Education Paradox: Equity as a Way to Excellence. *Harvard Educational Review* 61(2): 148–206.

Stiker, HJ (1999) *A History of Disability*. Ann Arbor, MI: Love Publishing House.

Tomlinson, S (1982) *A Sociology of Special Education*. London, UK: Routledge.

Tomlinson, S (2013) *Ignorant Yobs? Low Attainers in a Global Knowledge Economy*. London, UK: Routledge.

Von Tippleskirch, C (Producer & Director) and Linton, S (Producer) (2014) *Invitation to Dance* [Motion picture] USA: Metuffer Films.

Valle, JW, Connor, DJ, Broderick, A, Bejoian, L and Baglieri, S (2011) Creating Alliances Against Exclusivity: A Pathway to Inclusive Educational Reform. *Teachers College Record* 113(10): 2282–308.

Ware, L (2001) Writing, Identity, and the Other: Dare We Do Disabilities Studies? *Journal of Teacher Education* 52(2): 107–23.

Ware, L (2004) (ed) *Ideology and the Politics of (in)exclusion*. New York, NY: Peter Lang.

8 Economy, exploitation, and intellectual disability

Jihan Abbas

We owe much to Marta Russell's scholarship and commitment to exploring how economy shapes the experience of disability. Indeed, her ground-breaking analysis in *Beyond Ramps: Disability at the End of the Social Contract* (1998), and her work that followed, are increasingly relevant as neoliberalism aggressively reshapes disability policy, and in turn, reinforces dominant social constructions of disability that center on economic normality. Of specific concern in this chapter, are the many ways persons with intellectual disabilities have come to be known as unproductive, dependent, and idle, and how these misconceptions have powerfully influenced exclusionary and exploitive employment conditions and policies for this group. When Russell penned *Beyond Ramps*, she noted we were in a time of "extreme corporate domination, where 'the people' are conformed into corporate identities: consumers, clients, target populations, or potential consumers" (Russell, 1998: 8). As scholars, activists, and self-advocates work to bring attention to the many ways economy shapes the lived experience of disability, Russell's insights shed light on the role of these corporate identities in influencing how intellectual disability is increasingly understood and managed through policies and programs. Building on Russell's work, I argue throughout this chapter that intellectual disability and related supports increasingly promote an understanding of inclusion that centers on the needs of the economy, whereby inclusion is understood almost exclusively as an individual's capacity to meet economic norms, even under troubling forms of economic exploitation. This raises critical considerations with respect to how the bodies of those with intellectual disabilities are increasingly sought after as both a source of cheap labor and as poster children promoting problematic forms of "benevolence" for those who exploit them. It is here that Russell's insight into corporate identity most powerfully informs our collective understanding of how economy shapes the construction and experience of intellectual disability. In order to illustrate this process, this chapter will briefly explore connections between economy and disability, critique policy conceptualizations of inclusion that are centered on employment based solutions, illustrate how Goodwill Industries' use of the sheltered workshop practices connects this scholarship to the everyday lived experience of disability, and finally briefly explore how neo-liberal shifts exacerbate this economic exploitation. Throughout this chapter I will draw heavily on the scholarship of Russell as a means of situating these issues within the broader political economy of disability.

The role of the economy and the social construction of disablement

While the role of economy in shaping the construction of disability is well-established within disability studies and political economy literature, it is useful to briefly revisit some of this foundation to help situate Russell's scholarship and also to better understand the role of economy in the social construction of intellectual disability. Historical materialism serves as a critical foundation where disability and economy are concerned. It has been argued that industrialization shaped disability as the rise of capitalism was a powerful catalyst that changed the ways work, social relations, social attitudes, and family relationships were understood and experienced (Oliver, 1990). The underlying assumption within the materialist framework of disability is that the everyday experience of disability oppression becomes more obvious with industrialization (Gleeson, 1999). Indeed, the historical materialist perspective of disability recognizes that since the 18th century, the meaning of work in Western society has upheld values and principles which reinforce the maximization of profit and individual competition for wage labor (Barnes, 2000). Thus, as Russell argues "industrial capitalism imposed disablement upon those non-conforming bodies deemed less or not exploitable by the owners of the means of production" (Russell, 2001: 87). This is not to say that disabled bodies had achieved full inclusion pre-industrialization, but rather to draw attention to the reality that prior to industrialization many disabled bodies occupied spaces that allowed them to contribute based on their own abilities (Stewart and Russell, 2001).

While shifts that took place with industrialization and their impact on disabled bodies are a broad area of study, for the purpose of this chapter and understanding how the social construction of intellectual disability serves the economy, there are two key shifts I seek to highlight: the re-drawing of family obligations that takes place with industrialization; and the importance of the productive individual. As Michael Oliver argues, family and community were the primary sites where disabled people existed in feudal times, yet with industrialization, the gap between work-life and home-life had grown in ways that created cracks that made the growth of segregated institutions possible (Oliver, 1990). Amongst other social shifts then, industrialization led to the segregation of disabled persons from those members of the family and community who could and did enter new and formal forms of wage-labor (Harlan and Robert, 1998). This shift is significant where intellectual disability is concerned, as it powerfully shapes not only policy responses to intellectual disability, but also dominant social constructions of intellectually disabled bodies as idle and dependent. The second important change relates the role of industrialization in moving value away from collective contributions and towards isolated individual endeavors. For example, the capitalist economy required individuals to sell their labor, which was a dramatic change from the collective family and community-based forms of production pre-capitalism (Oliver, 1990). Therefore, the new emphasis on the individual is significant since traditionally the focus was not on the person, but rather on larger social units. Of significance here is how individuals come to be read and valued through the lens of productivity. Of note here are impacts that industrialization had on all disabled bodies. As Russell reminds us, capitalism (and related social policies) equally shapes the experience of disability for workers, those who want to work, and those who do not work (Stewart and Russell, 2001). Where disability is concerned, non-productive bodies came to be viewed as a social problem, which led to policy justifications for removal and segregation (Stewart and Russell, 2001). This is an important development, as it grounds our understanding of non-productive bodies as social problems, and speaks to the foundations of segregated sites as a solution to the "problem" of disability.

With a strong foundation in how industrialization reshaped the experience of disability, political economies of disability have reinforced the important and evolving threads between disability and economy. Circling back to Russell's important scholarship on this subject, we see the importance of identifying the structural problems that underlie the disability and employment debate (Russell, 2002). Here economy must be seen as central to the disability and employment debate, and as such, the kinds of individual interventions and advocacy that have historically failed to advance the disability and employment agenda are seen as unsuccessful because they rely on individual frameworks and tend to ignore structural barriers and the larger political and economic context that fuel marginalization (Russell, 2002). Russell's scholarship is significant here as it is useful in helping to explain how despite advances with respect to individual interventions, like employment rights, disabled bodies continue to experience disproportionate rates of economic marginalization and exploitation.

Thinking about Russell's insight into the importance of corporate identities, the role of disability as a business and the commodification of disabled bodies adds an important layer to the political economy of disability. For example, James Charlton has argued that even though they remain marginal within the workforce, people with disabilities experience commodification through the treatment of their disability as "whole industries have been set up to rehabilitate, transport, educate, house, employ, and service people with disabilities in 'special' settings" (Charlton, 1998: 47). Gary Albrecht, whose work has focused more generally on disability and the rehabilitation industry, has argued that identifying how the rehabilitation industry operates is crucial to understanding the place of disability:

> Furthermore, the specific production, definition, and response to disability in our society has major theoretical and policy implications. The 250-year-old story of disability and rehabilitation in the United States, although interesting and informative in itself, is illustrative of the larger social process by which selected sets of social relationships are judged undesirable, dysfunctional, or deviant and are targeted for intervention. This dissatisfaction with existing social conditions provides the impetus for the development of

> huge market segments within human service industries. Markets are created, products are developed, and profits are made.
>
> (Albrecht, 1992: 28–29)

The business of disability (Albrecht, 1992) has seen a proliferation in government, private, and voluntary sector responses to disability that work to define and address the issue, while at the same time actively creating more disability through businesses and government activities like wars, weapons, and harsh labor conditions (Albrecht and Bury, 2001). Russell's analysis is compelling as it not only draws attention to this exploitation, but also uses evidence of this marginalization, despite contradicting legislative frameworks like the *Americans with Disabilities Act (*ADA), to illustrate the need to have a more layered understanding of this oppression (Russell, 2002). What is appealing in her analyses, then, are the many ways she draws out these inherent contradictions as a means of illuminating oppressions that often go unseen. Through this lens, collective policy responses to disabled bodies are not neutral and benevolent, but rather these interventions are seen as firmly centered on the needs of the economy. Here then, persons with intellectual disabilities who do not work are naturally read as dependent and idle, while those who do work or carry out "work-like" activities (performing normalized economic activities) are framed as productive and contributing individuals. As inclusion as both policy and a process is increasingly framed as dependent on participation in normalized economic activities, persons with intellectual disabilities are increasingly vulnerable to various forms of economic exploitation packaged as a part of an individual's journey towards inclusion.

This is not to say that economic exploitation is a new phenomenon where intellectual disability and policy are concerned, as economic factors have always shaped disability policy. For example, within the institution, unpaid patient labor had a direct and important impact on the internal economy of these sites, as it reduced direct costs associated with paid care and produced outputs needed to maintain these sites (Reaume, 2000). It is important to note the deep roots economic exploitation has with respect to disability policy, in part because this is critical to understanding these important economic aspects, but also because this helps critically engage notions of inclusion and how easily they are made to serve the corporate bottom line. Here there are intersections with Russell's argument that disability, as a commodity, shapes social policies based on market value (Russell, 1998). This is useful to keep in mind when interrogating the concept of inclusion, as through this lens we can see how disability policies, specifically policies of inclusion, are shaped by market needs. While social inclusion, specifically for persons with intellectual disabilities, is generally understood as a process and an outcome (Frazee, 2005), in policy and practice inclusion remains ambiguous and problematic. For example:

> the social inclusion of people with [intellectual disabilities], along with other social groups, has centred on the economic and moral expectation to move from dependency on welfare payments into paid employment, to live

independently of the care system, and to be an active participant in 'normal' social activities in local communities.

(Hall, 2010: 51)

Coupled with dominant social constructions that frame persons with intellectual disabilities as idle and dependent, the tendency to see inclusion along a continuum that moves individuals away from "dependency" towards employment has created policy responses that are inherently economically exploitive. Under neoliberalism, this exploitation is exacerbated, as inclusion as a concept is hijacked and appropriated by corporate interests.

In part, Russell's important critique of sheltered workshops reflects this dynamic. While there are many sites in which the economic exploitation of persons with intellectual disabilities takes place, in this chapter I focus on the sheltered workshop for a few key reasons. First, these sites are actively promoted through policy frameworks to support those deemed "too disabled" to conform to the mainstream labor market. Second, sheltered workshops, often thought of as a relic of the past, are in fact shifting and changing under neoliberalism in ways that are troubling. I will return to this second point later towards the end of this chapter.

With respect to the role of sheltered workshops as a necessary policy response to disabled bodies, which do not or cannot conform to the workplace, much has been done to dismantle this argument. Yet, it has been argued that part of the problem in confronting sheltered workshops is that the nature of these sites allows them to operate both as a human service agency and as a business (Albrecht, 1992). While we will see this in greater detail with respect to Goodwill Industries, much of the argument to maintain these sites rests on the assumption that sheltered workshops provide valuable opportunities and disability-related supports for participants, including a sense of belonging and contributing, job training, and a reduction in isolation. While these benefits have been largely disproven and in fact exist in other human service models that are not reliant on sub-minimum wages, corporate interests masquerading as vital human services have made confronting these sites all the more challenging. With respect to their business function, sheltered workshops generate their revenue through sales and provide wages to their supervisory staff (Albrecht, 1992). The business side of disability services here seems to outweigh the employment interests of the clientele as, in order to operate more effectively as a business, managers often retain workers who are productive rather than helping to facilitate regular employment for these individuals (Albrecht, 1992). Indeed, managers of sheltered workshops are often "reluctant to lose their 'best' workers" (Hyde, 1998: 209). This conflict appears since it is integral to their survival that sheltered workshops gain contracts and raise capital (Elder et al., 1986). As Russell reminds us, "disabled people do promise a cheap source of labor" (Russell, 1998: 137) and the sheltered workshop capitalizes on this.

In keeping with Russell's illustration of the contradictions between the lived experience of disability versus policy and legislative rhetoric around inclusion and rights, it is important to note that sheltered workshops are generally not cost-effective in comparison to other frameworks (Conroy et al., 2010), although proponents will argue otherwise. A recent report by the National Disability Rights Network (NDRN) also outlined the many ways sheltered workshops continue to fail persons with intellectual disabilities as job seekers. Included in their critique of sheltered workshops are the following realities: this labor contradicts existing disability policy, including protection under existing laws; these sites reinforce the segregation of persons with intellectual disabilities in much the same way institutions once did (NDRN, 2011). As well, while employers experience the benefits of this labor, participants receive remuneration that is below the minimum wage which reinforces poverty and excludes workers from the kinds of benefits and protections non-disabled workers receive, and because sheltered workshops reinforce skills that are not transferable, this "training" does not lead to better job opportunities for persons with intellectual disabilities (NDRN, 2011). Furthermore, because of sub-standard wages, sizable subsidies, and their placement outside of the mainstream labor market, agencies that operate sheltered workshops have not been forced to evolve, innovate, or adapt in the same ways other businesses have (NDRN, 2011). There is also a general consensus among participants, academics, and advocates that because of their low wages and inability to "instill hope" there is general dissatisfaction with the sheltered workshop model (Menear et al., 2011). Yet, despite this sheltered workshops remain, and as I argue, are in fact increasingly appealing to policy makers under neoliberal regimes.

The example of Goodwill Industries

While Goodwill Industries has used the sheltered workshop model for some time with great success, recently the exploitive practices of Goodwill Industries in the United States hit the headlines (Adams, 2013). Goodwill promote themselves as leaders in providing "work" for persons with disabilities, yet, using a section of the *Fair Labor Standard Act* (FLSA) from 1938, Goodwill legally pays disabled employees below the minimum wage. The case of Goodwill Industries and how it treats disabled employees is important for a few key reasons. First, as Goodwill Industries is one of the first social enterprises with respect to creating employment for persons with disabilities (Parker Harris et al., 2014), and arguably one of the most successful, they carry a fair amount of authority where the issues of disability and employment are concerned. Second, this serves as a great case study to illustrate the "systemic economic discrimination against disabled workers in [the] capitalist economy" (Russell, 2002: 120). As such, the economic conditions facing disabled employees at Goodwill Industries must be seen not as an isolated occurrence, but rather as evidence of a broader and more coordinated system of economic injustices tied to the corporatization and commodification of disability that Russell's work sheds light on.

Of note are Goodwill's own efforts and support for the FLSA and the impact this has on disability policy and labor rights. For example, in an online policy paper promoting the FLSA as a means of creating employment opportunities for disabled employees, Goodwill positions itself as "North America's Leading non-profit provider of employment training, job placement services and other community based programs for persons with disabilities" (Walling, n.d.: 7). In this same paper, Goodwill Industries defends its use of s 14(c) of the FLSA and argues that these provisions in fact be strengthened. In this paper Goodwill frames these special certificates, that allow employers to pay employees with disabilities below the minimum wage, as a necessary means of supporting the employment and disability needs of those with the most significant disabilities, noting "unfortunately, those with significant disabilities have limited job opportunities, which would be even more limited if not for a special provision in the FLSA" (Walling, n.d.: 1). In the footnotes of this same paper the differences between disabilities that may impact productivity versus conditions that typically do not impact productivity are highlighted. This footnote is in itself of interest as it strongly reinforces a social construction of disability in which disabled bodies are presumed to be dependent, and one in which the lived experience of disability is universally one of idleness. For example, according to this footnote "blindness, mental illness, mental retardation, cerebral palsy, alcoholism and drug addiction" (Walling, n.d.: 4) are all linked to a reduced productivity in the workplace and thus reduced wages are warranted. What is of interest here is how closely this rationale mirrors foundational arguments in disability studies, explored earlier in this chapter, that measure and define disability based on perceived notions about economic capacity. Disability though, and the lived experience of disability, is not universal—there are multiple and layered experiences of disability that are individualized and shift over time and throughout the life course—and these need to be conceptualized separately from one's ability to conform to economic norms. Yet, in its own defense of its policy of paying disabled workers below the minimum wage, Goodwill reinforces these misconceptions as a means of justifying this exploitation. This is not surprising, as this line of reasoning is both popular and publicly palatable. For example, when news of Goodwill's practices recently made headlines, much of the public discourse around this issue revolved around this same justification with many proponents arguing similar variations of this argument that all reinforced the notion that disabled bodies are unproductive bodies and thus these sub-par wages are reasonable. Of note are also the important ways this line of reasoning negates the contributions of disabled bodies both within and outside of the formal labor market. Yet, for proponents of sheltered and exploitive work, there is a fundamental need to separate and mark certain disabled bodies as unproductive based solely on disability status, as this is necessary to continue to exploit this group.

In essence these sub-par wages hinge on the notion that wages should reflect productivity. Curiously, in this same paper the FLSA is linked back to the *National Industrial Recovery Act* (NIRA), which was declared unconstitutional in 1935 (Walling, n.d.). It was the NIRA then that established the notion of "productivity-based wage arrangements through a system of certificates for persons with disabilities" (Walling, n.d.: 4). The notion of "productivity-based wages" would be an absurd argument to make for justifying the economic exploitation of any segment of the population, yet where disability is concerned Goodwill Industries (and others who promote sheltered labor) actively use this same argument as one of their main justifications for this exploitation. This illustrates, once again, how contradictions within employment, rights, and disability discourse demonstrate Russell's important insights into the treatment of disabled bodies within capitalism. While many have rightly argued these wages are a gross violation of the rights of disabled workers, enforcement of these rights is an individual solution that ignores the macro-economic realities of the capitalist economy (Russell, 2002).

Goodwill Industries argues that if employers had to pay recipients of these special certificates the minimum wage, their payroll would skyrocket and additional disability supports their sheltered workshops provide would no longer be possible (Walling, n.d.). While this is often the argument used to maintain these exploitive arrangements, this is a problematic position as the wages of non-disabled bodies are rarely problematized in this same way. Indeed, Goodwill's own disclosure around senior executive wages and benefits illustrates that Goodwill does have the means to handsomely compensate its most senior employees. In fact the 2014 Form 990 reveals that the ten highest compensated employees at Goodwill Industries earned a combined $2,839,855. Given the pay gap that exists between senior executives and disabled employees, there is likely a more pressing conversation needed around executive wages and benefits and how this disproportionate gap may influence the kinds of disability supports Goodwill is able to provide.

It is also important to note that in material justifying sub-minimum wages, Goodwill refers to sheltered workshops as "center-based work centers", while in the footnotes they acknowledge the "pejorative" terminology of sheltered workshops (Walling, n.d.: 4). What is absent from this note is why "sheltered workshops" are pejorative. Indeed, it is not the terminology *itself* that is contemptuous but rather the economic exploitation inherent in these economic arrangements. I draw attention to this because it speaks to how disability exploitation and marginalization are often renamed and rebranded as part of wider efforts within neoliberalism to erase and sanitize disability history and oppression as a means of providing more palatable and modernized narratives that support these inherently oppressive practices.

If one were to believe Goodwill's argument, it would mean that without these special certificates and the sheltered work they enable, there would be no other opportunities for these individuals:

> Without Section 14 (c), people with significant disabilities deemed not qualified to work would be forced to stay at home, enter day habilitation centres (if a space were available) or live in institutions
>
> (Walling, n.d.: 8)

Yet there are alternatives to sheltered workshops. There are also options for disabled bodies to participate and contribute beyond sheltered work and in segregated or institutional settings. If Goodwill Industries were in fact a leader with respect to disability issues, they would recognize and promote these more progressive alternatives. This is not to say that neoliberal shifts are not a worry where disability supports are concerned, but rather to call attention to the hypocrisy of Goodwill Industries implying that without sheltered workshops and the exploitive labor that takes place within them, disabled bodies would experience greater forms of segregation and exploitation. Their solution is to support strengthening the FLSA while at the same time increasing penalties and enforcement. None of this however addresses the fact that disabled bodies are making below the minimum wage for their labor and that Goodwill Industries experiences impressive profits and success because of this exploitation.

While Goodwill Industries serves as an important case study to illustrate the connection between economy and disability, neoliberal shifts in part help explain how such an out-dated and clearly exploitive model persists and thrives. It is here where disability as both a commodity shaping social policy, and the sheltered workshop as an important function of capitalism, can be seen the most clearly. Indeed while often framed as a relic of the past, the recent rebranding and resurgence of sheltered work (whatever names it is given) speak to the importance of situating this labor within the broader political economy of disability. Here we can see how foundational shifts that took place alongside industrialization shaped both work and disability in ways that entrench this exploitation within capitalism.

The productive individual

First, we return to the importance of the productive individual, as the idea that individual worth is directly tied to participation in the labor process is a crucial aspect of understanding the prevalence and power of the sheltered workshop. For persons with intellectual disabilities this is also important, as policies have tended to promote participation as a part of the inclusion process whereby normalized work functions are prioritized over individual needs. Indeed, the "centrality of work to social inclusion and the importance of the income, self-esteem, social links and integration that are thought to occur through employment" (Mitchell and Shillington, 2002: 15) has been reinforced by many policy makers. Yet, there are obvious problems when we associate work with inclusion and conceptualize "non-work" as an undesirable state (Mitchell and Shillington, 2002). This form of policy promotes the false and "largely capitalist-induced" idea that work is a central requirement of membership, a notion that only serves to further oppress (Russell and Malhotra, 2001: 223). Indeed, the emphasis on the labor market through neoliberal citizenship debates has led to the reality for many that a failure to secure a job is a private moral failure (Soldatic and Chapman, 2010). Inclusion should not be conceptualized by policy makers as a process that ends with economic integration, as this leaves individuals who cannot or do not conform to the labor process ripe for exploitation. As Russell so thoroughly outlines throughout her scholarship, within such an unjust and exploitive economic system, disabled bodies are bound to be economic losers. Indeed, as the "corporate solution to disablement ... evolve[s] from the realization that disabled people [can] be made to serve profit because public financing [guarantees] the revenue" (Russell and Malhotra, 2001: 215), there is great incentive to continue to perpetuate exploitive systems and to understand disabled bodies as valued only when they serve the bottom line.

Under neoliberalism, these identities and conditions are exacerbated, as disabled bodies and related services are increasingly evaluated through an economic lens. Karen Soldatic and Anne Chapman's analysis, based on the experience of the Australian disability movement under the Howard government, demonstrate how key pieces within the neoliberal agenda do shape the experience of disability (Soldatic and Chapman, 2010). Their analysis highlights how a strategic realignment of funding through the lens of competition, free markets, and individualism in fact legitimized sheltered workshops (Soldatic and Chapman 2010). Of interest then are links between neoliberal actions and the reframing of sheltered workshops as "respectable" sites (Soldatic and Chapman, 2010). Thus, sheltered workshops are no longer relics of the past, but instead are brought out of the shadows to serve as models for sustainable charitable actions, as is the case with Goodwill Industries. Additionally, in the Australian context, a natural consequence of inviting capital in to shape disability policy allowed for a kind of rebranding that erased the exploitive history of sheltered workshops and instead reframed these sites as forms of "business service" (Soldatic and Chapman, 2010). This process of erasure and rebranding is important to note, as it reflects the shift in discourse and naming around sheltered work that was noted earlier in this chapter with respect to Goodwill's lobbying efforts. Again though, the problem does not lie with pejorative language but rather the exploitive practices that are upheld within capitalism.

Russell's scholarship was also critical of rights-based approaches to questions of disability and equity, as she noted their weaknesses within a capitalist economy as well as the powerful capitalist opposition that has grown persuasive under neoliberalism (Russell, 1998; Russell, 2002). While critiques of rights-based approaches are not unique within disability studies and/or political economy, Russell must be given credit for her early identification of these conditions and their impact on disabled bodies. Of note specifically are Russell's concerns around how rights are conceptualized and mobilized under neoliberalism and what this means in terms of their potential for success. Indeed, as neoliberalism has taken root we see the many ways it has worked to marginalize the disability movement from the broader political process (Soldatic and Chapman, 2010) by reshaping discourse to separate disability supports from the broader disability rights agenda. Through the neoliberal lens then, human rights "are the right and equality to compete, but not the rights to start from the same starting line, with the same equipment, or at the sound of the same gun" (Braedley and Luxton, 2010: 8). Here, there is a fundamental shift in terms of how rights are conceptualized, as under neoliberalism it is not social justice that advances but rather a perpetuation and intensification of injustice and disparity (Braedley and Luxton, 2010). While Russell keenly identified this outcome where capitalism is concerned, she was also able to articulate how these systems perpetuate a focus on micro-level issues rather than a much needed interrogation of the ways in which capitalism promote these injustices (Russell, 2002).

In speaking of the impact of these short-term labor market strategies (a staple within neoliberal policy) it has been noted, "the focus on social rights is 'relegated' to the needs of the market economy" (Parker Harris et al., 2012: 826). Thus, with capital interests driving and shaping disability policy, "participation" is applied in ways that are at odds with human rights frameworks, which address structural change, and instead is being framed as the need for individual change (Parker Harris et al., 2012). What is needed instead, is to answer calls for an "integrated analysis that takes account of the relations among and between markets, sites, families, and communities more effectively and captures the full range of regime effects" (Braedley and Luxton, 2010: 11). Thus, by framing the "problem" of disability as a failure for individuals to find paid work, employment-based policy solutions are promoted. Yet, the success of employment-focused policies rests on a government's ability to make rights and responsibility linkages that reflect that while "individuals may have responsibilities to participate in work-focused activities, the governments have the responsibility to offer programs and supports that will lead to parity of participation" (Parker Harris et al, 2012: 831–32).

The shifts noted above are taking place within a wider context of government withdrawal around services and assistance that has resulted in movement from the state towards the "community" (Chouinard and Crooks, 2008; Braedley and Luxton, 2010). Here, it is no longer the state's responsibility to provide disability services, but instead to support market solutions that address this exclusion. In these new funding and policy frameworks, it is the individual who is tasked with the weight of securing a standard of living with only minimal government support—a reality that has the greatest impact on those who experience the greatest barriers in the market, including disabled persons (Parker Harris et al., 2012). Where sheltered workshops are concerned then, while these wages raise important questions about the violation of the rights of these workers, these wages are also evidence of one of the many ways capitalism is crucial to understanding the economic marginalization disabled bodies experience.

Marta Russell sought to explore the broader political economy of disability in ways that explained why the movement had not made the gains it should have with respect to employment within rights-based frameworks. Through her scholarship she made a compelling case for why equity remained stalled not only within, but because of, capitalism. Her attention to detail and her reminders for us to look at the macroeconomics of oppression and exploitation provide a much-needed foundation for understanding disability oppression. Of specific interest are her observations about both neoliberalism and sheltered work, as these help contextualize sheltered work more broadly, as well as the success of entities like Goodwill Industries. As such, Russell's work is enduring in its ability to help us better understand how persons with intellectual disabilities have been socially constructed through capitalism, how this works to create bodies ripe for economic exploitation, and more importantly, why seemingly outdated and contradictory arrangements persist despite policy rhetoric about rights and inclusion. It is appropriate to end with Russell's own words on a possible way forward where these issues are concerned:

> Perhaps then disabled peoples' struggle for an equal place in the realm of work will be met with the class consciousness necessary to challenge the current disabled unemployment predicament.
>
> (Russell, 2002: 132)

Bibliography

Adams, S (2013) Does Goodwill Industries Exploit Disabled Workers? *Forbes Magazine*, 30 July, available online at www.forbes.com/sites/susanadams/2013/07/30/does-goodwill-industries-exploit-disabled-workers/ (last accessed July 15, 2015).

Albrecht, G (1992) *The Disability Business: Rehabilitation in America.* London, UK: Sage Publications.

Albrecht, GL and Bury, M (2001) The Political Economy of the Disability Marketplace. In Albrecht, GL, Seelman, KD, and Bury, M (eds) *Handbook of Disability Studies.* London, UK: Sage Publications.

Barnes, C (2000) A Working Social Model? Disability, Work and Disability Politics in the 21st Century. *Critical Social Policy* 20(4): 441–57.

Braedley, S and Luxton, M (2010) Competing Philosophies: Neoliberalism and the Challenges of Everyday Life. In Luxton, M and Braedley, S (eds) *Neoliberalism and Everyday Life*, Montreal: McGill-Queen's University Press.

Charlton, JI (1998) *Nothing About us Without Us: Disability Oppression and Empowerment*, Oakland, CA: University of California Press.

Chouinard, V and Crooks, VA (2008) Negotiating Neoliberal Environments in British Columbia and Ontario, Canada: Restructuring of State-Voluntary Sector Relations and Disability Organizations 'Struggles to Survive.' *Environment and Planning. C: Government and Policy* 26(1): 173–90.

Conroy, JW, Ferris, CS and Irvine, R (2010) Microenterprise Options for People with Intellectual and Developmental Disabilities: An Outcome Evaluation. *Journal of Policy and Practice in Intellectual Disabilities* 7(4): 269–77.

Elder, JK, Conely, RW and Noble, JH (1986) The Service System. In Kiernan, WE and Stark, JA (eds) *Pathways to Employment for Adults with Developmental Disabilities.* Baltimore, MD: Paul H Brookes.

Frazee, C (2005) Thumbs Up! Inclusion, Rights and Equality as Experienced by Youth with Disabilities. In Richmond, T and Saloojee, A (eds) *Social Inclusion – Canadian Perspectives.* Winnipeg, MB: Fernwood.

Gleeson, B (1999) *Geographies of Disability.* London, UK: Routledge.

Goodwill Industries Form 990 (2014) available online at www.goodwill.org/wp-content/uploads/2015/05/2014-Goodwill-Industies-International-Form-990.pdf (last accessed July 15, 2015).

Hall, E (2010) Spaces of Social Inclusion and Belonging for People with Intellectual Disabilities. *Journal of Intellectual Disability Research* 54(1): 48–57.

Harlan, S and Robert, P (1998) The Social Construction of Disability in Organizations:

Why Employers Resist Reasonable Accommodation. *Work and Occupations* 25(4): 397–435.

Hyde, M (1998) Sheltered and Supported Employment in the 1990s: the Experience of Disabled Workers in the UK. *Disability & Society* 13(2): 199–215.

Menear, M, Reinharz, D, Corbière, M, Houle, N, Lanctôt, N, Goering, P and Lecomte, T (2011) Organizational Analysis of Canadian Supported Employment Programs for People with Psychiatric Disabilities. *Social Science & Medicine*, 72(7): 1028–35.

Mitchell, A and Shillington, R (2002) *Poverty, Inequality and Social Inclusion*, Working Paper Series. Toronto, ON: The Laidlaw Foundation.

National Disability Rights Network (NDRN) (2011) *Segregated & Exploited: The Failure of the Disability Services System to Provide Quality Work*. Available online at www.disabilityrightstx.org/files/segregated-and-exploited_v18.pdf (last accessed August 7, 2015).

Oliver, M (1990) *The Politics of Disablement*. New York, NY: St. Martin's Press.

Parker Harris, S, Owen, R, and Gould, R (2012) Parity of Participation in Liberal Welfare States: Human Rights, Neoliberalism, Disability and Employment. *Disability & Society* 27(6): 823–36.

Parker Harris, S, Renko, M, and Caldwell, K (2014) Social Entrepreneurship as an Employment Pathway for People with Disabilities: exploring political-economic and socio-cultural factors. *Disability & Society* 29(8): 1275–90.

Reaume, G (2000) *Remembrance of Patients Past*. Toronto, ON: University of Toronto Press.

Russell, M (1998) *Beyond Ramps: Disability at the End of the Social Contract*, Monroe, ME: Common Courage Press.

Russell, M (2000) The Political Economy of Disablement. *Dollars and Sense* 231: 13–15.

Russell, M (2001) Disablement, Oppression, and the Political Economy. *Journal of Disability Policy Studies* 12(2): 87–95.

Russell, M (2002) What Disability Civil Rights Cannot Do: Employment and Political Economy. *Disability & Society* 17(2): 117–35.

Russell, M and Malhotra, R (2001) Capitalism and Disability. In Panitch, L and Leys, C (eds) *Socialist Register 2002: A World of Contradictions*. New York, NY: Merlin Press.

Soldatic, K and Chapman, A (2010) Surviving the Assault? The Australian Disability Movement and the Neoliberal Workfare State. *Social Movement Studies* 9(2): 139–54.

Stewart, J and Russell, M (2001) Disablement, Prison, and Historical Segregation. *Monthly Review* 53(3): 61–75.

Walling, L (n.d.) Employment of People with Disabilities through FSLA Section 14(c). Available online at www.goodwill.org/wp-content/uploads/2013/06/Goodwill-14c-Fair-Wages-Position-Paper.pdf (last accessed July 15, 2015).

9 Autonomism and the disabled and able working classes: a class composition approach to histories of resistance and destructuration

Zach Richter

I. The organization of work and the oppression of disabled people: a missing account in Marxian disability studies

What role does the organization of work during the course of modernity play in oppressing disabled people? Starting with Michael Oliver and going all the way to the later contributions from Marta Russell, an account is offered about how, constituent with modernity, the nature of work became standardized and in turn put many disabled people out of a job.

This chapter brings Autonomist Marxist historiography to the history of disability oppression in order to argue explicitly that the function of innovations in management and the organization of work have set new normative standards that both discipline able workers and mandate disabled sacrifice. Even the pre-Mercantile phase in Western Europe evinced more caring disability relations. The remainder from the feudal era in industrial times, the vagrant, is eliminated not through support, but through mandated work without pay, whose function is to restore value to the disabled advent of modernity and conceptualize the move of disabled people into rehabilitative colonies as a move into mandatory work without pay. When it becomes clear that the working of impaired bodies is not an unusual element of the rehabilitative institutions that contain disabled people, it is possible to conceptualize exclusion instead as dispossession. Then, modernity functioned for disabled people as an incarcerating moment and as a moment where their traditional community treatment and valorization as socialized workers was put to an end. To document the series of reductions from value and mechanisms of appraisal requires getting a sense of how the worker is manipulated by management. Bendix's *Work and Authority in Industry* (1956), a historiography of managerial ideology, is then a prime tool for analysis. An Autonomist Marxist disability analysis is used to read between the lines of Bendix's history and consider how changes in work and management always renegotiated labor so as to devalue disabled labor. It is important to highlight how Marta Russell's writing on organization of work foresaw this chapter's reversed reading.

For over 13 years, Marta Russell's foundational "What Disability Civil Rights Cannot Do" has served as an indispensable rebuttal argument to those celebrating the success of the disability civil rights movement (Russell, 2002). Key in her argument is the idea that the government could not offer full employment as part of the disability civil rights packages produced in the 1980s, in due part, because management and international capital had successfully shifted the economic policy program of the United States toward one that aimed to be supportive of business. Part and parcel of such a doctrine, Russell quotes major economists admitting that wages cannot go up without (what Marx might have called) "a reserve army of labor" to maintain the discipline of current workers based on their fear of slipping into chronic unemployment (Russell, 2002). The conclusion that one must come to from such analysis is the immense yet overlooked power of worker discipline and managerial ideology as a key part of both the oppression of disabled people and the ongoing maintenance of the capitalist class system.

A. Disability and class

While the social model of disability lacks an analysis of labor, much of Marxian thought is similarly unable to think of class in terms that are grounded enough to see past managerial representations of workers' labor power. Theorizing disability and class together means redefining class to be based on a shared economic fate that comes about from a shared appraisal within the managerial organization of work and then redefining disability to mean the negative appraisal of the labor power of impaired workers. This means that instead of limiting disability politics to the individually reduced set of capabilities caused by a disabling society, disability politics is able to imagine a collective set of class interests for its constituents. To conclude, thinking about disability and class together help in understanding the fundamentally capitalist basis for ableist inequality. Disability, when it is framed as a class issue that is explicitly about the appraisal of different kinds of work, is understood as a process of dispossession that occurs parallel with capital's move toward industrial standardization and efficiency.

In such a context, the refusal of work on the part of disabled workers whose labor is valued at next to nothing is not the same as their exclusion from work. Begging or not-working with purpose is and was what constitutes/ed in feudal stages of society a worthwhile way of existing for disabled people. In such circumstances, choosing to embrace positioning as charity due to the hyper-exploitative situation that devalues one's body is an agential move that invokes the class-consciousness of the disabled worker.

B. Towards an autonomist Marxist method in disability studies

In this chapter, the worldview common to Italian Autonomist Marxism is intermixed with Marxian Disability thought. Autonomist Marxism is itself a hybrid. It is considered simultaneously a Marxist and anarchist movement whose theories combined a Marxist focus on labor with an insurrectionist valorization of local resistance to power. The refusal of work that inhabits a crucial place in this chapter is also common to anarchist thought, but not all anarchist thought analyzes labor. Autonomist thought also inhabits a space of sympathy with the politics of identity as demonstrated in its affiliation with Marxist feminism work such as that of Dalla Costa, Silvia Federici and others. I hope to clarify here that Autonomist Marxism is both a set of arguments made by Italian Marxists in the latter half of the past century but also comprised a movement in Italy and a framework adopted by several other movements and types of activism globally (such as the German Autonomen). In the following paragraphs, two separate strands of Autonomist Marxism will be identified based on a division flagged by John Holloway between positive and negative Autonomisms.

Scholars of the Autonomist Marxist faction, such as Wright and Holloway, seem to identify two autonomias, one positive and one negative. Both become useful for a re-examining disability politics in the context of work. The positive Autonomism has had the principle effect of locating, in the developments of proletarian self-valorization, the gaps made by Capital's reactions (Negri, 2005). The negative Autonomism has drawn upon influences from identity politics and post-structuralism to critique the centrality of normative forms of labor and types of workers, resulting in Feminist reformulations of labor (such as Federici's "affective labor") as well as forms of labor more closely related to the demands of student and bureaucratic laborers (Federici, 2004; Bologna, 1972). For all the derision that this wide set of ideas has caught within some circles, it has presented itself simultaneously as a ruthless critique of dominant methods for resistance and a plan for a reconceptualization of the bounds of anti-capitalist thought.

The theory of class composition offered by the Autonomists separate the making of classes into two separate functions: technical and political. The technical refers to a topic brought up in this last section in terms of the contents of what actually makes the class, including the form of labor, the payment, and the positioning as well as the type of work involved. The political approaches levels of unity or disunity within the political classes structuring themselves against the capitalist mode of production. The three sections of this chapter analyze the technical and political composition, decomposition, and recomposition of the disabled and able working classes.

Combining the Autonomist legacy with a disability studies-based methodology will require drawing upon some of the Marxian Disability studies methodologies advanced by such voices as Erevelles and Gleeson. Gleeson calls attention to "chief defects" in historical disability studies analysis in terms of "brevity . . . theoretical underdevelopment . . . and reification (through idealistic tendencies)" (Gleeson, 1999: 23). While this analysis doubtlessly evades the demon of brevity and could easily be argued to avoid theoretical underdevelopment, it is very possible that the Autonomist Marxian disability studies methodology employed here does buy into more than a few idealistic tendencies. However, in an analysis of the disabled working class in the context of the able working class, one can be assured that the tendency toward ahistoricism and thinking of disability in a vacuum has been avoided. Erevelles' analysis on the other hand calls for something this chapter can account for, a historical dialectical analysis of disability in labor. A Marxian basis for disability studies analysis is then open for some of the methodological adjustments this chapter offers in the thread of Autonomism.

The terms of which this historical charting of dialectically entangled labors is engaged is based on the idea that ableness and disabledness, like capitalism, have an emergence point. To suggest that either is novel to industrial capital would be erroneous, but to say that the emergence of disability and ability in capitalist terms was a distinct event and process (composition) is not. My argument goes further to say that the self-valorization of abled workers had to lead eventually to a liquidation process by which the machinery of capital had to resolve losses through dramatic destructuration (decomposition), only to be revived strategically and resimulated as a product in the late capitalist economy (recomposition). Here, transcribed are the terms by which Autonomist thought is able to lay bare the drama of the working class, but unlike the Autonomists, whose subject's most formative moment was in struggle, the disability politic finds its repeated moment to contain domination. The definitional terms of class composition are applied to the development of abled and disabled classes to tell a story of suppression, but in the relaying of a tragic cycle, new pathways open up.

II. Composition

A. Political composition of the disabled class

Foucault identifies what he calls "the great confinement", marked by the 1656 great decree founding in Paris, the Hopital General, an establishment said by Foucault to house "the poor of Paris" (Foucault, 2013: 37). This institution and others of containment, Foucault says, were founded in the "simultaneous competition and complicity between the government and the church" but nearly 200 years later, Reinhard Bendix's analysis begins in the transition between the Feudal era and the Victorian period (Foucault, 2013: 42). While Foucault's work supports the notion of confinement as originating in rehabilitation of moral deficiency, by the early part of industrialization, it has an economic function. Bendix's argument concerning the development of a Taylorist ideology of management points out that early in the industrial era, elites of business, as well as the State and religion, began to worry that begging had become a career (Bendix, 1956: 61). Here, it is posited that the original ideological composition of the class of disability originated in an elitist need to securitize against begging as a job.

In continuity with the arguments of contemporary disability activist Sunaura Taylor's famous article "The Right Not To Work" and in critique of Brendan Gleeson's argument that the construction of disabled people as beggars in premodern times played into social policy narratives about disabled people as perpetually dependent, this chapter argues that the figure of the beggar is a form of working class resistance on the part of disabled people that brought them into existence as a class through proving that it was possible to receive money without working (Gleeson, 1999: 190). Negri's theory of the simultaneity of the self-valorization of one class and the destructuration of another help to explain how, in the same era of the rise of the beggar (the 1700s transition between feudalism and industrialism), capital had to go to great lengths to make unskilled labor productive through automation and the rise of Taylorism. The automation of labor in factory settings represents a quite powerful moment of destructuration as the former merchant and artisan classes upon whose productions mercantile capital was reliant were destabilized, leading to a massive decrease in the pay of such skilled workers and replacing them with unskilled and underpaid laborers, thus effectively creating the blueprint for what would later be done within the Fordist factory.

Sunaura Taylor's "The Right Not To Work" (2004) is used as a central text in this piece because it reveals both the historical context behind the emergence of disabled dependence as the founding composition of the class in capitalism as well as the resistant potentials which capital continually tries to sublate of merely being dependent. Sunaura Taylor notes that in the European feudal era because work was done through the family, disabled people could "contribute what they could" but that with the rise of early capitalism, there was a push for disabled people to fit in with efficiency schedules and to fit into factories (Taylor, 2004; Oliver, 1990; Schweik, 2009). The act of begging, in this situation, became a revolutionary rupture that forced the creation of a new category and would foresee over 100 years of changes to further punish the disabled for this transgression. Sunaura Taylor's advocacy for the right not to work as "the right not to have your value determined by your productivity as a worker" helps to place the presentation of disabled people as beggars as an early example of the Autonomist tactic of the refusal of work (Taylor, 2004). Autonomist Franco Bifo Berardi writes about the intensification of psychopathic behaviors as a symptom of the advance of cognitive labor in his famous essay "What is the meaning of Autonomy today?" (2003). We can refer back to Foucault in recognizing that the condition of not working was to be regarded as the original psychopathy in the feudal age, in terms of the dereliction of the old Feudal duty of labor. Then, the image of the beggar represents a radical negation of work through dependence; a form of self-valorization produced through the unity of medical claims of the truth of impairment and the experiential assertion of impairment by disabled people. It is clear that nearly 100 years of managerial policy may have been made in response to this constitutive moment in the story of work in Capitalist Europe. The negation of work by way of disability may have been the catalyst for exaggerated efforts to separate, institutionalize, and later sterilize disabled people. Further, the very nature of paid labor had to go through a major shift, starting with Frederick W Taylor, such that management could render financial gain from the invisibility and overall non-presence of disabled workers in common working roles (Taylor, 1914).

B. Technical class composition of the disabled class

The institution, it will be noted, offered a way for the resistant self-valorization strategy of the disabled beggar to be recouped by capital in a way that enabled the managerial class to capitalize on the refusal of work by disabled people. In creating a profit-based institution for the warehousing of unco-operative subjects as well as subjects for whom standardized labor was impossible, capital began the process of turning what was originally a rupture into a second-class form of labor, practically an unlabor, in which bodies that could not easily be integrated were in turn reformulated as commodities.

In Foucault's own analysis, the starting point for confinement in the modern era was an important distinction between "healthy poor" and "sick poor" that arrived after the end of the earlier European enthusiasm for confinement in the earlier part of the 1700s (Foucault, 2013: 411). Foucault states, "the difference between the healthy and the sick poor was not simply the degree of their poverty but their nature," then giving separate accounts of the healthy and sick, saying "misfortune . . . can be employed for the profit of the state and to the profit of the individual," but regarding impairment "a mass that one cannot get a grip on . . . a constant hindrance that never helps" (Foucault, 2013: 411). In the formation of this notion of "sick poor" and in the restriction of confinement, which had for a period been applied recklessly, strictly to those with biomedical diagnoses, we see that the power of medicine whose authority is deduced from the former sway of the church, takes on a classing function that designates who is in need of managerial expertise and who is doomed to work not for pay but against the garish weight of impossible impairment.

Once the disabled poor are established to have an origin and composition apart from that of the more typical worker, the next requirement is to understand how the labor of the disabled poor became designed. Foucault spends a great amount of time on the retreat cures thought of by the likes of Tuke. While cures have seldom been regarded as constituting work, it is quite clear that the supposed cures advocated in early modernity by Samuel Tuke involve the instantiation of emotional labor as a condition placed upon the life of the psychiatrically disabled. Here will be reconsidered, a passage in *History of Madness* in which, what Feminists later regard as emotional labor, is used as a restraining device:

> Samuel Tuke recounts the arrival of a maniac at the Retreat, a young man of prodigious strength, whose attacks brought panic to his entourage and even among his guards. He arrived at the Retreat handcuffed and in chains, with his clothes tied on with ropes. As soon as he entered, his fetters were removed, and he was allowed to eat with the superintendents, and his agitation disappeared immediately. . . . He was led to his room, and the superintendent explained how the house was set up for the greater freedom and comfort of all, and that he would never be restrained unless he broke the rules of the house, or went against the general principles of human morality. The superintendent assured him that he had no desire ever to use the means of coercion that he had at his disposal. 'The maniac was sensible of the kindness of his treatment. *He promised to restrain himself.* . . . The superintendent then repeated the threats and promises of the first day, saying that unless he calmed down, they would be forced to return to older means of punishment. . . . After such conversations, the patient was generally better

> for some days or a week.' After four months, he was released from the Retreat, entirely cured. Fear here was directed straight at the patient, not through any instrument but purely by means of discourse.
>
> (Foucault, 2013: 131)

It may be stated that what Foucault describes Tuke as doing is the building of the physical restraints formerly in material existence in the form of an emotional labor that must be done at all times by the patient. The demand of the simulation of normalcy in social performance is a kind of labor because for a person of unusual habits of mind and habits of socializing, to put on an act under threat of physical harm amounts to a daily effort. Arlie Hochschild defines "emotional labor" in her sociological sense as "filigreed patterns of feeling and their management" (Hochschild, 2003: 11). Hochschild offers that waitresses, secretaries, and bill collectors do emotional labor, but she ignores institutionalized people, whose communications with staff and reactions to the world around them must be sterilized to not be punished. While the nature of such emotive labors may seem milder on a moment-to-moment basis than physical work, such as that in a factory setting, it must be done nearly constantly in the institutionalized situation. Worse yet is the labor done in those institutions where actual restraint of one sort or another is practiced; Foucault's revelations here offer a baseline for the type of unwaged labor that institutionalized disabled people must endure.

C. Technical composition of the abled worker

It will be argued here that Frederick W Taylor's ideology of scientific management and use of the time study method of management was in its core essence, a way of deducing surplus capital from the ableness and therefore speed of hired workers. Taylor's attachment of the health of company profit margins to the abilities of employed workers occurs in passages such as those in which the "maximum prosperity" of the company are tied to the "development of each man to his state of maximum efficiency" (Taylor, 1914: 2). The eugenic implications of this discourse are further apparent when "scientific selection" and, in turn, the measurement of what are in various passages called "first rate men," enter the conversation in terms of necessary tasks of the manager. These dictates for managers' handling of working men and for the wider administration of work itself, prove to be exceptionally regressive in conceiving of work as an activity only doable by fit bodies. Further implications for the deduction of profits from the performance of ableness by workers would be the attachment of a prestige of ability (or what could be called a "wage of ableness") to the activity of work and of a sense of shame to workers whose inefficiency excluded them (as much by newly adopted managerial standards as anything else) from the honorable pursuit of labor.

Taylor's time study, which involves checking the movements taken by an employee to perform a small task, represent two separate dissections of human being and lived realities from the diversity of wider contexts in which they occur.

First, the work study is a poverty of temporality, as it reduces the time it takes to complete a task to the smallest possible subdivision, ignoring preparation and how the small task being done relates to the wider world. Second, the work study is a poverty of embodiment, viewing the labor strictly in terms or observable motions, ignoring planning and thinking time. In these two reductions, Taylorist thinking on work approaches a heightened similarity with medical diagnosis, as it observes a subject for a short period of time and draws wide evaluations from that observation. However, instead of spotlight forms of negative difference, the time study spotlights ableness as a generalization based on motion and time efficiency. Similarly, the product is inherently distinct: a positive result in the time study means the change of more money being paid to the worker in question.

D. Political composition of the able class

In Bendix's history of work, in the chapter on Enterpeneurial Ideology, Samuel Smiles is introduced as having authored the managerial creed but also having delivered a popular message about work, in his famous book Self Help (1878) in the 1800s. Smiles' work was originally meant to benefit managers, but due to its optimism, it was used as a template for the thinking being taught to the lower class workers. The content of Smiles' work amounts to a repeated claim about the civilizing nature of work. Another aspect to Smiles' platform is a glorification of self-help. In instilling a concept of work that punished dependence, Smiles' writing provided new guidance to workers that formed discipline out of career risk (Bendix, 1956: 111–13). It can be seen that the self-valorization in Smiles' ideology of management was not entirely averse to Marxists' positions, which place industrial labor at the center of social relations. Representations of the physical power and discipline of what has been called the "mass worker," re-entrench a view of ableness as a prerequisite for existence and elide the value extracted from disabled bodies who, when institutionalized, are dispossessed of personal value as well as property that might be present for the collective and are understood as deficient. Similarly, one can note the sterilization discussed in one of the next paragraphs as a dispossession of legacy.

The composition of the able class is generated in the lack of absolute or universal religious doctrine and the need for a new authoritative ideology for the arrival of factory production. Management as well as entrepeneurs in turn represent themselves in terms of diligence and generate a notion of minimum ableness as a given in successful communities. Through the embedding of work expectations with the more traditional feudal form of duty, Smiles and others encourage a claim of value as a production of bodily effort; in the political view, able work became conflated with personal and collective fulfillment. In turn, through workerism and consumerism alike the political making of able work as a celebrated status was a major driver behind unionization as well as other social reforms. But in the midst of the glorification of work, spokespersons for the able working class are only parroting the counter-revolutionary focus on independence and enthusiasm for self-annihilating labor. It is clear that these values were taught with the direct intention for the message to be offered by the rich to the poor. The political composition of the able class can then be chalked up to the over-valuation of normate bodies accompanied by an amnesia as to the degree society already depends upon the emotional labors of disabled people.

III. Decomposition

Marks, in his thoroughly useful "Autonomist Marxist Theory and Practice in the Current Crisis" offers a concept of the event of decomposition amidst the worker struggle, saying that decomposition consists of "the increasing division, weakness and contradiction among sectors of the class; the blocking of the circulation of struggles and their destruction, negation or recuperation as new forms of capitalist power" (Marks, 2012: 470). Autonomist historians note the Fordist era in general to be a period of decomposition, as labor becomes institutionalized in the United States and Europe. Similarly, disability histories often highlight the Fordist era at the turn of the century for the move forward in eugenics and institutionalization. The goal here will be to detail how the two classes became separate.

A. Political decomposition of the disabled class

Gramsci's section entitled "Americanization and Fordism" goes as far as to argue that Fordism has at its base "the need to elaborate a new type of man suited to the new type of work and productive process" (Gramsci, 2000: 279). While the processes creating this new type of work and man differ subtly based on the localities of Europe and the United States, Gramsci is adamant that "the new type of man demanded by the rationalization of production and work cannot be developed until the sexual instinct has been suitably regulated and until it too has been rationalized" (Gramsci, 2000: 282). In such a quotation and the pages before it, it becomes clear that the Fordist models of industrial standardization are impossible to detach from the eugenic enterprises that went on during the height of their proliferation. In Gramsci's understanding of Fordism, we see the economic basis for the Nazi Holocaust as well as the decomposition of the disabled worker in the United States by way of mandatory sterilization in the early to mid 1900s.

Gramsci's explanation helps to provide the economic rationale for the decomposition of the disabled class of workers and the further extension of the Taylorist ideology whose chief goal was to add greater value to able workers. In the rationalizing ideology of Fordism, there is an undercurrent of Malthusian logic in presuming that the sloughing off of reserve populations will heighten the production and wealth of the existing groups. In the work of Stubblefield, we get a sense that what this decomposition meant for disabled people was the passing, between 1909 and 1932, of statutes by over 30 states permitting involuntary sterilization of disabled people as well as laws permitting state hospitals, prisons, sanatoriums, and other facilities to sterilize their clients (Stubblefield, 2007: 165–66).

The political effect and meaning of sterilization upon a group of people may in fact have a greater weight than the actual act does upon a single individual. The logic leading to sterilization, which had decided that disabled people were of no use due to their ineffectiveness in modern working conditions, would likely have been profoundly disempowering to disabled people at the time. Further, it could not have divided the working class further, offering those out of nursing homes the relative confidence of having valuable genetic traits. It may be useful to consider the broader shadow of these policies in terms of disabled sexuality; after this program was carried out, disabled people would forever have their reproductive choices questioned. The acts of eugenic sterilization of disabled people as part of the Fordist creation of a new more efficient worker would forever re-articulate non-functioning bodies in the modern world as barren of productivity, life and value; as empty husks of failed non-humanity to be experimented on, gazed upon and used.

B. Technical decomposition of the disabled class

In John P Radford's (1991) "Sterilization Versus Segregation: Control of the Feebleminded, 1900–1938," an account is given of "the most visible eugenic segregationist ideology." Radford was describing the colony movement, an innovation in the custodial institutionalization of disabled people. What was distinct about the colony movement was two unusual differences: the colonies were self-supporting through mass agriculture, and were gender segregated. The colonies represent the grossest extension of eugenic ideology toward disabled people, in the form of unique conditions for disabled life: asexual and self-supporting. It will be my argument that the ideology of work employed in this eugenic case is one that views permanent impairment as an embodied monetary debt; this is exactly what Radford notes had been circulating in the political culture and were the thoughts of Galton who "advocated reducing birthrates among dependent populations so as to redress a perceived imbalance of inherent intelligence" (Radford, 1991: 452). The work that disabled people did was then destructured to its furthest extent when Fordist rationalization processes reached an extreme and forced disabled bodies to work to repay their existential debt. What is more, the gender segregation of disabled people represents a devaluation of impaired bodies to the status of mere functionality.

Radford is very clear about the honest economic calculus present in the eugenic agenda. Disabled work in the context of the colony is removed from even the sour parting gift of advancement in role; colony farming might be thought of as bleak and repetitive, with the knowledge of sex segregation, the environment could be thought of to be isolating. It is known that recreation time for such workers was regularly cut if ever present in such institutions. The rest cure of yesteryear is swapped with a work cure; the destructuring of work as a repayment for one's burden and in turn the creation of labors without end. The colony may be perhaps the most extreme example of the Fordist ideology intervening into, but doubtless some of its more extreme symptoms were present in, the wider institutional complex (Harbour and Maulik, 2010). In the Fordist decomposition of the disabled class, what was formerly a labor of rehabilitation became realized as having a stronger financial function. The Fordist eugenic policy was to limit waste, even human waste. In the pre-modern present, duty had still provided a girder that limited economic decision-making; Fordism represented a height of bourgeois innovation and the full dominance of capitalist ideology.

C. Political decomposition of the able class

Bendix's account of the rise of industrial psychology in the pre-World War II period emphasizes the popularity of two main features—testing and behaviorism—in the management style of that period. In the feature of testing, we see the formulation of the job interview, as it would appear in the modern age. According to Bendix, "the individual worker came to be known as a conglomerate of traits that could be measured by tests" (Bendix, 1956: 291). We see then the necessity that appeared was for workers to begin to define themselves based on their skills. The common assumption of ableness that Kumari Campbell references comes to life in this employer–employee formula; in the exigency of industrial psychology, workers would begin being forced to define themselves in terms of their skills (Campbell, 2009). The description of bodily and inhabited, and self-definition by functional attributes that is emphasized by the barrage of testing that became popular in the era of eugenics as well as the industrial psychology, would become in technocratic capitalism, a labor that exists as a precondition to labor. The testing practices innovated within industrial psychology were the origin of mandatory worker self-promotion; the labor of self-presentation would always be highly rewarded, to demonstrate and take pride in ability is to consistently reaffirm the system that relies upon the imagery of efficiency for its self-justification. These processes can be seen to come about in the Fordist era for two main significant reasons: to rejustify the impossibility of a valued life within Western capitalism in refusal of able work and to individualize the worker self-valorization process, so that it becomes incorporated into the very fabric of worker–management relations.

Traces of the behavioral psychology ideology in management are clear but were bracketed by a notion in the 1920s and 1930s, that the affect of workers had to be satisfied. Thus, the move toward thinking about work as an ultimate form of self-expression was born in this period, in part to fill the gap left by the strength of monarchical and nationalist ideas of duty. The positioning of work as an ultimate duty and as a location for the schooling of poor workers by wise managers came into being as a follow up to the Taylorist argument about the health of the worker's connection to the health of the work place. This political restructuring of the able worker or (as is referred by the Autonomists) "the mass worker" appears to both re-valorize able work and able workers and to restructure normate worker agency around a set of verifiable managerially controlled criteria.

D. Technical decomposition of the able class

Bologna's (1987) "The Theory and History of the Mass Worker in Italy," picks up on Gramsci's work in theorizing Fordism, noting that Gramsci's only shortfall is an ambivalence to the politics of technological rationalization of work during the Fordist era. In attempting to account for this gap in analysis, Bologna draws upon the work of Panzieri and questions the celebration of technology within Leninist, as well as trade union, circles, instead coming to the conclusion that during Fordism, "labour power was condemned to perpetual subordination to machinery" (Bologna, 1987). The decomposition of labor during Fordism was not limited to disabled workers, but was part of a dual incentivization and discipline strategy by managers to idealize able work according to smooth integration between labor and mechanization and to define disabled people as an exterior class on their inability to fit such a standard. Further extending the argument made by Panzieri, Bologna is very critical of the tendency by trade unions in the West to accept the conditions put forth by changes in technology. Bologna puts some consideration into how Prohibition laws, known as a principle feature of the American 1920s, served a hyper-Taylorist or perhaps Fordist goal, in ensuring a stability of habits by workers and as part and parcel of the cost-saving efforts made in automation. That unions failed to resist on these issues speaks to their subjection as well as their comfort in not experiencing the greater degree of destructuration by non-able workers.

IV. Re-composition

Brian Marks (2012) describes re-composition in terms of "the increasing concordance of action across a widening diversity of the class, occurring through the circulation of struggles, the transmission of forms of action and thought through the geographical and social diversity of the class" (Marks, 2012: 470). Re-composition will be treated here as a process by which a sub-class has a moment of reawakening. It will be crucial to note here that while the awakening of disability rights in the post-Fordist period does represent a renewed composition of the disabled as a class, that reawakening would be quickly slowed by capital, even as it succeeded in altering the stakes and increasing the survival and life chances of its cohort. As always, in the writing of this chapter we are obedient to Negri's gadfly: that every composition by one group is accompanied by a destructuration of another.

Within the Mayoist ideology of management, the goal is always to pursue extra-efficiency through worker co-operation. In such ideology, intensive communication, both between managerial personnel, workers and management as well as between workers is placed at a premium. As part of this new ethos for American workers, Mayo intended for emotive tensions to play a figural role in organizing worker behavior and ensuring worker productivity. In Mayo's open pursuit of co-operation as a managerial ideal, impression management becomes a principal aspect of the labor of the workplace. As a result, workers whose impressions are less under their control and workers whose impressions contained a sense of weakness or debility, took on an altogether different type of employment risk: the risk of being misread (Bendix, 1956). Overall, the social method used by Mayo replaced and innovated upon the Taylorist approach to measuring worker labor through placing informal social indicators over a more measurable task-based orientation. It is also notable that the social method allowed for better adaptation to a service-focused work environment or a work environment oriented more toward what the Autonomists referred to as immaterial labors, such as those involving the use of information.

A. Political re-composition of the disabled class

The political re-composition of disabled people as an independent section of the working class that could campaign for its own access needs began at least in the Western world in the 1970s. The website of the British group "Greater Manchester Coalition of Disabled People" offers a view of how the UPIAS or Union of Physically Impaired Against Segregation formed initially as a consumer group that viewed its identifying shared trait as political neutrality and stood largely against the repression that was unique to physically impaired people. In creating what disability theorists would later call "the social model of disability," the struggle of UPIAS was reactive in a way that the actions of Ed Roberts also were reactive. Both Roberts and UPIAS spearheaded a movement not toward the word disability but away from and out of institutions—an effort that had already begun according to Fleischer, in the 1950s (Fleischer and Zames, 2012). It is then important to the argument about the re-composition of the disabled class that it was not the triumphalist agenda of passing the *Americans with Disabilities Act* (or anything related to "disability rights") that recomposed what are now called disabled people—it was the movement for survival and freedom outside of institutions.

Deinstitutionalization for disabled people carries a historical resonance; it had been thought that the only way that disabled people could live without being subjects of state charity was as beggars. The disabled beggars as it was, had struck fear into the managerial class because the disabled beggar revealed a class of worker who could survive entirely on the auspices of duty alone. To free the disabled person from the institution would be to re-invoke this specter. The concept of independent living was then likely introduced as a bridge to soften this blow; instead of recognizing that disability, as a concept, requires interdependence, an ideology of independent living left the atomized capitalist notion of individualism stable.

B. Technical re-composition of the disabled class

If we are to regard deinstitutionalization in terms of a series of tricks of compensation achieved by impaired people to escape the institution, than a united crip counter-public may view it not as a moralism of parents and professionals, but as its own influence. While this series of tricks may have involved quite a bit of agency and political consciousness on the part of such people, they could in no way be understood as performed independently. In fact, the re-composition of disabled people as a class could only happen through the language of other re-compositions (and following recuperations). Fleischer notes that pioneering accessibility activist Ed Roberts learned from working with women's liberation organizations as well as meeting with Native American activists like Leonard Pelletier and black activist Stokely Carmichael (Fleischer and Zames, 2012). Through using the language of minority, it became possible for Roberts to move a struggle that would perhaps otherwise be misunderstood into an already understood lexicon. It is perhaps a mark of this remarkable ease that the work done initially by Roberts would become the major labor of the recomposed disabled class in the post-Fordist era. Self-advocacy or the labor of making necessary plans so that a given disabled person can fit into a given space was after Roberts' triumphant work of forming a CIL (Center for Independent Living) outsourced onto the disabled community, so that in every gap where disabled people would not otherwise be present, one group would have to do the emotional labor of making it possible to occupy the able-bodied spaces. This set the precedent for the *Americans with Disabilities Act* whose regulations are not enforceable without the outsourcing of access work onto disabled people. Judith Heumann, a once disability rights activist who found her calling in the career of state bureaucracy, is enthusiastic about this development in unpaid (and sometimes paid) labor, saying in Fleischer's quotation: "disabled people know what disabled people mean and want" (Fleischer and Zames, 2012: 41). The underside of this response was that it was only given after an unnamed bystander (conjured for the sake of dialogue by Heumann herself) mentioned the number of "rehabs" compared to standardized professional rehabilitation industries. The notion of the independent living center as pioneering the exchange of emotional labor for accessibility is then hardly shocking; a part of the political re-composition of the disability politic would mean the taking on of rehabilitation and normalization by a handful of well-connected disabled people and private stakeholders. An underside of the founding of the centers for independent living would be the further privatization of care. It is not surprising that the therapeutic sciences had a massive expansion in professionalization during this period. The response of capital to disability rights is to position deinstitutionalization as a mechanism for the private commodification of care and access.

C. Political re-composition of the able worker

Following the slow end of the Fordist era, a managerial ideology written by Elton Mayo and oriented around emotions became popular. Elton Mayo's thinking on management would be consistent with a set of wide spanning alterations to the concept of labor in the time period known as post-Fordist. The Mayo worker could not be convinced either by the efficiency calculations of Taylor nor by the behaviorist incentives of Fordism. Mayo's thinking on work was highly linked to the clinical professionalization of disciplines like psychology that would become prominent during the late Cold War period. It was Mayo's suggestion to have workers meet for interviews with someone in the employ of management who would help them to be rid of their personal thoughts and emotions. The Mayo School of Management played a major role in emphasizing social ease as a major factor in employment as well as founding the new corporate department known as Human Relations.

What Mayo's thinking would mean for able work would be the definition of social ease based on self-representation. It was now a worker's job primarily to make impressions properly and manage social interchange. The able worker was defined then according to Mayo as one who could relate to other employees; gone in this model were the factory discipline standards, gone also, was the conceptualization of work in terms of muscle and sweat. These workers would have to cope with an economy based on service. Then in the world of Elton Mayo, the wages of ableness were shifted into a praise of things like well-roundedness and flexibility as well as the obvious trait of reliability (Mayo, 2003). Autonomists detail this change on technical grounds in their work on concepts like "immaterial labor" and "the socialized worker."

D. The technical recomposition of the abled worker

Autonomist thinkers such as Negri and Lazzarato have already offered some basic foundations as to the technical composition of work in the post-Fordist period. In Toni Negri's "The Mass Worker and the Social Worker," one of the chief differences between the post-Fordist emotive worker and the mass worker is that the temporality of productive time is expanded outside of the rigid confines of hourly labor and social time becomes productive time. Implicit in this concept, from a disability perspective, is that the endurance to manage extended socializing without faltering, is positioned as a necessity for the able worker. In turn, the technical skill of the able worker must imply a nearly endless enthusiasm for this productive social work. Lazzarato's analysis, on the other hand, of what he refers to as immaterial labor, has more to do with how post-Fordist creative work requires the successful creation of social relations envelope workers themselves, in Lazzarato's language it "creates the ideological and cultural environment of the consumer" (Lazzarato, 1996: 5). In other words, the technical re-composition of the able worker means their taking on of a self-managerial role by way of their ideological labor.

The able worker as a member of a sub-class with distinct labor power gets its power through the attribution to it of powers of endurance and flexibility in the post-Fordist world. To be an able worker is to be able to represent ideology without wavering in body or losing the composure associated with a sane or clear-minded delivery. The able worker in their immaterial labor is gifted with a lasting temporality. Perhaps for Bifo Berardi, this gift is a fading one. Is the gift of self-management a license for the abled worker to make gestures toward ideological sabotage as the most optimistic bourgeoisie thinkers suggest? Or is it just a technology to get the laborer even more wrapped up in the labor, to the point that the body of the worker once more decomposes around the concentration of the senses instilled by the new ideological work?

V. Conclusion

In this chapter, I make a prolonged argument that instead of actually excluding disabled people from labor, managerial ideology's move of disabled people into pathology was a total dive in the value of disabled work and that rehabilitation as an industry forces disabled people to do certain kinds of work for free. In Western tradition, the pauper is socially valorized, so capital had to react against the commons and re-describe the disabled beggar as a burden. I place modernity at its basis as a reaction in the West against more communalist notions that supported the presence of disabled people in wider society without viewing them as disturbing to greater social impulses. Likewise, the reconfiguring of the classes pending the modern uniquely liquidated disabled bodies in terms of an array of moves toward institutionalization, sterilization, and eugenic population management. Finally, in the Mayoist phase, the emotional labors of the pathologized as well as more normative social labor associated with preserving face and seeking employment doubly exclude disabled people as therapeutic regimes both threaten and enable more normative work organization requirements.

An overall goal has been to confirm both Marta Russell's key recognition of the organization of work as an *a priori* force in limiting the possibilities of the impaired as well as to further elaborate Sunaura Taylor's positing of the right not to work as a resistant historical subjectivity. Negri's theory of the simultaneity of the self-valorization of one class and the destructuration of another help to explain how, in the same era of the rise of the beggar (the 1700s transition between feudalism and industrialism), capital had to go to great lengths to make unskilled labor productive through automation and the rise of Taylorism. The automation of labor in the factory setting represents a quite powerful moment of destructuration as the former merchant and artisan classes upon whose productions mercantile capital was reliant upon were destabilized. This led to a massive decrease in the pay of such skilled workers and replaced them with unskilled and underpaid laborers, thus effectively creating the blueprint for what would later be done within the Fordist factory. With the occurrence of the final step in the move of destructuration toward removal of more formal processes of worker management in favor of management by informal social status, the destructuration of modernity is taken to its ultimate conclusion and management is expanded. In the past paragraphs, I have considered in depth the ways in which the precedent begun by modernism has undone the care system that benefitted disabled people in traditional modernism and how modernity has systematically dispossessed disabled people of their labor value to the gain of the abled population. The continuation of this analysis will consider how the digital age either stops or continues this trend.

Bibliography

Bendix, R (1956) *Work and Authority in Industry: Managerial Ideologies in the Course of Industrialization*. New Brunswick, NJ: Transaction Publishers.

Berardi, Bifo Franco (2003) *What is the Meaning of Autonomy Today. Republicart.net.* Available online at http://republicart.net/disc/realpublicspaces/berardi01_en.htm (last accessed October 31, 2015).

Bologna, S (1972) Class Composition and the Theory of the Party at the Origin of the Workers Councils Movement. *TELOS* 1972(13): 4–27.

Bologna, S (1980) The Tribe of Moles. *Italy: Autonomia—Post-Political Politics.* In Lotringer, S and Marazzi, C (eds). New York, NY: Semiotext.

Bologna, S (1987) The Theory and History of the Mass Worker in Italy. *Common Sense.* Available online at https://libcom.org/library/theory-history-mass-worker-italy-sergio-bologna (last accessed October 31, 2015).

Campbell, FK (2009) *Contours of Ableism*. Basingstoke, UK: Palgrave Macmillan.

Davis, LJ (1995) *Enforcing Normalcy: Disability, Deafness, and the Body.* London: Verso.

Federici, S (2004) *Caliban and the Witch: Women, Capitalism and Primitive Accumulation.* New York, NY: Autonomedia.

Fleischer, DZ and Zames, F (2012) *The Disability Rights Movement: From Charity to Confrontation.* Philadelphia, PA: Temple University Press.

Foucault, M (2013) *History of Madness.* London, UK: Routledge.

Gleeson, B (1999) *Geographies of Disability.* London, UK: Psychology Press.

Gramsci, A (2000) *The Antonio Gramsci Reader: Selected Writings 1916–1935*, Forgacs, D (ed.) New York, NY: New York University.

Harbour, CK and Maulik, PK (2010) History of Intellectual Disability. In Stone, JH, Blouin, M (eds) *International Encyclopedia of Rehabilitation.* Available online at http://cirrie.buffalo.edu/encyclopedia/en/article/143/ (last accessed October 31, 2015).

Hochschild, AR (2003) *The Managed Heart: Commercialization of Human Feeling, Updated with a New Preface.* Berkeley, CA: University of California Press.

Holloway, J, Matamoros F and Tischler S (2009) Negativity and Revolution: Adorno and Political activism. *Adorno and Political Activism*, 1.

Lazzarato, M (1996) Immaterial Labour. In *Radical Thought in Italy: A Potential Politics, 1996* (eds) Virno, P and Hardt, Minneapolis, MN: University of Minnesota Press, 133–47.

Marks, B (2012) Autonomist Marxist Theory and Practice in the Current Crisis. *ACME: A International E-Journal for Critical Geographies* 11(3): 467–91.

Mayo, GE (2003) *The Human Problems of an Industrial Civilization.* London, UK: Routledge.

Negri, A (2005) *Books for Burning: Between Civil war and Democracy in 1970s Italy,* Murphy, T (ed) and Bove et al. (trans.) London: Verso.

Negri, T (1988) Archaeology and Project: The Mass Worker and the Social Worker. In Negri, T (ed) *Revolution Retrieved: Writings on Marx, Keynes, Capitalist Crisis and New Social Subjects (1967–83)*, St. Louis, MO: Left Bank Books.

Oliver, M (1990) *The Politics of Disablement: A Sociological Approach.* Basingstoke, UK: Palgrave Macmillian.

Radford, JP (1991) Sterilization Versus Segregation: Control of the 'Feebleminded', 1990–1938. *Social Science & Medicine* 33(4): 449–58.

Russell, M (1998) *Beyond Ramps: Disability at the End of the Social Contract.* Monroe, ME: Common Courage Press.
Russell, M (2002) What Disability Civil Rights Cannot Do: Employment and Political Economy. *Disability & Society* 17(2), 117–35.
Schweik, SM (2009) *The Ugly Laws: Disability in Public.* New York: NYU Press.
Smiles, S (1878) *Self-help: With Illustrations of Character, Conduct and Perseverance.* New York, NY: Harper & Brothers.
Stubblefield, A (2007) "Beyond the Pale": Tainted Whiteness, Cognitive Disability, and Eugenic Sterilization. *Hypatia 22*(2): 162–81.
Taylor, FW (1914) *The Principles of Scientific Management.* New York, NY: Harper.
Taylor, S (2004) The Right Not to Work: Power and Disability. *Monthly Review* 55(10): 30–44.

10 Disability community, policy, care and empowerment: "growing up" at MDA camp and the shaky social contract

Suzanne Stolz

No elevator

In 1989, as a 14 year old in rural Kansas, I faced a decision that I often recall when I consider my own progress as an activist. As I prepared to transition to secondary school, my IEP (Individualized Education Plan) team discussed what accommodations I would need at the local high school. My mother voiced her concern that, with a summer hip surgery scheduled, I would enter school using a wheelchair and would be unable to walk upstairs to the second level of the school. And even when I'd regain the strength to walk, the crowded stairways would be treacherous. A school representative suggested that I attend a school that had a special program for disabled students, 13 miles away. Having had the advantages of mainstream education with children from my own community up to that point, I refused to consider any aside from my local school and I told the team I no longer wanted an IEP either. I had come to see those meetings to do more in separating me than including me. That summer, my parents worried about how I would navigate the school. When my mother asked the school to install an elevator, the school district was reluctant and told her it would cost $60,000. "Do you think we should push it?" she asked me.

I imagined how it would play out . . . my parents demanding the installation, the financial burden on the district, and the reaction of the community. I imagined that all of the "trouble" would be just for me and would be attributed to me. I did not imagine how many others could benefit from an elevator. Although I was certain about my right to attend the school, I did not want to be a burden or be viewed as one. "No, let's not push it," I conceded.

Without the elevator, I completed my ninth grade lab science class without a lab and on my own in the counselor's office. After regaining the strength to walk, I did take classes on the second floor and cannot adequately measure the energy I used to negotiate stairs on crutches or to "make nice" with the peers who carried me and my books to class.

With its clear warning that neoliberal policies limit and work against the general welfare of disabled people, Marta Russell's writing and advocacy push us to be conscious of how our lives are manipulated by social and economic policy and to demand changes that lead to universal access. The still-prevalent view that disability is an individual medical issue serves to prevent, or at least delay, the demands of the disability community in a number of ways. It silences voices who have been taught to believe they are the only one, that their full participation in community is just not feasible or reasonable. It allows those in positions of power to justify exclusion. And it furthers society's conception of disability as burdensome, unacceptable, and pitiable.

In reflecting on the ways in which social and economic structures described in Russell's work have impacted my own life trajectory, I will explore how "growing up" at MDA Camp helped me to think about my place, my needs, my rights, and my responsibilities as a disabled woman. In this, I will critically problematize and synthesize ideas and efforts to support empowerment through community mentoring, acknowledging interdependence and challenging conceptions of disability.

Empowerment within sites of tension

Maton (2008: 8) defines empowerment to be, "[a] group-based, participatory, developmental process through which marginalized or oppressed individuals and groups gain greater control over their lives and environment, acquire valued resources and basic rights, and achieve important life goals and reduced societal marginalization." Asserting that empowerment is both a process and an outcome, his review of literature finds six main characteristics of empowering community settings.

The six characteristics are:

1. A group-based belief system that is strengths-based
2. Core activities in which members are productively involved
3. A relational environment that offers support, care, and a sense of belonging
4. An opportunity role structure open to the diversity of members' skills and interests
5. Shared leadership, talented and empowered, who can serve as role models
6. A setting maintenance that responsively handles conflict and change

(Maton, 2008: 8)

Thinking about my own process of empowerment, I question: how is it that I, as a teenager, had the agency to refuse being bussed to another school and to refuse an IEP and still felt unworthy to demand the full access of an elevator? Still in progress, I found myself in community settings that lacked some of the characteristics of empowering settings. How often do perfectly empowering settings really exist? Can settings have disempowering and empowering qualities? Many of the settings I've experienced have some empowering characteristics even while situated within oppressive systems. Many forces are at play, including forces that counter and question the status quo. Often, conflicting ideologies act in extremely close proximity, creating sites of tension that can illuminate the struggle that comes with empowerment.

Russell devotes a chapter of *Beyond Ramps: Disability at the End of the Social Contract* to "collisions" between the civil rights and charity mentality. In this, she sheds light on the duplicitous nature of organizations like the Muscular Dystrophy Association (MDA) in the way they claim to support disabled people while profiting from the exploitation of those same people. Russell describes MDA as a "cure charity" (Russell, 1998: 84) that perpetuates stereotypical images of disability while its telethons use pity to raise millions of dollars, some of which goes towards researching cures and some of which covers high salaries of top executives.

In this section, I reflect on my experience with MDA and consider the consequences of the conflicting ideologies within a community formed by a "cure charity." I consider mentorship and its potential to influence the possibilities we, as young people, saw for ourselves.

MDA camp as a site of tension

Ironically, many young people who attend MDA summer camps find their first experience of disability community within this setting. For me, my involvement with MDA was a significant site of tension during my formative years, as it helped me connect with disabled peer mentors and form community but also caused great discomfort in being misrepresented, patronized, and eventually discriminated against.

Malhotra and Rowe (2014) considered the role of segregated camps in the experience and identity formation of disabled youth and found that the majority of participants in their study did not see the need to challenge the lack of inclusivity. Interviewees who had attended camps described positive experiences like "sailing in a flat-bottomed pontoon boat which had been equipped with a ramp to allow children in wheelchairs to wheel on and off" (Malhotra and Rowe, 2014: 105) and having a "vacation from the otherwise everyday needs for advocacy" (Malhotra and Rowe, 2014: 110). Like the participants in their study, my peers and I did not question the segregated nature of the camp. In fact, the connection with other disabled youth, something I didn't have elsewhere, and the ease of participation is why I continued to return.

At age 10, I was selected to be the State of Kansas Poster Child for MDA, a position I was convinced was an honor. In this role, my family and I began to support fundraising efforts, appearing at Harley rides, Skate-a-thons, and the annual telethon. On camera, I was bashful and compliant, and somewhat unsure about the celebrity status. Around this time, I had also begun to attend MDA Summer Camp where I quickly made friends with other disabled children. Going to the telethon became a reunion of camp friends, eager to share more time together. We stayed up all night together, laughing, joking, and feeling a sense of belonging.

As we grew up together with camp and the telethon, we paid a price for membership in the MDA community. We tolerated the TV crews and interviews in which they asked, "Can you tell us about the day-to-day struggles you have?" and "Why do you love camp?" The film clips used on the telethon showed us in doctor's offices, with physical therapists, and in a very "special" and segregated setting of the camp. The lives depicted were overshadowed with sadness, and camp was viewed as the one good thing these kids had, thanks to the generosity of volunteers and the good people who gave money to MDA.

As teenagers, we confided with each other about the sick feelings we had when we returned to school and our classmates said they had seen us on the telethon. These narrow representations would help shape the way our home communities and our peers understood us. Our attempts to share stories that gave a fuller story of who we were never made the cuts that aired on TV. Ignoring the cost, we continued our involvement.

The time with our disability community provided us with access we hadn't found elsewhere. Within each other, we saw images of who we could grow to be. We found ways to value ourselves. At the first camp talent show I attended, I remember my feeling of surprise when I watched one of the older girls, dressed like a rocker, lip sync with such precision. She was beautiful and talented and I wanted to be like her. I had never before thought that about a disabled person.

The camp talent show and other activities gave us opportunities to perform and to lead. We created skits, organized groups, and recruited participants. Some of us joined a "camp committee" that met several times throughout the year to help plan the upcoming camp.

In each other's company, we also acknowledged our sexuality in ways we couldn't in our home communities. Openly, campers and attendants hugged, kissed, and flirted. The ritual of goodnight kisses brought male attendants into our cabins when we were tucked into bed. Likewise, female attendants visited the boys' cabins. We were encouraged to take dates to camp events and posed for photos as couples. However, we embraced a heteronormative and ableist sexuality in that the dates encouraged were between girls and boys, disabled campers and nondisabled camp volunteers. Most of us understood these dates to be an "act," nothing that would lead to a real relationship. Expectations for more could not be taken seriously. When some girls expressed ideas like "he might like me," some of us thought they were foolish. In general, campers had crushes that did not go anywhere; attendants had legitimate relationships. Among the girls I befriended, a preference for nondisabled partners was standard. We had either internalized our lack of value or fought against the idea that we should only date "our kind." And still, this limited view was a giant step above the lack of access to open sexuality we had in other spaces. Even the best of my friends at school often left me out of conversations about sexuality. In my home community, I felt a strong sense that I could not be a viable partner.

Within this disability community though, we could be more open to express our desires, to acknowledge experiences of oppression, and to address topics related to life and death that our nondisabled peers were not concerned with. A somewhat reserved student at school, I became a leader at camp, quick to share my ideas and apt to volunteer. The structure of the camp ensured that everyone had access to companionship and friendships thrived. In this space, we did not fear how our association with other disabled people might impact our perceived value.

Of the organizational characteristics Maton (2008) describes as empowering, the first three may be used to the highlight the strength we found in the MDA community. The group-based belief system focused on the organization's medical research goals of treating and preventing neuromuscular diseases and on families' need for support. Even though this belief system promoted the idea that cures would be the ticket to ultimately make life better for us, it also valued each of us as worthy participants in a common cause. The core activities of the telethon and camp productively involved all of us in fundraising and in recreation. And most importantly, we found caring relationships and a strong sense of belonging.

Critiquing the system

Despite our love for this experience, MDA camp was not a utopia all the way around. Along with the charity structure of the organization came a patronizing set of policies by which the camp was run. This provided an active text through which we, as preteens and teens, could together "read" and critique a system that oppressed us. In some cases, the community of shared experience and peer mentorship validated us enough to evoke activism.

One of the main critiques we made was in regard to the dichotomy established between "campers" and "attendants." Similar to the reification of differences created by special education (see Connor and Coughlin, Chapter 7), the differences at MDA camp were made clear. Campers were disabled; and, attendants were nondisabled, in theory. Each camper was assigned their own attendant who in some cases served as companions and in some cases served as personal care givers who helped with showering, dressing, and toileting. Unpaid volunteers, attendants were supposed to be at least 16 years old, but in special circumstances, were as young as 14, remarkably young for the responsibility of personal care-giving.

Policies were communicated during the attendant orientation; so as campers, we received the information secondhand in bits if attendants deemed it important for us to know. As young children, we accepted this hierarchy as the natural order of the camp. We accepted that all campers had a rest period each day while attendants went swimming or fishing without us. We begrudgingly accepted the much earlier bedtime set for campers and listened with envy when attendants returned whispering about who liked who, who had held hands, and who had kissed.

Some camp policies encouraged us to view each other in medicalized ways. The camp nurse required shower charts and BM charts to be hung in each cabin and expected attendants to track when campers had bowel movements. Pointing to roots in the mid-1800s, DasGupta (2015) describes the history of medicalizing disabled people as serving to classify and commodify bodies in growing capitalist systems "with productive bodies distinguished from those that were considered less productive or nonproductive" (DasGupta, 2015: 120). At camp, the public display told us our privacy was not respected and that our bodies needed to be monitored in ways other bodies did not. Some of us accepted the practice as something that perhaps other campers needed, even though we did not. We resisted creatively one year, posting an over-sized BM chart with the names of camp staff at the entrance of the dining hall. In Chapter 9 of this book, Richter describes society's "managerial ideology as a key part of . . . the oppression of disabled people" eventually leading to the confinement of disability to certain spaces, which is eventually what happened when some of us pushed against the ideology that limited us to acting in narrowly-prescribed nonproductive roles.

Camp was spoken about as "the campers' week," as if the other 51 weeks of the year did not belong to us really. The intention was to encourage attendants to make campers feel special and to feel as though their desires were priority, within certain G-rated limits anyway.

As teenagers, we became concerned though about what was being communicated to our attendants who were now our same-age peers and we began to fight against previously-accepted policies. Having recruited our nondisabled siblings and friends to come to camp as attendants, we asked for reports about what was said in orientation and in meetings. One year, camp leaders told attendants they should not "overstimulate" campers. Annoyed at the message that we had to be handled in a medicalized way, we mocked these rules and co-opted the term "overstimulate" to bring attention to our sexuality. Another year, camp leaders told attendants not to "lead on" campers. Comprehending that we were not expected to be recipients of genuine affection, we mocked this as well. Understanding that the camp rest period and early bedtime for campers excluded us from spaces with less adult supervision in which our nondisabled attendants more freely exercised sexual expression, we became aware of how social structures further distanced us from opportunity.

Building on the work of Foucault, Allan (1999) found that many practices used within special education often serve mainly to control and constrain disabled students. At MDA camp, we faced similar practices that required us to be in certain places within strict timeframes, allowed for hierarchical observation of our bodies, and set normalizing judgments, particularly around sexuality, that could shame anyone from behaving in certain ways.

In fighting the structures, we first pushed against being restricted by the rest period. Through negotiation, we changed the expectation that campers must be on a bed during rest period to one that allowed free movement between the rooms of our cabins and then to one that gave us space to congregate in the dining hall. We argued that our attendants could still take a break and we would attend to each other as needed.

The bedtime practices were harder to change. One senior counselor cried because she felt that our complaints about the bedtime showed that we didn't appreciate the work she had done, in the way oppressors in hierarchical systems sometimes react when challenged. A few of us violated our curfew by sneaking out, one or two at a time. Once outside the rules of bedtime, we still were not fully a part of the after-hours activities; and still, this ability to resist was meaningful to us. When evening activities ended, we lingered in spaces until we were escorted back to our rooms. Slowly, we loosened some of the restrictions and saw that together we could change an oppressive system.

The critiques we made call into question the reality of having the strong *relational environment* that can contribute to empowerment. How did we feel such a strong sense of community while we were viewed through a medical lens as a different population? Possibly, our sense came from believing the intentions of camp leaders were good, and that while they viewed us as different, they still valued us.

Our critiques also reflect the absence of a good *opportunity role structure*. As disabled people, we had a particular role to fill; nondisabled people filled other roles. We demonstrated our resistance to the strict role structure by mocking the staff's medicalized treatment of us and by breaking curfews. Because camp staff members were all nondisabled, many of us felt unrepresented in the *leadership*. However, the camp director began to understand that allowing some of us to serve in leadership positions as role models and mentors could be beneficial. She provided space for us to make changes.

During my later teen years, I participated more in camp planning meetings, began leading activities, and serving in the capacity of a volunteer rather than as a camper. With the maximum age for campers at 21, I escaped banishment. I became a unit leader, one who oversees one group of campers and attendants. At our camp, I was the first wheelchair user to be given the role and I saw it as a way to change the conceptions of what it means to be campers and attendants. One of my friends, also a wheelchair user, was allowed to serve as an attendant. For several years, we continued to fill various staff positions. In positions of power, we offered more flexibility to campers than we had been given. We took down the public BM charts. No longer were there spaces or time periods exclusively for the nondisabled. While the majority of volunteers were still nondisabled, young campers were able to see progress and feel represented. We felt good about being adult role models; we could give campers something we had not seen ourselves.

Disability as safety hazard

While our presence as staff members shifted practices and gave us some sense of empowerment, the underlying charity framework of the national MDA remained and eventually expelled us from serving at the camp. In 2002, MDA executives decided it was not beneficial to have disabled volunteers at camp. When we learned about the new policy, I sent an initial letter to the camp community:

> *Dear Friends,*
> *It has come to my attention that a major problem that will greatly affect our camp has been brewing. MDA now has a policy that says a camp volunteer must be able to "evacuate a camper" in case of emergency. The new camp application requires that volunteers can "lift and physically care for" a camper. Basically, this means a number of current volunteers will no longer be welcome at camp. Under this policy, Gina, Nick, Carla, and I (as well as others) will not continue to serve as sports director, newspaper staff, senior counselor, etc. This will also most likely prevent any current campers from growing up to serve as volunteers in the future. Here's the kicker . . . it seems Amber and Nancy in the Wichita*

office are supporting the change. Our camp director, Kim, has argued against this rule; but, the decision lies in the hands of those in positions above her.

Apparently, people in MDA's decision-making roles do not understand how volunteers with disabilities can contribute to making camp a great place. You've seen and know from firsthand experience how vital these volunteers are. Obviously, some do not understand our camp and do not realize the value of providing for campers role models, persons with disabilities who have a lot to contribute. Some do not see the value of a volunteer beyond the person's ability to lift weight.

As you can imagine, after years of volunteering myself and recruiting my family and friends, I am angered by the thought of all of this. I have spoken to Gina and Carla; and, none of us are ready to give in to this load of crap. When Kim expressed her concern about trying to plan a camp without us, one person at the office suggested that we could still be a part of camp by doing the pre-camp planning. What a joke!

We do have a plan and need your help. The first thing we will do is bombard the local and national offices with phone calls and letters, telling them what we think of this policy. We're starting this now. Feel free to tell them you heard about it from me. Tell them it's wrong, that it better change. If that does not take care of it, we will make this a public issue that would most likely have a negative impact on donations to MDA. Yes, we're serious about this because it means so much. Please forward to anyone I missed.

(Stolz, 2002)

With the letter, I intended to inform volunteers and families of the proposed change, to point out the value of having disabled adults participate at camp, and to request support. The response to my letter illustrated tensions created within a charitable framework when those being "served" step outside of submissive roles. Because MDA has relied on pity as a fund-raising technique, their interest in continuing the guise of our helplessness was shared by a number of families and individuals. One mother wrote, asking us to avoid making the issue public:

Remember, you would be hurting those who need help most, and not those who are in the position to change this policy. I will look into this ASAP. Please feel free to contact me, but PLEASE, PLEASE, PLEASE don't make any rash decisions about not giving or supporting our local MDA chapter. I would hope we could get this resolved quickly and without impacting the good work MDA does for kids, adults and families all year round.

(Stolz, 2003)

She did not want us to jeopardize the reputation of MDA as an organization that supported and cared for the best interests of disabled children and adults. In the same way that we, as young people, tolerated our exploitation in order to have the community, this mother asked that we tolerate discrimination in order to maintain the funding that provided medical support, medical support that was denied by many families' discriminatory insurance policies. Another long-time camp volunteer and family member of mine wrote to me telling me I should "grow up" and stop being selfish and ungrateful. He suggested that I accept the discriminatory policy and be quiet. If not, I would be viewed as one of the "ungrateful crips" (Russell, 1998: 86) who refuse to express thankfulness to those dear people who only mean to help.

The lack of support from some members of the community hurt and made us more aware of the divide within a group we had always called "family." However, the support we received told us that we were valued as contributors.

> *This is a bunch of bullshit. Camp is more fun with you guys there . . . I just can't see camp without you and Gina and Carla and everybody. I'm thinking if you guys can't go then I don't think I will go. I love seeing you guys . . .* (teenaged camper)
>
> *Growing up with a disability, I knew there were many things I could do, but I didn't have disabled adult role models to look up to and learn from. The kids who go to camp now are extremely lucky to have disabled adults with careers and real lives to look up to and learn from. I was clueless going out into the world on my own as a young adult and would have loved to have spent time with disabled adults that could lead me in the right direction.* (former camper)
>
> *I accompanied my daughter countless times at banks, airports, Dr. offices, when tellers, receptionist or brace makers address me instead of Suzanne simply because she is in a wheelchair. As a school teacher, she has been told that she commands less rights and respect because she is in a wheelchair. That physical disabilities reduce people's effectiveness as a valuable and able worker is the mindset of our society today. That has to change. I ask that you work with us to change that discriminatory mental attitude.* (my mother)
>
> *Where should I send my complaint??? I'm behind you guys 110%!!* (camp volunteer)
>
> *I'm confused, is this a local rule or a national rule? It appears to me to be something that totally disregards all the work you guys have done. . . If you could, please email me back with the scoop as far as whose rule this is, why it came about, and why all your years of service apparently don't mean crap. I'm not happy.* (camp volunteer)
>
> *This is a bunch of crap and will make what ever phone calls or letters to get this resolved, keep the e-mails coming and will let you know what I hear. Tell Suzanne we are behind her 100% I cannot begin to tell you how mad this makes me.* (financial supporter of MDA)
>
> (Stolz, 2003)

The positive responses we received acknowledged the importance of role models, the work we had contributed in planning, societal attitudes about disability, and confusion about why the change had been proposed in the first place. Taking these concerns to the local, regional, and national levels of the MDA, we failed to change to minds of those in positions of power. Representatives at the national office continued to argue that having adults with disabilities serve as activity leaders created a safety problem. Using post-September 11 discourse, they said the organization needed to be prepared for an emergency; and in an emergency, they would need all volunteers to be able to physically lift and carry campers in an evacuation. Our pleas to MDA's National Task Force on Public Awareness, who had publicly supported the enforcement of the ADA, revealed their positions as figureheads who could do nothing to sway the real policymakers within the organization. The local camp director argued against the policy as well, and subsequently was fired for not supporting it.

The fifth and sixth characteristics Maton (2008) counts as important in empowering settings, leadership and capacity to handle conflict and change, somewhat apparent at a local level, proved absent at the top of the hierarchy. While the camp director and a group of community members pushed to maintain the improvements we were making at the camp, they lacked the authority to challenge the higher-level executives in the MDA. Similarly, the same folks had the capacity for maintaining a responsive setting, but were prohibited from doing so when executives created a policy in direct contrast to the needed change.

Not covered under the ADA

Although the letters, phone calls, and community meetings did not prompt the MDA to change the policy, they did encourage us to fight for our rights to volunteer alongside nondisabled volunteers. Having served as role models to the young people at MDA for eight years, Gina Bauer and I were determined to continue setting an example, one that refused to accept a lesser place in our society. At the time, unaware of criticism of the ADA's "extraordinary limitations" (Russell, 1998: 109), we were hopeful.

Claiming unlawful discrimination under the ADA and the *Kansas Act Against Discrimination*, Gina Bauer and I filed a lawsuit against the MDA as our last effort to overturn the policy. The judge ruled that "as adult volunteer counselors at a summer camp for children, Plaintiffs were not covered under Title III of the ADA" and even if they were, the requirements to lift and carry "did not amount to unlawful discrimination because the criteria were necessary to fulfill the primary purpose of the camp and to ensure its safe operations" (*Bauer v Muscular Dystrophy Association*, Inc, 2003: 4). We were not protected because volunteers are not considered as intended beneficiaries to services of an organization. The judge also accepted the safety narrative, finding it reasonable to consider our presence a threat to the safety of the camp.

When the District Court sided with MDA, we followed the advice of our attorney and appealed the decision. The US 10th Circuit Court of Appeals upheld the decision, citing heavily from the testimony of MDA executives who had spent little, if any, time at camp. The final decision stated that we "were invited to participate in the camp program in other ways" (*Bauer v Muscular Dystrophy Association*, 2005: 8) and instead filed the lawsuit. Of course, this portrayed us as ungrateful and unreasonable cripples who could not be satisfied with a participation that would only be possible from a distance or within some imaginary world. How dare we understand what real participation is and expect it!

Although we did not bring the suit under Title I, the employment section of the ADA, it was considered in the discussion. A number of employment cases were cited to clarify that employers were not required to shift duties of positions to other employees if someone was unable to perform a function (*Bauer v Muscular Dystrophy Association*, 2005: 8). This was to point out that accommodating a worker by shifting the duty to lift campers to other capable workers was beyond expectation of the law. In the eight years prior to our exile from camp, two different camp directors had done just that. They had gladly made adjustments in order to make use of everyone's varied strengths, going well-beyond the expectation of the law. Most of us had come to view this as an acknowledgement of our interdependence and simply the right thing to do. In a review of the case, Attard (2006) argues that the ADA should in fact cover disabled volunteers and allow us to "enjoy the benefits of total participation" (Attard, 2006: 1101). She pointed out that the court did not consider benefits in having us at the camp:

> The benefits of having a positive role model with muscular dystrophy acting as a volunteer and caregiver outweigh the irrational fear that the plaintiffs could not react properly in the event of an emergency. The court instead accepted the MDA's contention that its stringent criteria were necessary for the camp's proper operation. Using a scare tactic, the camp exaggerated the potential benefits of the policy.
>
> (Attard, 2006: 1102)

While the benefit of positive role models and mentors is rarely questioned, the failure of the court to consider this likely stems from out-dated and still common views that disabled youth have medical and physical needs, but not social and learning needs. The outcome of the lawsuit taught me that a caring and determined community promises much greater integration than the ADA does. And unfortunately, that same community can be ruined rather quickly, especially when good practices are not backed with legal policy or with strong leadership who can create policy.

My MDA community today

The overall critique Russell (1998) makes is that capitalist systems turn disabled people into a commodity from which others can profit; this commodification, often disguised as care, serves to limit and often deny disabled people from having power over their own lives. She identifies MDA as one organization in this system in that the exploitation of disabled people becomes the mode of fund-raising to support the salaries of executives and a work force that minimally supports those they claim to be beneficiaries. In the MDA community I knew, tensions arose as some of us resisted the oppression created by the structure and others saw care, whether restrictive or not, as the primary need of disabled individuals. Among those using the social model of disability, care is often viewed as something that is disabling (Beresford, 2008), and a barrier to empowerment. Considering both feminist and disability perspectives, Watson et al. (2004) propose a more nuanced approach to care that recognizes that everyone has needs and will require care and support at different times and stages of life. Accepting this notion, Keyes, Webber, and Beveridge (2015) argue that care and empowerment can support each other in contexts where interdependence is acknowledged. With shared understanding that all people are dependent on others in some way, care does not have to be disempowering. Unfortunately, many folks who fought against having disabled adults volunteer at our MDA camp struggled to understand this interdependence and could only view us as receivers of someone else's care.

In 2003, many of us did not return to camp; some of us were not allowed; some refused to participate anymore. The local MDA lost their camp director, assistant camp director, about half of their long-time volunteers, and even a number of campers. Those trusty volunteers who could not in good conscience leave the organization without physical labor attended the much smaller camp and reported that it "just wasn't the same."

In the years that immediately followed, those who left during the schism planned reunions to keep connected; but the hurt feelings that resulted from people choosing to support MDA or to support those of us who had been excluded lingered and left us questioning who really was part of the "family."

Five years later, inspired by what we had been fighting for, several families and volunteers started the FUSE Foundation, completely separate from MDA, established "to provide opportunities for social networking, recreation and education for young adults with neuromuscular disease" (Fuse Foundation, 2015). The organization hosts events throughout the year, including a four-day retreat every summer. While their intention is good, the nondisabled board of directors has carried over much of the same social structure that we found oppressive at MDA camp. Although most of the disabled folks attending are now adults, they are called "campers," and regardless of support needed, each is paired with a nondisabled "attendant."

Conclusion

Marta Russell's work illustrates the complex ways in which political and economic structures limit and work against the general welfare of disabled people. She calls for systemic change that requires citizens to make demands of their governments. Although we who experience disability have intimate knowledge of how these structures impact our lives, empowerment to change conceptions and systems is not easily attained, especially when we are taught to view disability as an individual medical issue. In such imperfect community settings, in which elevator access at a high school is absent and certain groups are denied participation, mentorship is one avenue for educating our community, illuminating shared oppression, supporting empowerment, and formulating solutions. In this chapter, I have shared my experience in "growing up" at MDA camp to be, not dutifully accepting of a lower position, but instead to be making real sense of the social structures that have impacted my own life trajectory and that of others.

Aside from attending one Fuse Foundation event as a guest speaker when I had finished my dissertation, I have chosen to remain largely uninvolved in anything connected to MDA, still interested in the people, but unwilling to trade my dignity the way I did as a child and teenager. Although we worked to blur the lines between disabled and nondisabled, the dichotomy still exists; and, the idea that care is one-way, given charitably from the nondisabled, continues. I am privileged at this point to have found disability community outside of MDA and Fuse groups, among those who value the realities of interdependence, and therefore do not have the same need I did back then. Without faulting those who still make the trade, as we all must negotiate getting our needs met, I do sometimes question, "How can they stand it?" I suppose my years of study have heightened my sensitivity to ableist structures. And by living in California, my geographical distance has allowed me to dislocate easier. And perhaps I felt more wounded than others in fighting MDA's policy change and am just unwilling to be at ease with the tensions that forever surround charity-based programs.

Maton (2008) does not claim that an empowering community setting must have all six of the identified characteristics. My experience with MDA tells me that even charity-based programs can establish, intentionally or unintentionally, some of these characteristics; and even while their overarching ideologies come in conflict with empowerment, the benefits of these characteristics cannot be denied. Civil rights models and charity models exist and compete within the same spaces. While our positions as volunteers were denied, we were strong enough to make it public and to file a lawsuit, fighting against structures that medicalize and constrain our bodies. The ADA's devilish details could not protect us from discrimination; but, the law's intention did give us hope in affirming our expectation to fully participate.

Rejecting the notion that disability is a safety hazard, we moved on to mentor, serve as role models in other settings, and largely to lead lives we chose to live.

Bibliography

Allan, J (1999) Foucault's 'box of tools'. In *Actively Seeking Inclusion: Pupils with Special Needs in Mainstream Schools*. London, UK: Routledge, 7–17.

Attard, L (2006) "A Price on Volunteerism: The Public has a Higher Duty to Accommodate Volunteers," *Fordham Urban Law Journal*, 34(3): 1089–110, http://ir.lawnet.fordham.edu/ulj (last accessed August 25, 2015).

Bauer v Muscular Dystrophy Association, Inc., 268 F.Supp.2d 1281 (D.Kan.2003).

Bauer v Muscular Dystrophy Association, 2005 WL 2902588 (10th Cir. (Kan)).

Beresford, P (2008) *What Future for Care?* New York: Joseph Rowntree Foundation.

DasGupta, S (2015) Medicalization. In Adams, R, Reiss B, and & Serlin, D (eds), *Keywords for Disability Studies.* New York: New York University Press, 120-121.

Fuse Foundation, available online at www.fusefoundation.net (last accessed 20 August 2015).

Keyes, S, Webber, SH, and Beveridge, K (2015) Empowerment Through Care: Using Dialogue Between the Social Model of Disability and an Ethic of Care to Redraw Boundaries of Independence and Partnership between Disabled People and Services. *ALTER, European Journal of Disability Research* 9: 236–48.

Malhotra, R and Rowe, M (2014) *Exploring Disability Identity and Disability Rights Through Narratives: Finding a Voice of Their Own.* London, UK: Routledge.

Maton, K (2008) Empowering Community Settings: Agents of Individual Development, Community Betterment, and Positive Social Change. *American Journal of Community Psychology* 41: 4–21.

Russell, M (1998) *Beyond Ramps: Disability at the End of the Social Contract.* Monroe, ME: Common Courage Press.

Stolz, S (2002) "Camp Plea," Email (December 11, 2002).

Stolz, S (2003) "Dear task force on public awareness," Personal letter (January 10, 2003).

Watson, N, McKie, L, Hughes, B, Hopkins, D, and Gregory, S (2004) (Inter)Dependence, Needs and Care: the Potential for Disability and Feminist Theorists to Develop an Emancipatory Model. *Sociology* 38: 331–50.

Part III

Marta Russell and the humanities

11 Deafness as linguistic and economic subversion in Benjamin Sáenz's *Carry Me Like Water*

Emily Perkins

Throughout her career, Marta Russell explored the various connections between disabled bodies and capitalist economies. Our modern conception of disability, she explains, was, in fact, constructed upon the advent of industrialized labor. Since that time, disabled bodies have become devalued and economically oppressed because of their difficulty, and often, their inability, to participate in the industrial workforce. This oppression is inherently linked with exploitation; the severely disabled who cannot work are institutionalized and generate a steady stream of profit for the medical industry, and the less severely disabled who can work are often underpaid, denied accommodations, and abused in other ways by employers. Yet, the capitalist system justifies this oppression by placing the blame on disabled individuals' physical differences rather than placing it on a work system that does not provide accommodations for physical differences. Russell points out that the concept of normalcy lies at the heart of this justification. Within cultures that enforce normalcy, those bodies that are aberrant with respects to standards of the average are considered abnormal, and are therefore unfit and unworthy of social inclusion (Russell, 1998: 59–63). In her book *Beyond Ramps: Disability at the End of the Social Contract*, Russell poses a seminal question: who does the concept of "normal" serve? (Russell, 1998: 18). Her book is dedicated to answering this question, and throughout it, she explains that the concept of "normal" serves the capitalist labor market. However, in her book, she mainly conceptualizes disability as a cognitive or physical difference rather than a linguistic or cultural difference. To add to Russell's assertions, I argue that the concept of "normal" also serves those who have the ability to speak the national language, or the language of the dominant, and in the case of the United States, the language of the capitalists—oral English. Members of ethnic minority cultures who speak minority languages and speak little or no English are typically economically impoverished, either because they are unable to find work or because they are forced to work menial jobs that pay low wages. Although the Deaf are not usually thought of as an ethnic culture, some scholars claim that they indeed qualify as one, complete with their own minority language. Deaf individuals who use sign language to communicate are often among those who are economically impoverished by the capitalist system's failure to accommodate their language. Yet at the same time, the Deaf culture and its manual language can serve to empower deaf bodies and provide a progressive model of culture that encourages inclusion. A study of the navigation of linguistic minorities can foreground complex connections between language, national economy, and identity, and an exploration of deaf bodies, in particular, can reveal much about the economy in which linguistic minorities are entrenched.

This essay will explore narrative depictions of the deaf/mute/signing body in Chicano author Benjamin Sáenz's novel *Carry Me like Water* to argue that the deaf/mute/signing body functions as a site of resistance to the oppression inherent in the capitalist economy's enforcement of oral English. It further argues that the deaf/mute/signing body can serve to foreground and disrupt class barriers. In particular, it will explore the connection between language barriers and class barriers, a frequent topic in literature written by Chicanos (or Mexican-Americans who seek political empowerment). Spanish has occupied an important place in Mexican-American culture as a suppressed minority language within the American capitalist system. For this reason, this essay will draw comparisons between American Sign Language (ASL) and Spanish to underscore how minority languages can be both suppressed by, and subversive of, the enforcement of English in the United States. As his main objective, Sáenz foregrounds the violence created by the English-only movement and its defensive posture. He does not push for multilingualism as much as he encourages what he calls "generosity with languages," or the appreciation and sharing of languages (Mermann-Jozwiak and Sullivan, 2009: 51). With this measure, he counters nationalist attitudes toward language and promotes a way of viewing language from an internationalist, trans-nationalist context. Ultimately, this essay will explore how the deaf/mute/signing body can serve as a marker for capitalist economies' oppression of those who do not speak the national/ dominant language. It will also illustrate how the deaf/mute/signing body can disrupt the class structure inherent in capitalist economies, and how it can offer a solution to the oppressive standards of language enforced by those economies. This essay consists of four sections: 1) a discussion of the complex, tenuous relationship between deafness and disability; 2) an explanation of the methodology this essay will use; 3) a brief history of the deaf body and the Chicano body as they are connected with national identity, economics, and language; and 4) literary analysis of the novel.

Deafness versus disability

Both deafness and disability have been defined and redefined throughout history. Since the advent of the disability studies movement in the 1980s, these terms have changed in meaning. Scholars have debated about the extent to which these concepts are related and about the rhetoric that characterizes that relation. Some have argued that deafness constitutes a disability, and others have argued that it is altogether different. Though many aspects of deafness are debatable, Douglas C Baynton explains that it always entails an indisputable biological fact: "Being deaf . . . means most fundamentally that one occupies a different sensory world from those who hear, and this has certain consequences that cannot be constructed away" (Baynton, 1996: 160). But, as many scholars suggest, it is society's socially constructed reaction to the impairment that turns deafness into a disability. Scholars have also made more specific arguments about the relationship of deafness and disability. For example, the topic of education has long been a part of the debate, both the curriculum for deaf children and the language in which deaf children should be educated in order to avoid disablement. The American capitalist system has had a financial incentive to push for oral English-only education policies for the deaf because, as I will discuss in more detail later, oral English has been perceived as the most cost-efficient method of communication for the American national body. However, Ana Celia Zantella explains that:

> interrupting the learning and socialization process of one's first language and replacing it with another . . . results in a child who is neither fully socialized nor competent in either language. If instead the child is allowed to focus on their primary language for a while longer, many researchers believe that they will be far more successful in the long run. Thus even when the state actively tries to promote multiple languages, it is done in a way that hinders their continued use.
>
> (cited in Hieber, 2010)

Moreover, Gallaudet University, the first school of advanced learning for the deaf, reports that few profoundly deaf individuals who are given an education through oral communication will become proficient enough at oral communication to acquire a full education (Gallaudet, 1873: 200–06). MJ Bienvenu provides a succinct description of the relationship between deafness and disability where the suppression of ASL is concerned: "[f]or some deaf people, being deaf is a disability. Those who learn forced English while being denied sign emerge semilingual rather than bilingual, and they are disabled people. But for the rest of us, it is no more a disability than being Japanese would be" (Baynton, 1996: 158).

Some scholars use the deafness/ethnicity analogy to draw even more specific parallels between the two experiences than does Bienvenu, such as Paddy Ladd who claims that the Deaf minority can be seen as a colony in terms of its economic, political, and social relations to the hearing society (Ladd, 2003: 133). Similarly, Harlan Lane offers a model of deafness called the *linguistic minority model* which is based on similarities between the Deaf and ethnic minorities, and he contrasts it with the *disability model*, which is based on the concept of deafness as an impairment in need of rehabilitation. Advocates of the disability model believe that the hearing impaired should learn to participate in oral culture, and to accomplish this deaf individuals are medicalized. Hearing aids, psychologists, social workers, and speech therapists are part of the medicalization/rehabilitation process. Under this model, deafness is seen as a personal tragedy, and it is the responsibility of the disabled to try to achieve lives that are as "normal" as possible. This paradigm turns deafness into a disability, and as a result, hearing individuals come to see themselves as disabled (Lane, 2006: 80–85).

However, under the linguistic minority model, deafness is not seen as a disability. Manual language is encouraged, and it is believed that learning it will bring deaf individuals fully into the circle of Deaf culture. The capitalization of the first letter in the word *Deaf* designates a difference: While the word *deafness* is used to refer to biological hearing impairment, the word *Deafness* refers to a cultural identity. It is a term of self-recognition or recognition of others based on a shared use of a signed language. In fact, one need not necessarily be hearing-impaired to be Deaf, for the Deaf community does not exclude members based on biological makeup or function. To be Deaf, an individual must consider deafness to be positive and must share the values of Deaf culture, such as Deaf Pride. Under this model, deafness is not something that should be repaired through medical means. Rather than a personal tragedy, it is seen as a positive part of the identity, and unlike much of Western culture, the Deaf community is collectivist rather than individualist (Lane, 2006: 84–87).

In an effort to prove that deafness is not a disability, Paul Abberley points out that Deaf culture does not have the ambivalence that is called for in disability culture. He states that, within disability culture, "impairment must be identified as a bad thing, insofar as it is an undesirable consequence of a distorted social development, at the same time as it is held to be a positive attribute of the individual who is impaired" (Abberley, 1987: 9). Still, as Baynton explains, there are many similarities between the Deaf and disabled, but Deaf subjects usually think of themselves as having more similarities with ethnic groups than with the disabled (Baynton, 1996: 157–58). Several scholars have contrasted the values and traits of the Deaf and disabled in order to illustrate the Deaf culture as separate from the disabled culture. For example, many suggest that disabled people cherish autonomy and self-reliance much more than Deaf people, who prefer to focus on mutual dependence (or interdependence). The act of sharing, which is fundamental to the concept of interdependence, could be said to be the basis of the Deaf culture, and it is that sharing which is at the heart of *Carry Me like Water.*

Methodology

To avoid conflating deafness and disability, I will use the term *deaf* (as opposed to disabled) to refer to the hearing impaired, but because deafness and disability have many similarities, I will sometimes apply disability studies scholars' theories about disability to deafness, where it is applicable. For the purposes of this essay, I will use Lane's linguistic model, and I will propose that deafness is not a disability, but that it can become a disability in capitalist economies that exploit the hearing impaired. To illustrate how this occurs, I will apply the theory of materialism, which Nirmala Erevelles defines as "an historical understanding of social relations ensuing from exploitative labor practices, which informs a revolutionary praxis aimed at transformation" (Erevelles, 2011: 54). Michael Oliver explains how the materialist theory provides liberating potential for the disabled, stating that it offers them the opportunity to understand the ways that capitalist society oppresses them, the opportunity to transform their own lives, and the opportunity to transform their societies into ones in which all roles are valued (Oliver, 1999: 14). By applying the materialist theory to the linguistic model of deafness, I will approach Deafness as a unique culture bound together by common values and a common language, which is entrenched in an economy that treats the deaf body as a commodity. While it is true that the Deaf culture promotes special schools and even special living communities for those who identify as Deaf, I will concentrate on the broader aspect of Deaf culture, which is non-exclusionary.

History

The history of the Deaf culture and the Mexican-American culture have had similar trajectories, and a comparison of these cultures can illustrate how capitalist economies use linguistic oppression to dominate minorities. For centuries, both groups have been denied the right to an education in the language that is more natural for them, they have been forced to participate in oral/print English culture, they have experienced limitations placed on their expression and development, and they have been robbed of their linguistic heritages. Lane explains that this linguistic oppression has been used as "an instrument of empire" ultimately to create "homogeneity and fealty to a central power" and to minimize or eradicate diversity in the national body (Lane, 1999: 105).

Sign language has retained many different meanings throughout history. Baynton reports that, in the eighteenth century, manualism, or language that is communicated with hand gestures, was instituted in the educational setting and was seen as generally positive. But in America, in the second half of the nineteenth century, the deaf body became a metaphor for foreignness, as it became associated with the great influx of immigrants, which was pouring into the country at the time. Immigrants and their foreign languages were seen as threats to the national body, particularly after the Civil War when the United States increasingly encouraged national homogenization to bolster a unified national identity. Social space was shrinking and Americans feared the immigrants' new cultural beliefs, habits, and languages. Sign language, especially, was viewed with skepticism because of the mystery that surrounded the signing body. As a consequence, manual language was banned in the educational setting and oralism, which promoted lip-reading and speech, was enforced. ASL would thenceforth be considered inferior to oral language, and, by extension, the deaf, too, were considered inferior (Baynton, 1996: 29–33).

This enforcement of oralism was rooted in economic greed. For the first time, the education of the deaf became a commercial effort. Schools for the deaf were encouraged to teach practical vocational skills rather than a well-rounded education. With vocational skills, the deaf were expected to become "self-supporting, self-respecting citizens." Educators declared that deaf businesspersons would be more successful if they were able to speak and read lips (Baynton, 1996: 97–99) so they enforced oral language-only policies. These attitudes and policies justified the authority of the hearing over the deaf and reinforced deaf individuals' places on the lower rungs of the capitalist class system (Baynton, 1996: 150–51). This suppression of manualism persists even today in both the social and educational settings. Even though laws of the United States have mandated that children should be educated, transitionally at least, in their most fluent language, this provision has not been applied to ASL-using children, (Lane, 2006: 87) an act of neglect that, once again, reinforced the low socioeconomic status of the deaf.

Like the Deaf, Chicanos have a long history of linguistic suppression in the name of strengthening the national body. According to Jennifer Hurstfield, Spanish was the dominant language spoken in the Southwest from the mid-seventeenth through the mid-nineteenth centuries, but when the United States acquired the Southwest from Mexico in 1848, laws were enlisted requiring that all public affairs, including education, be conducted in English, even if native Spanish-speakers did not understand the language. Until 1968, it was illegal to teach in California in any language other than English (Hurstfield, 1975: 140–44). Then in the mid-1990s, an English-only movement established English as the official language of the United States, continuing their tradition of silencing the subaltern.

Literary analysis

Since the Chicano Movement of the 1960s, silence has functioned in many ways in Chicano literature, which is easy to understand in light of Chicano culture's long history with linguistic oppression. Benjamin Sáenz continued his predecessors' depiction of silence, but by exploring it as it is connected with the deaf body, he is able to examine it in new ways. *Carry Me like Water* is centered on a congenitally deaf man named Diego who is not mute but chooses not to speak because speech is unnatural for him. His past, like his deafness, continually haunts him because his mother died in a tragic accident. When he was a boy, he was crossing the street with his mother as he daydreamed. In his reverie, he neglected to watch the traffic. Because of his deafness, he did not hear the car approaching so his mother jumped in front of him and took the blow. He and his older sister Maria Elena were orphaned, and when he was age 19 his sister abandoned him, changed her name to Helen, suppressed her native Spanish tongue, and passed for Italian in order to escape her Chicana heritage and her working-class background. Diego, on the other hand, could not escape these aspects of his life. Helen chose to abandon him because she saw him as an anchor to her working-class Chicana background. For her, he represented foreignness, contagion, and a threat to the English-speaking, upper-class life that she pursued.

When the novel begins, Diego is nearly 30 years old but he is characterized as innocent, afraid, and isolated because he has had little life experience and social interaction. This lack of experience and interaction is due partly to his abandonment and partly to his being surrounded by people who communicate with oral language. His only support system consists of one friend, an older Chicana named Luz, who has no interest in learning sign language, so even though Diego has some knowledge of signs, he must participate in oral language through lip-reading and writing notes. The owner of the restaurant where he works exploits his hearing impairment, which keeps him poverty-stricken. Because Diego cannot hear his own voice, he hates himself and resents the hearing world. In fact, his obsession with his hearing impairment is the main facet of his characterization.

Throughout the first half of the novel, Sáenz uses images and words that signify heaviness and stillness to convey Diego's inescapable feeling of entrapment within the borders of his deaf body. These images of heaviness and stillness are meant to reinforce the descriptions of silence (or lack of hearing) that surround Diego's body. Sáenz also associates other pejorative concepts with Diego's deafness, including those which Lennard Davis explains are traditional metaphors for silence, like death, loneliness, confusion, ignorance, punishment, and spiritual disconnection from God (Davis, 1995: 108–09). Diego associates these pejorative metaphors with his deafness, and thus sees himself as hearing individuals see the deaf rather than the way that Deaf individuals see themselves. He has yet to think like the Deaf, who, according to Baynton, view silence as an empty signifier that is used by the hearing to signify absence, and as a way of dominating the hearing impaired (Baynton, 1996: 24). As a result, Diego feels as if he is not living but simply existing, and he blames his lack of hearing for everything negative in his life. He feels alone and punished, as though God has abandoned him.

While these depictions of lack may be stereotypical, discriminatory, and not necessarily based on the reality of the deaf experience, Sáenz uses them in order to illustrate how hearing individuals use these metaphors without realizing that they are man-made. By the end of the novel, he portrays deafness in a progressive, transgressive way when he critiques many of these pejorative depictions by revealing them to be based on prejudices and inaccuracies, especially the representation of the deaf/signing body as a threat to national identities. In other words, he presents an old order of thinking in order to introduce a new order.

This re-inscription is presented through a Marxian picture of the United States' and Mexico's ruling capitalist systems and their mechanisms of exploitation and maximization of profit. In this process, the similarities in the politics of ASL and Spanish are foregrounded such that re-inscription of one language brings about the re-inscription of the other. As a result, all minority languages that are suppressed by capitalism cease to be seen as foreignness or as threats to the national body. With this re-inscription, the deaf body is no longer a marker for lack or individual failure. On the contrary, it becomes a cultural/linguistic difference that is to be celebrated. In creating a culture where minority languages are freely expressed and the practice of them fosters a sense of pride, the characters in *Carry Me like Water* create an ideal society based on not only the free expression of languages, but the sharing of them. This sharing, Sáenz argues, is at the heart of liberation. While he realizes that the oppression caused by the greedy capitalist system seems insurmountable, he suggests that a revolution is necessary and that the sharing of languages is the starting point for this revolution. If a society can develop the kind of open-mindedness needed to share and appreciate all languages, then presumably, the sharing of material wealth will follow.

As the basis of his materialist critique, Sáenz illustrates how the deaf-mute body serves as a marker for how the capitalist system calculates the value of humans based on their abilities to master the national language. Americans are taught to subscribe to this line of thinking from an early age. The language of success is the language of the hearing, speaking Midwestern middle-class white male. Danny Hieber explains that America's adoption of only one national language is not surprising because it has been shown that having only one national language is cost efficient. English, in particular, is equated with material success. Especially since the advent of globalization, it has become the language of commerce, efficiency, and even prestige. National languages find incentive in violating the rights of minority language speakers (Hieber, 2010), and this violation enforces national chauvinism. It is this chauvinism that Sáenz seeks to expose and critique.

From the first few paragraphs of the novel, Sáenz alerts readers that the novel will present a Marxist view of deafness because he connects Diego's deaf body with economic and social immobility. He is constrained by what Russell calls an "economic straitjacket," squeezed between social and physical barriers to employment and a national ethic that equates human value with work (Russell, 1998: 71). Like many others with disabilities, his work system creates or allows social and/or physical barriers to hinder his productive potential, and at the same time, it judges him based on his ability to render a profit for his employer. This entrapment leads to a cycle of poverty for deaf or disabled individuals like him who, due to lack of accommodations, can never earn enough money to acquire social mobility, especially if they are both deaf and racialized.

This cycle of poverty becomes even more profound and inescapable when deaf individuals are intentionally and unjustly exploited by their capitalist employers in the pursuit of economic greed, and such is the case with Diego. Diego works as a cook at a Mexican-American restaurant. His boss, Gonzalo, also Chicano, is a despicable, arrogant man who verbally abuses Diego. Gonzalo withholds Diego's job benefits, pays him in cash at an hourly rate below the minimum wage, forces him to work long hours, and fails to report his labor to the Social Security system. The evidence of Diego's poverty can be seen in his simple food, inadequate housing, and lack of transportation. In an effort to flaunt his power over Diego, Gonzalo admits to Diego that he is exploiting him. He states, "I don't pay you enough to like me – I just pay you enough to eat. And that's why you're still here, isn't it?" (Sáenz, 2005: 306). When Diego gathers the courage to complain about this mistreatment, Gonzalo accuses Diego of being disobedient and disrespectful and he threatens to fire Diego. This type of threat is part of the abuse that capitalists like Gonzalo use to control employees who use minority languages. In this system of abuse, the deaf body is fetishized and treated as a commodity. Diego's labor power is exchanged for less than that of hearing individuals, a high relative surplus value is produced, and as a result, Gonzalo accumulates profit. But Diego is alienated from the capital that he produces, which places him in the lower class, socially, economically, and politically.

Karl Marx explains the inequity in the relationship between capitalist employer and exploited laborer in his analysis of the production of relative surplus value: "Within the capitalist system all methods for raising the social productiveness of labor are brought about at the cost of the individual laborer; all means for the development of production transform themselves into means of domination over, and exploitation of, the producers" (Marx, 1887). Certainly, the capitalist class benefits at the cost of Diego. Marx stresses the importance of this inequity in the capitalist work system, highlighting how the whole capitalist system is rooted in such unfair inequity: "Accumulation of wealth at one pole is, therefore, at the same time accumulation of misery, agony of toil slavery, ignorance, brutality, mental degradation, at the opposite pole, ie, on the side of the class that produces its own product in the form of capital" (Marx, 1887). Diego is the recipient of this misery, brutality, and degradation as long as he remains a commodity.

Sáenz depicts Diego as suffering from a lack of class and race consciousness, or in other words, an inability to see exploitation at work in society. This lack of awareness, which Marxist scholars call "false consciousness," perpetuates Diego's economic entrapment. Sáenz illustrates how capitalists shape the material and institutional processes of society in order to mislead the proletariat and control their ideological perceptions. The character Mundo is represented as the solution to this false consciousness. As a Chicano gang member who subverts the capitalist work system with his refusal to participate in a traditional job, he is the novel's voice of class and race awareness. Unlike Marx's discussion of false consciousness, Mundo's discussions necessarily involve race relations because in subjects of color, class and race are inextricably bound. He illustrates capitalist society's effects on the Chicano working class, racism's effects on Chicanos' places in the class system, and class effects on the Chicano nation. Through his discussions with Diego, Mundo points out how race is designed to maintain class barriers and how it is used as a commodity structure to exchange the work of the racialized for less, which results in accumulation for capitalists.

While Mundo provides good explanations of these power dynamics, Diego has difficulty understanding the larger picture, which can be explained by Erevelles' assertion that "it is the economic context (e.g. colonialism) that has blunted the capacity for the severely disabled desiring machine to realize its transgressive potential" (Erevelles, 2011: 60). Diego's failure to realize his potential can be seen when Mundo explains to Diego that capitalists hire Chicanos like him to do "dirty" jobs and pay them low wages, meanwhile they take the profit and use it to further accumulate wealth, further alienate the Chicano working-class from their production, and further depress their standards of living. When making his arguments, he shows Diego how his fear is keeping him entrapped, but each time, Diego responds by expressing his fear and desperation. His false consciousness becomes clear during these exchanges. Mundo states, "Man, [your boss] has you right where he wants – right under his foot." But Diego, thinking that he could never get a job anywhere else due to his hearing impairment says, "But being under my boss's foot keeps me from getting wet. It's kind of like an umbrella." Mundo replies that it does not rain in El Paso (Sáenz, 2005: 226). With these words, he suggests to Diego that he should not fear quitting his job because his employer is not truly providing economic protection for him, but is instead keeping him in a state of fear by constructing and reinforcing his sense of desperation.

In order to convey to Diego that he is not alone—that his exploitation exists on a collective level, not an individualist one—Mundo states, "The world is full of motherfuckers like that pinché—and it's not just you who works for people like that – it's everybody in the fuckin' barrio." He goes on to say that Gonzalo is even worse than a "gringo" (or white) capitalist because he "sold out his own people," which, according to Mundo is "the worst kind of pinché there is" (Sáenz, 2005: 226). By pointing out to Diego that there are other working-class Chicanos being taken advantage of, Mundo is trying to make Diego aware of the larger world order—the class hierarchy created by capitalism and how Gonzalo's betrayal of his own ethnic group hinders any possibility that the Chicano people could work together to achieve economic self-determination.

While many Chicanos may suffer from false consciousness of class and race, Diego's is particularly hard to dispel because his deafness reinforces it. Disability studies scholars explain that disability has its own version of false consciousness. In this process, disabled subjects blame their disabilities for their oppression even when such blame is misdirected. James I Charlton (1998) explains this process, stating that, "the majority of disabled people have been so psychologically oppressed by society that their oppression has become internalized. As a result, they have developed a Marxian notion of false consciousness through which they come to believe that they are less capable than others." He explains that this false consciousness is a mixture of self-pity, self-hate, and shame, which can obscure the true source of disabled people's oppression. As a result, it can keep them from recognizing their options and from understanding their needs and capabilities. When they suffer from false consciousness, they cannot recognize that their "self-perceived pitiful lives are simply a mirroring of a pitiful world order" (Oliver and Barnes, 2012: 112). Despite Mundo's attempts to explain the role of commodification of Chicanos in this "pitiful world order," Diego cannot understand the reason for his poverty beyond his own hearing impairment, for he asks, "Who is going to hire a deaf-mute with a high school education?" (Sáenz, 2005: 306). Further, he states, "As soon as I was old enough to know I was alive, I knew I would never be going too far" (Sáenz, 2005: 115).

Lane explains that deaf individuals' stigmatized self-perceptions are constructed out of paternalism, which is always rooted in economics. In this process, the dominant culture sets about to "rehabilitate" those who do not fit in order to "rescue" them. In other words, they force linguistic others to comply with dominant culture's standards in order to help them fit into the larger culture and retain a full range of social, political, and economic advantages. But in reality, this rehabilitation is the ruling class's effort to maintain its monopoly. Paternalism places its beneficiaries in a dependent position to perpetuate its own psychological and economic interests. In fact, most deaf people live in poverty because they must work menial jobs due to their communicative limits and lack of education (Lane, 1999: 38–39). Diego is the recipient of paternalistic efforts from authority figures. For example, after Mundo shows disrespect to an English-speaking police officer, in part, by speaking to him in Spanish, the police officer suggests to Diego that he should stop fraternizing with Mundo. While the officer seems to have Diego's best interest in mind, he is actually encouraging him to continue using English so that the police can maintain ownership of the streets, and thus retain economic, social, and political control.

Paternalism is also at work inside cultures of those who use minority languages, which can be seen in Luz's paternal treatment of Diego. When Diego requests that she communicate with him in Spanish so he can use the knowledge of Spanish that he worked so hard to gain in school, she refuses (Sáenz, 2005: 46). She understands the transgressive capabilities of Spanish but she feels that she must take care of Diego. Consequently, she insists that he participate in English so that he can prosper in an English-dominated culture. With this depiction, it is clear to see why suppression of minority languages happens decade after decade, century after century, especially when economic gain is involved.

Thus far I have looked at ways that the deaf body can serve as a marker for how capitalist economies oppress those who do not speak the national language, and more particularly, I have examined how the deaf body is turned into a disabled body through economic oppression created by the American capitalist system. My discussion has illustrated how the capitalist system turns deaf bodies into commodities, either because they cannot work or because they are exploited when they do work. However, the work system in America is even more complicated than I have suggested thus far, for the concept of self-reliance that is embedded in the American culture heavily influences the American work system, so bodies are expected to work and to be autonomous in that work. This expectation reveals much about the psychological underpinning of American attitudes toward dependence and independence.

Rosemarie Garland-Thomson provides insight into this underpinning, explaining that everyone in America is expected to be the same, and the democratic ideal of egalitarianism is based on this sameness. In fact, not only are citizens expected to be the same, but they are expected to be physically autonomous. The disabled figure troubles this fantasy because it is unique and ungovernable, and therefore it "refutes the fantasy of sameness implicit in the notion of equality" (Garland-Thomson, 1996: 41–43).

Bodies in the American work system are also affected by the Puritan ideals of work, which link hard work with moral virtue, and laziness with moral depravity. But with the foregrounding of disability, a moral dilemma emerges, which is the question of how responsible a disabled subject should be for his or her own social station and economic situation (Garland-Thomson, 1996: 43–48). In forming this question, the link between autonomy and virtue becomes destabilized and disabled bodies can be liberated from moral pressures. Furthermore, disability can become a marker for liberation. Garland-Thomson explains this aspect of what she calls the "extraordinary body":

> On one hand, the disabled figure is a sign for the body that refuses to be governed and cannot carry out the will to self-determination. On the other hand, the extraordinary body is nonconformity incarnate. In a sense then, the disabled figure has the potential to inspire with its irreverent individuality.
>
> (Garland-Thomson, 1996: 44)

The remainder of my discussion will explore the extraordinary, liberating qualities of the Deaf body and Deaf culture—specifically, the Deaf/mute/signing body's potential to disrupt the class structure inherent in capitalist economies.

As I discussed earlier, disability (and deafness) can reinforce the effects of colonialism and further impede the creation of class and race consciousness, but, as Garland-Thomson explains, it can also inspire change to a national body that expects homogenization, and I argue that it can decolonize bodies, dispel false consciousness, and create class and race consciousness. With these turns, the traditional associations with deafness disappear and they are replaced with more transgressive associations, such as subversion of the ruling class. Ironically, it is Diego's sister Helen who is the facilitator of this subversion, for her baby, Juan Diego, is born deaf—he is "nonconformity incarnate" and the character who inspires the manual language culture that Diego will need to finally develop his Deaf identity.

But before Diego develops his Deaf identity, Helen must create hers, as well as her Chicana identity because the two identities are bound together in Deaf Chicanos. Her identity lies at the intersection of the two cultures, and she must fully accept these cultures' values if she is to lead others on their journeys into what Paddy Ladd calls *Deafhood*, or the process of developing an acceptance of being Deaf. As Ladd explains, the term *Deafhood* is used to explain Deaf people's personal journeys to discover and understand themselves as Deaf people and understand their existences in the world. Through sharing their lives with each other as a community and enacting those explanations, Deaf people participate in a daily internal and external dialogue (Ladd, 2003: 3). Sáenz chooses Helen as the leader of the pilgrimage in order to underscore that members of the Deaf culture do not have to be deaf. By midpoint in the novel she begins to work on creating a Chicana identity by admitting to her husband Eddie that she is not Italian but is instead from a poor Mexican-American background. To reclaim this identity, she starts speaking the Spanish language to Eddie. This act of speaking is an important part of her decolonization and her formation of a Chicana identity because, according to Anzaldúa, "ethnic identity is twin skin to linguistic identity" (Anzaldúa, 1987: 81). To further her journey into what the Deaf community calls the *DeafWorld*, Helen—or now Maria Elena—admits to Eddie that she abandoned her deaf brother and has not been able to find him, and then she announces her plans to undertake a pilgrimage to find Diego and bring the family back together. But when her son Juan Diego is born deaf, she has difficulty understanding how deafness can be a source of cultural pride and she has to undergo a reevaluation of her attitudes toward deafness.

To undergo this reevaluation, she examines words that have meanings which are influenced by economic greed and that have had a detrimental impact on the deaf body, such as the words *normalcy*, *happy*, and *perfect*. The word *perfect* is used ubiquitously throughout the text, especially in regard to Maria Elena who lives the "perfect" upper-class lifestyle, marries the "perfect" wealthy Caucasian husband, and plans to have the "perfect" baby. After Juan Diego's birth, Maria Elena develops denial about his hearing impairment, so her husband Eddie breaks the silence between them by broaching the subject. With a twist, Eddie tells Maria Elena that their baby is "perfectly healthy in every way," but she responds by saying, "No. I said no. He's perfect" (Sáenz, 2005: 270). With her distinction between "healthy" and "perfect," she suggests that she does not want a healthy yet deaf baby. Instead, she wants a "normal" baby with hearing ability.

Then after some reflection, she wonders why she is so attached to this thing called *normalcy*, and this leads her to ponder her attachment to the word *perfect* (Sáenz, 1995: 271–72), an attachment that is prevalent in America. Marta Russell explains that the Western culture's fondness for perfection is related to economics, especially where the economy is connected with the "perfect" baby. In a section of *Beyond Ramps* called "the politics of perfect babies," Russell explains that unborn children with disabilities are exposed to a subtle system of eugenics when they are prenatally screened and then aborted because of their physical impairment (Russell, 1998). The medical culture and the media encourage these eugenic measures because disabled babies are seen as economic burdens. In this conception, the "perfect" baby is considered a commodity, and the disabled (or deaf) baby is considered "damaged goods" (Russell, 1998: 47–51). Sáenz draws a connection between the euthanizing of deaf babies in contemporary society and the euthanizing of deaf babies from the World War II era in order to underscore the brutality of this modern eugenics movement. To depict this connection, Eddie tells Maria Elena that dimples were seen as weaknesses during the Holocaust (Sáenz, 2005: 275). In other words, deafness is simply a physical characteristic like dimples—part of the human identity, and perhaps even a thing of beauty. He then asks Maria Elena if she would have aborted Juan Diego if she had known he would be deaf, and they agree that they would have "chosen" him (Sáenz, 2005: 275) because he is neither a weakness in any national body, nor an economic burden.

As Maria Elena considers the word *perfect* in relation to the deaf body, her memories of her Chicana background and her experience with deafness intersect. With this intersection, her own identity becomes further decolonized, her false consciousness is dispelled, and she develops race and class consciousness. Memories of her mother telling her that the family would speak for Diego because he could not speak for himself come rushing back to her. At the same time, visions of her family members' faces return to her, and she recalls her mother's saying that only the dead are perfect, because they are dead (Sáenz, 2005: 272). In other words, no living person is perfect, including the hearing and the upper class. With these two memories of her mother, Maria Elena understands that dependency is not necessarily a bad thing, neither is it un-American. Garland-Thomson explains how the disabled (or deaf) body can lead to such a realization with her statement that the disabled body (which society sees as "imperfect") "exposes the illusion of autonomy, self-government, and self-determination that underpins the fantasy of able-bodiedness" (Garland-Thomson, 1996: 69–70). After Maria Elena's illusions are exposed, she decides that the word *perfect* has no meaning (Sáenz, 2005: 272). Her consideration of deafness in relation to her Chicana heritage has created an awareness that the deaf are not imperfect, just different, and she and Eddie decide to study sign language together for their son.

While Juan Diego can be considered "nonconformity incarnate," Diego can be considered as the interrupter of the concepts of self-reliance and independence. He represents the move from individualism to collectivism after he develops an interdependent relationship with Mundo and his fellow gang members. In his new Chicano community, he is not subjected to paternalism, scorn, or discrimination, and he loses the fear that has kept him isolated from others. The images of stillness and heaviness disappear from the narrative as Diego develops a more positive attitude toward life and toward himself. Deafness is no longer the main facet of his characterization. Although his deafness is still part of his identity, it is not a negative aspect of it and it no longer overwhelms all other aspects of his identity. Mundo finally helps Diego to escape his exploitative boss, and Diego, in turn, vows that he will help the world by turning Gonzalo in to the IRS. In doing so, he will prevent Gonzalo from abusing other deaf or disabled individuals.

At the end of the novel, Maria Elena and Diego find each other again and, along with other characters, they form an interdependent community—a quasi-utopian society located in an El Paso mansion that Eddie and Maria Elena purchased with the intent of sharing. In fact, in their model system, all kinds of sharing occurs. Almost everyone in the house learns to use sign language, and economic wealth is also shared. As a result, class divisions and racism disappear. The house functions as a utilitarian shelter—a safe, happy place for family and friends. They even bring home a homeless stranger with AIDS because in their household, no one will be turned away. In their community, disablement is lifted, and hearing impairment does not entail oppression. Diego is no longer exiled because of his ethnicity or his hearing impairment, and Juan Diego will not become exiled because, in their society, all ethnicities are valued and all languages are for everyone. Maria Elena promises that Juan Diego and his little sister Elizabeth will learn ASL, English, and Spanish, and it is suggested that the children will teach future generations to have the kind of generosity with languages that Sáenz promotes.

This new society also erases confining borders in that it transgresses familial bonds. Sáenz refers to this group lifestyle as "living in a pack" (Sáenz, 2005: 378). This lifestyle signifies not only the Deaf culture, which often takes advantage of forming its own physical community, but also the Chicano lifestyle of large, extended families living together. Some Americans claim it is "unnatural" to live in packs, as Sáenz points out (Sáenz, 2005: 378), just as many Americans believe that ASL and Spanish are unnatural, but these assumptions privilege the individual over the community. Here, interdependence is valued over independence.

It is suggested that the duties of cooking and caring for the sick are shared, and to contribute financially, Diego finds new work delivering flowers for a local florist. While it may not be perfectly liberating, as he is still in an exchange system that relies on labor potential, it is a step in the right direction because Diego is no longer being exploited by a capitalist bully.

With the depiction of this ideal society, Sáenz suggests that if the United States would abolish its English-only policies, appreciate other languages, and instruct its children in the language that they know best, the poverty among linguistic minorities would disappear, along with class divisions and racism. Its citizens would support each other, no matter their skin color or ability, and employers would provide accommodations for all employees. With these accommodations, speakers of minority languages would earn higher wages and break free from the chains of poverty. After witnessing the difference that sharing languages can make, with hope, the citizens in power would understand the devastating oppression inherent in capitalism and would do even more to spread the nation's wealth. Ultimately, Sáenz envisions a world where every citizen economically prospers, rather than the few who maintain power through exploitation and the enforcement of English-only policies. Though these policies may confine speakers of minority languages now, Sáenz suggests that it will not always be the case. He states that "language is a fluid thing, and it belongs to everyone, and if you think you can legislate it, you've got another thing coming" (Mermann-Jozwiak and Sullivan, 2009: 59). In other words, language cannot be contained by legal restrictions, as we have seen in the last decade with the fast-growing use of Spanish among Latinos who come to the United States looking for work. Indeed, the internationalist, trans-nationalist, non-exclusionary society that Sáenz envisions may prove to be inevitable, bringing social, political, and economic equality to all.

Bibliography

Abberley, P (1987) The Concept of Oppression in the Development of a Social Theory of Disability. *Disability, Handicap, and Society* 2: 5–19.

Anzaldúa, G (1987) *Borderlands/La Frontera* (3rd edition) San Fancisco, CA: Aunt Lute Books, 2007.

Baynton, DC (1996) *Forbidden Signs*. London: University of Chicago Press.

Baynton, DC (2006) A Silent Exile Upon This Earth: The Metaphorical Representation of Deafness in the Nineteenth Century. In L Davis (ed.) *The Disability Studies Reader* (2nd edition) New York, NY: Taylor and Francis.

Charlton, JI (1998) *Nothing About Us Without Us: Disability Oppression and Empowerment*, Berkeley, CA: University of California Press.

Davis, LJ (1995) *Enforcing Normalcy: Disability, Deafness, and the Body*, London, UK: Verso.

Erevelles, N (2011) *Disability and Difference in Global Contexts: Enabling the Transformative Body Politic*, Basingstoke, UK: Palgrave MacMillan.

Gallaudet, EM (July 1873) 'Deaf mute' Conventions, Associations, and Newspapers. *Annals* 18: 200–6.

Garland-Thomson, R (1996) *Extraordinary Bodies: Figuring Physical Disability in American Culture and Literature*. New York, NY: Columbia University Press.

Hieber, D (2010) Language and the Socialist calculation problem. *Mises Daily*. 7 September, available online at https://mises.org/library/language-and-socialist-calculation-problem (last accessed May 28, 2015).

Hurstfield, J (1975) The Educational Experiences of Mexican Americans: 'Cultural Pluralism' or 'Internal Colonialism'? *Oxford Review of Education* (1)2: 137–49.

Ladd, P (2003) *Understanding Deaf Culture: In Search of Deafhood*, Bristol, UK: Multilingual Matters.

Lane, H (1999) *The Mask of Benevolence: Disabling the Deaf Community*. San Diego, CA: DawnSignPress.

Lane, H (2006) Construction of Deafness. In Davis, L (ed), *Disability Studies Reader*, 2nd edition, New York, NY: Taylor and Francis.

Markowitz, H and Woodward, J (1978) Language and the Maintenance of Ethnic Boundaries in the Deaf Community. *Communication and Cognition* 11: 2–17.

Marx, K (1887) Capital: A Critique of Political Economy, Moore, S (trans) and Aveling, E, (ed.) Engels, F. Moscow, Russia: Progress Publishers, available online at www.marxists.org/archive/marx/works/1867-c1/ (last accessed May 29, 2015).

Mermann-Jozwiak, E and Sullivan, N (2009) Between Belonging and Exile, in *Conversations with Mexican-American Writers: Languages and Literatures in the Borderlands*. Jackson, MS: University Press of Mississippi.

Oliver, M and Barnes, C (2012) *New Politics of Disablement*, Basingstoke, UK: Palgrave MacMillan.

Oliver, MJ (1999) Capitalism, Disability and Ideology: A Materialist Critique of the Normalization Principle, available online at www.independentliving.org/docs 3/oliver 99.pdf (last accessed May 29, 2015).

Russell, M (1998) *Beyond Ramps: Disability at the End of the Social Contract*. Monroe, ME: Common Courage Press.

Sáenz, B (2005) *Carry Me like Water*. New York, NY: Rayo.

Zantella, AC (1997) *Growing Up Bilingual: Puerto Rican Children in New York*, 1st edition, Hoboken, NJ: Wiley-Blackwell.

12 The left hand of Stalin: eugenics in the Soviet Union

Anne Finger

Eugenics—roughly speaking, the notion that the human population can and should be improved by controlled breeding—is commonly associated with the right, particularly with Nazi racial ideology. Marta Russell writes in *Beyond Ramps: Disability at the End of the Social Contract*: "[i]t must be noted that the 'defect question' did not fall neatly into 'left' or 'right' camps of political thought," and points out that in its heyday prior to World War II many on the left had fervently embraced eugenics (Russell, 1998: 65). Russell sees the eugenics movement as having been a linchpin of disabled people's oppression in capitalist society. Her insights were expanded in later works such as Sharon L Snyder and David T Mitchell's *Cultural Locations of Disability* and Ann Kerr and Tom Shakespeare's *Genetic Politics: From Eugenics to Genome*. Snyder and Mitchell write that the eugenics movement saw disability as "the master trope of human disqualification" (Snyder and Mitchell, 2006: 2–3) and argued that it still lurks like "a phantasm just below the surface" (Snyder and Mitchell, 2006: x).

While eugenics is now often described as a pseudo-science or a fringe movement, it in fact had widespread popular support and was inextricable from early genetic science. It seemed a "common sense" proposition, broadly supported in light of what had been learned about evolution as a result of the scientific revolution brought about by the work of Charles Darwin and Alfred Russel Wallace—who independently and concurrently developed many of the ideas we now think of as Darwinian. It was part and parcel of progressive initiatives which worked to improve living conditions for children, combat infant mortality, and fight for birth control and sexual freedom.

In the Soviet Union the eugenics movement took a very different tack from much of the rest of the world. For many of us, our initial—and erroneous—association to Soviet eugenics would be Lysenkoism, the theory prevalent from the 1930s to the mid-1950s, which held that acquired characteristics could be inherited; but Lysenkoism concerned itself with plant biology and never touched on human breeding. Soviet eugenics preceded Lysenokism by more than a decade, and had fallen into disfavor by the time Trofim Denisovich Lysenko, an agronomist of peasant stock, came on the scene. Prior to the Revolution, an anarchist prince, Petr

Kropotkin[1] proclaimed his own form of Social Darwinism which valued the "weak" and "infirm . . . as the most precious weapons used by humanity in its struggle for existence" (Kropotkin, 1955: 3); later, an American émigré to the Soviet Union—and later Nobel Laureate—would plead for humanity to seize control of reproduction, as it had seized control of production, and breed a new race: not just more intelligent, but more humane and cooperative. The Soviet eugenics movement did not call for the for racial purity as the Nazis did—those whom Leon Trotsky called "romantic numskulls . . . dreaming of restoring the old race of Europe's Dark Forest to its original purity, or rather its original filth"—but just the opposite: Trotsky looked to an America where "genuine scientific methods" would create, "out of your melting pot of races . . . a new breed of men—the first worthy of the name of man" (Trotsky, 1934).

In Nikolai Krementsov's chapter on eugenics in Russia and the Soviet Union in the *Oxford Handbook of the History of Eugenics* he notes how little attention has been paid to this eugenics in Russia and the Soviet Union, and the need for further research (Krementsov, 2010). "One of the largest holes," he writes, "in our knowledge is the influence that eugenic ideas exerted on actual policy-making in a variety of fields, from social hygiene to family planning and from abortion to immigration policies" (Krementsov, 2010: 413). I would add; "and, most importantly, what its impact was on disabled people."

Most historians of science write histories of scientists. These are, of course, valuable, but in this essay I consider how the understandings of scientists rippled out beyond their laboratories, their journal articles, their institutes, to the broader culture, and how these ideas affect the actual lives of disabled people. While I may have some preliminary answers to the first part of that question, I have few to the latter, but hope that future writers will be able to answer to what I have only been able to ask.

Before the revolution

While theories about evolution can certainly exist without eugenics, the eugenics movement could not have existed without the widespread acceptance of Darwin's evolutionary theory. The first printing of the Russian translation of *The Origin of Species* in 1864 sold out rapidly and ideas about evolution were enthusiastically taken up by Russian radicals. Darwin's work first came to the attention of the Russian intelligentsia in a long review by the influential social critic Dmitry Pisarev, written from the Peter and Paul Fortress where he was a political prisoner. As Daniel P Todes writes, the Darwinian notion that humans were first of all animals "struck at the core of tsarist ideology, particular at its tenet that an immaterial 'spiritual aspect' separated man from the animal world and tied him to God, the Church, and the tsarist social order" (Todes, 1989: 29).

1 An anarchist prince may seem like a contradiction, but recall that at the end of the nineteenth century, nearly two million Russians bore noble titles, including one Vladimir Ulyanov—later to be known, of course, as Lenin.

Russian leftists of the nineteenth century relied heavily on a positivist faith in science. As Pisarev put it: "[m]ankind has only one evil—ignorance; and against this evil there is only one medicine—science" (Graham, 1993: 56–57). Many—although certainly not all—adherents of Marxism, Engels among them, had come to regard Marxism itself as a science. Moreover, there was a widespread belief among radicals that the laws of nature could not be fundamentally different from the laws of society, a notion, which would come into strange play in the era of Lysenkoism, when the "law" of dialectical materialism was applied to the wheat harvest.

However, Russians were often troubled by Darwin's reliance on the doctrines of Malthus, ideas which were crucial underpinnings of eugenic thinking in much of Europe and North America. In his 1798 *An Essay on the Principle of Population*, Rev Thomas Malthus had argued that unchecked population increases geometrically, while resources increase only arithmetically, and used this as a basis to argue against charity and parish poor laws, and for human life as a brutal contest, with the winnowing of humanity inevitable (Malthus, 1809). Malthus' ideas—lucid, clear, and coinciding with British ruling class views—were widely accepted in Britain, becoming part of the common-sense understanding of the nature of life, and were almost inevitably incorporated into the notions of "struggle for existence" and "survival of the fittest" which grew out of Darwin's writing (Malthus, 1809). Russians, on the other hand, wondered what "the great Darwin" could have in common with "the pastor thief" and specifically rejected his notion of life as a struggle within species and the survival of the fit. Pisarev, it should be noted, was an exception: in his review of *Origin* he wrote: "The overwhelming majority of organic beings come into the world as into a huge kitchen where the cooks are chopping, disemboweling, stewing and frying one another" (Todes, 1989: 30).

As Todes has pointed out both Darwin and Wallace formed their ideas about evolution and natural selection in the fecundity of the tropics and both had grown up on the crowded island of Britain during the era of unbridled and ruthless industrialization (Todes, 1989). In Russia, however, wilderness was not found in colonized, far-off lands teeming with life but in the vast and sparsely populated wastes of Siberia where bitter cold and torrential rains made life perilous for the few species that managed to eke out an existence there. Kropotkin was a noted geographer before he became an anarchist, and his writing is rich with detail about what he observed in the Russian steppes. In the opening of his *Mutual Aid: A Factor of Evolution*, he writes:

> Two aspects of animal life impressed me most during the journeys which I made in my youth in Eastern Siberia and Northern Manchuria. One of them was the extreme severity of the struggle for existence which most species of animals have to carry on against an inclement Nature. . . . And the other was, that even in those few spots where animal life teemed in abundance, I failed to find—although I was eagerly looking for it—that bitter struggle for the means of existence, *among animals belonging to the same species*, which was

> considered by most Darwinists (though not always by Darwin himself) as the dominant characteristic of struggle for life, and the main factor in evolution.
> (Kropotkin, 1955: vii [emphasis in original])

Instead, Kropotkin found abundant evidence of animals of the same species assisting one another to survive. Especially when animals were studied, not in laboratories or in museums "but in the forest and prairie, in the steppe and mountains" one saw that "[s]ociability is as much a law of nature as mutual struggle" (Kropotkin, 1955: 5). He explicitly critiqued the passage in Darwin's *Descent of Man* in which Darwin wrote:

> With savages, the weak in body or mind are soon eliminated; and those that survive commonly exhibit a vigorous state of health. We civilised men, on the other hand, do our utmost to check the process of elimination; we build asylums for the imbecile, the maimed, and the sick; we institute poor-laws; and our medical men exert their utmost skill to save the life of every one to the last moment. . . . No one who has attended to the breeding of domestic animals will doubt that this must be highly injurious to the race of man.[2]
> (Darwin, 1981: 168)

In *Mutual Aid*, Kropotkin answered Darwin's argument: "As if thousands of weak-bodied and infirm poets, scientists, inventors, and reformers, together with other thousands of so-called 'fools' and 'weak-minded enthusiasts,' were not the most precious weapons used by humanity in its struggle for existence by intellectual and moral arms which Darwin himself emphasized in those same chapters of *Descent of Man*" (Kropotkin, 1955: 3).

While he agreed with Darwin that "[l]ife *is* struggle; and in that struggle the fittest survive," he also argued that:

> it is sociable species, where all individuals live in solidarity with one another, that prosper, develop and reproduce; while those which live by brigandage, like the falcon, for example, are decaying throughout the world . . . the investigations of Darwin and his successors comprise, on the contrary, an excellent argument to the effect that animal societies are best organized in the communist-anarchist manner.
> (Kropotkin, 1955: 130)

2 Darwin did not practice what he preached. The father of ten children, he had what Victorians called "a weak constitution," and was, again in the terminology of the times, "a reclusive invalid," suffering from a chronic illness which has variously been seen as being psychosomatic in origin or as being cyclical vomiting syndrome, Chagas disease, Crohn's disease, arsenic poisoning, lupus erythematosus, adrenal disease, and giardiasis, which may tell us more about the vagaries of retrospective diagnosis than anything else (see Bowcott, 2009; McNeil Jr, 2003; Orrego and Quintana, 2007; Thomson, 2009). It is difficult to say whether diagnosis of Darwin's malady is helped or hindered by the fact that he kept voluminous notes on his own health, applying to his own excreta the same keen and precise scrutiny that he applied to the beaks of finches.

At the First International Eugenics Congress held in London in 1912, Kropotkin, having reminded the other delegates that Dostoevsky was an epileptic, and spoken of the dysgenic effects of war and poverty, called upon them to "[d]estroy the slums, build healthy dwellings . . . pave the streets . . . bring a supply of water to a city . . . and you will have improved the germ plasm of the next generation much more than you might have done by any amount of sterilization" (Kropotkin, 1912: 356–57). He went on to ask, "[W]ho are the unfit. . . ? The workers or the idlers? The women of the people, who suckle their children themselves, or the ladies who are unfit for maternity because they cannot perform all the duties of a mother? Those who produce degenerates in the slums, or those who produce degenerates in palaces?" (Kropotkin, 1912: 357).

Despite all this, Kropotkin was a eugenicist. He had begun his speech by speaking of "the great question, which we all have at heart—the prevention of the deterioration and the improvement of the human race by maintaining in purity the common stock of inheritance of mankind" (Kropotkin, 1912: 354). His questions about whether the unfit are the workers or the idlers, the women of the people or those who produce degenerates in palaces, leave in place the notion that there are those who *are* unfit.

Kropotkin was not alone in his views. As Nikolai Krementsov notes, Russia was "huge, sparsely populated, predominately agrarian, [and] autocratic," lacking the socioeconomic conditions—rapid urbanization and industrialization, immigration, population density—which had spurred the rise of eugenics elsewhere (Krementsov, 2010: 414). Russian eugenicists were critical of the racist and classist ideas of foreign eugenicists, and strongly emphasized environmental change as a necessary tool for the improvement of the human race. In a country where underpopulation was seen as a curse, negative eugenic measures such as marriage prohibition and sterilization were largely rejected.

Russia had a long tradition of *yurodivye* or holy fools, many of whom today would be seen as mentally ill or intellectually disabled, some of whom were canonized by the Russian Orthodox Church. One such holy fool, II Koreisha, lived as a patient for almost half a century in a Moscow hospital, receiving visits and dispensing advice and blessings to Moscow's merchant class, and even being called upon by Nikolai Gogol. This was certainly not the only tendency at work in pre-revolutionary Russia: Peter the Great had forbidden members of the nobility with mental disabilities from marrying and limited their property rights. While Russian trends in building asylums mirrored those in other Western countries, the proportion of the population institutionalized in Russia tended to be smaller, and many of those defined as mad were cared for in peasant homes, in a system known as *patronage familial.* Julie V Brown writes: "[M]adness was never segregated in Russia to the extent that it was elsewhere. Hence, it was not transformed into a strange and fearsome state, associated primarily with thick walls and barred windows, but remained a relatively ordinary feature of everyday life" (Brown, 1989: 34). When Kropotkin wrote of 'fools' and 'weak-minded enthusiasts' his Russian audience doubtless conjured up those amongst whom they lived, those who were sometimes the objects of worship rather than a fearsome other.

But that was hardly the only tendency in Russian thought relevant to the emergence of eugenics. Twenty years before Zarathustra spake the word *übermensch* (often translated into English as "superman," although "overman" is perhaps a less felicitous but more accurate translation), Nikolai Chernyshevsky wrote the novel *What Is to Be Done?*, subtitled *Tales of New People* (1863) which had its own superman, a character named Rhakmetov. It is difficult to overstate the importance this novel had on Russian culture—its impact (and its literary skill) have been compared to that of *Uncle Tom's Cabin*. Both Lenin and Tolstoy later wrote books titled *What Is to Be Done?* Lenin called Chernyshevsky:

> the greatest and most talented representative of socialism before Marx. . . . Under his influence hundreds of people became revolutionaries. . . . After my brother's execution [for having taken part in an unsuccessful conspiracy to assassinate Tsar Alexander III], knowing that Chernyshevksy's novel was one of his favorite books, I really undertook to read it, and I sat over it not for several days but for several weeks. Only then did I understand its depth. . . . It's a thing that supplies energy for a whole lifetime. . . . He plowed me up more profoundly than anyone else.[3]
>
> (Valentinov, 1951: 193–94)

Yes, Lenin captivated by a book in which the goddesses Astarte and Aphrodite appear in the dream of the heroine, Vera Pavlovna. "Greetings, sister," they say. *I am not making this up.*[4]

In the dreams there are goddesses, but in the novel's daylight world there is Rakhmetov, a sort of socialist Paul Bunyan, who appears about two-thirds of the way through the book. At 17, having been "an ordinary youth of somewhat above-average height and strength," he decides to become physically strong: hauling water and firewood, undertaking gymnastics, cutting rock, mining and forging iron. He eats a boxer's diet—raw beefsteak—and works as a "plowman, carpenter, ferryman . . . barge hauler along the whole length of the Volga, from Dubovka and Rybinsk, buckled into a harness" (Chernyshevsky, 1989: 279). Thereafter, he applies himself to his studies with the same vigor. Having been given a reading list, he walks along the Nevsky Prospekt at eight in the morning, waiting for the bookstores to open, and then reads for more than three days and nights in a row, before finally, on the fourth night, collapsing onto the floor (Chernyshevsky, 1989).

Rakhemtov plays almost no role in the story, seeming to exist merely as an exemplar. Cherneshevsky addresses those he is fond of calling his Perspicacious

3 More proof that one's political acumen and one's literary taste need not bear any relationship. Nelson Mandela loved William Ernest Henley's poem "Invictus." I rest my case.

4 In Victor Shklovsky's *Mayakovsky and His Circle*, writing of the time of widespread hunger in the early Soviet Union, he notes: "Horse meat is better fried than boiled; if you have no oil to fry it in, you can use soap and vinegar, for the vinegar neutralizes the taste of the soap," and adds, "I am not making this up" (Shklovsky, V (1940) *O Mayakovsky*. Feiler, L (trans) (1972) *Mayakovsky and His Circle*. New York, NY: Dodd, Mead & Co., p. 138).

Readers: "If I hadn't shown you the figure of Rakhemtov," he says, we would have seen the main characters of this novel as "heroes, people of a higher nature, perhaps even idealized figures, maybe even inconceivable in reality because of their very great nobility. No, my friends, my mean, base, pitiful friends, you're quite mistaken: it's not they who stand too high, but you who stand too low. . . . Come up out of your godforesaken underworld, my friends, come up." We must have people like Rakhmetov: "There are only a few of them, but they make it possible for all people to breathe; without them people would suffocate. . . . But these few people are within that mass, as theine is in tea, as bouquet is in fine wine. They are its strength and its aroma. They are the flower of the best people, the movers of the movers, the salt of the salt of the earth" (Chernyshevsky, 1989: 312–14). The line of descent from Rakhmetov can be traced to the New Soviet Man and to Alexey Stakhanov, the Soviet coal miner whose prodigious feats in the 1930s would not only lend his name to a movement, Stakhanovism, but get his picture on the cover of *Time* magazine, and the fictional heroic Polish bricklayer of Andrzej Wajda's film *Man of Marble*.

For the Russian intelligentsia, both strains—acceptance of the disabled and a desire for the superman—would feed into the Russian version of eugenics.

Eugenics is the religion of the future

Prior to the October Revolution, eugenics had been an ad hoc tendency, without organization or an institutional setting. That situation changed dramatically. The Russian Eugenics Society was formed in November of 1920, chaired by Nikolai Kol'tsov, and launched its *Russian Eugenics Journal* in 1922. Its emblem was a genealogical chart of the linked pedigrees of Darwin and Galton. Kol'tsov wrote in that journal:

> The ideals of socialism are bound up with our earthly life: but the dream of creating a perfect order in the relations between people is also a religious idea, for which people will go to their deaths. Eugenics has before it a high ideal which also gives meaning to life and is worthy of sacrifices: the creation, through conscious work by many generations, of a human being of a higher type, a powerful ruler of nature and creator of life. Eugenics is the religion of the future and it awaits its prophets.
>
> (Adams, 1990a: 162)

Kol'tsov was not the first to use the concept of religion in reference to eugenics: Galton had referred to it as a "civic religion."

Kol'tsov spoke of three key areas of eugenics: the task of gathering further knowledge of human heredity, applying that knowledge to improve the genetic quality of future generations, and, finally, the above-referenced eugenic religion, comparable, in Koltsov's opinion, to nationalism, Christianity, Islam and socialism, and would inspire people to both ardor and sacrifice. What did not change was the tendency expressed in Kropotkin's speech to the Eugenics Conference to blend eugenics with other schemes for social improvement. Sterilization was largely (although not entirely) rejected: it seemed to make little sense in a country where scarcity of population was a problem, and also conflicted with the notions that "defectives" could be raised up with proper education and guidance. The concepts of "innate criminality" and "hereditary feeblemindedness," both of which served as a linchpins for eugenics in the US and Western Europe, were largely rejected, and Russian eugenicists tended to be critical of those in other countries who adopted them, although in 1924 the *Russian Eugenics Journal* did publish a plea by a German physician who appealed to his "colleague-physicians both in the cities and in the countryside to search for defective persons, taking advantage of the help of local authorities, teachers, philanthropic institutions, medical personnel, and to sterilize as many of them as possible" (Graham, 1977: 1148–49).

Other eugenics proposals did find support. Several such measures were enshrined in the 1926 Soviet Civic Code, including prohibition of marriages between close relatives and between mentally ill persons, along with the requirement that marriage registration agencies collect written depositions stating that couples had informed one another of their medical histories (Krementsov, 2010: 419).

Instead of focusing on negative eugenics, which largely preoccupied the US and German movements—and, as Loren R Graham has pointed out, to their own peril—eugenicists often studied "the fit," particularly the inheritance of creative talent, often seeing links between creativity and "hereditary dysfunctions," such as epilepsy and psychoses (Graham, 1977). In the early 1920s, the *Russian Eugenics Journal* was publishing genealogies of aristocratic Russian families and papers, which expressed despair about the dysgenic effects of the Russian Revolution and the subsequent emigration of upper-class families. It also published favorable reviews of German texts which were establishing the field of race hygiene, and both Kol'tsov and Filipchenko, who ran the Petrograd counterpart to Kol'tsov's Moscow eugenics society, wrote articles for the leading German eugenics journal. The fact that the USSR, because of its revolutionary path, and Germany, because it was seen as the instigator of World War I, were both treated as pariah states served to bring the eugenics movements of those two countries closer together.

It is hardly surprising that by the mid-1920s these studies brought criticism of eugenics as a "bourgeois science," ill-suited to the egalitarian Bolshevik state. In 1925 an article in the theoretical journal *Under the Banner of Marxism* criticized the Russian eugenics movement for emphasizing the biological determinants of behavior, and pointing out that conservative thinkers had always seen human actions as caused by innate qualities, since to look at the social determinants of behavior inevitably led to revolutionary conclusions. Such attacks were answered by, among others, the commissar of public health who published an article, "Eugenics, Theirs and Ours," which sought to distinguish between eugenics as it was practiced in the proletarian state and in bourgeois societies (Graham, 1977).

"As elsewhere in the world," as Krementsov notes, "the institutionalization of eugenics went hand in hand with the institutionalization of genetics" (Kremenstov, 2010: 417). Leading texts on heredity concluded with lengthy chapters on eugenics. Filipchenko's Institute began in 1921 as the Bureau of Eugenics, became in 1925 the Bureau of Genetics and Eugenics and in 1927 morphed into the Bureau of Genetics.

The links between genetics and eugenics are shown by the fact that when eugenics was suppressed under Stalinism, so was genetics. In the post-Stalin thaw, genetics at last began to emerge as a legitimized science. If geneticists in the post-World War II US often knew little of the historical connection between their own field and eugenics, in the Soviet Union the suppressed science and the movement linked with it re-emerged whole. In the late 1960s and early 1970s, a leading genetics textbook—and, of course, no textbook could be published without official approval—called on the Soviet authorities to breed superior people. The inside cover of another textbook depicted the tree of genetics, with its various branches: human genetics had "eugenics" at its tip. (Adams, 1990b).

During the first ten years of the Russian Revolution, hope about the future was enormous. Vladimir Mayakovsky spoke for his generation when, in his 1918 "Open Letter to the Workers," he wrote:

> No one knows what huge suns will illuminate the life of the future. It may be that artists will transform the grey dust of the cities into hundred-coloured rainbows; that the never-ending thunderous music of volcanoes will be turned into the sound of flutes resounding from mountain ranges; that ocean waves will be forced to play on nets of chords stretching from Europe to America.
>
> (Pullman, 2013)

In his conclusion of *Literature and Revolution*, originally published in 1923, Trotsky spoke of how:

> [T]he psycho-physical molding of new generations . . . will take its place as the crown of social thinking. . . . Communist life will not be formed blindly, like coral islands, but will be built consciously, will be tested in thought, will be directed and corrected. . . . The shell of life will hardly have time to form before it will burst open again under the pressure of new technical and cultural inventions and achievements. Life in the future will not be monotonous.
>
> More than that. Man at last will begin to harmonize himself in earnest. . . . Even purely physiologic life will become subject to collective experiments. The human species, the coagulated *Homo sapiens*, will once more enter into a state of radical transformation, and, in his own hands, will become an object of the most complicated methods of artificial selection and psycho-physical training.
>
> (Trotsky, 1960: 206)

Trotsky goes on to write of how "dark elements" had been driven out of industry and ideology, out of politics; the "blind elements" still exist in economic relations, but are being driven out by socialism (Trotsky, 1960). He states:

> Finally, the nature of man himself is hidden in the deepest and darkest corner of the unconscious, of the elemental, of the sub-soil. Is it not self-evident that the greatest efforts of investigative thought and of creative initiative will be in that direction? The human race will not have ceased to crawl on all fours before God, kings and capital, in order later to submit humbly before the dark laws of heredity and blind sexual selection.[5]
>
> (Trotsky, 1960: 207)

Tales of new people

Mark B Adams notes:

> Eugenics fit ideally the new emphasis on science as a way of undermining religion and improving the human condition; it entailed a scientistic, materialist, biosocial concept of human beings; it sought to apply the results of genetics to benefit society; and it emphasized the human power to shape the future.
>
> (Adams, 1990a: 162)

Ideas about eugenics spread beyond the ranks of scientists and indeed beyond the intelligentsia. Filipchenko gave popular lectures on eugenics in 1917, and between 1921 and 1925 produced four mainstream books on eugenics, including a comparative biography of Galton and Mendel. In 1926, "the eugenic society of perfectionists" in southern Russia wrote to Kol'tsov for aid in putting "eugenic marriage" into practice. Eugenics, melded with questions of maternal-child health and early childhood education, found a ready following among gynecologists, who were often restyled as eugenic-gynecologists.

Alexandra Kollontai—revolutionary, writer, People's Commissar for Social Welfare—published an article in *Kommunistka* in 1921 with the decidedly unsexy title, "Theses on Communist Morality in the Sphere of Marital Relations" (Kollontai, 1921). Beginning with the statement, which few historians of the family would disagree with, that family and marriage were not categories which existed outside of history, Kollontai went on to argue that under communism, the family as an economic unit would cease to exist, and the legal system would not concern itself about consensual sexual relations, although that did not suggest an amoral free for all. "The satisfaction of healthy and natural instincts only ceases to be normal when the boundaries of hygiene are overstepped," and gave

5 I cannot help but note how blindness is used as a negative image, as are darkness and crawling (one of my favorite at-home means of locomotion). While metaphors of darkness, blindness, and pathology saturate language, that hardly means they should go unremarked.

us an example sexual excess that might leave one too tired for productive labor, as well as unnatural sexual restraint (Kollontai, 1921: 19). Sexual radicals such as Alexandra Kollontai, having argued for the separation of love from marriage and conception from sexual activity, argued that reproduction could logically also be separated from loving relationships and organized on a rational and eugenic basis.

Slaves of the past or captains of the future?

Throughout the 1920s, a lively debate was going on within the Soviet Union about whether acquired characteristics could be inherited. Paul Kammerer, an Austrian biologist and socialist who argued for such inheritance, wrote:

> If acquired characteristics cannot be passed on, as most of our contemporaneous naturalists contend, then no true organic progress is possible. Man lives and suffers in vain. Whatever he might have acquired in the course of his lifetime dies with him. His children and his children's children must ever and again start from the bottom.
>
> (Kammerer, 1924: 30)

However,

> [i]f acquired characteristics are occasionally inherited, then it becomes evident that we are not exclusively slaves of the past—slaves helplessly endeavoring to free ourselves of our shackles—but also captains of our future, who in the course of time will be able to rid ourselves, to a certain extent, of our heavy burden and to ascend into higher and ever higher strata of development.
>
> (Kammerer, 1924: 31)

He did concede, "If a definite scientific perception destroys our hopes of evolution in such a manner, we would have to bow before the truth, be it ever so disconsolating. A revolt against facts would be of no avail" (Kammerer, 1924: 30).

Kammerer conducted experiments on a genus of frogs which are popularly known as midwife toads—so called because the males carry a string of fertilized eggs on their backs—which he claimed offered evidence of such inheritance; however, his work was subsequently shown to have been faked, and Kammerer committed suicide in 1926. A film called *Salamandr*—the scenario was written by Commissar of Enlightenment Anatoly Lunacharsky—portrayed Kammerer as having been hounded to his death for his Communist sympathies, with nefarious elements from the Catholic Church—Gregor Mendel had, after all, been a monk—playing a role. For a long time it has been easy to dismiss Lamarckians, but new studies in the field of epigenetics suggest that advocates of inherited characteristics may have glimpsed a truth, even if much of what they said was wrong. Darwin himself—writing before genes were known—believed in the possibility of inheritance of acquired traits, as did the great Russian scientist and Nobel Laureate Ivan Pavlov, who offered experimental evidence for the theory.

The great break

In 1928, with Stalin's power in the Soviet Union consolidated, a period known as the Great Break, the Cultural Revolution, or the revolution from above began. Abandoning Lenin's New Economic Policy—a limited revival of the market economy—and the period of great artistic ferment that had accompanied the first decade of the Soviet Union, the government undertook forced collectivization of agriculture and pushed for rapid industrialization. Along with this revolution from above came a suspicion of, and sometimes an outright hostility towards, technology and technocrats. Mark B Adams notes that, "As a bourgeois, biosocial, technocratic field, eugenics was doomed" (Adams, 1989: 881). To biologize (*biologizirovat'*)—to extrapolate from the biological to the social—became a pejorative. The same could not be said of extrapolation from the social to the biological. As Mark B Adams notes, "Genetics was seen as being incompatible with revolutionary Marxist materialism: an immortal germ plasm, subject only to rare, random, unpredictable, and generally harmful mutations, seemed to preclude social control" (Adams, 1989: 100).

Despite the disapproval that was beginning to be expressed for eugenics, some scientists continued to advocate for it. In 1928, the Party called for proposals for implementing the first Five Year Plan. Alexsandr Serebrovsky, a student of Kol'tsov and a prominent geneticist, put forth a proposal, which said that a program of socialist eugenics would enable the Five-Year-Plan to be fulfilled in two and a half years. He advocated, "the widespread induction of conception by means of artificial insemination using recommended sperm, and not at all necessarily from a beloved spouse" (Adams, 1990a: 180). Such technology, he pointed out, was already widespread in animal husbandry, and "one talented and valuable producer could have up to 1000 children" (Adams, 1990a: 180–81). Exactly how this would enable the Five-Year-Plan to be achieved in half that time was not spelled out: after all, these "new forms of human beings" would barely be out of diapers in two and a half years. Serebrovsky's plan was denounced as a "psychotic delusion." Other eugenicists, such as Filipchenko, tried to erase the connection between eugenics and genetics altogether, taking the word "eugenics" from his bureau and declining to renew its membership in the International Federation of Eugenic Organizations.

In June of 1930, a poem entitled "Evgenika" appeared in *Izvestiia*, written by Demian Bednyi—known as the Bolshevik Edgar Guest—which mocked eugenics, asking if Serebrovsky was proposing a new slogan—"Genes of the World, Unite!" and imagining shock brigades masturbating in such a "productive frenzy" that they ended up with callouses—whether on their hands or the nether parts of their anatomies not made clear (Joravsky, 1959). While doggerel did not bring down a field, the poem's presence in the newspaper of record signaled a decisive shift in the official attitude towards eugenics.

Despite these attacks, eugenics did manage to survive, albeit in a more subdued fashion, renaming itself medical genetics, and including in its public pronouncements denunciations of "bourgeois eugenics."

Kids on show, a man with the heart of a dog, and giant ostriches attack Moscow

While the history of Soviet eugenics has largely been written as part of the history of science—which scientist proposed what theory and when, the creation and destruction of various institutes and journals, which scientists were executed and deported to camps, and who somehow managed to survive—eugenics had a much broader reach, into popular culture and broader understandings.

Sergei Tretyakov's *I Want a Baby* was written in the late 1920s but not produced until long after Tretyakov had been shot as an enemy of the people in 1937. Although he is almost unknown today, he was hailed by Brecht as his teacher and much of what today would be called Brechtian had its roots in Tretyakov's work: he did not want to write plays which would "end with some kind of approved maxim" after which "the spectators can go and put their galoshes on in peace" nor did he want audience members to identify with the characters, aiming for the engagement of their critical faculties rather than their sympathies (Tretyakov, 1995: x).

As Eric Naiman writes in his *Sex in Public*, "Control over previously elemental behavior is very much the play's central issue" (Naiman, 1997: 110). That said, the play itself is the antithesis of controlled. It is crowded with characters—an undertaker, a self-styled poet ("the houses bill and coo like amorous hippopotamuses"), an inventor who comes up with, among other things, a device for getting the mold off pickled mushrooms, an old woman who pledges not to die until she's seen—peeking through a crack in the wall of communal house—"how these Bolsheviks fornicate," along with Milda, an ardent party member, more than a bit of a pill, who during the course of the play will recruit the "100% proletarian" Iakov[6] to father her child (Tretyakov, 1995: 65). But while characters in the play make pro-eugenics speeches, Milda, who explains her dislike of flowers by saying "They're the plant's sex organs" (Tretyakov, 1995: 65) and declares "There's no such thing as human solidarity. There are well-equipped factories. A correctly laid-out day. . . . A precise railway timetable and a truly charted course to socialism," no one puts their ideological galoshes on in peace at the end of the play (Tretyakov, 1995: 20). Whether the play got in trouble for its portrayal of eugenics, abortion (one character says "I want a little son. And what have I had? Fifteen abortions"), or gang rape is unclear.

In the mid-1920s, Mikhail Bulgakov, who would later become famous for his great satiric work, *The Master and Margarita*, wrote two short novels, *The Heart of a Dog* and *The Red Ray*—the title of the latter rather strangely translated into English as *The Fatal Eggs*, given that redness seems to hold roughly the

6 The auto-correct on my iPad kept trying to make this "Iacocca."

same place in this book as whiteness does in *Moby Dick*.[7] These two early novels by Bulgakov have traditionally been read as an anti-Soviet satire or as a warning against scientific hubris à la *Frankenstein*; a reading of them as texts about eugenics has been suggested by Yvonne Howell, in her "Eugenics, Rejuvenation, and Bulgakov's Journey into the Heart of Dogness" (Howell, 2006). Bulgakov had been a medical student and was well-acquainted with the scientific milieu in which eugenicists worked.

The Fatal Eggs is the earlier—and far cruder—of the two works. Set in the year 1928—slightly in the future, the book having been first published in 1925—Vladimir Ipatyevich Persikov, a Moscow zoology professor, happens to discover that a red ray, aimed at a disc of amoebae, causes amazing changes: "In the narrow red strip life was on the boil . . . [The amoebae] made their way in hordes and fought with one another for a place in the ray. Inside the ray, there was no other word for it, *furious* reproduction was taking place. . . . The best ones and the strong ones were victorious. And these best ones were horrific." The ray is then tried on frog spawn: "In the course of two days thousands of tadpoles hatched from the grains of roe." Within a single day, they have grown into frogs "so vicious and gluttonous that half of them were gobbled up on the spot by the other half (Bulgakov, 2010: 15–21).

The Fatal Eggs serves as a warning about the hubris of scientists and the dangers of tampering with biological processes, even with the best of intentions. Shortly after the discovery of the miraculous red ray, a plague strikes the country's chickens. A screen on the roof of *The Workers' Newspaper* shows piles of chicken corpses being burned. Persikov's miraculous device is sent to "The Red Ray" model state farm, to which foreign eggs, free from blight, have been imported (Bulgakov, 2010).

Alas, the red ray has not been directed at chicken eggs but at anaconda and ostrich eggs—oops!—and has created gigantic rampaging ostriches and serpents as tall as a Moscow electricity pole and three times as thick. The latest weaponry—electric revolvers and sub-machine guns—prove powerless against the marauding mutants. Soon panicked refugees are rushing away from the disaster, crowds calling to the military forces setting out, "Help us brothers! Kill the reptiles! Save Moscow!" A mob attacks Persikov's laboratory, smashing glass, killing innocent frogs, and the professor himself—he who was once the savior of the world now having become the enemy of the people. Moscow is only saved by an untimely frost—minus 18 degrees in August (Bulgakov, 2010: 88).

Bulgakov's later short novel, *The Heart of a Dog*, in which a self-proclaimed eugenicist amalgamates a human and an animal, wrestles with similar questions about scientific "improvement" of life. Before discussing this novel, it is worth describing an actual series of experiments carried out by a Soviet eugenicist.

In the mid-1920s, zoology professor and eugenicist, Ilia Ivanov had not only

7 Early on in the novel, Professor Persikov is called on by a journalist whose satin calling card identifies him as a contributor to *The Red Light*, *The Red Journal*, the *Red Searchlight*, *The Red Evening Newspaper*—and *The Red Pepper*.

proposed creating human-ape hybrids via artificial insemination, but traveled to French Guinea (now the Republic of Guinea) where the Pasteur Institute had an experimental primate station, accompanied by his son as his assistant, and attempted to inseminate apes with human sperm. Ivanov was an internationally acclaimed expert in artificial insemination, having had great success in applying his methods to purebred horses before the revolution. Alexander Etkind notes "[i]t is important to recognize that Ivanov's ideas were perfectly in tune with his time and circle": his work was supported by the Pasteur Institute and the circle of Bolsheviks centered around the Commissariat of the Enlightenment, the optimistic and futuristic wing of the Bolsheviks (Etkind, 2008: 205–10). The success of these experiments would not only have offered proof of evolution, but might also have laid the groundwork for the biological creation of the New Socialist Man.

In Africa, the two Russians carried out their work in secret, fearing that if the "native staff" found out what they were doing, they would arouse "the suspicions and interpretations by the Negroes . . . this could have led to very unpleasant consequences for us" (Rossiianov, 2002: 297). The apes, not surprisingly, had little truck with being used in this way. Two of them, named Babette and Syvette by their keepers, fought back against the brutal inseminations. The work with the apes proved so difficult that Ivanov decided that inseminating human women with the sperm of male apes would be easier, and approached the head of the colonial health service in Brazzaville, asking him for permission to experiment on hospitalized women, planning to do this without the women's knowledge (Rossiianov, 2002: 299). His plan did not come to pass—when the Russian Academy of Sciences learned about it, its members were aghast, although Ivanov "angrily reported to his sponsors in the Kremlin about the primitive fears of the blacks and the bourgeois prejudices of the French" (Etkind, 2008: 205).

Instead, primates were brought to the Soviet Republic of Georgia—although only four of 20 animals survived the trip—with its subtropical climate and palm trees. A call was made for women to volunteer to become the mothers of hybrids. Five women were selected for the experiment and inseminated with the sperm of a 26-year old orangutan named—*I am not making this up*—Tarzan. Needless to say, no pregnancies resulted. Tarzan died.

As a former doctor and a member of the intellectual circles of Moscow, Bulgakov would have been well aware of the currents linking rejuvenation, eugenics, and the hopes for a "New Soviet Man." Howell writes, "the science fictional layer of the novel is [the] very real world of scientific debates that occupied intellectuals, health officials, and policy-makers in NEP [New Economic Policy]-era Moscow" (Howell, 2006: 558). Eugenicists often had a particular interest in whether the changes induced in endocrine glands could be inherited; Geneticist II Agol, who will appear below as the unfortunate collaborator of HJ Muller, worked on inheritance of induced changes in the thyroid glands of chickens.

In *The Heart of a Dog*, a eugenicist and rejuvenation specialist, Professor Philip Philipovich Preobrazhenskii, performs an experiment involving glandular transplantation from a human to a mongrel dog, which he has rescued—or perhaps kidnapped—from the streets of Moscow (Bulgakov, 1968). The experiment, intending to bring about rejuvenation, instead brings about humanization: Sharik—the word is a common Russian dog's name—the hound, is reborn as Sharikov, a dog who raises himself up on his hind legs and strides around the professor's seven room flat, uttering a word salad of all the curses which were flung at him in his previous canine incarnation. The professor's assistant notes in his journal: "Oh, what a glorious confirmation of the theory of evolution! Oh, the sublime chain leading from a dog to Mendeleyev the great chemist" (Bulgakov, 1968: 67).

The novel often has been read through the lens of Cold War politics, in what might be termed the Dwight Eisenhower School of Literary Criticism. Certainly, Bulgakov pokes fun at the ardent proletarian members of the housing management committee—who track mud across the poor professor's Persian carpets and have the temerity to suggest that the professor give up his dining room in order to increase the occupancy of the apartment building. They point out that he could eat in his bedroom, since no one else in Moscow—not even Isadora Duncan—has a dining room.

But the novel is anything but an allegory, with Professor Preobrazhensky as the fiendish eugenicist and Sharik as the pure and good icon of Nature with which the Evil Scientist tampers. Sharik is something of a eugenicist himself: like Cesare Lombroso, who could read innate criminality from the shape of a forehead or an earlobe, Sharik, speaking of the cook who burned him, wonders what one can expect from a man whose mug is wider than it is long. He nails the professor as gentleman not from the fact that he's wearing a coat—why even the proletarians have coats these days!—but from his eyes. As Howell points out, the dog biologizes. At the end of the novel, he decides "there was something shady in my ancestry. There must have been a Newfoundland. She was a whore, my grandmother," adding, "may she rest in the Heavenly Kingdom" (Howell, 2006: 551).

Dear Comrade Stalin, I come to you with a matter of vital importance

HJ Muller was an American geneticist who, in 1946, would win the Nobel Prize for his work on mutations in fruit flies induced by radiation. His family had Americanized their name by removing the umlaut from Müller, so it rhymed with "duller." Hounded for his Communist associations at the University of Texas where he was a faculty member and seeing Russia as the socialist future, he emigrated to the Soviet Union in 1933. In *Out of the Night: A Biologist's View of the Future*, he voiced a fervent plea for humanity to seize control of reproduction, as it had seized control of production, and breed a new race via artificial insemination: more intelligent, more humane, more cooperative. He had his book translated into Russian and sent it with a cover letter to Stalin, which encapsulated the book's main arguments. "Dear Comrade Stalin," Muller wrote, "As a scientist with confidence in the ultimate Bolshevik triumph throughout all possible spheres of human endeavor, I come to you with a matter of vital importance . . . the control by man of the hereditary material lying at the basis of life in man himself" (Glad, 2003). He went on to speak of "bourgeois misconstructions" of eugenics, stating that eugenics which could only truly be realized in "a socialized economic system . . . it will be possible within only a few generations to bestow the gift even of so-called 'genius' upon practically every individual in the population—in fact, to raise all the masses to the level at which now stand our most gifted individuals. . . . And this need only be the beginning. . . . [I]n place of the accidental, wavering and painful processes of natural selection prevalent in the distant past," socialism could bring about "a relatively high rate of multiplication of the more favorable gene," by allowing individuals to obtain "the best genetic equipment obtainable . . . for use by artificial insemination" (Glad, 2003). After 20 years, if capitalism still existed beyond the Soviet borders, "this vital wealth of our youthful cadres . . . could not fail to be of very considerable advantage for our side" (Glad, 2003).

Not only was Stalin not converted to Muller's ideas, his majesty was not amused. Certainly, the association of eugenics with the ideas of Trotsky was a mark against it, as was its association with "bourgeois science." Stalin is reported to have two webbed toes, and certainly had a left arm that was withered enough to have kept him out of the Tsar's army, although the cause of it is disputed, with some seeing it as the result of an infection and others—notably his French biographer Boris Souvarine—attributing it, along with two toes grown together, to the effects of his father's alcoholism, and perhaps even to his father being inebriated at the moment of conception. Perhaps his own association with rural backwardness and being scorned for his physical difference fed into his distrust of eugenics. Colleagues arranged to spirit Muller out of the country before he could face Stalin's wrath. His collaborators were not so lucky. Several of them were shot, including II Agol, and the secretary who had undertaken the translation of his book.

In 1948, Lysenkoism became the official policy in the Soviet Union. Muller published a two part article on the destruction of science in the USSR and what he termed a "return to barbarism" in the *Saturday Review of Literature* in that year, calling to task the Soviet authorities for having "officially repudiated the entire science of genetics and approved in its stead a group of superstitions that hark back to ancient times" (Muller, 1948b: 31). Lysenko's work was defended in the *Saturday Review* by none other than George Bernard Shaw (Muller, 1949; Shaw, 1949). The photos of the two men included with their articles show Shaw with a long white beard, his head inclined downwards, looking sage; while a grinning and bespectacled Muller appears to be a man who could well be an accountant in Babbit's Zenith. If one worries about Muller-rhymes-with-duller clashing swords with a man whose wit was—well, Shavian, Muller more than held his own.

Nearly two decades after Muller left Russia, during the US McCarthy era, two FBI agents were waiting for Muller when he arrived at his office at the University of Indiana, there to serve him with a subpoena to appear before the House Un-American Activities Committee. One of them apologized for bothering him—I can't help wondering if the agent showed this unexpected deference given that he was serving a Nobel Prize winner. Muller replied: "This morning I heard that Stalin died and nothing can make me unhappy today" (Carlson, 1981: 372–74).

"There are no invalids in the Soviet Union!"

And where, one may well ask, were the disabled people in this debate about eugenics that so directly concerned them? I have searched for their voices in vain. In Trotsky's *The History of the Russian Revolution*, we learn that in a Moscow amphitheater in 1918, "a meeting of invalids was called, soldiers and officers together" (Trotsky, 1932). Trotsky goes on to describe how:

> An orator-cripple began to cast aspersions on the officers. A noise of protest arose, a stamping of shoes, canes, crutches. "And how long ago were you, Mr. Officer, insulting the soldiers with lashes and fists?" These wounded, shell-shocked, mutilated people stood like two walls, one facing the other. Crippled soldiers against crippled officers, the majority against the minority, crutches against crutches.
>
> (Trotsky, 1932)

Trotsky paints this scene not in order to tell us anything about the self-organization of "invalids," but in order to make the point that "[t]hat nightmare scene in the amphitheater foreshadowed the ferocity of the coming civil war." Later on, in his *History of the Russian Revolution*, the All-Russian League of Crippled Warriors appear, again almost in an aside, where Trotsky sees them as "tragic specters of the past . . . [t]he handless, the legless, the blind" (Trotsky, 1932).

While many have seen the eugenics movement as foundational to the oppression of disabled people, the repudiation of eugenics in the Soviet Union hardly meant that institutionalization and other forms of segregation did not exist. Sarah D Phillips notes that policies which excluded and stigmatized those with disabilities, both physical and mental, ended up making disability invisible. Those with impairments called into question the notion that the body of the New Soviet Man was being created under state socialism. This segregation was so complete that a government official, queried by a Western journalist about Soviet participation in the first Paralympic games in 1980, could respond: "There are no invalids in the USSR!" (Phillips, 2009). Russian writer Ruben Gallego—the grandson of the head of the Spanish Communist Party, which accounts for the un-Russian name—paints a grim portrait of what life was like for those whose existence had been expunged from public consciousness in his autobiographical novel, *White on Black*.

In *Eugenic Design: Streamlining America in the 1930s*, Christina Cogdell makes a surprising—and persuasively argued—case that eugenic ideals were intrinsic to the development of the 1930s design style known as streamline, and marshals much evidence about the convergence of design and eugenic ideology. Could similar arguments be made for the radical art movements, such as constructivism, which rested on "precision, impersonality, a clear formal order, simplicity and economy of organization?" (Scher, 2015). There were two great systems of concentration camps and mass murder in the Global North in the twentieth century. The role of eugenics played a fundamental role in the Nazi genocide, as has been explored by Robert J Lifton in his *The Nazi Doctors: Medical Killing and the Psychology of Genocide* and amplified in the works of Henry Friedlander and Benno Müller-Hill, among others. Did Soviet eugenics play any role in creating the ideological underpinning for the Gulag and liquidations under Stalinism?

These questions about the role of disability and eugenics in the Soviet Union remain to be answered by disability studies scholars who can further delve into the long-term effects of Soviet eugenics.

Bibliography

Adams, M (1989) The Politics of Human Heredity in the USSR, 1920–1940. *Genome*, 31.

Adams, M (1990a) Eugenics in Russia, 1900–1940. In *The Wellborn Science: Eugenics in Germany, France, Brazil, and Russia*, Adams, M (ed). Oxford, UK: Oxford University Press.

Adams, M (1990b) The Soviet Nature-Nurture Debate. In *Science and the Soviet Social Order*, Graham, L (ed). Cambridge, MA: Harvard University Press.

Bowcott, O (2009) Doctor Offers Diagnosis in Charles Darwin Medical Mystery. *Guardian*, December 13, 2009.

Brown, J (1989) Societal Responses to Mental Disorders. In *The Disabled in the Soviet Union: Past and Present, Theory and Practice*. McCagg, WO and Siegelbaum, L (eds). Pittsburgh, PA: University of Pittsburgh Press.

Bulgakov, M (1968) *The Heart of a Dog* (trans. M Glenny). London: Harvill Press, 1999.

Bulgakov, M (1925/2010) *The Fatal Eggs* (trans. M Karpelson). Thornhill, ON: Translit Publishing.

Carlson, E (1981) *Genes, Radiation, and Society: The Life and Work of H.J. Muller*. Ithaca: Cornell University Press.

Chernyskevsky, N (1863/1989) *What Is To Be Done?* (trans. M Katz). Ithaca: Cornell University Press.

Darwin, C (1981) *The Descent of Man, and Selection in Relation to Sex*. Princeton, NJ: Princeton University Press.

Etkind, A (2008) Beyond Eugenics: The Forgotten Scandal of Hybridizing Humans and Apes. *Studies in History and Philosophy of Biological and Biomedical Sciences* 39.

Friedlander, H (1995) *The Origins of Nazi Genocide: From Euthanasia to the Final Solution*. Chapel Hill, NC: University of North Carolina Press.

Gaissinovitch, AE (1980) The Origins of Soviet Genetics and the Struggle with Lamarckism, 1922–1929. *Journal of the History of Biology* 13(1).

Glad, J (2003) Hermann J. Muller's 1936 Letter to Stalin. *The Mankind Quarterly*, 43(3): 305–19, available online at http://mankindquarterly.org/muellersletter.pdf (last accessed November 8, 2015).

Graham, L (1977) Science and Values: The Eugenics Movement in Germany and Russia in the 1920s. *The American Historical Review* 82(5).

Graham, L (1993) *Science in Russia and the Soviet Union: A Short History.* Cambridge, UK: Cambridge University Press.

Howell, Y (2006) *Heart of a Dog*: Eugenics and Bulgakov's Journey into the Heart of Dogness. *Slavic Review*, 65(3).

Joravsky, D (1959) Soviet Marxism and Biology Before Lysenko. *Journal of the History of Ideas* 20(1).

Kammerer, P (1924) *The Inheritance of Acquired Characteristics* (trans. AP Maerker-Branden). New York, NY: Boni and Liveright.

Kerr, A and Shakespeare, T (2002) *Genetic Politics: From Eugenics to Genome.* Cheltenham, UK: New Clarion Press.

Koestler, A (1972) *The Case of the Midwife Toad.* New York, NY: Random House.

Kollontai (1921) *Theses on Communist Morality in the Sphere of Marital Relations.* Available online at www.marxists.org/archive/kollonta/1921/theses-morality on (last accessed on April 7, 2014.

Krementsov, N (2010) Eugenics in Russia and the Soviet Union. In *The Oxford Handbook of the History of Eugenics,* Bashford, A and Philipps, L (eds). New York, NY: Oxford University Press.

Kropotkin, P (1912) The Sterilization of the Unfit. *Mother Earth* 7(1): 354–57.

Kropotkin, P (1955) *Mutual Aid: A Factor of Evolution.* Boston, MA: Porter Sargent Publishers.

Lifton, R (1986) *The Nazi Doctors: Medical Killing and the Psychology of Genocide*, New York, NY: Basic Books.

Malthus, T (1809) *An Essay on the Principle of Population.* Washington, DC: Robert Chew Weightman, available online at www.esp.org/books/malthus/population/malthus.pdf (last accessed November 8, 2015).

McNeil, D Jr (2003) Rare Infection Threatens To Spread in Blood Supply. *New York Times,* November 18.

Muller, H (1935) *Out of the Night: A Biologist's View of the Future.* New York, NY: The Vanguard Press.

Muller, H (1948a) The Destruction of Science in the USSR. *The Saturday Review of Literature*, December 4 1948.

Muller, H (1948b) Back to Barbarism—Scientifically. *The Saturday Review of Literature*, December 11, 1948.

Muller, H (1949) It Still Isn't a Science: A Reply to George Bernard Shaw. *The Saturday Review of Literature*, April 16, 1949.

Müller-Hill, B (1998) *Murderous Science: Elimination by Scientific Selection of Jews, Gypsies, and Others.* Danvers, MA: Cold Spring Harbor Laboratory Press.

Naiman, E (1997) *Sex in Public: The Incarnation of Early Soviet Ideology.* Princeton, NJ: Princeton University Press.

Orrego, F and Quintana, C (2007) Darwin's Illness: A Final Diagnosis. *Notes and Records of the Royal Society,* 61(1).

Phillips, S (2009) 'There Are no Invalids in the USSR!': A Missing Soviet Chapter in the New Disability History. *Disability Studies Quarterly* 29(3).

Phillips, S (2012) Citizenship and Human Mobility: Disability and the 'Etatization' of Soviet and Post-Soviet Space. In *Russia in Motion: Cultures of Human Mobility Since 1850,* Randolph, J and Avrutin, EM (eds). Chicago: University of Illinois Press, available online at www.dsq-sds.org/article/view/936/1111 (last accessed November 8, 2015).

Pullman, P (2013) 'How Children's Books Thrived Under Stalin', *Guardian*, October 11,

2013, available online at www.theguardian.com/artanddesign/2013/oct/11/russian-children-books-illustration-stalin (last accessed November 17, 2015).

Rossiianov, K (2002) Beyond Species: Il'ya Ivanov and His Experiments on Cross-Breeding Humans with Anthropoid Apes. *Science in Context* 15(2): 277–316.

Russell, M (1998) *Beyond Ramps: Disability at the End of the Social Contract*. Monroe, ME: Common Courage Press.

Scher, P (2015) *Russian Constructivism*, available online at http://paulastribute.weebly.com/russian-constuctivism.html (last accessed November 26, 2015).

Shaw, George Bernard (1949) Behind the Lysenko Controversy. *The Saturday Review of Literature*, April 16, 1949.

Shklovsky, V (1940) *O Mayakovsky*. Feiler, L (trans) (1972) *Mayakovsky and His Circle*. New York, NY: Dodd, Mead & Co.

Snyder, S and Mitchell, D (2006) *Cultural Locations of Disability*. Chicago, IL: University of Chicago Press.

Todes, D (1989) *Darwin Without Malthus: The Struggle for Existence in Russian Evolutionary Thought*. Oxford, UK: Oxford University Press, 1989.

Thomson, K (2009) Darwin's Enigmatic Health. *American Scientist*, May/June.

Tretyakov, Sergeĭ Mikhaĭlovich (1995) *I Want a Baby* (trans. R Leach). Birmingham: University of Birmingham Press.

Trotsky, L (1932) *History of the Russian Revolution* (trans. M Eastman, M). Available online at www.marxists.org/archive/trotsky/1930/hrr/ (last accessed April 4, 2014).

Trotksy, L (1934) If America Should Go Communist. *Liberty* available online at www.marxists.org/archive/trotsky/1934/08/ame.htm (last accessed November 8, 2015).

Trotsky, L (1923/1960) *Literature and Revolution*. Strunksy, R (trans). Ann Arbor, MI: University of Michigan Press.

Valentinov, N (1951) Chernysevsky i Lenin. *Novyi zhurnal*, 27: 193–94.

Vucinich, A (1988) *Darwin in Russian Thought*. Berkeley, CA: University of California Press.

What disability civil rights cannot do: employment and political economy

Marta Russell

ABSTRACT *The Americans with Disabilities Act is both a liberal civil rights bill and a labour economics bill meant to increase the employment of disabled persons. It identifies the source of unemployment in discriminatory attitudes of employers and physical barriers in the work environment, and promotes inclusion through the establishment of regulations that are intended to create 'equal opportunity' in the labour market. Such liberal reforms primarily focus on 'irrational' discriminatory attitudes. Operating within an individualist framework, civil rights have not given sufficient attention to structural barriers, which 'rational' business practices, the economic system and class power relationships erect. This paper will both micro- and macro-economic realities of US capitalism, which directly impede disabled peoples' employment and perpetuate a disabling society. The failure of rights legislation to increase disabled people's employment exposes the contradictions of promoting equal opportunity in a class-based (unequal) society.*

Introduction

Given that a decade has passed since the passage of the ADA and 5 years since the enactment of the British Disability Discrimination Act, it seems a fitting time at which to examine the civil rights employment impasse against the larger political economy backdrop. Since my expertise lies with US capitalism, this paper will detail structural problems underlying disability employment issues in the US only.

In the US it is now evident that disability civil rights do not equate with a lowering of the disabled unemployment rate. Despite a growing economy—the best possible scenario for increasing the employment of disabled persons—and a low aggregate national official unemployment rate (4–5%) presiding over much of the 9 years the Americans with Disabilities Act (ADA) employment provisions have been in effect, the unemployment rate for working-age disabled population has barely budged from its chronic state—hovering at 70%.[1]

1 During the pre-ADA research phase, Congress found that 'two thirds of all disabled Americans between the age of 16 and 64 [were] not working at all.' Hearing on H.R. 2273, The Americans with Disabilities Act of 1989: Joint Hearing before the Subcommittee on Select Education and

Over two-thirds of working-age disabled adults say they would prefer to work (Harris *et al*, 1998), yet US Census data suggests that in 2000 only 30.5% of those with a work disability between ages 16 and 64 were in the labour force and only

27.6% were employed, while 82.1% of non-disabled persons in this age group were either employed (78.6%) or actively seeking work for pay. According to a recent study, while many Americans reaped higher incomes from an economy that created a record number of new jobs during 7 years of continuous economic growth (1992–1998), the employment rates of disabled men and women continued to fall so that by 1998, they were still below the 1992 level (Burkhauser *et al.*, 2001). A Boston Globe headline news story 'Access and Closed Doors: Despite Federal Act, Number of Disabled with No Job is Rising' noted that Pollster Louis Harris & Associates found that 71% of people with disabilities who are of working age were unemployed in 1998, 5 percentage points higher than in 1986, when the study was first conducted (Lewis, 1999).

What does the empirical data show has happened to employment during the economic expansion of the 1990s with full implementation of the ADA's employment provisions? The Congressional Research Service found that the employed share of 18–64-year-olds with disabilities who reported they were able to work grew from 70.2% in 1992 to 72.3% in 1996. Over the same period, the proportion of the non-disabled working-age population who were employed rose from 78.5% to 80.5%. The job prospects for the disabled population improved to the same degree as the non-disabled population, meaning the gap in employment rates did not narrow. Study author Linda Levine concludes 'this suggests that the ADA did not provide an extra boost to the employment situation of working-age adults with disabilities through the mid-1990s' (Levine, 2000, p. 12).

The Disability Rights Movement (DRM) in the US has largely conceptualised disability as a minority group, which is disadvantaged and denied majority rights status (Hahn, 1985; Zola, 1994). Identifying the source of disabled persons unemployment in discriminatory attitudes of employers and physical barriers in the work environment, the DRM has sought to alter the historical exclusion of disabled persons from the workforce through the establishment of individual legal rights and remedy under the liberal theory of 'equal opportunity' to employment—which essentially means equal access to a job not available to all.

The Americans with Disabilities Act of 1990 (ADA)[2] is both a civil rights bill intended to end employer discrimination and a labour economics bill, intended to increase the relative wages and employment of disabled persons. The Act states '[T]he Nation's proper goals regarding individuals with disabilities are to assure . . . economic self-sufficiency[.] Discrimination . . . costs the United States billions of dollars in unnecessary expenses resulting from dependency

Employment Opportunities of the House Committee on Education and Labor, 101st Congress, 1st Session (July 18 & September 13, 1989; two hearings). S. Rep. No. 101–116, at 9.

2 42 U.S.C. § 12101–12213 (1994).

and nonproductivity.'[3] The ADA bans discrimination on the basis of disability through the establishment of constitutional law and regulations which are geared to 'level the playing field' for disabled job applicants and to induce employers to accommodate impairments on the job. It gives disabled persons redress against work-based disability discrimination in the courts and through the Equal Employment Opportunity Commission (EEOC).

There is consensus, however, amongst scholars and analysts that the US courts have failed to enforce the ADA as civil rights proponents intended and that EEOC enforcement has fallen short. A study by the American Bar Association's Commission on Mental and Physical Disability Law, for instance, shows that disabled workers bringing discrimination suits are unlikely to succeed in court (Mental and Physical Disability Law Reporter, 1998). Of the more than 1200 cases filed under the employment provisions of the ADA 1992–1998, disabled employees prevailed only 8% of the time. By 2000 employers prevailed 95% of the time. Another study by Ohio State University Law Professor Ruth Colker shows similar results, finding that employers successfully defend more than 93% of reported ADA employment discrimination cases at the trial court level and succeed in 84% of cases appealed (Colker, 1999, p. 99).

So far, disabled plaintiffs have faced great difficulty prevailing in court on key issues. The US Commission on Civil Rights notes that many disability experts ascribe the problem in judicial and administrative confusion over interpretation of the employment statutes (US Commission on Civil Rights, 1998, p. 5). Professor Matthew Diller explains that legitimate plaintiff cases are being thwarted often for nonsensical reasons (such as medical conditions are not granted the legal standing of 'disability' under the law), and that courts are resistant to both comprehending and accepting equal rights and reasonable accommodation as applied to disablement (Diller, 2000, p. 23). Arlene Mayerson, an attorney with the Disability Rights Education and Defense Fund, characterises ADA case law as 'hyper technical, often illogical interpretations of the ADA', which have generated a 'disturbing trend' of court precedents (Mayerson, 1997, pp. 587, 612). Robert Burgdorff, Jr, one of the drafters of the ADA, concludes that 'legal analysis has proceeded quite a way down the wrong road' (Burgdorff, 1997, p. 409). Burgdorff points to a judicial tendency to view ADA plaintiffs as seeking *special* benefits and treatment instead of equal rights (Burgdorff, 1997, p. 413). Bonnie Tucker theorises that there is an inherent flaw in the civil rights paradigm when it comes to equal rights for disabled persons. She suggests that judges may be viewing the provision of reasonable accommodation as an 'extra' requirement, an expansion of traditional civil rights concept and, consequently, rejecting the legitimacy of disability rights under equal rights principles (Tucker, 2001).

To explain such outcomes, I have sought to examine the relationship between politics, policy and economics—particularly with regard to the interests of business. Disability scholars such as Victor Finkelstein, Michael Oliver, Colin Barnes, Paul Abberley, Nirmala Erevelles, Lennard Davis, Brendan Gleeson and others

3 42 U.S.C. § 12101(a)(8)–(9) (1994).

have advanced the position that the capitalist system—particularly the commodification of labour—is a crucial contributing factor to the lack of economic advancement of disabled people. Going back to Marx's theory of absolute impoverishment, Ernest Mandel clarifies Marx's observation that capitalism 'throws out of the production process' a section of the proletariat: unemployed, old people, disabled persons, the sick, etc. (Mandel, 1962, p. 151) Marx calls these groups a part of the poorest stratum 'bearing the stigmata of wage labor'. As Mandel says, 'this analysis retains its full value, even under the "welfare" capitalism of today' (Mandel, 1962, p. 151).

While others have made links between capitalism and disablement my purpose has been to expose how modern capitalism perpetuates this substratum in the face of disabled peoples' struggle for their place the US labour force. In this vein I have sought to expose systemic economic discrimination against disabled workers in a capitalist economy that the ADA cannot address or remedy and will return to this matter below. I have also argued that ADA court failures have been prompted by capitalist opposition made more powerful in a neoliberal era, where conservative forces have politically achieved a more *laissez faire*, deregulated economy, successfully targeting regulationships they view as interfering with business for weakening or repeal (Russell 1998; pp. 109–111; 2000, p. 341). The philosophical momentum for social justice that spurred the Civil Rights Act of 1964, and subsequent progressive court decisions in the 1960s and 1970s was well into decline by the 1990s when the ADA was passed. For example, in the era following passage of civil rights laws in 1957, 1960, 1964 and 1968, the Republicans made dramatic inroads into Democratic victories that forged the civil rights movement, established the Office of Economic Opportunity and initiated the War on Poverty during the Great Society. Presidents Reagan and Bush dismantled the entire Community Services Administration, responsible for driving much of the 1960s social change agenda by advancing human services, occupational safety, consumer protection and environmental protection laws.

On the way out were civil rights and economic entitlements, replaced by a conservative thrust to reduce 'big bad government'. The dominant agenda of the late 1970s and 1980s was bolstered by corporate goals, which emphasised globalisation and political dominance of government (McMahan, 1985). Increased international capital mobility and liberalised international trade have resulted in the transfer of more power to management, at the expense of labour. (Parenti, 1995, pp. 99–119, 271) Conservative forces targeted protective regulations for repeal or rollback that, in their view, interfered with business (Wolman & Colamosca, 1997; Mishel *et al.*, 1999). Economic policy in the post-1979 period moved decisively toward a more *laissez faire*, deregulated approach. Industries like transportation and communications have been largely deregulated. Social protections, including safety, health and environmental regulations, the minimum wage, government transfer payments (welfare) and the unemployment insurance system all have been weakened. The ADA was no exception. It was watered down substantially to achieve Congressional consensus and Bush's presidential approval (Pheiffer, 2000, p. 43). The most recent evidence that these forces remain intact: the Supreme Court's weakening of the ADA in *Garrett*, *Sutton*, *Murphy* and *Albertson's* disability employment decisions; the striking down of the Age Discrimination Act in *Kimel v Florida*; and the invalidation of the Violence Against Women's Act in *United States v Morrison*.

After years of dedicated civil rights activism in the 1950–60s the American civil rights leader Dr Martin Luther King, Jr outgrew the liberal view that economic justice for blacks was possible through the enactment of civil rights laws geared to make race-based employment discrimination against the law. King realised that civil rights (even when coupled with economic expansion) could not solve the mass unemployment of black Americans.

At the 1967 Southern Christian Leadership Conference convention Dr King implored the movement to:

> address itself to the question of restructuring the whole of American society. There are 40 million poor people here. And one day we must ask the question, 'Why are there 40 million poor people in America?' And when you begin to ask that question, you are raising questions about the economic system, about a broader distribution of wealth. When you ask that question, you begin to question the capitalistic economy. (Washington, 1991, p. 250)

For King, the theme of job creation in a capitalist economy was an ongoing and primary part of his peoples' struggle for justice. 'We need an economic bill of rights. This would guarantee a job to all people who want to work and are able to work' (King, 1968, p. 24). Today, almost 40 years since the passage of the Civil Rights Act of 1964, no economic rights have been enacted and black unemployment remains twice (8%) that of the official national rate (4.2%). This is so even when civil rights have been accompanied by affirmative action measures designed to promote hiring and remedy past race discrimination. The ADA was not followed by affirmative action for disabled workers. There is no reason to believe disability civil rights outcomes will fair better.

In practice, civil rights, which primarily focus on attitudes and prejudice, have not given sufficient attention to the barriers that the economic structure and power relationships erect against the employment of disabled persons. This paper explores the shortcomings of the liberalist 'equal opportunity' approach to employment. My emphasis will be on the political economy of disablement, on micro- and macro-economic realities systemic to capitalism, which contribute to the high disabled unemployment rate. Class interests perpetuate the exclusion of disabled persons from the workforce through systemic business accounting practices and compulsory unemployment. If we conceptualise disablement as a product of the exploitative economic structure of capitalist society; one which creates the so-called disabled body to permit a small capitalist class to create the economic conditions necessary to accumulate vast wealth, then it becomes clear that anti-discrimination legislation, by failing to acknowledge the contradictions of promoting equal opportunity in class-based (unequal) society, is insufficient to solve the unemployment predicament of disabled persons. Instead, the liberal rights model serves to forestall criticism of relationships of power at the centre of the exclusion from employment and inequality that disabled persons face. This paper will offer such a criticism.

The Relevance of the Political Economy

Political economy is a term used for nearly 300 years to express the interrelationship between the political and the economic affairs of the state. In terms of economics, liberals tend to believe that the current system is basically just, and that injustices and unemployment, low pay, inequality and poverty that occur within that system are mere unintended consequences of an otherwise beneficent economy. They are reformists who believe that gross inequalities can be leveled through legislation and other measures aimed at correcting 'market failures'. In the US and elsewhere the DRM similarly has largely accepted the foundations of free market ideology by framing the terms of the justice debate as the rights of disabled people entitled to receive equal treatment from the existing labour market (Russell & Malhotra, 2002). In contrast, left political economy looks to the laws rooted in the ongoing reproduction and expansion of this system of material accumulation as the source of the ills. Radical economists believe that the economic system itself is the problem: the system of profit does not create hardship as the unfortunate mishap of an otherwise just social order; rather, the pain experienced by people under such a system is very much integral to that system, and is required by it in order to function. People, including many disabled people, are excluded from work in such a system, and thus poor and even destitute, not because the system is breaking down, but because it is working exactly as intended.

The notion of the US as a meritocracy where individual failings are deemed the result of personal shortcomings is a seductive ideological posture. The appeal to rugged individualism—that we can be anything we want if we persevere—is an American tradition and perhaps a comforting notion, but barriers to advancement and achievement are often unrelated to individual effort, ability or motivation. Disability civil rights laws (or any civil rights) do not subject that assumption to a challenge. Civil rights, for instance, are based on the premise that the individual citizen is an equal actor in the judicial process with the legal power to redress injustice through court challenges to discrimination, but what if the individual, due to her class position, lacks the money to hire an attorney, or has not the education or circumstance to secure those rights? Gender and race are also known determinants of lack of access to the courts. Furthermore, rights depend upon court interpretation. What if the political climate of the courts is such that her rights are likely to be thwarted by judges acting in opposition to the ideological premise of those rights? What if rights are in direct class conflict; if for instance, the business class has amassed such political power that the civil right has essentially become moot through defeat after defeat in the courts and few attorneys will risk taking such cases because they have little prospect of winning (and getting paid)? In these instances individual action and individual 'right' is blocked and nulled by class and politics outside the control of the individual.

> [when 'rights-bearing persons'] lack the power and resources to properly 'compete', rights can do nothing but reinforce the status quo, as those left powerless can do nothing [but] make sporadic and/or symbolic claims. (Young & Quibell, 2000, p. 757)

The economic system presents a similar set of obstructions. The founding principle for the dominant economic model of our day or 'pure economics' (what is falsely referred to as neoclassical economics[4]) is 'methodological individualism', which treats society as nothing more than the apolitical aggregate of its component individuals, and strips the economic structure of any social dimension except the interaction of sole individual activity and projects. While both pure economic and left economic theories might allow that individuals can act independently and according to their wants, left economists recognise that behind these private wants stands an objective structure of reproduction whose requirements dominate the individual in the carrying out of her private interests. While the pure economists hold onto their theory that maximisation of well-being occurs because of individual merit, left economists recognise that structural barriers dominate individual wants. As the economist Samir Amin notes 'real society, far from being built up out of direct encounters among individual behaviors, is an infinitely more complex structure combining social classes, nations, states, big businesses, collective projects and political and ideological forces' (Amin, 1998, p. 134).

A left economic perspective does not concede disablement as an socio-attitudinal construct that can be corrected by erasing incorrect attitudes or prohibiting prejudiced-based employment discrimination. It places a different set of questions at the apex of concern, as Dr King posed. Why are there millions of persons both with and without impairments who are willing to work left unemployed in our economy? Why in the richest nation in the world are people still impoverished and working at below living wages, and why are 'deserving' disabled persons severed from the means of making a livelihood and subjected to bare survival on at or below poverty disability benefits? Left political economy reflects on the limits of the market as an institution for want satisfaction and that is the approach taken here.

Compulsory Unemployment

The capitalist economy inherently restricts the liberal application of 'equal opportunity' to employment for all because unemployment is not an aberration of capitalism, rather, it is a built-in component of the market economy that requires

4 Classical political economy was practiced by theorists such as Adam Smith, Ricardo, Karl Marx, and John Keynes who accepted politics as an inherent component of economics. Neoclassical economists reduce economics to an ahistorical and apolitical mathematical technique.

many people be unemployed against their will (Keynes, 1936, p. 249; Kalecki, 1966, p. 131; Marx, 1967, pp. 589–592) Not every person will be employed, not every person's material needs will get met through employment. Rather the system is like a giant pyramid scheme in which many 'surplus' persons in the labour market will be intentionally left out of the game. This reserve army of labor includes the official unemployed and all those parts of the population, whether part of the work force at a given time or not, who might become part of the work force if the demand for them grew. The surplus population and reserve army overlap; the slums of Mexico City are part of the US reserve army of labour—and they are also a surplus population. The reserve army has historically included women and minority workers. Marx designated disabled persons in the group least likely to become employed; the 'stagnant' or passive reserve army of labour. Now that more disabled people expect to participate in paid employment there is the potential for many to join the active reserve army.

Disabled persons, however, are the last identity group to enter the workforce, seeking the right to share in the wealth of the nation at a time when unemployment levels are as low as they have been in nearly 40 years and may be below what the investor class traditionally will tolerate. The employment expectations of disabled persons are likely to outstrip material gains due to the limits economic policy makers place on growth (Russell, 2001a, p. 226).

To illustrate how US capitalism preserves the reserve army of labour, the focus here will be on the role of the state in augmenting the reserve army.[5] US monetary policy as carried out by the Federal Reserve, a system of quasi-independent banks, overseen by a Board of Governors appointed by the President sets interest rates and for many years now has essentially been running the economy of the nation.

Large numbers of people are left jobless in part because mainstream economists believe that a threshold of unemployment is necessary to avoid inflation and maintain the health of the American economy (Friedman, 1968; Akerloff *et al.*, 2000). The theory of a 'natural rate of unemployment' or non-accelerating inflation rate of unemployment (NAIRU) has dominated macroeconomics for about 25 years. The Full Employment and Balanced Growth Act of 1978 (the Humphrey– Hawkins Act) mandates that the Federal Reserve Bank promote full employment, but the Federal Reserve connects low unemployment with inflation in disregard of the Humphrey–Hawkins Act. Since the 1970s, the Fed has assumed the task of fighting inflation by raising interest rates, slowing economic growth and keeping unemployment in check. When the unemployment rate drops, the Fed adjusts interest rates upward to discourage more growth (employment) with the intent of preventing inflation. (Greenspan, 1997; Henwood, 1998, p. 219).

5 There are many sources of the reserve army of labor, some of them, like the destruction of precapitalist societies, the detailed division of labour and mechanisation internal to the process of capital accumulation and others, such as the manipulation of credit availability by the US Federal Reserve System, intentional mechanisms of state policy.

From 1999 to May 2000, for instance the Federal Reserve raised interest rates about two points. As Federal Reserve Chairman Alan Greenspan explained it, the economy was too healthy, unemployment had fallen too low and wages had started to inch upward, thereby raising the spector of inflation.

Greenspan told congress:

> At some point in the continuous reduction in the number of available workers willing to take jobs, short of the repeal of the law of supply and demand, wage increases must rise above even impressive gains in productivity. This would intensify inflationary pressures or squeeze profit margins, with either outcome capable of bringing our growing prosperity to an end. (Greenspan, 2000)

It became necessary, according to the view of the Federal Reserve, to raise the cost of borrowing money, thereby cooling off the expansion and hiring, and nudging the unemployment numbers back up to slow wage increases. This deserves repeating. The Federal Reserve sought to raise (not lower) the unemployment rate, to put a halt to both hiring and better wages for workers.

Why? Tight labour markets—a 'labour shortage' or a smaller active reserve army—mean pressure for wage increases from labour; as unemployment goes down, labour costs go up because there is more pressure for wage increases.

There is solid empirical evidence for the negative correlation between wage levels and unemployment. Two mainstream economists, David Blanchflower and Andrew Oswald have produced evidence that, all things being equal, unemployment depresses wages (Blanchflower & Oswald, 1994). Economist James Galbraith has also shown that power, and particularly market or monopoly power, changes with the general level of demand, the rate of growth, and the rate of unemployment. He explains that 'in periods of high employment, the weak gain ground on the strong; in periods of high unemployment, the strong gain ground on the weak' (Galbraith, 1998, p. 266). Even Greenspan, the mouthpiece for Wall Street investors, admits a class relationship: a primary purpose of US monetary policy is to keep wages down (Greenspan, 1997).

Since full employment undermines labour discipline and the social position of management, political economist Michel Kalecki posits that capitalists accept unemployment 'as an integral part of the normal capitalist system' (Kalecki, 1971, pp. 140–141). Economist Michael Piore explains government's reluctance to pursue full employment objectives; they believe that such policies would create rising expectations among workers—expectations that would not be met and so result in social and political instability (Piore, 1978). Positive unemployment rates, then, become the outgrowth of class struggle over the distribution of income and political power (Pollin, 2000, p. 98).

In time, the US unemployment rate did go up from 3.9% in April 2000 to 4.5% in April 2001. About 763,000 people lost their jobs.

How does this affect the disabled unemployment rate? The implications of a decision-making class engineered slow down are perhaps greatest for disabled persons, whether one is seeking a job or already employed. The existence of an extremely tight labour market is generally a positive environment for previously unemployed populations to get a job. This is because a low supply of workers forces business to hire and train workers that they may not have been willing to hire or might have avoided at another point in the business cycle (Conlin, 2000). A downturn of the economy, however, means that disabled workers who have a job may be laid off. 'Disabled workers are usually last in/first out', explains Peter Blanck, Professor and Director Law, Health Policy & Disability Center, University of Iowa College of Law. For example, economists Edward Yelin and Patricia Katz show that disabled individuals experienced proportionally larger gains during periods of labor market expansion than nondisabled individuals and suffer proportionally greater losses during times of contraction than their nondisabled counterparts (Yelin & Katz, 1994, p. 36). Overall, persons with significant disabilities are hurt by negative changes in the economy evidenced by the fact that disability benefits claims rise during recessions (Disability Policy Panel, 1994).

There are further implications. Enlarging the active reserve army of labour is 'good' for business because it disciplines labour. Having more people desperate for work keeps competition for jobs high and workers' wages down, thereby protecting the corporate profit margins and class privilege, which are sacred to the interests of capital. Former President Clinton made this macroeconomic link when he told CNBC 'you can bring more people from welfare or from the ranks of the disabled into the work force [to keep inflation (wages) down' (Insana, 1999). *The Personal Responsibility and Work Opportunity Reconciliation Act of 1996*, which ended federal welfare entitlements and ensconced welfare-to-work as a primary goal of federal welfare policy, and pushed millions of women into the low pay labour force was one such tool. Former Labour Secretary Alexis Herman explained that disabled workers could be put to a such purpose as well: 'as President Clinton has said: The last big group of people in this country who could keep the economy going strong with low inflation are Americans with disabilities . . . who are not in the workforce' (Herman, 1999). Hence, it is no surprise that in the late 1990s Washington politicians engaged in policy reforms, such as the Return-to-Work (TWWIIA) legislation, a supply side measure, which promises feed the disabled population on Social Security benefits into the labour force, but does not mandate a jobs creation programme where disabled persons would actually become employed.

How large is the reserve army? It is much larger than the officially unemployed. The Bureau of Labor Statistics puts official unemployment at 5.5 million (2000), but another 3.1 million people work part-time when they would rather have a full time job and 4.4 million who need jobs are off the recording charts because they gave up looking and are not counted.[6] The real jobless rate

6 Under current US definitions of employment, one must be actively looking for work to count as unemployed. People are classified as unemployed if they meet all of the following criteria: they had no employment during the reference week; they were available for work at that time; and

is closer to 13 million or 8.9% of the population—more than twice the official rate.

How many disabled persons are there to potentially join the active reserve army? The Economic and Social Research Institute finds 2.3 million unemployed disabled people could be working with accommodations (Meyer & Zeller, 1999, p. 9). However, this appears to under-estimate the disabled reserve army. Seventeen million working-age people have disabilities, 5.2 million of whom are working (Trupin *et al.*, 1997). This leaves about 11.8 million either officially unemployed or not in the labour force. Over two-thirds of disabled persons age 16–64 who are not employed say that they would prefer to be working (Harris *et al.*, 1998). Thus, as many as 8.3 million workers could be enlisted in the active reserve army and the labour force would expand by about 8%.

Furthermore, there are indications that disabled persons may be significantly under-employed, preferring to work full-time when they are only employed parttime. Between 1981 and 1993, the proportion of disabled persons working full-time declined by 8%, while the number working part-time for both economic and non-economic reasons increased disproportionately (Yelin & Katz, 1994b). There is a very large pool of disabled persons to utilize as buffers against higher wages and lower profits (Russell, 2001a, p. 228).

Essentially, about 20 million working people are condemned, by federal anti-inflationary policies which ration employment, to either compulsory unemployment or employment at low wages. This demonstrates clearly that economic suffering, low wages and poverty are not the result of individual moral failings or a pathological 'dependency' nor a decline in the Protestant work ethic, but rather, are built-in to the structure of modern capitalism. It is easy to see why Nobel laureate William Vickrey, in his presidential address to the American Economics Association in 1993, called the 'natural' unemployment rate 'one of the most vicious euphemisms ever coined' (Collins *et al.*, 1994, p. 10). Pure economics rationalises unemployment—as 'voluntary'—without addressing the economic system or social relations that create it.

Micro-Economic Matters: capitalist calculus

Mainstream economists have traditionally devoted (and limited) themselves to the 'trade-offs' between equality and market efficiency. I have already discussed the macro-economic 'trade-off' between inflation and employment. In this segment I will focus on the micro-economic matter of economic discrimination

they made specific efforts to find employment sometimes during the 4-week period ending with the reference week. If one has given up the search for work as hopeless, he is not counted as jobless. Prisoners, a growing population, are not included in the unemployed figures. In addition, US unemployment statistics may tend to undercount the poor and unemployed more than most European statistics. The BLS uses headcount rather than full-time equivalent (FTE) to account for employment. Since a person who is employed only 10 hours a week counts the same as one who is employed 40 hours a week, significant numbers of the under-employed can skew the employment rates upward as compared to the FTE approach.

in the labour market. Economic discrimination occurs when persons of equal productivity are offered unequal wages or unequal opportunities for employment (Johnson, 1997, p. 161).

Liberal society promotes equality by establishing social and political rights that are, in theory, but rarely ever in reality, distributed equally and universally. That is individual rights are considered to be above the rules of the market. There is, however, an interrelationship between market institutions, inequality and equal opportunity.

Policy makers are keenly aware that rights affect the functioning of the economy and at the same time, their operation is affected by the market. An entitlement, for instance, is more likely to be established as a right when it has a relatively low cost. When congress enacted the ADA, it recognised that the traditional civil rights model would not serve to provide equal opportunities for disabled people in the labour force. The DRM articulated the need for accommodations in the workplace and Congress determined that the provision of a 'reasonable accommodation' was a necessary component of civil rights for disabled persons in order they might be integrated into mainstream employment.

Considerable discussion flowed during the ADA debates over the cost that equal rights for the disabled population posed. Senator Paul Simon stated during the congressional hearings, for instance, that congress was going to 'do the right and decent thing' by enacting the ADA despite the costs that would be incurred (Americans with Disabilities Act; Hearings, 1989, p. 22). Former President George Bush was intent upon 'containing the costs that may be incurred' (Mashek, 1990, p. 4). Indeed, the right to a 'reasonable accommodation' was watered down significantly with the injection of the 'undue hardship' clause to alleviate business concerns. The employer is not mandated to pay for an accommodation if doing so would create 'undue' financial hardship on the business; the disabled worker's theoretical 'right' is not a right, it is determinant upon the employer's calculus. This and other exemptions in the ADA catering to the business class has led me to refer to the ADA as a free-market civil rights bill (Russell, 1998, p. 114) because the business owner's right to property (wealth) is weighted more heavily than the disabled individual's 'right' to accommodation on the job and, hence, to employment.

Even so, the year the ADA was signed, the Cato Institute, a Libertarian think tank, called on President Bush 'to ask Congress to reconsider' the ADA since from the standpoint of free enterprise, it represented a re-regulation of the economy that was harmful to business (*Disability Rag*, 1992, p. 28). Paul Craig Roberts, a supply-side economist at the Center for Strategic and International Studies in Washington, warned on the day the Act was signed that '[the ADA] will add enormous costs to businesses that will cut into their profits' (Shogun, 1990, p. A26).

While we may believe that disabled workers should not be denied civil rights simply because employers may incur costs, while attempting to comply with the ADA, business objections are informative because they reveal labour market mechanisms endemic to capitalism. Business practices clearly demonstrate that the economic structure does generate obstacles to the employment of disabled people. Capitalism is a system of social relations in which profit-maximisation and a constant need to revolutionise the forces of production are basic and inescapable conditions of survival, as they have never been in any other social form. Capital is only interested in labour that will increase material wealth. From the standpoint of an individual capitalist, productive labour is simply labour that generates profits— surplus—for the employer engaged in the exploitation of that labour (Marx, 1967, p. 167). Surplus refers to the difference between output and the necessary costs of its production. Typical business accounting practices weigh the costs of employment against the profits to be made. Business calculates what it can gain from the worker productivity against what it pays in wages, health care and benefits (the standard costs of having an employee). The surplus created in production is then appropriated by the capitalist. profits (Marx, 1967, pp. 184–186). The worker receives wages, which in theory cover socially necessary labour or what it takes to reproduce labour-power every working day.

Disabled workers face inherent micro-economic discrimination within the capitalist system, stemming from employers' expectations of encountering additional production costs when hiring or retaining a non-standard (disabled) worker as opposed to a standard (non-disabled) worker who has no need for job accommodations,[7] interpreters, readers, environmental modifications, liability insurance,[8] maximum health care coverage (inclusive of attendant services) or even health care coverage at all (Russell, 2000, p. 349). 'Disability' is a (historical) social creation of capitalism that defines who is offered a job and who is not, and what it means varies with the level of economic activity.

This is so because a root cause of the work-place discrimination experienced by disabled people is to be found in an accountant's calculation of the present cost of production versus the potential contribution the employment of a given worker will make to future profits. Pure economic theorists conclude then that if disabilities among the direct producers add to the cost of production without increasing the rate of profit, owners and managers will necessarily discriminate against them. Expenses to accommodate 'disabled' persons in the workplace will be resisted as an addition to the fixed capital portion of constant capital.[9]

This plays out in many ways. The US Commission on Civil Rights noted in a 1998 report that employers continue to express concerns about increased costs of employing disabled workers (US Commission on Civil Rights, 1998, p. 4).

7 The equal pay and reasonable accommodation requirements of the ADA increase the costs of labor for individuals with disabilities. Hiring and firing costs would also increase (see Donohue & Siegelman, 1991).

8 ADA provisions allow disabled people may be classified and written up as a 'risk' in private insurance, an added costs employers may pay [42 U.S.C. Section 12111(c) (1994)].

9 'Given a choice between two equally productive workers, one requiring the expenditure of significant sums in order to accommodate him and one requiring no such expenditures, the profit-maximizing firm would prefer the worker who is less costly to hire,' (see Donohue, 1994).

Whether the employers' calculus is based on proven data or based on false projection in any given individual circumstance, employers anticipate extra costs in the form of providing reasonable accommodations, anticipate extra administration costs when hiring non-standard workers and speculate that a disabled employee may increase worker's compensation costs in the future. (Baldwin, 1997, pp. 42, 49). Employers, if they provide health care insurance at all,[10] anticipate elevated premium costs for disabled workers (US Commission on Civil Rights, 1998, p. 134). Insurance companies and managed care health networks often exempt 'pre-existing' conditions from coverage or make other coverage exclusions based on chronic conditions, charging extremely high premiums for the person with a history of such health care needs (Baldwin, 1997, p. 47; Johnson, 1997, p. 171). Employers, in turn, tend to look for ways to avoid providing coverage to cut costs (Carrasquillo *et al.*, 1999). In addition, employers characteristically assume that they will encounter increased liability and lowered productivity from a disabled worker (Baldwin, 1997, pp. 46–47).

Historically, managers and owners have only tolerated the use of 'disabled' workers when they can save on the variable portion of cost of production, e.g. by paying low wages to disabled workers, or through tax breaks and other subsidies. Not-for-profit employers who run sheltered workshops are known to pay well below-minimum wages, but data from the Census Bureau shows a negative association between earnings and disability generally. In 1995, workers with disabilities holding part time jobs (disabled persons are more likely to work part time) earned on average only 72.4% of the amount non-disabled workers earned annually (Kaye, 1998, p. 2). An employee who is too costly (i.e. significantly disabled) to add to net profits at the current level of output will not likely become (or remain) an employee at all. US Census data tend to support this view. Among working-age persons with no disability 82.1% have jobs; among people with a non-severe disability 76.9% have jobs; but for those with a significant disability the level of employment is only 26.1% (McNeil, 1997).

Neoclassical economist Richard Epstein echoes the view emanating from the business sector at large when he states that the employment provisions of the ADA constitute 'a disguised subsidy' and that 'successful enforcement under the guise of "reasonable accommodation" necessarily impedes the operation and efficiency of firms' (Epstein, 1992, pp. 484, 485).

Ruling for the employer-defendant in the 7th Circuit in 1995, Judge Richard Posner relates the business schematic of cost/benefit analysis to the ADA:

> If the nation's employers have potentially unlimited financial obligations to 43 million disabled persons, the Americans with Disabilities Act will have imposed an indirect tax potentially greater than the national debt. We do not

10 One in five US workers are uninsured. A primary reason (aside from no US universal health care as exists in most developed nations) is because health care benefits are not offered by employers. The coverage rate has decreased in the past decade, dropping from 73% in 1989 to 67% in 1996 (see Kaiser Family Foundation 1999, p. 30).

> find an intention to bring about such a radical result in either the language of the Act or its history. The preamble actually 'markets' the Act as a cost saver, pointing to 'billions of dollars in unnecessary expenses resulting from dependency and nonproductivity' ß12101(a)(9). The savings will be illusory if employers are required to expend many more billions in accommodation than will be saved by enabling disabled people to work. (*Vande Zande v State of Wisconsin*, 1995)

Employers and investors rely on the preservation of the status quo labour system, which does not require them to absorb the non-standard costs of employing disabled workers under the current mode of production, let alone the 800 million people who are totally or partially unemployed in the reserve army of labour worldwide. Consequently, disabled individuals who are currently not in the mainstream workforce, who are collecting disability benefits and who could work if their impairments were accommodated, are not tallied into employers' costs of doing business (Russell, 2001b) The disability benefit system thus serves as a socially legitimised means by which the capitalist class can avoid hiring or retaining non-standard workers and 'morally' shift the cost of supporting the 'deserving disabled' onto poverty-based government programmes—thereby perpetuating their immiseration.

Public policy which then condemns disabled persons to poverty serves another class function. At base, the inadequate safety net is a product of the owning class' fear of losing control of the means of production. The all-encompassing value placed on work is necessary to produce wealth. The American work ethic is a mechanism of social control that ensures capitalists a reliable work force for making profits. It workers were provided with a federal social safety net that adequately protected them through unemployment, sickness, disability and old age, then business would have less control over the workforce because labour would gain a stronger position from which to negotiate their conditions of employment, such as fair wages and safe working conditions. American business retains its power over the working-class through a fear of destitution that would be weakened if the safety net were to actually become safe. This, in turn, causes oppression for the least valued non-working members of our society; those deemed 'disabled' who do not provide a body to support profit-making (for whatever reason) are relegated to economic hardship to shore up the capitalist system (Russell, 1998, pp. 81–83).

Civil rights laws have historically demanded equal treatment designed to remedy the 'irrational' acts of employers. In the case of employment and disability, civil rights laws operate within a capitalist labor market where profit maximisation is 'rational'. Civil rights laws envision equal treatment, but do not acknowledge the full impact of competition and efficiency governing capitalist economies. The market transgresses on nearly every liberal right, including the right to a job accommodation. Furthermore it needs to be recognised that productivity is at the centre of capitalist accumulation. Capital holds labour as always, *a priori*, the retarding factor of productivity because labour can never produce fast enough or equivalently, at a low enough valued rate, to suit the expectation of an accelerating profit curve. Therefore, it is likely that impaired persons' labour will continue to be perceived as less than what is desirable to maximise profit.

Equal opportunity laws such as the ADA must fall short of remedying disabled peoples' employment predicament. For equal opportunity to be truly equal, biases (including economic biases) must be eradicated (Russell, 2000, p. 351). However, historically, capitalism has not been a system of material production that has taken into account the human consequences of its development. It is unlikely that disability discrimination can be eradicated under the current mode of production.

Beyond Equal Opportunity

Some economic theorists,[11] ignoring the damaging capitalist super structure, have sought to alter the way neoclassical economics treats disability by attempting to show that it miscalculates the value of disabled workers. In this view, the capitalists need to 'correct' their irrational (stereotypical) approach to avoid market failure. What galls these theorists is the 'unfairness' of particular markets. They hope through information dissemination to employers to act rationally and create 'fair' markets of perfect competition. However well intended, this seems a futile ploy in a fixed game where disabled workers are at the bottom of the competitive labour market and that labour market is, by design, structured to leave millions of workers under-employed and unemployed.

Further says economist Amin, pure economics is not rational, it is a parascience (not a science as it claims to be), which needs replacing with a reality-based approach. Why give it any credence by persuading business they aren't acting 'rationally'? Politically, pure economics is based on a single preoccupation. Amin writes:

> [Pure economics is] a preoccupation with showing that 'the market' rules with the force of natural law, producing not merely a 'general equilibrium' but the best of all possible equilibria, guaranteeing full employment in freedom, the 'social optimum' and this preoccupation is nothing but the expression of a fundamental ideological need, the need to legitimize capitalism by making it synonymous with rationality—which, in conformity with bourgeois ideology, is seen as nothing more that the use of technically rational means for the individual pursuit of mercantile profit. (Amin, 1998, p. 144)

11 See references for Michael Stein, 2000, concluding that biases against hiring disabled workers based on inflated costs constitute a market failure deterring employers from making rational decisions, and Peter Blanck, 1998, reporting a beneficial 'ripple effect' to hiring disabled workers; in part, accommodation costs are 'minimal'.

By contrast, left political economy holds:

> no prior assumptions attributing to the system any tendency toward equilibrium. It does not hold that class struggles upset any really existing equilibrium, or even a really existing, yet provisional, disequilibrium. In sum, Marxist political economy is realistic—whereas there is no realism at all about pure economics, which abstracts from reality (classes, states, the global system) so that its discourse, emptied or reality, is left a mythical fable. (Amin, 1998, p. 144)

The ADA and equal opportunity (a fable) is a 'demand-side' solution for a capitalist society, wherein the disabled workers and would-be workers, by definition, do not have the social or political power to realise their economic wants. Power lies at production, with the owners of capital. Productive capital is privately owned and owners are not forced to make capital available for the employment of the labour of others. Denial of access, therefore, is an important property right of capitalists to which workers do not have an equal legal rebuttal, since there is no 'right to a job'.

The failure of liberalism forces the need for a new discourse of liberation. We need a radically different approach. Disability, being a reflection of social class—in this instance, proletariats shoved out of the labour force—presents an opening to force a broader discussion about the legitimacy of the organisation of work and or our economy. We cannot ignore private ownership of the social economy. There is no 'equal opportunity' when the most important economic decisions about investment, choice of technology, work processes and the organisation of work itself are in the hands of a tiny elite of corporate owners and monetary policy makers. Nor can economic (or any other) democracy be realised when this elite can effectively block progressive public policies by threatening or carrying out disinvestment from the progressive jurisdiction as has happened in the conservative US courts with the ADA employment provisions.

Both pure economics and liberal civil rights law remedies are based on the 'atomistic individual' and as such need to be seen as products of bourgeois ideology.

Perhaps then disabled peoples' struggle for an equal place in the realm of work will be met with the class consciousness necessary to challenge the current disabled unemployment predicament.

References

Akerloff, G.A., Dickens, W. & Perry, G. (2000) Near rational wage and price setting and the optimal rates of inflation and unemployment. Available on-line at: http://elsa.berkeley.edu/ users/akerlof/docs/inflatn-employm.pdf. Date accessed 13 February 2002.

Americans with Disabilities Act (1989) *Hearings Before the Subcommittee on the Handicapped of the Senate Committee on Labor and Human Resource*, 101st Congress, p. 22.

Amin, S. (1998) *Specters of Capitalism: a critique of current intellectual fashions* (New York, Monthly Review Press).

Baldwin, M. (1997) Can the ADA achieve its employment goals? *Annals of the American Academy of Political & Social Science*, 549 (January), pp. 37–52.

Blanchflower, D. & Oswald, A. (1994) *The Wage Curve* (Cambridge, MIT Press).

Blanck, P. (1998) *The emerging Role of the Staffing Industry in the Employment of Persons with Disabilities: a case report on Manpower Inc. 7* (Annenberg Washington Program Publication).

Burgdorff, R., JR. (1997) 'Substantially limited' protection from disability discrimination: the special treatment model and misconstructions of the definition of disability, *Villanova Law Review*, 42, pp. 409–414.

Burkhauser, R.V., Daly, M.C. & Houtenville, H.J. (2001) How working age people with disabilities fared over the 1990s business cycle, in: P. Budetti, J. Gregory & R.V. Burkhauser (Eds) *Ensuring Health and Income Security for an Aging Workforce* (Kalamazoo, W.E. UpJohn Institute for Employment Research). Available on-line at: www.frbsf.org/econrsch/wklyltr/2000/e1200028.html. Accessed 13 February 2002.

Carrasquillo, O., Himmelstein, D.U., Woolhandler, S. & Bor, D.H. (1999) A reappraisal of private employer's role in providing health insurance, *New England Journal of Medicine*, 109, pp. 109–114.

Colker, R. (1999) The Americans with Disabilities Act: a windfall for defendants, *Harvard Civil Rights—Civil Liberties Law Review*, 34, pp. 99–162.

Collins, S.D., Ginsburg, H.L. & Goldberg, G.S. (1994) *Jobs for All: a plan for the revitalization of America* (New York, Apex Press).

Conlin, M. (2000) The new workforce: a tight labor market gives the disabled the chance to make permanent inroads, *Business Week*, March 20, p. 19.

Diller, M. (2000) Judicial backlash, the ADA, and the civil rights model, *Berkeley Journal of Employment and Labor Law*, 21(1), pp. 19–52.

Disability Policy Panel, National Academy of Social Insurance (1994) Rethinking disability policy: the role of income, health care, rehabilitation, and related services in fostering independence, *Social Security Bulletin*, June 24.

Disability Rag (1992) Read 'em and weep, July–August, p. 28.

Donahue III, J.J. (1994) Employment Discrimination Law in Perspective: three concepts of equality, *92 Michigan Law Review*, 2583, p. 2609.

Donahue III, J.J. & Siegelman, P. (1991) The changing nature of employment discrimination litigation, *43 Stanford Law Review*, 983, pp. 1023–1025.

Epstein, R. (1992) *Forbidden Grounds: the case against Employment Discrimination Law* (Cambridge, Harvard University Press).

Friedman, M. (1968) The role of money policy, *American Economic Review*, 58(March), pp. 1–17.

Galbraith, J. (1998) *Created Unequal: the crisis in American pay* (New York, Simon & Schuster).

Greenspan, A. (1997a) *Federal Reserve Board Humphrey–Hawkins Report*, February 26. Available on-line at: www.federalreserve.gov/boarddocs/hh/1997/february/reportsection1.htm. Date accessed April 25 2001.

Greenspan, A. (2000) *Federal Reserve Board Humphrey–Hawkins Report*, February 26. Available on-line at: www.federalreserve.gov/boarddocs/hh/1997/february/reportsection1.htm. Date accessed April 25 2001.

Hahn, H. (1985) Towards a politics of disability: definitions, disciplines and policies, *Social Science Journal*, 22(4), pp. 87–105.

Harris, L. & Associates & National Organization on Disability (1998) *Americans With Disabilities Still Face Sharp Gaps in Securing Jobs, Education, Transportation, and in Many Areas of Daily Life*. Available on-line at: www.nod.org/pressurvey.html. Date accessed April 25 2001.

Henwood, D. (1998) *Wall Street* (New York, Verso).

Herman, A.M., US Secretary of Labor (1999) *Remarks before the National Council on Independent Living, the National Association of Protection and Advocacy, and the National Council on Disability*, June 24.

Insana, R. (1999) *CNBC interview with President Bill Clinton*, Waterfield Cabinet Company, Clarksdale Mississippi, July 6.

Johnson, W. (1997) The future of disability policy: benefit payments or civil rights? *Annals of the American Academy of Political & Social Science*, 549, January, pp. 160–184.

Kaiser Family Foundation & Health Research and Educational Trust (1999) *Employer Health Benefits 1999 Annual Survey* (Menlo Park, Kaiser Family Foundation).

Kalecki, M. (1966) *Studies in the Theory of Business Cycles 1933–1939* (New York, A.M. Kelley).

Kalecki, M. (1971) Political aspects of full employment, in: *Selected essays on the dynamics of the capitalist economy*, chap 12, pp. 138–145 (Cambridge, Cambridge University Press).

Kaye, H.S. (1998) Is the status of people with disabilities improving? *Disability Statistics Abstract* 21(May), pp. 2–4.

Keynes, J.M. (1936) *General Theory of Employment, Interest, and Money* (New York, Harcourt, Brace and World).

King, M.L., JR (1968) Showdown for nonviolence, *Look*, 32, April 16, pp. 23–25.

Levine, L. (2000) *The Employment of People with Disabilities in the 1990s* (Washington, Congressional Research Service, Library of Congress).

Lewis, D.E. (1999) Access and closed doors: despite federal act, number of disabled with no job is rising, *Boston Globe*, July 4, p. G7.

Mandel, E. (1962) *Marxist Economic Theory Vol. 1* (New York, London, Merlin Press).

Marx, K. (1967) *Capital: a critical analysis of capitalist production Vol. I–III* (New York, International Publishers) (Original work published 1867).

Mashek, J.W. (1990) To cheers, Bush signs rights law for disabled, *Boston Globe*, July 27, p. 4.

Mayerson, A.B. (1997) Restoring regard for the 'regarded as' prong: giving effect to congressional intent, *Villanova Law Review*, 42, pp. 587–612.

McMahan, J. (1985) *Reagan and the World: imperial policy in the new Cold War* (New York, Monthly Review Press).

McNeil, J. (1997) *Americans with Disabilities: 1994–95* (Washington, DC, United States Bureau of the Census). Available on-line at: www.blue.census.gov/hhes/www/disable/sipp/ disab9495/oldasc.htm. Date accessed April 12 2001.

McNeil, J. (2000) *Employment, Earnings, and Disability*, p. 129 (Washington, DC, United States Bureau of the Census).

Mental and Physical Disability Law Reporter (1998) Study finds employers win most ADA Title I judicial and administrative complaints, 22, May–June, pp. 403,404.

Meyer, J.A. & Zeller, P.A. (1999) Profiles of disability: employment and health coverage, in *Kaiser Commission on Medicaid and the Uninsured* (Menlo Park, Kaiser Family Foundation).

Mishel, L., Bernstein, J. & Schmitt, J. (1999) *The State of Working America 1998–1999* (Ithaca, Cornell University Press).

Parenti, M. (1995) *Democracy for the Few* (New York, St Martin's Press).

Pheiffer, D. (2000) The art of political manipulation and the ADA, *Disability Studies Quarterly*, 20(1), pp. 43–46.

Piore, M. (1978) Unemployment and inflation: an alternative view, *Challenge*, 21, pp. 28–34.

Pollin, R. (2000) The 'reserve army of labor' and the 'natural rate of unemployment': Can Marx, Kalecki, Friedman, and Wall Street all be wrong? in: R. Baiman, H. Boushey & D. Saunders (Eds) *Political Economy and Contemporary Capitalism* (New York, M.E. Sharp, Inc).

Russell, M. (1998) *Beyond Ramps: Disability at the End of the Social Contract* (Monroe, Common Courage Press).

Russell, M. (2000) Backlash, the political economy, and structural exclusion, *Berkeley Journal of Employment and Labor Law*, 21(1), pp. 335–366.

Russell, M. (2001a) The new reserve army of labor? *Review of Radical Political Economics*, 33(2), pp. 224–234.

Russell, M. (2001b) Disablement, oppression, and the political economy, *Journal of Disability Policy Studies*, 12(2), pp. 87–95.

Russell, M. & Malhotra, R. (2002) Disability and capitalism, in: C. Leys & L. Panitch (Eds) *Socialist Register 2002: a world of contradictions*, pp. 211–228 (Suffolk, Merlin Press).

Shogun, R. (1990) Halt Bush's tilt to left, conservatives tell GOP, *Los Angeles Times*, July 14, p. A26.

Stein, M.A. (2000) Labour markets, rationality and workers with disabilities, *Berkeley Journal of Employment and Labour Law*, 21(1), p. 333.

Trupin, L., Sebasta, D.S., Yelin, E. & Laplante, M.P. (1997) Trends in the labor force participation among persons with disabilities, 1983–1994, *Disability Statistics Report 10*, June (San Francisco, Disability Statistics Center).

Tucker, B.P. (2001) The ADA's revolving door: inherent flaws in the civil rights paradigm, *Ohio State Law Journal*, 62, 1. Available on-line at: www.osu.edu/units/law/Law Journal/ tucker.htm. Date accessed 30 July 2001.

United States Commission on Civil Rights (1998) *Helping Employers Comply with the ADA: an assessment of how the United States Equal Employment Opportunity Commission is enforcing Title I of the Americans with Disabilities Act* (Washington, US Commission on Civil Rights).

United States Current Population Survey (1998) *United States Census Bureau, Current Population Survey*, March. Available on-line at: www.census.gov/hhes/www/disable/disabcps.html. Date accessed 21 May 2001.

Vande Zande v State of Wisconsin Department. of Administration (1995) 7th Circuit, 44 Federal 3d, pp. 538, 543.

Washington, J.M. (1991) *A Testament of Hope: the essential writings and speeches of Martin Luther King, Jr* (San Francisco, Harper Collins).

Wolman, W. & Colamosca, A. (1997) *The Judas Economy: the triumph of capital and the betrayal of work* (New York, Addison-Wesley).

Yelin, E. & Katz, P. (1994a) Labor force trends of persons with and without disabilities, *Monthly Labor Review*, 117, October, pp. 36–42.

Yelin, E. & Katz, P. (1994b) Making work more central to work disability policy, *Milbank Quarterly*, 72, pp. 593–619.

Young, D.A. & Quibell, R. (2000) Why rights are never enough, *Disability & Society*, 15 (5), pp. 747–764.

Zola, I.K. (1994) Towards inclusion: the role of people with disabilities in policy and research issues in the United States—a historical and political analysis, in: M. Rioux & M. Bach (Eds) *Disability is Not Measles*, pp. 49–66 (North York, Ontario, Roeher Institute).

Index